McCOOK COLLEGE
WITHDRAWN

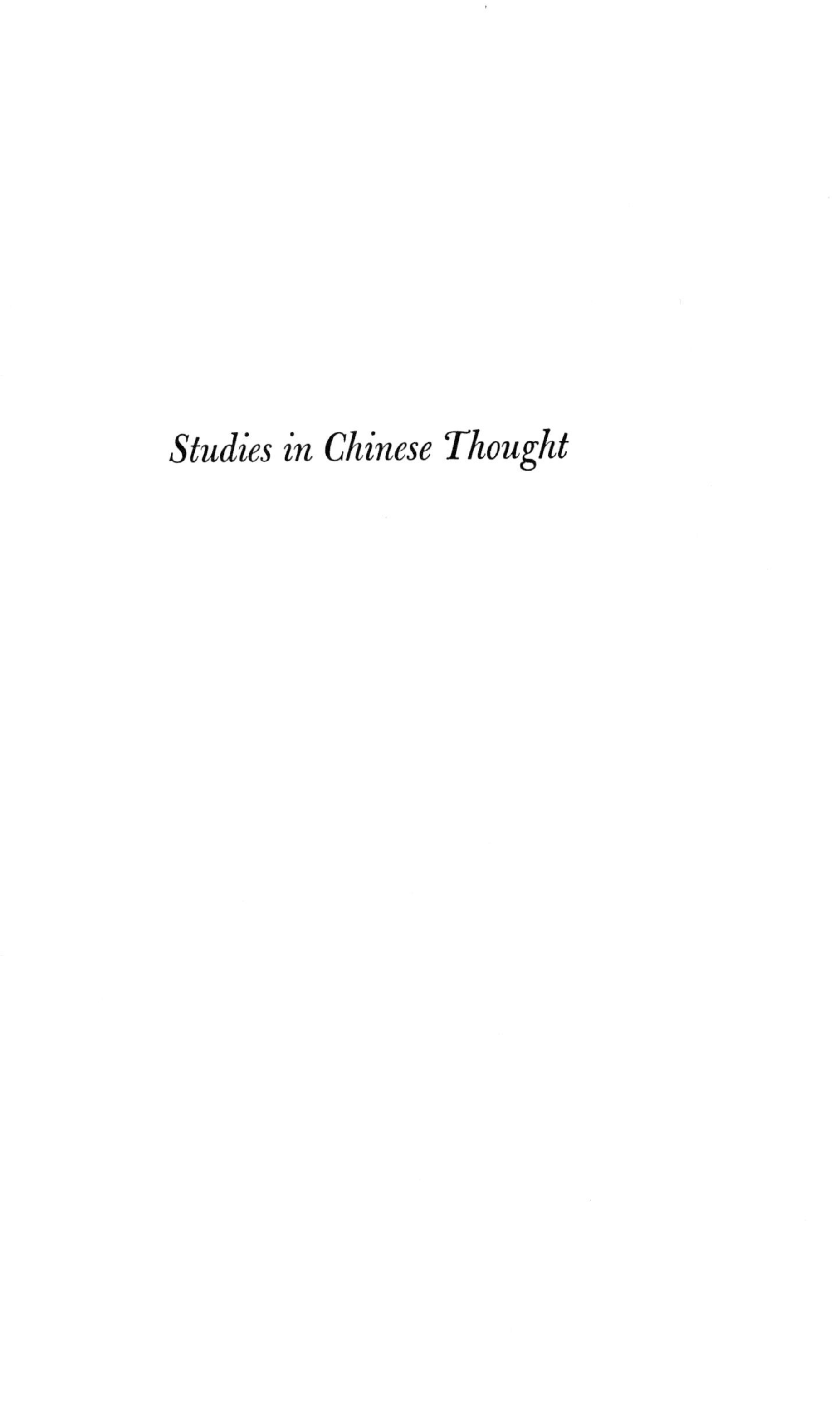

Studies in Chinese Thought

Comparative Studies of Cultures and Civilizations

Editors

ROBERT REDFIELD *and* MILTON SINGER

Studies in Chinese Thought
Edited by ARTHUR F. WRIGHT

Language in Culture
Edited by HARRY HOIJER

The Little Community
ROBERT REDFIELD

Unity and Variety in Muslim Civilization
Edited by GUSTAVE E. VON GRUNEBAUM

Village India
Edited by MCKIM MARRIOTT

Chinese Thought and Institutions
Edited by JOHN K. FAIRBANK

PLATE I

Courtesy of the American Museum of Natural History

COSMIC SYMBOLISM IN JADE

The interlocked *yin* and *yang*, forming the *T'ai-chi t'u*, surrounded by the *Pa kua*, on the base of an eighteenth-century imperial calendar.

STUDIES IN CHINESE THOUGHT

Edited by

ARTHUR F. WRIGHT

With Contributions by

DERK BODDE

ARNOLD ISENBERG

SCHUYLER CAMMANN

J. R. LEVENSON

W. THEODORE DE BARY

DAVID NIVISON

ACHILLES FANG

I. A. RICHARDS

ARTHUR F. WRIGHT

THE UNIVERSITY OF CHICAGO PRESS

Chicago & London

This volume is also published as Memoir No. 7 of The American Anthropological Association

THE UNIVERSITY OF CHICAGO PRESS, CHICAGO & LONDON
The University of Toronto Press, Toronto 5, Canada

Published 1953. Third Impression 1967
Printed in the United States of America

FOREWORD

In a recent book (*The Taming of the Nations: A Study of the Cultural Bases of International Policy* [1952]) F. S. C. Northrop finds the essential differences among the world's peoples to lie in the conceptions each has, as a deep part of its tradition, of the nature of the world. To him the differences that matter are not political but cultural. He thinks of these basic differences as irreconcilable as a basis for present policy; for him the just and peaceful world to which we may look forward is one of cultural pluralism restrained by agreement to respect the cultures other than one's own.

Where Northrop thinks of a culture or civilization as a way of life obedient to premises as to the nature of things, Toynbee (*The World and the West* [1953]) thinks of it as a complex of ideas and institutions with incompletely detachable parts. While Northrop prepares us for a residuum of basic differences among peoples, Toynbee emphasizes the impact of Western civilization upon all peoples and the tendency of the institutions and ideas of the West to follow its technology into other cultures and civilizations and so in great part to displace them.

The wave of influence from the West has apparently passed its crest, and in the weakening or withdrawal of this impact new national states have recently arisen in India, Pakistan, Africa, the Middle East, Indonesia, Indochina, and China. This immense and multiple event would seem to contradict Northrop's dictum that "culturalism" rather than nationalism is the rising fact of the world today. Yet there is a plausible sense, explicated in Toynbee's recent book, in which the eruption of nationalism is itself part of a cultural revolution. We may think of the idea and institution of the national state as one part of the complex of institutions that has been associated with the history of the West. In this complex, science and technology, mechanized warfare, industrial economic organization, and aspirations for social and political democracy or equality are the interlocking parts of a coherent culture pattern. Where one part goes, the other parts tend to go.

How are we to judge the worth of such large ideas as those given us by a Northrop or a Toynbee for the understanding of the contemporary affairs of mankind? To accept either one is to raise difficulties, both of scholarship and of practical consequence. Toynbee's views would probably not be accepted in any degree of fulness by most historians, nor would most philosophers readily accept Northrop's. Indeed, most specialized scientists or scholars would retreat from consideration of the problem of characterizing the world's civilizations and their interrelationships as much too large and unmanageable for the methods and data of their special disciplines.

To the leaders of those new states that are now struggling with the question of how far to Westernize their countries and how much to retain of their ancient traditions, the implication that they must choose all or none of the Western complex is bound to be disturbing. What Toynbee writes will also disturb the Westerner who seeks to take a more selective and less unilateral attitude in these new encounters with civilizations of the Orient or of Africa. And all who seek to change the minds of men in the direction of universal understandings will be given pause by Northrop's conclusion that the most fundamental differences within mankind will not soon yield to any common understanding but that of mutual tolerance and respect.

While we hesitate to accept fully either of the two comprehensive views just mentioned, or any other, the encounter of diverse cultures and civilizations has come to reach unprecedented proportions, to give rise to immense problems pressing for solution. The problems are already familiar: how to reconcile the competing claims of tradition and progress; the impact of programs of technical assistance and industrialization on preindustrial ways of life; the question as to the minimum of common value sufficient to make possible a peaceful and mutually comprehensible intercultural relationship within a world community of different languages, religions, races, and ideologies.

There is no systematic body of scientific knowledge that will much help us to solve these problems. No single scientific or scholarly discipline is by itself competent to deal with them, since their scope encompasses the whole range of the humanities and the social sciences and borders on some of the natural sciences. Under these circumstances it is not surprising that specialists in this or that field find fault with the bold syntheses of a Toynbee or a Northrop. But such criticism will not lead to the improvement of basic knowledge or of practical wisdom in this field unless the specialists see the importance of the big problems and join in a common effort for their solution. The accumulation and refinement of information about particular historical periods and particular civilizations is but one part of the effort. Another and perhaps greater part is the development of valid methods for the generic characterization and comparison of the world's cultures and civilizations.

The common effort does not start from nothing. Something toward that effort has been done by the historian of art or of culture, the philosopher of history and of culture, the sociologist of religion, and the geographer and cultural anthropologist. The work of Burckhardt and Woelfflin, Dilthey and Cassirer, Durkheim and Max Weber, Vidal de la Blache and Kroeber—to mention only a few of the pioneers—is sufficiently convergent to serve as a first foundation for the construction of a common framework of cross-cultural categories.

Cultural anthropologists, in particular, have concerned themselves with the development of categories by which total cultures may be described and compared. "Configurations of culture," "themes," "ethos," "eidos," "world view," and "basic" and "modal personality" are among some of the concepts which are being proposed for this purpose. These have usually been applied first to small communities in primitive cultures, but their range of application is intended to include civilized cultures as well. And many anthropological studies have already been inaugurated within this wider range. In the United States the "national character" studies directed by Ruth Benedict and Margaret Mead, the basic personality studies stimulated by Kardiner and Linton, and the comparative study of "value systems" directed by Kluckhohn are among the most recent.

To these studies the anthropologist brings the method of systematic observation which he has developed in the study of small communities. And because it is a method which is at once comparative and holistic, it leads to a study of the historic civilizations as developed cultures rather than as sequences of discrete events. The anthropologist does not of course possess an exclusive monopoly of the proper method for the conduct of comparative studies and is, in fact, self-critical about the whole problem of comparative method. Although he has a special contribution to make to it, he has also drawn fruitfully upon other disciplines. His use of concepts like "implicit philosophy," "world view," "value system," "cultural change," and some of his methods of analyzing linguistic and nonlinguistic symbolism indicate an increasingly mutual exchange between those disciplines like philosophy, history, philology, and iconography, which have developed in relation to the "great traditions," and the anthropologists' methods which have been mainly developed for the study of the "little traditions" of primitive cultures.

While it would be premature—and perhaps undesirable—to urge that these varied disciplines be merged into a single unified science of culture, there are some immediately practicable forms of interdisciplinary co-operation which this monograph series hopes to encourage. Through critical analysis and testing of the methodology of comparative cultural studies, through the exploration by groups of specialists of new methods for making the systems of thought and value of the major civilizations more nearly intelligible to one another, and through the encouragement of original research whose methods are likely to have wide cross-cultural applicability, we hope to achieve, not yet a unified science of cultures, but at least a set of co-ordinates within which we can order and evaluate the studies already made, a framework of concepts and hypotheses to organize and direct future research, and possibly some new and valid methods for characterizing and comparing cultures.

With the help of a grant from the Ford Foundation, the editors have during the last two years been pursuing these limited objectives through interdisciplinary seminars, conferences, symposiums, and the support of original research. They have sought to enlist the co-operation of students of the world's major civilizations (Sinologists, Islamicists, Indologists), of students of particular ingredients of civilization (language and literature, philosophy, religion, art, science, etc.), as well as that of the anthropological specialists in primitive cultures. To make progress reports of these activities available to interested scholars and scientists quickly and inexpensively, the present series of monographs is initiated. In the next two years we hope to publish about ten monographs. These include a critical analysis by the editors of some of the major concepts and methods in comparative studies, papers from a conference on language and culture edited by Professor Harry Hoijer, papers from two conferences on Islamic culture studies edited by Professor Gustave von Grunebaum, papers on the world view of primitive cultures, and others which are now being planned.

It is particularly fortunate that we can launch the series with these *Studies in Chinese Thought*, so conspicuously successful an example of interdisciplinary co-operation and so creative of new vistas for the understanding of Chinese culture. Since Professor Wright, who organized the conference out of which these papers grew, has in his excellent Introduction commented on the significance of these studies for Chinese thought, we shall not anticipate him here. We only venture the prediction that the many new methods explored in the following papers may prove equally fruitful for the study of other civilizations and cultures.

ROBERT REDFIELD
MILTON SINGER

CHICAGO, ILLINOIS

PREFACE

IT IS BY no means as usual as it should be in this world of easy and rapid communication that a group of scholars with certain common interests are brought together in fruitful collaboration. The papers in this volume are the result of one of those fortunate and still fortuitous conjunctures of congenial scholars, challenging problems, and an opportunity to work together. In the early spring of 1951 John Fairbank sent word to a number of people who, he felt, might share an interest in Chinese thought and a sense of the challenge it presents to modern scholarship. Some of those he approached were able to meet at Philadelphia later that spring, and, as a result of discussion, a committee on Chinese thought was organized and attached as a subcommittee to the Committee on Far Eastern Studies jointly sponsored by the American Council of Learned Societies and the Far Eastern Association. Correspondence ensued, and it became clear that the Sinologues, philosophers, and social scientists in the group were deeply interested in fresh approaches to the many problems of Chinese thought and that they shared an inclination to explore and to experiment.

It was our good fortune that Professor Redfield interested himself in the subcommittee's activities and, through funds provided by the Ford Foundation, made it possible to plan a conference. Papers were written, and a conference on Chinese thought was held at Aspen, Colorado, September 7–14, 1952. The discussions at the conference were lively and illuminating. As a result the participants gained valuable suggestions toward the revision of their papers, a new feeling for the ramifying problems of this field of study, and some inkling of the great variety of ways in which those problems may be studied. The essays in the present volume are the result of individual research and thinking enriched by the discussions at Aspen. The editor's Introduction owes much to the suggestions on methodology and problem formulation advanced at the conference.

We are indebted to many friends who helped in the conference and editorial tasks. Among them are Mr. Bernard Taper, who served as editorial consultant; Mrs. Althea Miller, who prepared many of the manuscripts; and Mr. John Manning, who acted as conference *rapporteur*.

A. F. W.

TABLE OF CONTENTS

CONTRIBUTORS

DERK BODDE did graduate work in Chinese in Peiping and Leyden and holds the Ph.D. degree from Leyden. He is now Professor of Chinese at the University of Pennsylvania. His principal interests are the history of Chinese thought, intellectual relations between China and the West, and Chinese folklore. His books include *China's First Unifier*, *Tolstoy and China*, *Annual Customs and Festivals in Peking*, and a two-volume translation of Fung Yu-lan's *History of Chinese Philosophy*.

SCHUYLER CAMMANN did graduate work in Chinese in Peiping, at Harvard, and at Johns Hopkins, from which he received his doctorate in 1949. He has done extensive field work in West China, the Tibetan borderlands of China and India, Inner Mongolia, Siam, and Afghanistan. He is now Associate Professor of Chinese Studies at the University of Pennsylvania and Associate Curator of the Oriental Department of the University Museum. His writings include numerous articles on Chinese art and symbolism, on China's relations with other countries of Asia, and on the peoples of China's frontiers. He is the author of *The Land of the Camel*, *Trade through the Himalayas*, and *China's Dragon Robes*.

WILLIAM THEODORE DE BARY received his doctorate from Columbia University, where he is now Assistant Professor of Chinese and Japanese and Chairman of the General Education Program in Oriental Studies, Columbia College. His major interest is in Chinese and Japanese thought. He has recently completed a study on seventeenth-century Chinese political thought entitled "A Plan for the Prince, the *Ming-i Tai-fang Lu* of Huang Tsung-hsi."

ACHILLES FANG was for some years on the editorial staff of *Monumenta Serica* and has been a Research Fellow in Chinese at Harvard since 1949. His major interest is in comparative literature. In addition to articles and reviews in *Monumenta Serica*, the *Harvard Journal of Asiatic Studies*, and literary journals, he has recently published *The Chronicle of the Three Kingdoms*.

ARNOLD ISENBERG has taught at Cornell, Harvard, and Queens College and is at present Acting Associate Professor of Philosophy at Stanford University. His principal interests are ethics, aesthetics, and the history of ideas, and he has published in such journals as the *Philosophical Review*, *Philosophy and Phenomenological Research*, the *Shakespeare Quarterly*, and the *Journal of Philosophy*.

JOSEPH R. LEVENSON received his Ph.D. degree from Harvard, where he was a member of the Society of Fellows. He is now Assistant Professor of History at the University of California. His major interest is the intellectual history of modern China. In addition to numerous articles and reviews, he is the author of a forthcoming book, *Liang Ch'i-ch'ao and the Mind of Modern China*.

DAVID S. NIVISON received his doctorate from Harvard and is now Acting Instructor in Chinese at Stanford University. His special interest is in the history of Chinese thought, particularly of the period 1644–1911. He has completed a study entitled "The Literary and Historical Thought of Chang Hsueh-ch'eng (1738–1801)."

IVOR ARMSTRONG RICHARDS is University Professor at Harvard and Fellow of Magdalene College, Cambridge. Among his books are *Principles of Literary Criticism*, *Practical Criticism*, *Interpretation in Teaching*, and *Mencius on the Mind*.

ARTHUR F. WRIGHT did graduate work in Chinese studies at Oxford, Harvard, Kyoto, and Peiping and holds the doctorate from Harvard. He is now Associate Professor of History at Stanford University. His principal interests are the intellectual history of China and the history of Chinese Buddhism. He has published reviews and articles in the *Harvard Journal of Asiatic Studies*, *Asiatische Studien*, the *Far Eastern Quarterly*, and *World Politics*.

INTRODUCTION

ARTHUR F. WRIGHT

WESTERN INTEREST in Chinese thought has persisted for more than three centuries. Despite that interest there has been to date little sustained, objective, and systematic study of Chinese thought. Part of the explanation for this anomaly lies in the history of Western learning, with its peculiar segmentation of fields of inquiry. Other, and perhaps more decisive, reasons are to be found in the motives with which Westerners turned to this study. Some sought confirmation of their own beliefs or opinions, some pursued the exotic for its own sake, while others hoped that China might yield some wisdom not to be found in their own heritage.

Leibniz, for example, regarded the formulations of Chinese philosophers as verifications of some of his major propositions, demonstrating their universal validity. Voltaire maintained that Chinese thought and history exemplified the triumph of reason over superstition and the enthronement of the rational man in state and society. The Jesuits and some of the Protestant missionaries believed they had found in that heathen land striking evidence of the working of God's grace: his guidance of the minds of the Chinese sages to the discovery of eternal moral truths. For all these, and for other Westerners down to recent times, there was strong appeal in the fact that Chinese thought as a system of values and as a guide to action had found expression in a great, self-sufficient, and enduring order such as no other people had created. Even in the face of the decline and disintegration of that order, some in the West have continued to seek in the dicta of Chinese sages those distillations of immemorial wisdom which, they hoped, might serve as guides to life in the shaken and uneasy world of the West.

Such interests as these, though understandable, have served to focus attention on scattered and discrete aspects of Chinese thought; they have tended to produce premature and biased judgments based on data that were inadequate or imperfectly understood. The purpose of this volume is to point to some of the problems which, in terms of Chinese thought itself, seem important and to suggest and illustrate some approaches to these problems, particularly some of the more promising methods of study that have thus far not been applied to Chinese material.

Such an effort as this may also suggest ways in which studies in Chinese thought can find their proper place in comparative study and help to refine its methodology.

Cross-cultural comparative studies have shown great vitality in recent years, and they have tended increasingly to include material from Chinese history and thought. Thus, for example, Arnold Toynbee analyzes Chinese history in his search for universal patterns and regularities. Max Weber sought in the study of Chinese and Indian sociology a "control" for his analysis of the dynamics of Western society. Masson-Oursel has propounded a theory of comparative philosophy and has used Chinese thought to illustrate its application. The Chinese language, so different—and so illuminatingly different—from our own, has gained an important place in comparative linguistics. In recent years the symposiums, through which American scholars seek to focus a variety of special skills on a common problem, have included increasing quantities of material from Chinese history and culture. The efforts of UNESCO, of the great foundations, and of the East-West philosophy conferences have been increasingly directed at comparative studies of thought and values which might contribute to some eventual world community of understanding. Yet the Chinese data included in many of these comparative and synthetic studies are frequently inadequate and often misleading. If comparative studies are to take proper account of Chinese history, thought, and values, if they are to be enriched as they should be by the record of Chinese experience, then far more intensive studies of that experience are needed. Comparison and synthesis are likely to be false and misleading if the Chinese ingredient remains ill analyzed and ill understood.

One of the functions of intercultural comparative studies is to ask large and important questions about man and his life on earth. Students of particular cultures must respond to these large questions or abdicate in favor of bolder but less qualified men. The scholar of China or some other non-Western area may make a further contribution to comparative studies. He can suggest modifications in the question or the hypothesis, or in the techniques of inquiry, when these seem ill suited to the culture he studies. When all such questions are seriously made and seriously considered, any comparative scheme gains greater relevance and validity.

I suppose that the ultimate goal of all studies of Chinese thought is a characterization of Chinese thought in terms which would accurately describe and interrelate every mental production of the Chinese both past and present. There are two main ways to approach this goal. One way is the historical or genetic study of thought, which seeks in a sequence of related mental productions the configurations of persisting ideas and values, the dynamics of their change, and their significance for the society in which they developed. The other way is the analytical study which aims, through the use of some existing system of analysis, to characterize Chinese thought as a whole or in part. Obviously neither type of study is completely independent. No one can analyze a sequence of ideas without some theoretical assumptions, and no one can successfully characterize without a knowledge of historical development, a sense of the depth and variety of a people's intellectual heritage.

At the present level of our general knowledge of China, the historical method, broadly experimental in terms of theory, seems the more promising of the two. Some of the reasons for this may be worth stating. First, such preliminary characterizations as have been made tend to obscure the importance of the dynamics of Chinese thought, to perpetuate the dubious notion that Chinese thought is "unchanging." Second, Chinese thought is so predominantly a sequence of answers to questions raised by the course of human events and the evolution of Chinese institutions that it is not readily understood apart from the factors which produced the questions. In addition, historical studies of Chinese thought can serve as keys to the understanding of little-known periods, groups, and institutions which have played significant roles in the formation of a distinctively Chinese civilization. In the paragraphs which follow I shall first discuss various types of historical studies which seem promising; I shall then take up the present state of studies in the "analytical" category and the possibilities they offer. I shall conclude with a brief discussion of some of the problems of communication which arise when one tries to analyze and interpret the thought of so alien a people as the Chinese.

In what follows many of the ideas are those of the authors of papers in this volume, but this does not mean that they share the responsibility for the ways in which those ideas are developed or for the suggestions that are made for further studies.

The History of Philosophy and the History of Thought

Philosophy, in terms of its Western foci of interest and breakdown of problems, is not a particularly useful framework in which to consider formal Chinese thought. To attempt to fit Chinese thought into Western philosophic categories tends to do violence both to the nature and to the hierarchy of problems with which Chinese thinkers have been concerned. For example, epistemology is a major focus of interest for Western philosophers; it is subordinate or irrelevant for most Chinese thinkers.

Yet, even if Western patterns of the organization of philosophic knowledge are abjured, the writing of a history of Chinese philosophy faces serious difficulties. Some of these arise from the inadequacies of Western historiography of philosophy; others, from the nature of Chinese formal thought. The history of philosophy has been, in the West, something of a stepchild of both history and philosophy. It may be useful to recall some of George Boas' criticisms of the conventional history of philosophy; all of them apply equally well to existing histories of Chinese philosophy.[1]

Boas points out that histories of philosophies have tended to string together *Kerngedanken;* they have been written in terms of essences, "in which logical patterns may be outlined but not the birth and decay of ideas as psychological and biological events." They have tended to consider philosophic ideas apart from the total intellectual life of a time and to ignore the reasons why an idea arises or becomes obsolescent or lingers on long after its utility is lost. They have usually ignored protophilosophy, the assertions which a philosopher took for granted. They have failed notably to take account of biographical factors, for example: Does a philosopher seek "unity" in philosophy when his personal life is disintegrated? Is a philosophy the idealization of a thinker's desires? Is a philosopher's thought rationalization? If so, of what economic or erotic appetites?[2] Many of these challenges have been taken up by scholars of the history of ideas, but no comprehensive history of philosophy which meets even some of these criticisms has yet appeared. This suggests that studies in the development of Chinese philosophy might well abandon the conventional "history of philosophy" pattern and proceed along different lines. They might begin to relate philosophic ideas to the context—intellectual and psychological as well as physical—in which those ideas developed. They might well attempt to relate philosophic issues to the problems of a developing society and to changing group and individual attitudes.

The shift of attention which I am suggesting amounts to substituting the history of thought for the history of philosophy. The history of thought encompasses much of the history of literature, of science, and of the arts. It gives special attention to the relation between political, social, and biographical events and the development of ideas. It would assume the sort of relation between philosophic and ordinary thought that is described by Kristeller: "Philosophy proper emerged from the much broader area of general thought through the development of a conscious and elaborate method and tradition. As the technical terms of philosophy are based on the words of the general language, so the problems and solutions of philosophical thought are often transformations and elaborations that correspond to the trends and currents of general thought."[3]

An even more intimate relation between the history of philosophy and the history of thought exists in respect to China than to the West. This relation is so intimate and of such a character that it seems to argue for a greater emphasis on the history of thought. One must remember that Chinese philosophers were generally members of the official class concerned with the management of social, economic, and political affairs. They were always near enough to authority to promote the embodiment of their ideas in programs of action. And many of their abstract formulations are intelligible only in terms of programs of action for specific social and political ends. It is this characteristic which has influenced Granet to call the formulations of the classical Chinese thinkers not "philosophies" but "recipes" or "prescriptions." This of course is less relevant in regard to many later thinkers, but the relation between the thinker and the problems of his age remains close.

This close relationship may be viewed in terms of that characteristic of Chinese society which might be called, in MacIver's words, a "community-wide synthesis of doctrines and institutions." Chinese philosophers were concerned that this harmony or synthesis be maintained. As philosophers they reiterated and reinterpreted values; as literary men they gave pleasing and persuasive form to statements of values; as officials they saw to the integrity of the institutions which were the expression of those values. They were the perpetuators of the synthesis which was the core of Chinese civilization, and what they said was never irrelevant to it.

It would seem, then, on the merits of the method itself and because of its peculiar applicability to Chinese intellectual history, that a history of thought has much to recommend it. But such a history presupposes organized knowledge in such diverse fields as the history of literature, of institutions, and of technology. For long reaches of Chinese history only fragmentary studies in a few of the necessary fields have appeared. Thus a satisfactory history of thought is a remote desideratum whose attainment depends on the advance of a wide variety of other studies. But, in the meantime, a number of studies could be made which would contribute to such an eventual synthesis and, at the same time, serve to refine our methods of analysis and throw light on important periods and themes of China's history. In the paragraphs that follow I shall discuss some of the types of study which in themselves are illuminating and which together might contribute to an eventual history of Chinese thought.

History of a Group of Thinkers

The history of a group of thinkers of a particular period is a valid and promising field of study. Such a study should analyze interpersonal relations within the group as well as the interplay of ideas among the individuals. It should relate the group and its ideas to the principal problems of its day. A full understanding of the difference in views from one member of the group to another would usually be found not in differing social origins—since the members were usually of the same class—but in the personalities of individuals, their peculiar responses to the heritage of Chinese thought, and the roles which each believed he should ideally play in the official and political life of his time. For China such studies have only recently been attempted. Étienne Balázs has written a penetrating study of a little-understood group of thinkers of the third century A.D.[4] In the present volume Mr. De Bary's contribution is an effort to reappraise a group of thinkers who, perhaps more than any others in Chinese history, are responsible for formulating the dominant Neo-Confucian orthodoxy of the last seven hundred years. His essay points to the need for many further studies of groups of thinkers in the Neo-Confucian tradition, particularly of the seventeenth and eighteenth centuries, for these thinkers established the orthodoxy on which Western ideas acted to produce the ideological and philosophic ferment of modern China. Studies of this kind would, I believe, raise interesting questions of a comparative nature. For example, in different societies, what are the motives and environmental influences which bring several thinkers into a recognized group? What, in different societies, holds such groups together? Is "the strife of systems" a key to the history of Chinese thought, as Boas believes it is to the history of Western thought? What are the essential beliefs and assumptions which form the core of a community of view among a group of thinkers, and to what extent would such an essential core be different in its components and their relative weights for a group of Chinese thinkers and a school of Western philosophers?

The History of Ideas

The history of ideas has proved to be one of the most illuminating approaches to an understanding of Western thought. Such studies can, when sufficiently developed, constitute the vital threads that hold together and give continuity to the history of thought as a whole. Each such history is, in itself, a case study of the way a given people expresses and develops its ideas. These studies involve enormous difficulties, even in the well-cultivated field of Western thought, for they demand of the scholar a thorough knowledge of successive contexts—historical and discursive—within which and from which an idea takes on its changing meanings. The history of a Chinese idea is infinitely complicated by our ignorance not merely of successive contexts but often of the bare facts of history. Nevertheless, even with these limitations such studies can be made. Mr. Nivison's paper in this symposium is an effort to explore the history of the problem of the relation between "knowledge" and "action"—a problem which has had a peculiar fascination both for philosophers and for modern political leaders. This paper suggests some of the possibilities of this approach and points to some of its difficulties; I believe it demonstrates that a number of similar studies would contribute substantially to our knowledge of Chinese thought.

A comparative history of ideas may appear unfeasible at the present time. But, if a concept or a group of concepts which have a core of common meaning in China and the West were subjected to historical study, we should gain considerable insight into the critical ways in which the two traditions differed and the divergent ways in which ideas changed in the volatile society of western Europe and in the relatively stable society of China. The works of Lovejoy and Boas on Western primitivism provide a challenge and an opportunity for the historian of Chinese thought.[5] An exploratory study shows that most of the types of primitivism analyzed by Lovejoy and Boas occur in Chinese thought. This raises a variety of interesting questions: What types of people in differing societies tend to think in primitivistic terms? Do similar or different social crises produce this variety of thought? What relation, in the two traditions, does the primitivistic strain have to other kinds of thinking—in the thought of individuals and in the thought of an age?

The History of Values

At certain times in the life of a society an idea becomes the object of interest and esteem and thus becomes a value; it then attains a certain place and a certain relative weight in the group of values which characterizes the society. The principal values which a people collectively recognize and on which or for which they act in common are their ideals. "Ideals are ideas or beliefs when these are objects not only of contemplation or affirmation but also of hope, desire, endeavor, admiration, and resolve. Or . . . one may limit the term to the case in which ideas, by evoking a community of emotion and will, play a social and not merely an individual role in human affairs."[6]

The histories of major Chinese values or ideals would resemble in some respects Karl Popper's *The Open Society and Its Enemies*, which traces, from antiquity to the present, a persisting ideal of Western man—an ideal which, he shows, recurs in diverse contexts and in changing terminological guises. But, because of the social role of Chinese thinkers and because of the state of our knowledge of Chinese history, such studies would be bound to take somewhat greater account of institutional and historical factors in the life-history of an ideal.[7] For example, the history of the ideal, "government by men of merit," is inseparable from the history of the system of state examinations through which certain Chinese thinkers and statesmen sought to realize that ideal. This relationship is, in fact, a help to such a study, for the memorials and essays and records of discussion of Chinese scholar-statesmen on the institution are clear and highly relevant records of their thinking about the ideal.

The difficulties of this type of study are obviously formidable, but my own recent, very tentative, experiment with it has persuaded me that it holds great promise.[8] Mr. Bodde's study in the present volume, while not wholly in a historical framework, contains rich and well-analyzed data for a history of the ideal of harmony. His translation of Fung Yu-lan's *History of Chinese Philosophy* is a valuable guide to the successive formal, more or less systematic, statements of values.

Histories of values would contribute directly to our understanding of the changing ideals of Chinese society and of the role of ideals in social and institutional change. In comparative terms one might well discover certain qualitative differences between the role of ideals and values in the development of Chinese and Western civilizations, certain illuminating contrasts in the life-histories of comparable ideals. Such studies would, of course, contribute directly and substantially to those analytical schemes which seek to characterize and to compare cultures in terms of values.

History of Situations of Intellectual Choice

This type of study is represented in the present volume by Mr. Levenson's paper.[9] It is essentially a history of an interconnected sequence of situations of intellectual choice in modern China. The term does not imply that no factors other than the intellect were involved in these choices but rather that those who stated the choices were intellectuals and did so in intellectual terms. Indeed, the appeal of each alternative is profoundly affected by such nonintellectual factors as the march of events, the ebb and flow of pressure on China from the West, and emotional attitudes toward events and toward one or another element in the Chinese cultural heritage. These were harsh and momentous choices—choices between the conflicting values of two civilizations in which the survival of one is at stake. They are paralleled in the West perhaps by such epic inner struggles as those of Julian the Apostate between the claims of pagan and Christian civilizations.

There is a special historical significance to such choices as these, for, as Ralph Barton Perry puts it,

> acts of choice and agreement are not in themselves *sufficient* causes. They do not operate in vacuo, but in conjunction with some set of necessary conditions. The adoption of an ideal is said to be *the* cause of an event in situations in which it is the culminating condition. The other necessary conditions being present, the ideal may pull the trigger, ignite the spark, or tip the scale—being fateful in the sense that the event hangs in the balance until the weight of the ideal is added. Such situations are characteristic of human conduct, sets of conditions being present which with a slight supplemental force will precipitate far-reaching and widely divergent trains of events.[10]

It must be admitted that for China we have an imperfect knowledge of the sets of necessary historical conditions which are the contexts of such choices as these. Yet a preliminary study of a sequence of situations of choice may not only shed light on some momentous problems of an age; it may also point to the very facts and factors in a historical epoch which demand the most careful investigation.

For comparative purposes this type of study has wide implications. Thoughtful men throughout Asia are now torn between the persisting appeals of their own traditions and the sharp challenges of the modern world. If we were to study comparable situations of choice in these changing societies, we might be able to come up with a typology of responses and perhaps also a useful guide to the understanding of present and possible behavior of Asian leaders.

Histories of Foreign Ideas

What has happened to foreign ideas in China? What has been their impact? What can their life-histories tell us about Chinese thought? Studies of the histories of foreign ideas can, it seems to me, show the relative strength, persistence, or intractability of some Chinese ideas and the adaptability of others; this comparison may sometimes show which Chinese ideas are associated with major values and, indirectly, the relative strength of those values. Such studies can suggest which Chinese ideas are potentially universal, that is, easily interchangeable with comparable ideas in other systems, and which are relatively parochial. Such histories presuppose a reliable estimate of contextual factors in a period of the invasion of foreign ideas: What were the strengths and weaknesses of the social and political orders? What was the vitality of the prevailing ideology?

They further require a knowledge of the media of the communication of foreign ideas within Chinese society, of the history of translation and publication. Yet, even with incomplete knowledge of these factors, it is now possible to make comparative studies of the histories of different foreign ideas in three periods covering some seventeen hundred years. Studies in the history of Buddhism in China are advancing; material on Catholicism in the Ming and early Ch'ing dynasties is abundant; and the impact of Western Christian and secular ideas in the nineteenth and twentieth centuries is now beginning to get the attention it deserves.

Studies of foreign ideas in the modern period should, however, be greatly expanded. If we are to come to a real understanding of modern China, we must know something of the history of the influential ideas of modern science and, indeed, of "scientism" and their effects on Chinese society and values. We must be able to assess the ephemeral popularity of Deweyan pragmatism and come to some understanding of the seemingly implacable advance of materialism which won so many of China's intellects before political communism rose to power. Which traditional ideas and mental habits have survived these waves of foreign ideas, which are gone forever, and which are merely submerged? These are questions that should be answered. It is clear that throughout Asia the emergent national states have, each in its own way and against a background of its own traditions, gone through a prolonged period of invasion by foreign ideas. Our understanding of all these situations of cultural contact and cultural change would be greatly deepened if we were able to see them comparatively, if we could analyze historically the relative strength and appeal of different foreign ideas in relation to the inherited values and patterns of thought of each of the cultures affected.[11] Such analyses would seem to be essential if, as one often hears, the struggle for Asia is "a struggle for the minds of men."

The History of Symbolism

Both ideas and values may, as Mr. Cammann's paper suggests, be expressed in nonlinguistic symbols. A history of symbols, then, is in a measure a history of the ideas and values which were their referents. For the early periods of Chinese history studies of symbols may shed light on the meaning of proto-philosophic ideas. For later ages artistic symbols provide a valuable check on formal statements of ideas.[12] And since these art symbols generally moved from the lower to the upper strata of society—sometimes returning to the lower—they can suggest, as literary evidence often does not, the prevalence of certain ideas and values in various strata of Chinese society.

As a clear example of the way in which the history of symbolism can corroborate analysis of formal thought, note that in Mr. Cammann's study symbols of secular desiderata predominate, while similarly in Mr. Bodde's independent account of some leading Chinese ideas there is an almost total absence of other-worldly reference.

The history of symbolism may also provide suggestive indexes to shifts in the meaning of ideas and in the relative weights of different values. For example, Mr. Cammann notes the shift, in the T'ang dynasty, in the interpretation of the symbols on the imperial robe; the new interpretation stressed moral and human significance rather than the old nature-magic connotations. This shift is paralleled by a contemporaneous change in the nomenclature of era names (*nien-hao*) away from magic and portent symbols and toward symbols of moral and secular desiderata.[13] And, in the intellectual sphere, the same period saw the beginnings of the new moral-rationalist synthesis which was to dominate Chinese thought down to recent times.

Mr. Cammann's paper shows that the history and typology of Chinese art symbolism is a large and rewarding field of study; it suggests that investigations of both the symbolism of literary ornament and the symbolism of formalized behavior would yield a wealth of valuable insights. Methodologically the point to be noted is that a knowledge of the total culture in historic depth is more likely to produce valid results than a ready-made system of analytic categories without that knowledge. Comparative study of the key symbols of different cultures is in its infancy; the richness of the available Chinese material and the wealth of parallel literary sources suggest that China should have a major place in any comparative study.

The types of historical studies just discussed all seem useful in themselves as well as being contributions to that possible history of thought which would illumine the whole nature and development of Chinese ideas in relation to developing Chinese cultural patterns. We shall now turn to the other broad category of studies, which we have called the analytical.

Analytical studies of Chinese thought may have a variety of purposes: (1) they may use Chinese data in order to test and refine some comparative scheme for the classification of cultures in terms of thought; (2) they may analyze the Chinese "mode of thought," isolating and using it as a criterion for the comparative characterization of cultures; and (3) they may study what the Chinese thought *about* as part of an effort to determine Chinese values and a Chinese world view. Both values and world view may also serve as criteria for the characterization and comparison of cultures.

Granet's *La Pensée chinoise* is the most serious analytical study yet produced.[14] It is worth discussing because its errors and shortcomings are instructive and because its major points can provide the hypotheses for further analytical studies. Granet came to the study of Chinese thought and society with the analytical concepts of the Collectivist school of sociology. It would seem at this date that the result of his application of Collectivist principles forces the drastic modification, if not the rejection, of those principles. For example, the "collective representation," the symbolic representation embodying the self-image of the culture,[15] is difficult to establish in a country of multitudinous subcultures. And, since Granet wrote, studies of Chinese history have made considerable progress. These studies suggest that many of Granet's characterizations of "Chinese thought" are less acceptable for the thought of later ages than they are for what he regarded as the formative period up to the first century B.C.

The notion of "prelogicality" shared by Granet and Lévy-Bruhl has been seriously challenged, perhaps nowhere more pointedly than in Malinowski's dictum, "Every primitive community is in possession of a considerable store of knowledge, based on experience and fashioned by reason."[16] An even more far-reaching criticism is that Granet failed to recognize different levels of thought and that he consequently compared Chinese traditionalized ritual conceptions with our everyday matter-of-fact technical and scientific notions. For example, did the Chinese *act as though* the earth was square and heaven round, or did they make different informal and common-sense assumptions as a basis for action?[17]

The controversy over Granet's method has served to clarify many of the theoretical problems involved in such an inquiry. It enables the investigator to reformulate as hypotheses many of Granet's brilliant generalizations. We had hoped to have in this volume an experimental effort to take some of Granet's characterizations of Chinese thought and test them by an analysis of the thought content of a group of Mongol Dynasty dramas. Unfortunately this study has not been completed. But if a series of such analyses were carried through, using various types of literature—particularly of early modern and modern date—a series of defensible characterizations might well emerge.

Mr. Bodde's paper in this volume is an analytical study of the dominant Chinese world view as expressed by Chinese philosophers. It avoids one of the defects of Granet's approach by making its comparisons of like levels of Chinese and Western thought. It avoids another by taking account of the development and modulations which this nexus of ideas acquired through time. The author believes that such studies as these might usefully form part of a comparative study in which differences in world view of diverse cultures are first clarified; from there, he suggests, it might be possible to develop some general theory of the genesis and development of such divergencies.

For the testing of generalizations about Chinese values and the Chinese world view, some promising techniques have been developed in the last fifteen years. Both community studies and the investigations of the linguistic geographers had begun to yield important results. Had they continued, we might have looked forward to the day when every type of generalization about Chinese thought patterns and Chinese values had been tested in a broad sampling of communities throughout China. Not only would such generalizations have been refined but variations among the subcultures would have become clear, and we would have gained a far clearer picture than we now have of the relation between formal thought and everyday language and behavior among the peasantry. These promising lines of inquiry are now barred, and none of the makeshift substitutes, such as the use of expatriate informants, seems likely to be satisfactory. We are thus forced to concentrate on those analytical and historical studies which can be made from written sources.

A recent and very ambitious attempt to analyze the Chinese mode of thought and world view on the basis of literary material is that of Hajime Nakamura. This is part of a fourfold comparison involving the modes of thought of the Indians, Chinese, Japanese, and Tibetans.[18] In describing the indigenous mode of thought of the Chinese, Mr. Nakamura is subject to many of the same criticisms as Granet. There is the same rigid conception of "logical" and "nonlogical," the same ahistorical selection of data, and a similar lack of differentiation of the "levels" of thought. What is new and interesting, possibly susceptible of further development, is his study of Chinese thought in interaction with the alien ideas of Indian Buddhism. By this means he attempts to show which indigenous thought patterns changed under its influence and in what ways and which proved resistant both to change and to assimilation with alien ideas. He thus uses Buddhism as a device for isolating or precipitating that which is most persistent and unchanging in Chinese thought. It might be that one of the other alien systems which has come to China could be similarly used or that comparative study of the reaction of Chinese thought to, say, Catholicism and communism would be illuminating. But, at present, our knowledge of the base points from which changes in Chinese thought did or did not occur (e.g., Chinese thought of the late 1500's and the 1920's) is inadequate. And ignorance of the dynamics of indigenous Chinese thought introduces a further uncertainty. Further testing of Nakamura's method might well await the completion of some of the other types of study suggested above.

The late Benjamin Lee Whorf took much the same view of the relation of language to thought as Granet and, indeed, as Nakamura. The field of study which has grown up under his influence—metalinguistics, or, as some now prefer to call it, ethnolinguistics or exolinguistics—has produced hypotheses susceptible of testing against Chinese data. Perhaps the most challenging of these is to be found in Whorf's statement of the relation between language and culture:

> In the main they [language patterns and cultural norms] have grown up together, constantly influencing each other. But in this partnership the nature of the language is the factor that limits free plasticity and rigidifies channels of development in the more autocratic way. . . . Language thus represents the mass mind; it is affected by inventions and innovations, but affected little and slowly, whereas to inventors and innovators it legislates with the decree immediate.[19]

If there is any validity to this approach, then Chinese vocabulary and linguistic structure must be freshly studied with the aim of discovering whether the peculiar segmentation of experience found in its vocabulary and the peculiar relationships suggested by its structure are indeed the primary determinants—or even "indicators"—of the Chinese mode of thought and of the Chinese world view. A preliminary investigation along Whorfian lines might be fruitful; it could produce a sharper awareness of the relation between language and thought; it might well contribute to the abandonment or the modification of the Whorfian hypotheses in their present form. The relation between linguistic forms and culture which Whorf tentatively establishes for the Hopi would be far more difficult to establish for China, with its complex civilization and its multitude of subcultures. But such a study of the Chinese language might prove rewarding in terms of one of Whorf's less debatable propositions: that, if we seek to discover which of our own categories of thought are the result of our language community, the best approach is through an exotic language, "for in its study we are at long last pushed willy-nilly out of our ruts. Then we find that the exotic language is a mirror held up to our own."[20]

Any study in Chinese thought depends on translation. To the degree that translators lack a sense of their task or a grasp of its techniques, distortion and misunderstanding result. Indeed, the most brilliant analyses, the most painstaking research, can be vitiated by inadequate translation.

Mr. Richards' paper in the present volume seeks, first of all, to place translation within the broad framework of the communication process. His analysis of that process leads to the specification of seven different functions of an utterance, as he puts it, the seven "sorts of work" an utterance may be doing. If the translator is dealing with mathematical or scientific works, his difficulties are fewer because the functions of the utterances—the sorts of work they are doing—are few. But, when the translator deals with literary and philosophic writings, the functions of each utterance are many, and what Mr. Richards calls "utterances-within-situations" vary enormously from Chinese to English; and, of course, the "situations" or contexts are another variable. Therefore the translator faces the necessity of compromise, the essence of his practical art. From his knowledge of the communication process in the two cultures and of the two sets of verbal and other contexts, he chooses that function of the original utterance which seems the most important. He then in his translation consciously subordinates the unimportant functions to the important. This is the process by which he reaches his compromises. In effect, Mr. Richards urges the substitution of conscious choice for instinct or accident. He believes that by such a procedure the translator gains a keener sense of just what he is sacrificing for precisely what gain, a fuller understanding of his key role in the process of communication. Systematic translation theory may thus contribute to man's self-realization as well as to better mutual comprehension between users of different tongues.

Translators of Chinese face a range of difficulties which may not be qualitatively different from those of other translators. But each type of difficulty is increased by the almost total absence of common customs, language elements, ideas, and values. And each is further multiplied by the monstrous weight of a millennial literary tradition. The first stage in every act of translation is, as Mr. Fang points out, adequate comprehension of the text to be translated. Chinese has suffered more than most languages from translators who did not comprehend the text under consideration. Mr. Fang analyzes the weaknesses of various translators in terms of deficiencies in various categories of knowledge, perception, and technique. For example, many mistranslations are the result of an inability to distinguish between rhetoric and sentiment. Others, at a more technical level, arise from inept use of admittedly imperfect tools, such as dictionaries and so-called "grammars." But perhaps the greatest number of failures stem from inadequate knowledge of context—literary, historical, sociological, or psychological. Mr. Fang's analysis will be of use to the translator in specifying the types of error he can learn to avoid. Together with Mr. Richards' essay, it should make him more conscious of the process in which he is engaged. Further, it may serve as a warning to those who use translations for scholarly purposes that these, at their best, are but "the most direct form of commentary."

The reverse of this process, in a few of its aspects, is dealt with in my paper. While Mr. Fang shows some of the hazards in the communication of Chinese ideas in Western languages, I attempt to sketch some of the barriers which the Chinese language has put in the way of foreign ideas. In their linguistic quandaries the Buddhist missionaries of the fourth century, the Christian missionaries, and the propagandists of modern ideologies have this in common: they all seek terminology that conveys the sense of the original, that is not outlandish and preferably ingratiating, and that will not, in its Chinese context, be subject to gross misinterpretation. The degree to which they attain one or more of these ends varies, and one gains some sense from a study of their dilemmas of the range of ideas which can least easily be communicated in Chinese. This in turn is fully explicable only in terms of the values and institutions of the society as a whole. But it also suggests some of the things that are most intractably Chinese, some of the persisting barriers to adequate communication.

The problem of intercultural communication through translation is particularly difficult; it is peculiarly difficult for the interchange of concepts. Yet it may be well to recall, as Mr. Isenberg does for us, that the problems of communication do not differ *qualitatively* from those within a single culture. He suggests, for example, that we may more easily comprehend some ancient Chinese political concept than the views of our political opponents. He introduces a further dimension to the study of Chinese thought, "the domain of verification." That is the consideration of whether a statement is, in the light of known experience, generally true. In his analysis of the relation between the domain of verification and the field of historic-genetic explication he suggests one of the reasons why the serious student of Chinese thought is so reluctant to assay the validity of Chinese statements which are meant by their authors to be universally true. It is only by a study of historical and contextual elements that one can determine the scope and the nature of the reference of the supposedly "general" or "universal" proposition. Take as an example the Confucian dictum, so often quoted out of context as an assumed parallel—and sharing the assumed validity—of the Christian ideal of brotherliness, "Within the four seas all men are brothers." Any judgment of validity must wait upon the answer to at least three historical and contextual questions: What did the author of the statement mean by the area "within the four seas"? The known world? The limited world of the Chinese culture of his day? Second, when he used the compound expression for "brothers"—literally "elder and younger brothers"—what did his social milieu lead him to mean by the expression? And did he really mean "all men" or only all gentlemen of specific moral attainments? Thus at least one of the requisites for serious considerations of validity is the type of historical analysis suggested earlier in this Introduction.

In the pursuit of international understanding well-meaning efforts are often made to find among another people ideals which resemble our own. Or, sometimes, people seek in an alien heritage some statement with pretensions to universal validity and find in it an ideal or a principle which they feel may contribute to the creation of a world community of values. Perhaps enough has been said in this Introduction—and it is underscored by the essays which follow—to suggest the hazards of such an approach to the Chinese and their heritage of thought. A specious affinity broadcast and insisted on can lead to more ramifying misunderstandings than a host of simple misstatements of fact. We should, at this stage of our studies and in this moment of world history, study the distinctive phenomena of Chinese thought in and for themselves. Once detached and disinterested inquiries guide us to an understanding of the precise ways in which Chinese thought and behavior are different from our own, we shall have gained two indispensable requisites of intercultural understanding: a knowledge of the roots and nature of difference, which is the basis of tolerance, and a knowledge of the whole range and context of Chinese thought, which must form the basis for any search for affinities.

NOTES

1. I refer particularly to Alfred Forke's three-volume work, *Geschichte der alten chinesischen Philosophie*, . . . *der mittelalterlichen* . . . , and . . . *der neuern* . . . (Hamburg, 1927, 1934, and 1938), and to Fung Yu-lan's *History of Chinese Philosophy*, first published in Chinese in 1934–35 and now available in Derk Bodde's translation (2 vols.; Princeton, 1952–53).

2. Cf. George Boas, "The History of Philosophy," in Y. H. Krikorian (ed.), *Naturalism and the Human Spirit* (New York, 1946), pp. 133–53, *passim*.

3. Paul Kristeller, "The Philosophical Significance of the History of Thought," *Journal of the History of Ideas*, VII (1946), 364.

4. "Entre Révolte nihiliste et évasion mystique: Les Courants intellectuels en Chine au IIIe siècle de notre ère," *Études asiatiques*, I/II (1948), 27–55.

5. Arthur Lovejoy and George Boas, *Primitivism and Related Ideas in Antiquity* (Baltimore, 1935); George Boas, *Essays on Primitivism and Related Ideas in the Middle Ages* (Baltimore, 1948).

6. Ralph Barton Perry, *Puritanism and Democracy* (New York, 1944), p. 19.

7. An example of such a study is Albert Guérard, *The Life and Death of an Ideal: France in the Classical Age* (New York, 1928). This work has a special interest for the historian of Chinese values because it deals with a self-conscious effort to reinvigorate an antique ideal—the sort of effort which characterizes many different periods in the intellectual history of the Chinese.

8. Arthur F. Wright, "Struggle versus Harmony: Symbols of Competing Values in Modern China," to appear in a forthcoming symposium, *Symbols and Values*. Homer H. Dubs's essay, "The Concept of Unity in China," suggests the potentialities of the history of this value. Cf. *The Quest for Political Unity in World History*, Vol. III of *The Annual Report of the American Historical Association for the Year 1942* (Washington, 1944), pp. 3–19.

9. For a less elaborate but penetrating study of intellectual choices in a time of crisis cf. Étienne Balázs, "La Crise sociale et la philosophie politique à la fin des Han," *T'oung Pao*, XXXIX (1949), 83–131.

10. *Op. cit.*, p. 23.

11. For a tentative effort in this direction see the symposium, "Religion and Modernization in the Far East," *Far Eastern Quarterly*, Vol. XII (1953).

12. Cf., e.g., Schuyler Cammann, "The 'TLV' Pattern on Cosmic Mirrors of the Han Dynasty," *Journal of the American Oriental Society*, LXVIII (1948), 159–67.

13. Cf. Arthur F. Wright and Edward Fagan, "Era Names and *Zeitgeist*," *Études asiatiques*, V (1951), 113–21.

14. Marcel Granet, *La Pensée chinoise* (Paris, 1934). Compare the much less sophisticated work of Alfred Forke, *The World Conception of the Chinese* (London, 1925).

15. Cf. Milton Singer, "Total Culture Patterns" (Chicago, 1952), p. 27. (Hectographed.)

16. B. Malinowski, "Magic, Science and Religion," in Joseph Needham (ed.), *Science, Religion and Reality* (New York, 1925), p. 28.

17. Cf. Robert K. Merton, "The Sociology of Knowledge," in Gurvitch and Moore (eds.), *Twentieth Century Sociology* (New York, 1945), p. 388.

18. Hajime Nakamura, *Tōyōjin Shii Hōō* ("Modes of Thought of East Asian Peoples") (2 vols.; Tokyo, 1948–49). It should be noted that a considerable tradition of Japanese scholarship lies behind Mr. Nakamura's analysis.

19. B. L. Whorf, "The Relation of Habitual Thought and Behavior to Language," in *Language, Culture and Personality* (Menasha, Wis., 1941), p. 91. Harry Hoijer has recently restated this thesis in modified terms: "The fashions of speaking peculiar to a people, like other aspects of their culture, are indicative of a view of life, a metaphysics of their culture, compounded of unquestioned, and mainly unstated, premises which define the nature of their universe and man's position within it" (quoted in Singer, *op. cit.*, p. 26).

20. Whorf, *op. cit.*, p. 77.

HARMONY AND CONFLICT IN CHINESE PHILOSOPHY

DERK BODDE

THE TWENTY-FIVE centuries separating Confucius (551–479 B.C.) from the present day have seen the appearance of many Chinese philosophical schools, of which only a few (Confucianism, Taoism, Buddhism) have survived as organized movements until modern times, though ideas from others have been perpetuated by being absorbed into these three main schools. Despite this long time span, with its numerous and often conflicting bodies of thought, I believe that it is possible to detect certain concepts or patterns which, because of their frequent appearance in widely separated times and contexts, may fairly be regarded as basic in Chinese philosophical thinking.

The purpose of this article is to analyze a few of these patterns, with the hope of demonstrating that, though far from all of them appear with equal prominence in all schools of thought, owing to the inevitable differences of interest among these schools, they nevertheless display sufficient universality and interrelatedness to constitute a homogeneous and therefore significant world view. The title of the article only imperfectly suggests the center of focus of this world view. More fully descriptive, but also more cumbrous and hence ultimately discarded, was the title I had originally planned: "Permanence and Change, Harmony and Conflict, in Chinese Philosophy."

At the outset it should be clearly understood that what we are here primarily concerned with is Chinese thinking on a sophisticated philosophical level rather than its manifestations in such fields as nonphilosophical literature, art, or popular religion. It is probably correct to say that ideas in these fields tend, in many cases, to correspond to prevailing philosophical thinking; yet there are also sometimes important deviations—for example, the idea of a personal creator of the universe, which is wholly absent from Chinese philosophy and yet occurs in Chinese popular religion. Even within Chinese philosophical speculation itself, furthermore, the dominance of the thought patterns to be described below has not prevented the appearance of occasional exceptions and countertendencies, some of the more striking of which will be noted as we proceed.

Finally, the reader may wonder why the name of Confucius is mentioned so infrequently in the following pages. The explanation is simple: The ideas of early Confucianism, as preserved in Confucius' own very fragmentary recorded sayings, are usually found expressed with much greater detail and clarity in the works of his two major followers, Mencius and Hsün Tzŭ.*

1. The Cosmic Pattern

In a recent article Needham has demonstrated a phenomenon of signal importance which differentiates Chinese from Western patterns of thinking.[1] We in the West, he points out, have been dominated by a world view in which the cosmos, far from being a self-contained, self-operating organism, is conceived of as having been initially created, and since then externally controlled, by a Divine Power who "legislates" the phenomena of the nonhuman natural world. This conception, from which has arisen our idea of the "Laws of Nature," is, of course, not of European origin, being traceable all the way back to ancient Mesopotamia.

In China, on the contrary, quite a different situation prevailed. The most important divinity of the ancient Chinese, to be sure, was a purposeful ruling power known as *T'ien*, or "Heaven," capable of exercising control over natural and human events alike. Such seems to have been the kind of *T'ien* believed in by Confucius, and traces of the old conception survive in Mencius (371?–279? B.C.). Even in pre-Confucian literature, however, the anthropomorphic qualities of *T'ien* were not strongly emphasized, nor was this divinity described as being the creator of the natural universe. Moreover, passages can easily be found in which the word does not have a religious significance at all but is simply used as a name for the physical sky. With the rise of philosophical speculation, therefore, it became possible for the old theistic conception to give way (save for certain exceptions to be discussed later) to a much more naturalistic and depersonalized point of view.

The result, for China, was momentous, for it meant that there, unlike the West, the theory of the "Laws of Nature" failed to gain a foothold. "The Chinese world-view," Needham observes, "depended upon a totally different line of thought. The harmonious cooperation of all beings arose, not from the orders of a superior authority external to themselves, but from the fact that they were all parts in a hierarchy of wholes forming a cosmic pattern, and what they obeyed were the internal dictates of their own natures" (*op. cit.*, p. 230).

In the present section we propose to analyze the nature of this cosmic pattern in terms of its concept of change. For this purpose we shall first turn our attention to the two major cosmological schools of early Chinese philosophy, those of Taoism and of the *Yin* and *Yang* and Five Elements, and then, for later times, to the Confucian New Text school of the Han dynasty (206 B.C.–A.D. 220), to Neo-Taoism (3d–4th centuries A.D.), to Buddhism (4th century onward), and to Neo-Confucianism (11th century onward). Prominent in all these schools is the belief that the universe is in a constant state of flux but that this flux follows a fixed and therefore predictable pattern consisting either of eternal oscillation between two poles or of cyclical movement within a closed circuit; in either case the change involved is relative rather than absolute, since all movement serves in the end only to bring the process back to its starting point.

Perhaps the earliest expression of the oscillation theory is the famous statement by Lao Tzŭ (prob. 4th–3d centuries B.C.): "The movement of the *Tao* (the universal course or Way) is that of reversal" (chap. 40). This general principle explains many of Lao Tzŭ's seeming paradoxes, such as: "Passing on means going far away, and going far away means reverting again" (chap. 25), or "If diminished, it will increase; if increased, it will diminish" (chap. 42).[2]

In the appendixes (prob. 3d–2d centuries B.C.) of the *Book of Changes*—writings representative of the *Yin-yang* school in its early stages—we find a similar concept, expressed, however, in terms of the eternal interplay of two cosmic forces, the *yang* and the *yin*.[3] Thus in Appendix III of this work we read: "The alternation of the *yin* and *yang* is what is called *Tao*" (Legge, p. 355). Or again: "Shutting a door is called *k'un*. Opening a door is called *ch'ien*.[4] One opening following one shutting is called change. The endless passing from one of these states to the other may be called the constant course (of things)" (Legge, p. 372).[5]

For early expressions of the cyclical concept of change, we should turn to the *Chuang-tzŭ* (attributed to the Taoist of the same name, *ca.* 369–*ca.* 286 B.C.), passages from which have been used by Hu Shih to illustrate what he calls ancient Chinese "theories of natural evolution."[6] Such a term is misleading, however, if by it is implied anything similar to modern Western theories of natural evolution, since Chuang Tzŭ himself indicates quite clearly that what he has in mind is a process of endless return within a closed circle rather than of forward movement along a straight line. Thus we read in his twenty-seventh chapter (Giles, p. 365): "All things are species which, through variant forms, pass one into another. Their beginnings and endings are like those in a ring—incapable of being definitely located. This is called the Equilibrium of

Heaven." Or, again, Hu Shih has quoted another passage from the eighteenth chapter (Giles, p. 228), which, though difficult and possibly corrupt, seems to describe a process of biological evolution starting from water-borne germs, passing through a series of plant and animal forms, and culminating when the *ch'eng* (unidentifiable) "produces the horse, which produces man." Here too the significance lies in the closing sentences: "Then again man reverts to the germs. All things come from the germs, and all return to the germs."

In the Five Elements school (originally distinct from the *Yin-yang* school, with which, however, it became amalgamated by the 2d century B.C.), we find other cyclical theories based on the successive flourishing of the Five Elements (earth, wood, metal, fire, and water). One such theory, in which these elements are correlated with historical epochs, will be discussed in the next section. Another theory correlates these same elements with the annual cycle of the four seasons in such a way that each season flourishes owing to the activities of its associated element. In its earliest form this theory is found in the *Yüeh Ling*, or *Monthly Commands*,[7] but it soon reappears, considerably elaborated, in the fifth chapter of the *Huai-nan-tzŭ* (compiled shortly before 122 B.C.). There we find the Five Elements, four seasons, five directions, five colors, ten "stems" or cyclical signs (used for dating purposes), and five notes of the Chinese scale, all correlated in an endlessly recurring cycle to form the following spatiotemporal cosmological framework:

Element	Season	Direction	Color	Stems	Note
1. Wood	Spring	East	Green	*chia* and *yi*	*chiao*
2. Fire	Summer	South	Red	*ping* and *ting*	*chih*
3. Earth	Summer (3d month)	Center	Yellow	*wu* and *chi*	*kung*
4. Metal	Autumn	West	White	*keng* and *hsin*	*shang*
5. Water	Winter	North	Black	*jen* and *kuei*	*yü*

Numerous variations of this theory occur in the writings of this and later periods down to recent times. Perhaps the most complex is that of Tung Chung-shu (179?–104? B.C.), major representative of the New Text school (the Han dynasty form of Confucianism, which, however, was heavily influenced by the Five Elements and *yin-yang* theories). He accepts the foregoing correlations, save that for him the element earth, being the central of the Five Elements, no longer has its activities confined to the third month of summer but acts throughout the year to assist the other elements in their seasonal duties. Furthermore, he introduces the *yin* and *yang* into his system by conceiving of them as two forces whose annual revolution successively takes them through the four compass points and their associated four seasons. In this way they function, together with the elements stationed at these compass points, to bring about the seasonal changes marking the passage of each year.

A special feature of Tung's system is that the *yang* and *yin*, in doing this, move not in the same but in opposite directions: the *yang* clockwise, the *yin* counterclockwise. Thus the *yang*, starting from the north just after the winter solstice, at which time it is at its lowest ebb, moves clockwise toward the south, passing through spring in the east en route, and steadily growing in strength as it does so, until it reaches its culmination in the south at the time of the summer solstice; thereafter it returns to the north, this time, however, passing through autumn in the west, and steadily diminishing in strength until it arrives once more at the north at the time of the winter solstice. Meanwhile the *yin* follows a contrary course: from the north, where, at the time of the winter solstice, it has reached its topmost power, it moves counterclockwise through the west (from which, however, it does not operate upon autumn but upon spring on the opposite side of the circle); then it continues to the south, there reaching its lowest ebb, after which it again returns to the north, gaining strength as it does so and passing en route through the east (from which, again, however, it does not operate upon spring but upon autumn in the west).

In this way the *yin* and *yang* annually meet each other in the north at the winter solstice, when the *yin* is dominant and the *yang* subordinate, and again in the south at the summer solstice, when the reverse is true. They are annually opposite each other at the spring equinox, when the *yang* is in the east and the *yin* in the west, and again at the autumn equinox, when their positions are reversed; on both occasions they are exactly equal in strength. All this, says Tung Chung-shu, constitutes "the course of Heaven," which, "when it has been completed, begins again."[8]

So far we have not discussed the question of what first set these pulsating or cyclical movements into operation. In other words, how did the universe as a whole come to be what it is now? First of all, it should be stressed that no Chinese thinker who discusses the subject admits the possibility of any initial *conscious* act of creation. By all of them the process bringing the universe from initial simplicity and disorder to its present state of complexity and order is conceived of in purely naturalistic terms. Lao Tzŭ's explanation, for example, is that "*Tao* produced Oneness. Oneness produced Duality. Duality evolved into trinity, and trinity evolved into the myriad things" (chap. 42). In this connection we should keep in mind that for Lao Tzŭ, as for all the Taoists, *Tao* is a wholly spontaneous principle, without any trace of personality. He says of it, for example, that "*Tao*'s standard is the spontaneous" (chap. 25).

When Lao Tzŭ here speaks of *Tao*, he apparently has in mind what he elsewhere calls "non-being," while by "oneness" he means the state of undifferentiated being, and by "duality" the further state in which this same being became differentiated into Heaven and Earth. This, at least, is the deduction we may draw from another passage (chap. 40), in which he says: "Heaven and Earth and the myriad things are produced from being; being is the product of non-being." The *Chuang-tzŭ* (chap. 12; Giles, pp. 143–44) tells us very similarly that "at the Great Beginning there was non-being," that from this non-being there then came oneness, and that this finally resulted in the existing world of separate objects. Many other Chinese thinkers have likewise accepted the theory that the universe as we now have it is the result of a naturalistic process of development starting from an impersonal first cause.[9]

At this point, however, we are faced with a dilemma. If the universe originated from a first cause, this means that in its early stages, at least, it underwent a process of progressive evolution. But if this be true, and if, nevertheless, the cosmic pattern today consists of oscillation or cyclical movement, then we must suppose that at some unknown period in the past the evolutionary process came to a halt and was replaced by the existing one of repetitive movement. How, when, and why did this shift take place?

Most Chinese thinkers do not even seem to have been aware of this problem, which, if faced squarely, would seem to lead logically to the alternative assertion that the whole idea of evolutionary development from a first cause is nothing more than a myth. If the basic pattern of the universe is today that of cyclical movement, then it would be reasonable to suppose that it always has been so in the past.

Hints of such a bold hypothesis are found already in the *Chuang-tzŭ*.[10] However, it is more particularly in a famous commentary on that work, attributed to the Neo-Taoist Kuo Hsiang (d. A.D. 312),[11] that we find such a theory presented with clarity and vigor. Thus in Kuo Hsiang's philosophy the term "non-being" means literally what it says, "nothingness." Hence, for him, there is no such thing as non-being, while being is the only reality. It follows, therefore, that this being could never have been evolved from non-being, as the earlier Taoists maintained, nor can it ever conceivably revert to non-being: "Not only is it that non-being cannot become being, but being also cannot become non-being. Though being may change in thousands of ways, it can never change into non-being. As this is so, there is no time when there is no being; being eternally exists" (Fung 2, p. 209).

Since the universe consists of being, this means that it likewise eternally exists and therefore can have no first cause. On the contrary, as pointed out by Kuo in several passages, one of the basic principles of the universe is that all things in it are self-produced; none of them whatsoever depends for its being on some external Creator:

> I venture to ask whether the Creator is or is not? If He is not, how can He create things? If He is, then, (being one of these things), He is incapable of creating the mass of bodily forms. Hence only after we realize that the mass of bodily forms are things of themselves, can we begin to talk about the creation of things. . . . The creating of things has no Lord; everything creates itself. Everything produces itself and does not depend on anything else. This is the normal way of the universe [Fung 2, p. 210].

Thus Kuo's cosmology is one of permanence in change: the individual things of the universe are in a perpetual state of flux—this is its change—but the universe as a whole is eternal and self-creating—this is its permanence.

With the spread of Buddhism in China, this concept was powerfully reinforced, for one of Buddhism's fundamental tenets is that

> there has been no single act of divine creation which has produced the stream of existence. It simply is, and always has been, what it is. Even the gods in the Buddhist heavens are attached to the wheel of life and death and are not its creators. Thus the wheel is permanent and unchanging in the sense that it goes on eternally. It is impermanent and changing, however, in the sense that everything in it is in a state of flux.[12]

As a single example of this thesis, let us turn to the Mere Ideation school, as represented in China by Hsüan-tsang (596–664). According to the subjective idealism of this school, all things in our universe, including both the seemingly objective phenomena of the external world and the seemingly subjective ego of the individual, are "mere ideation." That is to say, they are the products of a stream of consciousness which, for each individual, continuously takes its rise from a basic nexus of consciousness known as the *ālaya*, and continuously flows back to that *ālaya* in a closed circuit. The question arises, therefore, whether this stream of consciousness is itself to be regarded as permanent or impermanent? Hsüan-tsang replies, in typically Buddhist manner, that it is neither the one nor the other, by which he really means that it has aspects both of permanence and of impermanence:

> It is neither permanent nor impermanent, for it is in perpetual revolution. By "perpetual" is meant that this consciousness, from time without beginning, has constituted a homogeneous successive sequence. . . . By "revolution" is meant that this consciousness, from time without beginning, is born and perishes again from moment to moment, ever successively changing. As cause it perishes and as fruit it is then born. . . . Because these effects are born, it is not impermanent; because these causes perish, it is not permanent. . . . That is why it is said that this consciousness is in perpetual revolution like a torrent [Fung 2, pp. 311–12].

On a more prosaic level, Buddhism shares with other Indian schools of thought a belief in *kalpas*, or "world periods." That is to say, the universe as such is eternal and uncreated, but it passes through recurring cycles of formative growth, organized existence, disintegration, and annihilation, in the course of which successive worlds, including that in which we now live, are born and die. Each phase in this fourfold cycle constitutes one *kalpa* and has a duration of 1,334,000,000 years.[13]

With the rise of Neo-Confucianism, we find this Buddhist theory being taken over by Shao Yung (1011–77), who, however, made it more acceptable to the Chinese mind by replacing the Indian *kalpa* with what he called a *yüan*, or "cycle," and reducing its astronomical length to a more manageable duration of 129,600 years. He furthermore gave the theory a Chinese coloration by expounding it in terms of the alternating growth and decay of the *yin* and *yang*, as symbolized by the hexagrams of the *Book of Changes*. This theory was thereafter widely accepted in Neo-Confucianism, notably by the famous Chu Hsi (1130–1200).[14]

Another famous Neo-Confucian theory of cycles, in which, likewise, no starting point is postulated for the universe, is that of Chang Tsai (1020–77). The entire universe, says Chang, consists only of *ch'i*, or "Ether" (lit., "gas"), which, however, undergoes alternating phases of dispersion and condensation. In its state of dispersion it is invisible and intangible and is then known as the Great Void. At that time, therefore, there is only the Ether as such, but no organized world of discrete objects. But, with the condensation of the Ether, such a world comes into being, only to suffer dissolution, however, at which time the Ether again disperses and reverts to its former state. To quote Chang himself: "The Great Void cannot but consist of Ether; this Ether cannot but condense to form all things; and these things cannot but become dispersed so as to form (once more) the Great Void. The perpetuation of these movements in a cycle is inevitably thus" (Fung 2, p. 497).

This theory is echoed in later times by several thinkers, such as Liu Tsung-chou (1578–1645)[15] and Huang Tsung-hsi (1610–95).[16] Even as late as the nineteenth century, in fact, we find T'an Ssŭ-t'ung (1865–98) enunciating a similar theory, to which, however, under the influence of Western physics, he gives a modern touch by abandoning the word *ch'i* and coining a new term, *yi-t'ai*, which is simply a transliteration of the Western word "ether." This ether, he says, passes through alternating phases of seeming production and destruction, as the result of which individual objects exist and cease to exist. Yet the ether as a whole is never destroyed thereby, and thus the process continues eternally: "If we look at the past, the process of production and destruction has never had a beginning. If we look at the future, the process will never come to an end. And if we look at the present, it is constantly going on. . . . The cycle of production is followed by that of destruction; as soon as there is this destruction, it gives way to production" (Fung 2, pp. 696–97).

2. *The Pattern of History*

In the Christian world, historical events are dated from the birth of Christ; in the Islamic world, from the Hejira; among the Jews, from the Creation. In China, on the contrary, history has no such fixed starting point. Events are dated either according to their occurrence within a recurring sixty-year cycle (each year having its own appellation) or according to their position within the reigns of successive rulers. These chronological techniques are perhaps symptomatic of a Chinese world view which sees the human world as a part of the universal macrocosm and hence as conforming, like the latter, to an inherent pattern of cyclical rather than linear movement.

Besides this cyclical interpretation of history, however, there is another one, equally widespread, which sees the days of the ancient sage-kings as a truly golden age, and all human history since that time as a process of steady degeneration. Between this and the cyclical view there would seem to be a contradiction, inasmuch as the latter denies all forward movement save in relative terms, whereas the former affirms such movement of a sort, though in devolutionary rather than evolutionary terms.

Of the two, that which exalts antiquity seems to be earlier and less philosophical and was no doubt reinforced among its proponents during the late Chou dynasty (6th–3d centuries B.C.) by their sad awareness of the actual political disorder in which they lived. With the rise of the later cyclical theory, we find both views sometimes expressed by the same thinkers without apparent awareness of the possible contradiction between them. Certain men, however, as we shall see, reconcile the two views very simply by maintaining that history does indeed move in cycles but that we moderns are unfortunately living in the downswing of one such cycle. No doubt many other thinkers, if they had been specifically asked, would have given a similar answer to the problem.

Praise of antiquity and disparagement of modernity is so widespread among early Chinese thinkers as to require no extended comment here. For the Taoists, however, its motivation differed from that of the other schools. For them antiquity was golden, not because it was a time of universal government, but because it was one in which government was lacking. All men then lived at peace with one another precisely because they lived in a state of nature which required no government; their subsequent degeneration has been solely due to the increasingly complex and artificial civilization with which they have surrounded themselves.

The Confucians, on the other hand, inevitably reasoned quite differently. For them antiquity was admirable because it was the age of universal rule of the all-wise sage-kings. Hsün Tzŭ (*ca.* 298–*ca.* 238 B.C.), the third major figure in early Confucianism, is no exception to this general Confucian attitude. He, however, perhaps more than any other Chinese thinker, justifies his veneration for the past by a peculiarly static view of history, in which the many are like the one, and past and present are the same. In his own words:

> Abandoned and incorrigible people say: Ancient and present times are different in nature; the reasons for their order and disorder differ. . . . But why cannot the Sage be so deceived? I say it is because the Sage measures things by himself. Hence by himself he measures other men; by his own feelings he measures their feelings; by one kind he measures other kinds. . . . Past and present are the same. Things that are the same in kind, though extended over a long period, continue to have the self-same principles [chap. 5; Dubs, pp. 73–74].

In later times, as one among innumerable examples of continuing reverence for the ancient sages, we need cite only Han Yü (768–824). He maintains that anciently there was an esoteric truth, the *Tao*, which was transmitted through a series of early sage-kings to Confucius, and by him to Mencius (371?–289? B.C.), but that thereafter this *Tao* has ceased to be transmitted (Fung 2, p. 410).

The roots of this theory actually go back to Mencius himself, in whom we find the earliest attempt to reconcile such an exaltation of antiquity with a more sophisticated view of history as a continuing sequence of ebb and flow. "Since the appearance of the world of men," says Mencius (III*b*, 9), "a long time has indeed elapsed, consisting of alternating order and disorder." In this and other passages (II*b*, 13; VII*b*, 38) he further describes history as having already passed through three such periods of order and disorder, each with a duration of roughly five hundred years, and consisting of initial sage-rule, followed by disorder, and then concluded by the rise of new sages. These cycles, as outlined by Mencius, were as follows: (1) from the sage-kings Yao, Shun, and Yü (trad. 24th–23d centuries B.C.) to the founder of the Shang dynasty (trad. 18th century); (2) from the founder of the Shang to the founders of the Chou (trad. 12th century); (3) from the founders of the Chou to Confucius (551–479 B.C.).

Implicit in this theory of Mencius, as in any other theory of cyclical change, are two basic concepts: (1) History is dynamic, not static; it is a continuing process, not a timeless uniformity. (2) Its changes, however, do not occur sporadically but follow a fixed and therefore knowable pattern. There is no doubt that Mencius, inasmuch as he tacitly accepts these two concepts, holds a position much closer to the central stream of Chinese thinking than does Hsün Tzŭ, who rejects them. That his underlying attitude toward history may, in fact, already have been held by Confucius himself is perhaps inferable from the passage in the *Analects* (II, 23) in which, responding to a disciple's question as to whether the future can be foreseen, Confucius replied: "The Yin (i.e., Shang dynasty) perpetuated the civilization of the Hsia; its modifications and accretions can be known. The Chou perpetuated the civilization of the Yin, and its modifications and accretions can be known. Whatever others may succeed the Chou, their character, even a hundred generations hence, can be known."

However, for a theory which for the first time provides a naturalistic interpretation for the existence of historical cycles, we must turn from Confucianism to the Five Elements school. Prominent in this school is the doctrine that human affairs and natural phenomena are closely interlinked, each period of history being under the domination of some one of the Five Elements in an endlessly recurring cycle. For example, the *Shih Chi*, or *Historical Records* (chap. 74), tells us concerning Tsou Yen (3d century B.C.), the founder of this school: "Starting from the time of the separation of Heaven and Earth and coming down, he made citations of the revolutions and transmutations of the Five Powers (Five Elements), arranging them until each found its proper place and was confirmed (by history)" (Fung 1, p. 160). As formulated by his successors, the correlations established between the elements, their accompanying colors, and the early periods of Chinese history were as follows:

Element	Color	Period
1. Earth	Yellow	Yellow Emperor (trad. 3d mill. B.C.)
2. Wood	Green	Hsia dyn. (trad. 2205–1766 B.C.)
3. Metal	White	Shang dyn. (trad. 1766–1123 B.C.)
4. Fire	Red	Chou dyn. (trad. 1122–256 B.C.)
5. Water	Black	Ch'in (255–207 B.C.) or Han dyn. (206 B.C.–A.D. 220)[17]

In the second century B.C. we find Tung Chung-shu advancing several cycles of his own invention, among which that of the Three Sequences (black, white, and red) is the most important. Equated with actual history, these sequences go as follows:

Sequence	Dynasty
1. Black	Hsia
2. White	Shang
3. Red	Chou

Tung also propounds a four-phase cycle consisting of *Shang*, *Hsia*, Simplicity, and Refinement, each of which has either Heaven or Earth as its "guiding principle." (The terms *Shang* and *Hsia*, though identical with the dynasties so named, are abstract conceptions, and hence not to be taken as literally denoting these dynasties.) Equated with history, this cycle operates as follows:

Sequence	Guiding Principle	Dynasty
1. *Shang*	Heaven	Shun (3d mill. B.C. legendary ruler)
2. *Hsia*	Earth	Hsia
3. Simplicity	Heaven	Shang
4. Refinement	Earth	Chou

Another of Tung's cycles is based upon the alternation of Simplicity and Refinement alone, and he also has cycles consisting of five or nine phases. In all these he explains that the shift from one period to another is to be manifested by various ritualistic changes, such as proclaiming a new color for the official robes and other paraphernalia used at court, instituting a new calendar, building a new capital, and creating new titles of nobility. Such changes, however, all merely serve to demarcate one historical period from another but do not affect their basic principles of government, for "the great source of right principles derives from Heaven; Heaven does not change, nor do these principles."[18]

Wang Ch'ung (A.D. 27–*ca.* 100), iconoclastic member of the Old Text school which followed Tung's New Text form of Confucianism, seems at first sight to stand apart from the general ideological pattern we have been describing. Attacking the prevailing view that the present is inferior to the past, he argues vigorously that "the people of early ages were the same as those of later ages." Indeed, he points out that, judged in terms of size and political stability, his own Han dynasty is even superior to the earlier Chou period.[19] Yet, despite this seeming indorsement of the idea of progress, closer examination shows that he, like most of his countrymen, looks at history in terms of cycles. Thus he writes further in his *Lun Heng:*

> Each age has its prosperity and its decay; the latter, when prolonged, leads to ruin. The case is like that of a man's clothing or food: when first made, (the clothing) is fresh and intact, but after being used for a while it wears out; when first cooked, (the food) is fragrant and clean, but after the lapse of several days it acquires a bad smell. . . . This principle applies to antiquity, and not solely to the present day [chap. 56; Forke, I, 474].

Taking a long jump forward to Neo-Confucianism, we there find expressions of the compromise theory mentioned earlier, namely, that history moves in cycles but that we moderns are living in the downswing of one such cycle. Ch'eng Yi (1033–1108) writes, for example:

> As for successive epochs, those of the Two Emperors (the legendary Yao and Shun) and the Three Kings (founders of the Hsia, Shang, and Chou dynasties) were ones of growth, and later ages have been ones of decay. . . . There may be some cases in which decay is checked by (momentary) renewed growth, as well as ones in which such revival does not take place. . . . Generally speaking, however, if we consider the great revolutions of the universe, their principle is one of steady decay and decline (following a peak) [Fung 2, pp. 519–20].

This theory may have been influenced by that of Ch'eng's contemporary, Shao Yung, who, as we have seen in the previous section, took from Buddhism its theory of *kalpas* or world periods and translated it into Confucian terms. According to Shao, the cycle of 129,600 years in which we are today living began at a date corresponding to 67,017 B.C.; living creatures first came into existence *ca.* 40,000 B.C.; and the cycle reached its peak *ca.* 2330 B.C., a period corresponding to the reign of the legendary sage-emperor Yao. Since then there has been a steady decline which has taken mankind through four descending forms of government: those of the sovereign, the emperor, the king, the tyrant (in the Greek sense), and still lesser imitations of these. Living creatures will cease to exist *ca.* A.D. 46,000, and our present world will come to an end in A.D. 62,583. A new cycle will then begin. "From Emperor Yao until today," Shao concludes sadly, there has "sometimes been unity and sometimes division," but "never has there been anyone who could give a (real) unity to the manners and customs for a period of more than one generation" (Fung 2, pp. 474–76).

So far we have been dealing with thinkers all of whom deny the idea of progress by asserting either that the present is inferior to the past or that it is a mere repetition of the past. There are, however, a few conspicuous exceptions to this point of view. Most notable in early times were the Legalists, who, as practical statesmen keenly aware of the forces destroying the feudal system of their day (4th–3d centuries B.C.), were anxious to build a new power structure in its place. They never tired, therefore, of attacking the other schools for their reverence toward the past, and themselves insisted that changing political forms are needed for changing conditions. "Former generations did not follow the same doctrines," they exclaimed, "so what antiquity should one imitate? . . . There is more than one way to govern the world, and there is no necessity to imitate antiquity in order to take appropriate measures for the state."[20]

The most famous of the Legalists, Han Fei Tzŭ (d. 233 B.C.), explains the reason for these changes in a passage of his works (chap. 49) which has a curiously Malthusian ring. In ancient times, he says, "there were few people and plenty of supplies, and therefore the people did not quarrel." Hence it was easy to maintain good government without resorting to large rewards or heavy punishments. Today, however, the growth of population is so rapid that "before the death of the grandfather there may be twenty-five grandchildren. The result is that there are many people and few supplies. . . . So the people fall to quarrelling, and though rewards may be doubled and punishments heaped up, one does not escape from disorder" (Fung 1, p. 328). From this it would appear that even the Legalists, despite their insistence on the need for political change, agreed with other schools (though for their own sociological reasons) that conditions of the past were better than those of today. If this interpretation be correct (and perhaps it is unwise to try to read too much into a single passage), it would seem doubtful that the Legalist insistence on the need for change was based on any genuine belief in historical progress.

For such a theory we must turn to the Han dynasty expositors of the *Ch'un Ch'iu*, or *Spring and Autumn Annals*—a small chronicle history of Confucius' native state of Lu covering the years 722–481 B.C., and traditionally, though probably erroneously, attributed to Confucius himself. Tung Chung-shu classifies the 242 years of this history into three groups: events of which Confucius learned through transmitted records (722–627 B.C.); events of which he learned through the oral testimony of older contemporaries (626–542); and events which he personally witnessed (541–481).

Ho Hsiu (A.D. 129–82), a commentator on the *Ch'un Ch'iu*, further elaborates this theory by describing these divisions as constituting the Three Ages of Disorder, Approaching Peace, and Universal Peace. Confucius, he says, when narrating events of the earliest Age of Disorder, of which he learned only through transmitted records, concentrated his attention on his native state of Lu, while dealing only sketchily with the rest of China; in recording the next Age of Approaching Peace, he dealt in detail with China but disregarded the surrounding barbarian tribes; but concerning the third age, which he personally witnessed, "he made evident (in his recording) that there was an order arising of Universal Peace," in which "the barbarian tribes became part of the feudal hierarchy, and the whole world, far and near, large and small, was like one."[21] Devoid though this theory is of historical reality, it seems to be the first in Chinese thought which explicitly recognizes the possibility of positive human progress according to a fixed pattern of historical evolution.

Turning to the Neo-Taoist, Kuo Hsiang, we find him insisting that the principle of change, to which the whole nonhuman world is subject, operates equally strongly in the world of man, and that therefore it is folly for man to try to resist this change:

> The events of antiquity have already perished with that antiquity. Though attempts may be made to transmit them, who can cause them to happen again in the present? The past is not the present, and what happened today is already changing. Therefore we should give up the study (of the past), act according to our nature, and change with the times. This is the way to perfection [Fung 2, p. 219].

As a Taoist, Kuo Hsiang refrains from expressing any opinion as to whether this change is for the better or not. Rather than attempt such value judgments, the really important consideration, in his eyes, is that such change is inevitable and natural, and hence that human "perfection" consists in conforming to it. By thus acknowledging, however, that modern social institutions, despite all their complexity, are just as "natural" for their own age as were the simpler forms of life for former days, Kuo diverges significantly from early Taoism, and, in so doing, he undoubtedly reflects centuries of Confucian influence. Yet, by refusing to interpret this growing complexity as necessarily synonymous with human progress, he seems to remain within the prevailing Chinese point of view.

We find a very different situation centuries later when we consider the Confucian, Wang Fu-chih (1619–92), better known as Wang Ch'uan-shan. Not only in his approach to history but also in his nationalism (see Sec. 5 below) he is one of the most "un-Chinese" of all Chinese thinkers. There is nothing accidental, he says, in the shift from one historical epoch to another. Every event is the result of historical forces, which operate according to a definite pattern, irrespective of the intentions of the historical individuals concerned. The actions of these individuals, indeed, no matter how seemingly haphazard and accidental, all contribute in the end to the unfolding of this pattern. Furthermore, the resulting changes are not piecemeal but affect the social institutions of each epoch in their totality. Hence it is futile to argue whether the Chinese bureaucratic empire created in the third and second centuries B.C. was better or not than the feudal hegemony preceding it. Each system was equally inevitable for its own age, and it was likewise inevitable that the one should give way to the other at the precise moment it did. Even a sage, therefore, had he been living in the earlier period, would have been unable to hasten the shift to bureaucratic empire, just as the several attempts at feudal restoration, made soon after the founding of the empire, were all equally doomed to failure.

Not only are such changes inevitable, however, but they belong to a definite pattern of social improvement which has moved China forward from tribalism to feudalism and from feudalism to centralized empire. Though Wang Fu-chih does not deny the greatness of the early sage-kings, he breaks sharply with tradition by asserting that the times in which they lived, despite their efforts, were crude and dark and that there has been a steady subsequent growth in civilization.

When he comes to discuss civilization on a world-wide scale, however, Wang seems to retain a hint of the old cyclical concept. Thus in a remarkable passage he points out that civilization is not the exclusive possession of the Chinese alone, nor does it evolve at the same rate in all places. Hence just as in China itself there has been a gradual cultural shift over the centuries from north to south, so it is possible that in very early times there may have lived non-Chinese peoples as civilized as are the Chinese today, and likewise it is possible that a day will come when the Chinese themselves will revert to barbarism. This view, however, holds only a small place in Wang's total philosophy of history, and elsewhere he vigorously criticizes the cyclical theories of Tung Chung-shu and Shao Yung alike.[22]

For the next exceptions to the prevailing Chinese historical view, we must turn to the nineteenth-century revival of the New Text school of Confucianism, headed by the famous reformer, K'ang Yu-wei (1858–1927). As part of this revival, K'ang refurbished the two-thousand-year-old theory of the Three Ages of Disorder, Approaching Peace, and Universal Peace (originally applied to the *Ch'un Ch'iu*, or *Spring and Autumn Annals*) and, in so doing, brought it up to date and gave it a world-wide context by ascribing the Age of Disorder to the time of Confucius, the Age of Approaching Peace to his own (K'ang Yu-wei's) day, and the Age of Universal Peace to a period yet to come. Not only China, K'ang asserted, but the entire human race, has been steadily moving from Disorder, through Approaching Peace, and thus toward the common goal of Universal Peace, which will inevitably be reached two or three centuries hence. In his *Ta-t'ung Shu*, or *Book of the Great Unity*, K'ang describes the coming millennium with apocalyptic fervor as one in which there will be no political or racial divisions, no social classes, and no exploitation of man by man.[23]

In K'ang's associates, T'an Ssŭ-t'ung (1865–98) and Liao P'ing (1852–1932), we find curious attempts to reconcile this ardent belief in evolutionary meliorism with the prevailing Chinese belief in devolutionary cyclicism. To do this, T'an Ssŭ-t'ung interprets the six lines of the first (*ch'ien*) hexagram of the *Book of Changes* as graphically symbolizing a twofold historical cycle, the first phase of which consists of devolution (prehistoric times to Confucius), and the second phase of evolution (Confucius to an age still in the future). The lower half of the *ch'ien* hexagram, called by T'an its "inner trigram," pertains to its devolutionary phase, and the upper half, called by him its "outer trigram," to its evolutionary phase. This theory (see Fung 2, pp. 699–702) can best be shown through the following table (to be read from bottom to top):

Lines of *Ch'ien* Hexagram		Sequence of Three Ages	Absolute Time Sequence
Outer trigram	6	Age of Universal Peace	Distant future
	5	Age of Approaching Peace	Near future
	4	Age of Disorder	Confucius until today
Inner trigram	3	Age of Disorder	Hsia dynasty until Confucius
	2	Age of Approaching Peace	Three Sovereigns and Five Emperors
	1	Age of Universal Peace	Prehistoric

Liao P'ing's solution is somewhat different. "The evolution of the world," he writes, "is, culturally, from barbarism to civilization, and, geographically, from the lesser to the greater." Politically, this means that mankind has passed through five ascending forms of government: those of the lord, the tyrant, the king, the emperor, and the sovereign. The process will culminate with "the unification of the entire globe," which "must take place 10,000 years hence."

Confucius, though living long ago, had prophetic insight that this was going to happen and therefore, according to Liao, when editing the classics, used them to convey this information. In so doing, however, he deliberately reversed the true picture, attributing to remote antiquity the Age of Universal Peace, which actually still lies in the future, and portraying the above-mentioned five stages of government in descending rather than ascending order. Confucius' idea in so doing was, says Liao, "to set up an inverted image which, while showing retrogression, would, by telling men about the past, thereby inform them of the future."

As a graphic portrayal of this theory, Liao has a table consisting of two diverging columns of statements, one of which, arranged in usual sequence from top to bottom, is inscribed: "The classics are all abstract words and not real history," while the other, arranged in reverse sequence so that it can be read only by turning the page upside down, is inscribed: "Progress is something actual and historical."[24]

All three of these nineteenth-century Confucianists, as we know, were acquainted to varying degrees with Western literature. Hence there is every reason to suppose that their insistence on progressive evolution—so at variance with traditional Chinese belief—very probably reflects Western influence, in the form either of scientific writings on the theory of evolution or of theological literature about a coming millennium.[25]

It seems fair to conclude, therefore, that, of the men discussed above as possible exceptions to prevailing Chinese historical theory, some are only seemingly so, some have expressed their views in rather rudimentary form, some have been under outside influence, and only one—Wang Fu-chih—has created a really well-rounded theory stressing historical progress.

Most thinkers, on the other hand, when they have expressed themselves on the subject, have either asserted the superiority of antiquity to later ages or have maintained that historical movement, though an actual fact, operates only in the form of recurrent cycles. A few have tried to combine these two prevailing points of view by asserting that we moderns happen to belong to the downswing of one such cycle. All such theories, irrespective of other differences, obviously agree in their implicit denial of the possibility of long-term historical progress. On the other hand, however, it should be noted that only one major Chinese thinker—Hsün Tzŭ—has seemingly gone to the opposite extreme by denying that in history there occurs any appreciable movement at all.

3. Good and Evil

In the preceding sections we have seen that the universe, in Chinese eyes, is a harmonious organism; that its pattern of movement is inherent and not imposed from without; and that the world of man, being a part of the universe, follows a similar pattern. What, then, may be asked, is the origin of evil in such a universe? Before trying to answer this question, it will be helpful if we first survey the prevailing Chinese views on the subject of human nature.

A. THE GOODNESS OF HUMAN NATURE

One of the major problems in Chinese philosophy has been that of the goodness or badness of human nature. Most of all, it has been a Confucian problem, because the Confucianists, more than others, have been primarily concerned with the relation of the individual to society. For the Taoists this problem did not pose itself in the same way, since, in their eyes, what is good means what is natural, and therefore the extent of the individual's goodness depends upon the extent to which he is permitted by society to follow his natural instincts. "Do not let what is of man obliterate what is of Nature," was the Taoist slogan (*Chuang-tzŭ*, chap. 17; Giles, p. 211). As for the Buddhists, they, if anything, were even less interested in social relationships per se, believing as they did that these are among the ties binding us to the painful wheel of life and death. We shall have something more to say about Buddhist attitudes later.

The Confucianists, on the other hand, were par excellence men whose minds centered on political and social relationships, and therefore it was inevitable that sooner or later they should find themselves confronted with a major problem: to what extent is man's behavior conditioned by the social institutions under which he lives and to what extent does it spring directly from his own innate qualities? Hints of an awareness of this problem may be found already in Confucius, but Mencius (371?–279? B.C.) was the first to venture a clear-cut answer. Man, he maintained—and in so doing it is conceivable, though not provable, that he may have been influenced by Taoist ideas—is a being born for goodness; in him at birth, therefore, there exists a natural tendency for goodness, as inevitable as the natural tendency of water to flow downward (*Mencius*, VI*a*, 3). This means that social institutions do not produce, but merely give refined expression to, the shoots of goodness already innate in every man.

This optimistic view was far from universally shared in ancient China. Kao Tzŭ, who debated with Mencius on the subject, advanced a theory seemingly closer to the findings of modern psychology. Man's nature, he said, is at birth simply a bundle of instincts, of which those concerned with food and sex are primary; left to itself, therefore, it is as indifferent to either good or evil as water, left to itself, is to the direction it will eventually take when a passage is opened for it either to the east or to the west (*ibid.*).

The Legalists, for their part, were quite uninterested in abstract problems of metaphysics or psychology as such. They were, however, shrewd observers of human behavior as manifested in the disordered China of their time, and, on the basis of what they saw, they concluded cynically that within a state not more than ten people can be found who naturally do good of themselves; almost all men act only through motives of self-interest. This is why, the Legalists argued, no government can be effective unless it be based on a stern system of rewards and punishments, by means of which it can manipulate men's desires and fears for its own purposes (Fung 1, pp. 327–30).

The most formidable opponent of Mencius was, however, his fellow-Confucian of a later generation, Hsün Tzŭ. More than any other Chinese thinker, perhaps, Hsün Tzŭ preached what may be called a philosophy of culture. All morality, he maintained, is a product of culture and education and therefore would not exist were it not for the civilizing institutions created long ago by the sage-kings through their enlightened self-interest. "The nature of man is evil. His goodness is only acquired training." Man at birth possesses desires which, if unchecked, inevitably lead to strife; only under the constant influence of the mores of his group does he gradually learn to do what is right (chap. 23; Dubs, p. 301). In the next section we shall see how Hsün Tzŭ stressed the need for a structured society in order to curb and harmonize the otherwise anarchic desires of the individual.

Hsün Tzŭ's theory influenced many later Confucianists in varying degrees. Tung Chung-shu, for example, tried to harmonize Mencius with Hsün Tzŭ by saying that man's nature initially contains both selfishness and altruism and therefore can never become wholly good unless subjected to further human training: "Goodness is like a kernel of grain; the nature is like the growing stalk of that grain. Though the stalk produces the kernel, it cannot itself be called a kernel, and though the nature produces goodness, it cannot itself be called good. The kernel and goodness are both brought to completion through man's continuation of Heaven's (work)" (Fung 2, p. 34).

Yang Hsiung (53 B.C.–A.D. 18) asserted somewhat similarly that, "in man's nature, good and evil are intermixed. If he cultivates the good elements, he becomes a good man, but if he cultivates the evil elements, he becomes an evil one" (Fung 2, p. 150). A more deterministic view was expressed by Wang Ch'ung, who said: "There are in truth some (natures) that are good and some that are bad. The good ones are definitely so of themselves, whereas the bad ones may be caused to become good by undergoing inculcation which leads them to exert themselves" (*Lun Heng*, chap. 4; Forke, I, 374). During the next several centuries of Neo-Taoist and then Buddhist intellectual domination, little more was said on the subject until Han Yü, in the eighth century, proclaimed even more deterministically than Wang Ch'ung that men's natures fall into three categories: the superior, which is wholly good; the medium, which may be made to be either good or bad; and the inferior, which is wholly evil (Fung 2, p. 413).

With the rise of Neo-Confucianism in the eleventh century, however, Hsün Tzŭ's pessimistic view, together with the theories influenced by it, was definitely rejected, and that of Mencius became supreme. From then until recent days all major thinkers, regardless of other differences, have agreed that man is by nature good. The only partial exception is Tai Chen (1723–77), a thinker of materialistic tendencies who reacted strongly against the earlier Neo-Confucianists. Thus he denied their contention that man's nature is a metaphysical principle implanted in man at birth, describing it instead in physical terms as consisting simply of "blood, breath, and the mental faculty." There is a difference, he maintained, between what is natural to man and what is morally necessary, and, though man's nature at birth is potentially good, his ability to rise from the natural to the morally necessary sphere depends upon the extent to which he succeeds in developing his mental faculty. Thus Tai, like Hsün Tzŭ, attaches great importance to education and knowledge as molders of human morality.[26]

B. ORIGIN OF EVIL

What is the reason for this insistence—well-nigh universal during the last nine centuries—on man's innate goodness? Any consideration of this question must begin with a recognition of the Chinese conviction, already repeatedly referred to, that the universe is a harmony, the basic principle of which is therefore one of goodness; that the human world is an integral part of this harmony; and that man's nature is the vital link between the two.

On this point it is illuminating to contrast the attitudes of Mencius and Hsün Tzŭ. Thus for Mencius, in whom there is a mystical awareness of the oneness of man and the nonhuman universe, the metaphysical justification for the doctrine of human goodness is the fact that man's nature is "what Heaven has given us" (VI*a*, 15). For Hsün Tzŭ, on the contrary, human goodness has no such metaphysical basis but is solely the result of man's own efforts. It is thus unrelated to *T'ien*, or "Heaven," which, by Hsün Tzŭ, is interpreted as simply the name for a wholly naturalistic process.[27]

For this reason Hsün Tzŭ urges men not to exalt and conform to Heaven but rather to depend on themselves and to utilize the manifestations of Heaven for their own advantage (chap. 17; Dubs, p. 183). This denial by Hsün Tzŭ of the cosmic unity of man and nature, together with his theory of human nature and static view of history (see preceding section), represents a world view which in later times was decisively rejected by most Chinese thinkers.

If, however, the universe is actually a natural harmony, and therefore imbued with a principle of goodness which, contrary to Hsün Tzŭ, provides the basis for human goodness, we are then again faced by the question which was raised at the beginning of this section: What is the origin of evil? Is it, as has so often been asserted in the West, a matter of original sin or of a devil—figurative or otherwise—who struggles to gain men's souls? The former thesis is, on the face of it, impossible for anyone who, like Mencius, believes that man is *born* good. But the latter is equally unacceptable to him and his followers, since the very idea of forces of good and evil being engaged in a *struggle* with one another violates the basic concept of a self-contained harmonious universe.

Mencius himself does not analyze the problem from a metaphysical point of view. He merely says that men do wrong because of carelessness—they forget to preserve and nourish the goodness that lies within them and thereby allow it to be stripped from their natures, just as a once-beautiful mountain may be stripped of its trees until it becomes bare and barren. "But is this," Mencius asks, "the (original) nature of the mountain?" (VI*a*, 8). Thus, he says, "if men do what is not good, it is not the fault of their natural powers" (VI*a*, 6).

Though this answer may be unsatisfying in its failure to explain *what it is* that thus causes men to forget their original natures, it at least seems clearly to avoid the idea of good and evil as two contending forces and to point instead toward another conception much more congenial to Chinese thought. This is, that what we call "evil," far from being a positive force trying to destroy the cosmic harmony, is, on the contrary, just as much a part of that harmony, and just as necessary for its functioning, as what we call "goodness." Or, looked at from a slightly different point of view, it is an occasional falling-away from the harmonious centrality of all things—arising, in the case of man, because of his inadequate understanding of the cosmic pattern.

Formulations of this idea occur both in Taoism and in Buddhism. The Taoists, for example, never tire of pointing out that what men call right and wrong, good and evil, are purely relative concepts, without validity from the standpoint of the universal *Tao*. In Chuang Tzŭ's words: "Because of the right there is the wrong, and because of the wrong there is the right. . . . The right is an endless change. The wrong is also an endless change. . . . Therefore the Sage harmonizes the systems of right and wrong, and rests in the Evolution of Nature" (chap. 2; Giles, pp. 18 and 21).

Chinese Buddhism, too, though from its own point of view, denies the existence of evil as a positive force. Men endure the sufferings of life and death simply because of ignorance; they gain release from suffering through an understanding of its true nature. In either case the world itself remains unchanged; the only change lies in the individual's own understanding. Hence sin has no objective existence but is only a state of mind. Indeed, it is even possible for enlightened beings to perform acts without incurring retribution for them, which, if performed by other beings, would certainly be sinful.[28]

The clearest statements on good and evil, however, are those of the Neo-Confucianists. Li Ao (d. *ca.* 844), for example, one of the precursors of Neo-Confucianism, maintains that man's nature per se is wholly good but that, when the nature comes to be externally manifested in the form of the feelings or emotions (*ch'ing*), this goodness becomes obscured. This, however, "is not the fault of the nature," any more than it is the fault of an originally pure stream of water that it later becomes muddied by sediment. To prevent the feelings from operating, therefore, is the way to enable "the nature to gain its fulfilment," whereas "when the movements of the feelings continue unceasingly, it becomes impossible to return to one's nature and to radiate the infinite light of Heaven and Earth" (Fung 2, p. 414). Though Li thus distinguishes sharply between the original nature and its external emotional manifestations, he then goes on to say that "the nature and the feelings cannot exist one without the other"; in other words, that they are not diametric opposites, since both are equally aspects of the same universal whole. This doctrine, as Fung Yu-lan points out (*ibid.*), not only stems back to Mencius, but also owes much to Buddhism.

Chou Tun-yi (1017–73) agrees with Li that, though man's nature is originally good, its manifestations in actual conduct do not always conform to the mean; defective conduct of this sort we then call "evil" (Fung 2, p. 446). At about the same time we find the Ch'eng brothers insisting on the fact that goodness and evil are both inherent in the cosmic pattern and therefore cannot be disassociated from one another. Thus Ch'eng Hao (1032–85) says: "That some things are good and some evil is all equally a result of Heavenly Principle. For in Heavenly Principle it is inevitable that some things be beautiful and some ugly" (Fung 2, p. 518). And Ch'eng Yi (1033–1108) says similarly: "Within the universe, all things have their opposite: when there is the *yin*, there is the *yang;* when there is goodness, there is evil" (*ibid.*). These remarks possibly reflect the views of their uncle, Chang Tsai, who said that "the feelings of love and hatred are both equally products of the Great Void" (Fung 2, p. 483).

In the philosophy of Chu Hsi (1130–1200), the great synthesizer of Neo-Confucianism, there is a dualism between *li*, or "Principle," which is metaphysical, and *ch'i*, or "Ether," which is physical. The *ch'i* is the physical substance of which the universe consists. However, what gives meaning and order to the *ch'i*, and makes an organized universe possible, is the immanence in each physical object, whether animate or inanimate, of the metaphysical *li*, or "Principle." In the case of man, this *li* is known as his nature, which, therefore, in itself is invariably good. As externally manifested, however, this goodness can be actualized only imperfectly, owing to the impediments laid upon the nature by the surrounding physical *ch'i*. This *ch'i* differs in its purity (i.e., in the extent to which it allows *li*, or "Principle," to manifest itself) not only as between different species of creatures but also as between individual human beings. This is the reason for the moral differences externally found among different men. As to why the *ch'i* should thus have such differences, Chu Hsi can say nothing more than that they are natural and inevitable. Thus a disciple once asked: "Since *li* is everywhere good, how is it that the *ch'i* is differentiated into the pure and the turbid?" To which Chu replied: "Because, if one speaks only of the *ch'i*, there is some that of itself is cold and some that is hot, some fragrant and some bad smelling" (Fung 2, p. 553).

Here, as far as the *ch'i* alone is concerned, we find the view expressed that so-called "evil," like so-called "goodness," are both inherent elements in a larger whole. In Chu's greater dichotomy between the *li* and the *ch'i*, however, there seems at first sight to be a dualism of the sort so familiar to us in the West. Yet even here, as we shall see in Section 6, this seeming similarity breaks down on closer examination.

Wang Shou-jen, better known as Wang Yang-ming (1472–1529), was the greatest figure in Neo-Confucianism after Chu Hsi, with whom he differed in many important respects. In his concept of evil, however, he conforms to the general line of thinking we have been describing. Thus he says:

> The highest good is the mind's original substance. Whatever goes beyond this original substance is evil. It is not a case of there being something good, and then of there being something evil standing in opposition to it. Thus good and evil are only a single thing. . . .What we call evil is not original evil, but results either from transgressing or falling short of our original nature [Henke, pp. 156–57].

Somewhat later Yen Yüan (1635–1704) strongly attacks Chu Hsi's dichotomy between the metaphysical *li* as being wholly good and the physical *ch'i* as being the source of evil. Actually, Yen maintains, *li* and *ch'i* are inextricably bound together into "a single continuum," of which, therefore, it is impossible to say that one part is good and another evil. "How then," he asks, "can it be said that Principle (*li*) is uniform and single in its goodness, whereas the physical endowment deviates toward evil?" This would be like saying that the eye's (nonphysical) power of vision is good, whereas the physical eye itself, possessing this power, is evil. In actual fact, however, "it is only when its (the eye's) vision is led astray by improper things, or blocked or beclouded by them, that its view of things becomes wrong, so that evil can first be spoken of." Thus, for Yen, evil is not to be associated solely with the *ch'i*, nor is it a positive quality in itself. Rather, it is simply a deflection from "Heaven's correct pattern," caused by "enticement, delusion, habit, and contagion."[29]

From this survey of Neo-Confucian opinion, let us turn back for a moment to the Han Confucianist, Tung Chung-shu. He, it will be remembered, partially agreed with Hsün Tzŭ by saying that man's nature, at birth, contains selfishness as well as altruism and, therefore, that it cannot be made wholly good save through human institutions and education. His explanation for this initial mixture of good and evil is that man's goodness corresponds to the *yang* principle of Heaven, and his evil to Heaven's *yin* principle. Heaven imposes restraints upon the movements of the *yin*, and man should likewise confine the operation of the evil aspect of his nature, using for this purpose his intelligence, by means of which he creates his civilizing institutions (Fung 2, pp. 32–35).

Here we should keep in mind the thesis first suggested at the beginning of this paper—that in the West the universe has commonly been regarded as under the control of an external Divine Power, whereas in China it has been regarded as a self-contained organism functioning according to its own inherent pattern. At this point, however, it is necessary to make a further qualification by pointing out that this latter conception, while *generally* true of Chinese thinking, is not necessarily invariably true.

The *Yin-yang* and the Five Elements schools, for example, commonly explain the interrelationship alleged by them to exist between natural phenomena and human behavior in terms of an impersonal and automatic sequence of cause and effect. At other times, however, and without any explanation for the resulting contradiction, they interpret abnormal natural phenomena as the deliberate manifestations of a Divine Power, used by it to warn men of their improper behavior (Fung 1, p. 165).

In Tung Chung-shu, who was heavily influenced by the *yin-yang* ideology, a similar contradiction appears (Fung 2, pp. 55–58). Sometimes, as a result, Tung seems to use the word *T'ien*, or "Heaven," in a naturalistic sense, signifying a natural universe whose movements take place through their own inner necessity, without external guidance; at other times, however, he seems to regard *T'ien* as a conscious power, acting deliberately to control the movements of the *yin* and *yang*, the Five Elements, etc.

The latter concept, as we have seen, provides the metaphysical basis for Tung's belief that man's nature initially contains evil as well as goodness, so that the former must be repressed in order to allow the latter to realize its full potentialities. For as soon as one believes that Heaven acts from without to insure the proper functioning of the universe, it would seem to follow that this universe, if left to itself, would no longer function properly. However, Tung Chung-shu is neither clear nor consistent on this point, so that in his philosophy there remains an unresolved contradiction between a teleological and a naturalistic trend of thinking, of which he himself appears to be unconscious.

This leads us to a final consideration of some importance: Hsün Tzŭ, who denies the innate goodness of human nature, also stresses man's separateness from the nonhuman universe, which he conceives of in naturalistic—seemingly almost mechanistic—terms. Tung Chung-shu, on the other hand, while sharing Hsün Tzŭ's views about human nature to a limited extent, nevertheless affirms the unity of man with nature, to which, however, he apparently sometimes attributes volition and even personality. The prevailing Chinese belief in human goodness, for its part, seems to stem from yet a third, peculiarly Chinese, world view, different from that of either of these two men. Unlike that of Hsün Tzŭ, this view asserts that man is an integral part of a larger cosmic pattern, the goodness of which it accepts as axiomatic, simply because it *is* the cosmic pattern; but, unlike Tung Chung-shu's view, it asserts that this goodness is something inherent and spontaneous and not dependent on the volition of any external controlling Power.

C. UNIVERSAL SALVATION

The natural corollary of the foregoing ideas is a firm belief in the universal perfectibility of all men. This, for the Confucianists, means that every man can become a sage and, for the Buddhists, that every man can achieve Buddhahood. Such, at least, is the theory, though, as clearly realized by Confucianists and Buddhists alike, it is one rarely achieved in actual life.

For the Taoists the situation is somewhat different, since, with their relativistic outlook on human affairs, they not only accept the existence of differences between individual human beings as inevitable but insist that true goodness lies in the preservation rather than the obliteration of these differences. In other words, the Taoists maintain that men are necessarily unequal in their external achievements but that they are nevertheless all equally good in so far as they all equally conform to their true natures. Hence they believe it is folly for anyone to strive to become a sage, unless it is truly in his nature to be such. This point of view explains why the Taoists, unlike the Confucianists and Buddhists, are uninterested in the possibilities of universal sagehood or salvation.

Among Confucianists, on the contrary, the belief in this possibility is shared with few exceptions. It is natural that Mencius should give his hearty approval to a saying possibly already current before his time: "All men may become a Yao or a Shun (legendary sage-rulers)" (VI*b*, 2). More unexpected, however, is Hsün Tzŭ's utterance (chap. 23; Dubs, p. 312) of an almost identical saying: "The man in the street can become a Yü (another sage-ruler)." If Hsün Tzŭ, despite his pessimistic view of man's original moral state, could nevertheless have such confidence in the possibility of human improvement through education, it is not surprising to find almost all later Confucianists voicing similar confidence. Thus Wang Shou-jen, to cite but one example, assures us that "the unifying quality of love is as surely possessed by the little man" as by the great one (Henke, p. 204).

It is the Buddhists, however, especially those representing the more peculiarly Chinese developments in Buddhism, who lay greatest stress on universal salvation. For example, Tao-sheng (*ca.* 360–434), who was very instrumental in shaping Chinese Buddhism, boldly asserted that even the *icchantikas* (nonbelievers in Buddhism), since they are sentient beings, are therefore like other men endowed with the Buddha nature and hence capable of achieving Buddhahood (Fung 2, p. 271).

This trend of thought is most spectacularly developed by the T'ien-t'ai school (6th century onward), in which the startling doctrine is advanced that all beings, even the Buddhas, possess two kinds of nature, the one pure, the other impure, and that these natures, for the Buddhas and other beings alike, remain forever immutable: "The mind-substance of each and every sentient being, and of each and every Buddha, originally contains the two natures, without the slightest distinction for all. Throughout they are exactly of the same sort, and have remained indestructible from antiquity until the present" (Fung 2, p. 379).

The only difference between the Buddhas and ordinary sentient beings, therefore, is that the former check the outward manifestations of the impure nature, whereas the latter do not. Even the Buddhas, however, can merely keep latent, but cannot actually eliminate or change, the impure nature, and, conversely, even depraved beings cannot eliminate or change the pure nature. The necessary corollary is that Buddhahood is open to all beings, provided only that they practice spiritual cultivation. This universalistic theory reached its logical culmination with Chan-jan (711–82), ninth patriarch of the T'ien-t'ai school, who proclaimed that "even inanimate things possess the Buddha-nature." "Therefore," he wrote, "we may know that the single mind of a single particle of dust comprises the mind-nature of all sentient beings and Buddhas. . . . All things, being immutable, are the *Bhūtatathatā* (the Absolute), and the *Bhūtatathatā*, responding to causation, is all things" (Fung 2, pp. 384–85).

This powerful affirmation contrasts significantly with the doctrine of the Mere Ideation school, as propounded in China by Hsüan-tsang. According to this school, the evolutions of all beings throughout successive existences are determined by "seeds"—some of them tainted, others untainted—which are imbedded in the consciousnesses of the beings concerned. These differing kinds of seeds, however, are not distributed among all beings equally: some beings are wholly devoid of the untainted seeds, some possess seeds qualifying them merely for the lower stages of Buddhism, and only a few possess the untainted seeds of Buddhahood itself. This, says the Mere Ideation school, is the reason for the differences in nature found among different beings and explains why not all men, but only a few, are capable of achieving Buddhahood (Fung 2, pp. 307 and 339). It is no mere accident that not only in this respect, but in others as well, the Mere Ideation school is the least Chinese and most purely Indian of all Buddhist schools in China. Indeed, it might better be termed "Buddhism in China" than "Chinese Buddhism."

4. *Social Harmony*

According to Chinese thinking, the world of man is, or should be, a reflection of the nonhuman universe, and man's nature is the essential link between the two. It is time now to examine in detail what has been the major Chinese conception regarding the social order.

Society, in Chinese eyes, consists of a large number of small social units (the family, the village, the guild, etc.), each of which consists in turn of individuals varying greatly in their intellectual and physical capabilities. Because of these inequalities, it is inevitable that class differences should exist. The social order, in other words, is a rationalization of existing human inequalities.

It does not follow, however, that there should be conflict between social classes. On the contrary, the welfare of the social organism as a whole depends upon harmonious co-operation among all of its units and of the individuals who comprise these units. This means that every individual, however high or low, has the obligation to perform to the best of his ability those particular functions in which he is expert and which are expected of him by society. Thus the ruler should rule benevolently, his ministers should be loyal yet at the same time ready to offer if need be their frank criticism, the farmers should produce the maximum of food, the artisans should take pride in their manufactures, the merchants should be honest in their dealings, and no one should interfere needlessly in the tasks of others for which he himself is not qualified. In other words, society should be like a magnified family, the members of which, though differing in their status and functions, all work in harmony for the common good.

It is in Confucianism that we find greatest insistence on this conception of society as a graded but harmonious organism. For example, the typically Confucian idea that government is the function of a specialized ruling group, and that in it, therefore, there can be no popular participation, goes back to Confucius in his assertion: "The people can be made to follow it (probably meaning a policy decreed from above); they cannot be made to understand it" (*Analects*, VIII, 9). Or, again, the view of society as a corporate body of responsible individuals appears in the answer given by him when asked the way of good government: "Let the ruler be ruler, the minister minister; let the father be father, and the son son" (*Analects*, XII, 11). In other words, let each individual fulfil in practice the obligations ideally expected of him according to his social position.

Mencius has given one of the most candid enunciations of Confucian class theory in two passages of his works:

> Some labor with their brains and some labor with their brawn. Those who labor with their brains govern others; those who labor with their brawn are governed by others. Those governed by others, feed them. Those who govern others, are fed by them. This is a universal principle in the world [III*a*, 4].

> If there were no men of a superior grade, there would be no one to rule the countrymen. If there were no countrymen, there would be no one to support the men of superior grade [III*a*, 3].

But it is Hsün Tzŭ, perhaps more than any other Confucian, who has supplied a theoretical justification for social inequality. Strife arises, he says, because all men are born with desires, whereas things are insufficient to satisfy all these desires equally: "People desire and hate the same things. Their desires are many, but things are few. Since they are few there will inevitably be strife." The primary reason for instituting social distinctions, therefore, is that such distinctions are needed in order to insure an orderly distribution of the good things of life without undue exploitation of one group by another:

> If the strong coerce the weak, the intelligent terrorize the stupid, and the people who are subjects rebel against their superiors; if the young insult the aged, and the government is not guided by virtue—if this be the case, then the aged and weak will suffer the misfortune of losing their subsistence, and the strong will suffer the calamity of division and strife. . . . Hence for this reason intelligent men have introduced social distinctions [chap. 10; Dubs, pp. 152–53].[30]

This view of society as an ordered inequality has been taken for granted by all later Confucianists, so that it is sufficient if we quote only the following single typical statement by Tung Chung-shu:

> The Sage observes what it is in the nature of the generality of men that leads to disorder. Therefore in his governing of men he differentiates between upper and lower (classes), permitting the rich to have enough to display their noble position, but not to the point of arrogance, and the poor to have enough to support life, but not to reach the point of anxiety. If a harmonious balance be maintained according to this rule, there will then be no lack of material resources, and upper and lower (classes) will be mutually at peace. Therefore good government will be conducted with ease [Fung 2, p. 53].

If we turn from Confucianism to other early schools, we find in Mo Tzŭ (*ca.* 479–*ca.* 381 B.C.) one of the most striking antitheses to the Confucian way of life. In a manner almost Marxian, he emphasizes the fact of conflicting group interests and waxes bitter over "the large state which attacks small states, the large house which molests small houses, the strong who plunder the weak, the clever who deceive the stupid, the honored who disdain the humble" (chap. 16; Mei, p. 87). Nor does he hesitate to make many sarcastic attacks on the "gentlemen of the world" who condone this state of affairs (Mei, pp. 49, 135, 151, 246). Yet, unlike Marx, he draws no conclusion that the weak should unite to dispossess the strong. On the contrary, he remains well within the major current of Chinese thought by upholding the sanctity of the existing class structure and insisting that reform must come from above through moral indoctrination—which, for him, primarily means his famous doctrine of Universal Love, supported by certain religious and political sanctions. In the latter field, indeed, he goes further in the direction of authoritarianism than the Confucians themselves, by urging the complete intellectual conformity of inferior to superior in an ascending hierarchy consisting of clan members, clan patriarchs, state rulers, the king of the Chinese hegemony, and finally the Will of Heaven. This is his well-known doctrine of Agreement with the Superior (chap. 13; Mei, pp. 72–75).

The real totalitarians of ancient China are the Legalists, however, and it is they who are farthest removed from the Confucians in their insistence that men are inherently selfish and that therefore their unquestioning obedience to the state cannot be gained except through fear. Thus the Legalists, while fully as anxious as the Confucianists to maintain a clearly gradated class structure, see it in terms of a rigid conformity based on force rather than of a voluntary co-operation based on suasion. This fact undoubtedly goes far to explain their subsequent disappearance from Chinese thought as an identifiable group, even though certain of their political devices were perpetuated in modified form under the Confucian state.

Among the early Taoists there is a mixed point of view. Whereas the anarchistically minded Chuang Tzŭ would like to do away with government entirely, Lao Tzŭ accepts it, though grudgingly, and with the proviso that it be made as simple as possible. Much of his little book, as a consequence, is intended as advice for the Taoist sage-ruler. Hence when he says that "the Sage rules the people by emptying their minds" (chap. 3) or that he "treats them all as children" (chap. 49), he shows himself as much a believer in class distinctions as any Confucian, though from a different point of view.

A marked mellowing toward social institutions—undoubtedly the outcome of centuries of Confucian influence—appears in the Neo-Taoist Kuo Hsiang. Not merely does he, like Lao Tzŭ, accept organized government and society as unavoidable evils; as we have seen in Section 2, he even goes so far as to find no necessary incompatibility between the order of nature and the growing complexities of human civilization. Thus the following passage, though undoubtedly not intended by Kuo merely to justify the social status quo, nevertheless is as suitable for that purpose as any to be found in Confucian literature:

> Error arises when one has the qualities of a servant but is not satisfied to perform a servant's duties. Hence we may know that (the relative positions of) ruler and subject, superior and inferior, . . . conform to a natural principle of Heaven and are not really caused by man. . . . Let the servants simply accept their own lot and assist each other without dissatisfaction, . . . each having his own particular duty and at the same time acting on behalf of the others. . . . Let those whom the age accounts worthy be the rulers, and those whose talents do not meet the requirements of the world be the subjects, just as Heaven is naturally high and Earth naturally low. . . . Although there is no (conscious) arrangement of them according to what is proper, the result is inevitably proper [Fung 2, p. 227].

In another statement Kuo eloquently describes the harmony that emerges from seeming disharmony when the above principle is followed:

> Just as the spider and scarab, despite their humble surroundings, can spread their net or roll their ball without seeking the aid of any artisan, so for all creatures, each has that in which it is skilled. Although their skills differ, they themselves are alike in that they all practice these skills. This, then, is the kind of "skill that looks like clumsiness." Therefore the talented employer of men uses those who are skilled in squares to make squares, and those who are skilled in circles to make circles, allowing each to perform his particular skill, and thus to act in accordance with his nature. . . . That is why, being different from one another, their multitude of separate skills seem like clumsiness. Yet because everyone in the world has his own particular skill, the result seems like great skill [Fung 2, pp. 220–21].

Basic in the many attacks made on Buddhism by non-Buddhists during the next several centuries was the conviction that this alien ideology is dangerous to the Chinese way of life. On the one hand, it was felt, the Buddhist teaching that life is suffering is a denial of the Chinese conception of cosmic harmony; on the other, the Buddhist monastic order—an *imperium in imperio*—draws men away from their normal duties and thus destroys the fabric of Chinese society. This attitude appears clearly, for example, in the attacks made by one of the most famous of the critics, Fan Chen (*ca.* 450–*ca.* 515), a man who himself shows both Confucian and Taoist influence. "Buddhism," he begins by pointing out, "is injurious to government and its monks do harm to custom." Then, after going on to criticize the Buddhists for refusing to accept the ordinary round of human existence as natural and therefore desirable, he concludes by saying:

> Lesser people should find sweetness in their cultivated acres, and superior men should preserve their quiet simplicity. Let food be grown and it will not be exhausted. Let clothing be spun and it will not come to an end. Let inferiors present their surplus to their superiors, and superiors practice non-interference toward their inferiors. By the use of this principle there will be sufficiency for life and support for the parents; it will be possible to act for oneself and also for others; the country will remain in order and the ruler will be in his place [Fung 2, pp. 291–92].

There is little doubt that Fan's point of view, reiterated by many later critics, was a primary factor in the ultimate decline of Buddhism in China.[31]

It is not until the nineteenth century, therefore, that we find any Chinese so "un-Chinese" as to advocate the transformation of a class society into a classless society. This, however, is precisely the bold proposal made by K'ang Yu-wei and T'an Ssŭ-t'ung, both of whom, as we have seen in the first two sections, were directly influenced by Western thought. Thus K'ang exhorts: "Let us eliminate the class sphere and bring equality to all men. . . . Let us eliminate the sphere of the family and become 'citizens of Heaven.' . . . Let us eliminate the occupational sphere and foster means of livelihood common to all" (Fung 2, p. 689).

With similar fervor T'an Ssŭ-t'ung describes the coming Age of Universal Peace as one in which distinctions between ruler and subject and rich and poor are all to be obliterated: "Poverty and wealth are equalized. Within a thousand or a myriad miles it is as if there were but a single family or a single individual. . . . It is like the Millennium spoken of in Western books, or the Great Unity found in the *Evolutions of Rites*" (Fung 2, pp. 698–99).

Before concluding this section, we should not overlook a seeming contradiction between the Chinese belief in a strongly hierarchical society and the other Chinese belief, discussed in the preceding section, in the universal perfectibility of all men. In other words, there here seems to be a clash between the practical need of the Chinese for social stability and their theoretical advocacy of social mobility, as implied by their belief in the moral worth of the individual. Undoubtedly, the latter concept explains why certain writers have tried to read a "democratic" meaning into Confucianism, even though the former shows clearly why such "democracy" cannot possibly be equated with Western political definitions of the word.

On the theoretical level the Chinese solved this contradiction by recognizing that, whereas classes are necessary to society and must remain forever immutable as such, the possibility always exists for particular individuals to move upward or downward between these classes. Here, therefore, is another manifestation of the Chinese fondness for solutions which permit lesser change to occur within a greater permanency.

On the practical level the exemplification of this concept was the Chinese examination system—a device whereby all members of society, with trifling exceptions, were given the opportunity of entering the ranks of the ruling scholar-bureaucracy. In practice, unfortunately, this institution fell short of its avowed aim, owing to the failure of the Chinese state to provide equally broad opportunities for acquiring the education without which success in the examinations was impossible. This meant that most examination candidates came from a relatively restricted group of gentry families, whose political power, as a result, tended to become hereditary as a class, even though the individual members of this class had to prove their intellectual worth anew from generation to generation. Even this situation, however, is remarkable when compared with prevailing Western conditions before modern times, and to the Chinese mind, with its strong preference for working compromises in place of unworkable absolutes, it must have seemed sufficient. The net result, therefore, is that, though the Chinese social system theoretically left a place open for individual mobility, such mobility was infrequent in practice, save in times of war or political disintegration.

5. *Peace and War*

Since war is the most violent disrupter of social harmony, it is natural enough that it should be overwhelmingly condemned in Chinese philosophy. This is particularly true of the early period, when no unified empire existed, and war between the feudal states was endemic. Thus not only did the Confucians and Taoists denounce war, but also the hitherto unmentioned Dialecticians, whose leaders, Hui Shih and Kung-sun Lung (4th–3d centuries B.C.), were both known as pacifists (Fung 1, pp. 195 and 203). So too were such minor contemporaries as Yin Wen and Sung K'eng, who "proposed disarmament in order to save their generation from war" and preached that "it is no disgrace to be insulted" (Fung 1, pp. 148 ff.). The most famous indictment of war, however, is undoubtedly that of Mo Tzŭ, who in unsparing terms attacked it on both moral and economic grounds. Even for the victors, he said, the cost is so great that "when we consider the victory as such, there is nothing useful about it. When we consider the possessions obtained through it, they do not even make up for the loss" (chap. 18; Mei, p. 102).

Yet it would be incorrect to conclude that all these ancient thinkers were unalterably opposed to war under any circumstances. This, indeed, was made difficult by an embarrassing circumstance, namely, that, among the universally revered sage-kings of early times, several were known to history as having engaged in military campaigns. This fact forced Mencius, Mo Tzŭ, and Hsün Tzŭ alike into the familiar but dangerous doctrine that wars are sometimes "just," provided they be waged by the right person. The ancient sages, these thinkers said, occasionally found it necessary, despite their abhorrence of conflict, to take punitive measures against notorious tyrants or rebels. Such measures, however, would better be described as "chastisement" than as "attack," since their aim, in Hsün Tzŭ's words, was to "stop tyranny and get rid of injury." To this reasoning based on history, Mo Tzŭ added the further argument that the arming of the weak is justifiable as a deterrent to the aggression by the strong. This is why his book, which contains perhaps the most vehement denunciation of warfare in Chinese literature, also contains a group of chapters devoted to the defensive tactics to be used against aggression.[32]

There was only one group of men in ancient China, however, that deliberately exalted war as a political instrument, and this was the Legalists. As followers of *Realpolitik*, engaged in a ruthless struggle for power, they were interested in one thing only: how to create a strong and centralized apparatus of government. To achieve this end, all else must be subordinated, they said, to the two basic occupations of agriculture and war. Yet both, especially the latter, are arduous and poorly rewarded. Therefore, in order to induce people to serve readily in the army, "ordinary conditions should be made so hard for them, that they look upon war as a welcome release from their toil and as a good opportunity for earning rewards. Then they will fight with all their energy."[33] The cold-blooded realism of the Legalists is well expressed in the following passage from the *Han-fei-tzŭ* (chap. 49, middle):

> What are mutually incompatible should not co-exist. To reward those who kill the enemy, and at the same time praise acts of mercy and benevolence; to honor those who capture cities, and at the same time believe in the doctrine of universal love; . . . to depend on agriculture to enrich the nation, and on the soldiers to resist the enemy, and at the same time encourage men of letters; . . . strong government will not thus be gained.

Significantly, however, even the Legalists made no attempt to glorify war. For them it was simply a necessary means to a desired end. In the entire range of Chinese philosophy there has been nothing comparable to Nietzsche's exaltation of the superman and praise of war as morally desirable.

Only one later Chinese thinker, so far as I know, in any way compares with the Legalists in his acceptance of warfare. This is Wang Fu-chih, whose militant attitude stems from his nationalism, which, in turn, combines with his view of history (see Sec. 2 above) to set him sharply apart from the general current of Chinese thought. There are good historical reasons for this phenomenon, inasmuch as Wang lived at a time (the seventeenth century) when China was overrun by the Manchus, and this event embittered him so greatly that he spent much of his life in retirement rather than hold office under the alien rulers.

The ideological result, for him, is an ardent nationalism which causes him to extol the glories of the Chinese race and to laud China's periods of military expansion as expressions of manifest destiny. To bring the barbarians under Chinese rule is, he says, "to expand the virtue of Heaven and Earth and establish the apogee of man." Any means toward this end seems to be justifiable to him, the more so as the barbarians, in his eyes, may scarcely be accounted members of the human race at all: "As for the barbarians, destroying them means no lack of benevolence, attacking them means no lack of righteousness, and tricking them means no lack of good faith. Why so? Good faith and righteousness are principles to be practiced between one man and another, but they are not to be extended to an alien species."[34]

Before leaving this topic, there is one matter that should give us pause, and that is the seeming discrepancy between the attitudes we have been describing and those on a more popular and less philosophical level. On the one hand, to be sure, it is quite true that the soldier did not even hold a recognized place among the traditional classes of Chinese society—a fact implied by the well-known saying (rhyming in the original):

> Good iron isn't beaten into nails;
> A good man doesn't become a soldier.

Yet, on the other hand, it is also true that many of the most popular Chinese novels and dramas—from which, until recently, the ordinary man derived much of his knowledge of Chinese history—deal in most colorful fashion with famous wars and military figures of the past. This, no doubt, can largely be explained by fondness—widespread in China as elsewhere—for gallant deeds of derring-do, especially when sufficiently remote from the present as to become enshrouded in a haze of romantic glamour. Another factor of some sociological importance is that many of China's historical military heroes began their careers as bandits and have become identified in the popular mind as Robin Hood-like protagonists of the people against a corrupt social order. Even in these exciting novels and dramas, however, it is noteworthy that chief applause is often reserved for the man who prefers guile to force for gaining the submission of his opponent.[35]

6. *The Harmonizing of Opposites*

By now it should be evident that basic among Chinese thought patterns is the desire to merge seemingly conflicting elements into a unified harmony. Chinese philosophy is filled with dualisms in which, however, their two component elements are usually regarded as complementary and mutually necessary rather than as hostile and incompatible. A common feature of Chinese dualisms, furthermore, is that one of their two elements should be held in higher regard than the other. Here again, therefore, we have an expression of the concept of harmony based upon hierarchical difference, such as we have already seen in the Chinese view of society.

In the following pages we shall discuss only a few of these dualisms: man and nature, being and non-being, quiescence and movement, the *yin* and the *yang*, and *li* and *ch'i*.

A. MAN AND NATURE

The theme of the oneness of man with nature underlies so much of Chinese art and literature, and is so well known, that it scarcely needs reiteration. Here, therefore, we shall merely cite a few typical examples to illustrate the various ways in which it has been expressed by different schools.

In Taoism, of course, the approach is mystical, as typified by Chuang Tzŭ's statement (chap. 2; Giles, p. 23): "Heaven and Earth came into being with me together, and with me, all things are one." Chuang Tzŭ's contemporary, the Dialectician Hui Shih, expresses a similar sentiment when he says (chap. 33; Giles, p. 451): "Love all things equally; the universe is one." The same theme, expressed in terms of Confucian ethics, is repeated by Mencius (VII*a*, 4) in the words: "All things are complete within us. There is no greater delight than to find sincerity (*ch'eng*) when one examines oneself." The rationalistic Hsün Tzŭ, as we have seen, rejects this mystical approach, but the *Doctrine of the Mean*—a Confucian work probably partially reflecting Mencius' ideas—reaffirms it by saying (chaps. 20 and 22): "Sincerity (*ch'eng*) is the way of Heaven. To attain to that sincerity is the way of man. . . . (Able to do this), he can assist the transforming and nourishing operations of Heaven and Earth. Capable of assisting in these transforming and nourishing operations, he can form a trinity with Heaven and Earth."

In the *Yin-yang* and Five Elements schools, mysticism gives way to a wholly concrete and matter-of-fact attitude, in which, however, emphasis is given to the delicate balance believed to exist between natural phenomena and human behavior. Thus the *Yüeh Ling*, or *Monthly Commands* (Legge, *Book of Rites*, I, 257), tells us that "if in the first month of spring (the sovereign) follows the regulations pertaining to summer, the rain will be unseasonable, plants and trees will drop (their leaves) early, and the state will constantly have something of which to be afraid. If he follows the autumn regulations, his people will suffer great pestilences." In similar fashion the text goes on to describe the results of other unseasonable behavior for this and other months.

This sort of thinking culminates in Tung Chung-shu, who, with fervor combined with almost painful literalness, proclaims the following correlations, *inter alia*, between man and the nonhuman world:[36]

Man	Nature
head	Heaven's countenance
hair	stars and constellations
eyes and ears	sun and moon
breathing	wind
body	Earth's thickness
four limbs	four seasons
five viscera	Five Elements
orifices and veins	rivers and valleys
12 larger joints	12 months of year
360 lesser joints	360 days of year
ruler's likes and beneficence	warmth of spring
ruler's joy and rewarding	heat of summer
ruler's dislikes and punishing	coolness of autumn
ruler's anger and executing	coldness of winter
four official ranks (each with three officials, or a total of 12 officials)	four seasons (each with three months, or a total of 12 months)

We have already seen how some Chinese criticized Buddhism for its renunciation of life and thereby, in their eyes, its denial of the unity of man with the cosmic process. In part, at least, the reformist Buddhist movement known as *Ch'an* (Japanese *Zen*) was an attempt to answer this criticism. In many ways this school represents the most distinctively Chinese movement in Buddhism. It revolted against the complex cosmological and psychological theories of other Buddhist schools, calling them "arguments which are the ordure of nonsense." Likewise it rejected the deliberate striving for enlightenment through meditation and similar techniques, maintaining instead that "spiritual cultivation cannot be cultivated." By this it meant that enlightenment cannot be forced; it either comes naturally, in the course of one's ordinary humdrum round of life, or it does not come at all. "In carrying water and chopping wood: therein lies the wonderful *Tao*," was the Ch'anist slogan. In the words of Yi-hsüan (d. 867): "You followers of the Way (*Tao*), there is no need for you to devote effort to the Buddhist teaching. Only do the ordinary things with no special effort: relieve your bowels, pass water, wear your clothes, eat your food, and, when tired, lie down. The simple fellow will laugh at you, but the wise will understand."[37]

In this stress on enlightenment as something to be found within the natural round of life (a subject to which we shall recur in Sec. 7), there is much of the spirit of Taoism. In several respects, indeed, the Ch'an school may well be termed a kind of Taoism in Buddhist dress.

Finally, both in Neo-Confucianism and in nineteenth-century Confucianism there are innumerable expressions of a mystic awareness of oneness between man and the nonhuman universe:

> Chou Tun-yi is said to have refrained from clearing away the grass from the front of his window, "because," said he, "its impulse is just like my own."[38]

> "Heaven and man are to each other as the inner and outer sides (of a garment)," says Shao Yung [Fung 2, p. 468].

> "A state of functioning in which differentiation is made between Heaven and man cannot adequately be said to be 'sincerity.' A state of knowledge in which differentiation is made between Heaven and man cannot be considered as the utmost 'enlightenment,' " says Chang Tsai [Fung 2, p. 493].

> "The man of love (*jen*) takes Heaven, Earth, and all things as one with himself," says Ch'eng Hao [Fung 2, p. 521].

> "The mind of a single person is the mind of Heaven and Earth," says Ch'eng Yi [Fung 2, p. 531].

> "It is not the case that man, as the being possessed of the highest intellect, stands alone in the universe. His mind is also the mind of birds and beasts, of grass and trees," says Chu Hsi [Bruce, *op. cit.*, p. 61].

"The universe is my mind, and my mind is the universe," so that "if I can develop completely my mind, I thereby become identified with Heaven," says Lu Chiu-yüan (1139–93) [Fung 2, pp. 573–74].

"The great man is an all-pervading unity with Heaven, Earth, and all things," says Wang Shou-jen [Henke, p. 204].

"The bringing of all things into equable conformity, tranquilizing Earth, giving completion to Heaven, and bringing great harmony to the entire universe: these are my nature's final results," says Yen Yüan [Fung 2, p. 646].

"Heaven is a single spiritual substance, and man too is a single spiritual substance. Though different in size, they both share the vast energy derived from the Great Origin," says K'ang Yu-wei [Fung 2, p. 685].

"The ether functions in its most spiritual and subtle aspects when it constitutes the brain in the human body. . . . It is the electricity in the atmosphere, . . . that unites Heaven, Earth, the myriad creatures, the self, and other men, into a single organism," says T'an Ssŭ-t'ung [Fung 2, pp. 693–94].

B. BEING AND NON-BEING

The terms "being" (*yu*) and "non-being" (*wu*) occur only sporadically in Confucian literature and then most commonly in the course of diatribes against Taoism or Buddhism. In the latter two schools, on the other hand, both terms are in frequent use, though with a strong and characteristic preference shown for "non-being" as against "being." This preference, as Fung Yu-lan observes, runs quite counter to the Western point of view:

> When a student of Chinese philosophy begins to study Western philosophy, he is glad to see that the Greek philosophers also made a distinction between Being and Non-being, the limited and the unlimited. But he feels rather surprised to find that the Greek philosophers held that Non-being and the unlimited are inferior to Being and the limited. In Chinese philosophy the case is just the reverse.[39]

We have already read in Section 1, for example, Lao Tzŭ's statement that "being is the product of non-being" (chap. 40), with which may be compared the passage in the *Chuang-tzŭ* (chap. 23; Giles, p. 304): "All things issue forth from non-being, for since being itself cannot, by means of its own being, cause being, it must necessarily issue forth from non-being." The same idea appears in the Neo-Taoist Wang Pi (226–49), when he says: "Though Heaven and Earth, in their greatness, are richly endowed with the myriad things; though their thunder moves and their winds circulate; though through their evolving operations the myriad transformations come to be—yet it is the silent and supreme non-being that is their origin" (Fung 2, p. 181).

In these and similar Taoist passages, non-being definitely does not mean actual "nothingness." It is simply a convenient name for what is really indescribable and, therefore, strictly speaking, unnamable: the state which is different from, or ontologically prior to, the state of being of our own organized, finite universe. In the same way the Buddhists commonly refer to the world of fluctuating phenomenal existence as that of being, but to the permanent reality underlying this phenomenal flux as non-being.

In the passages quoted so far, being and non-being are apparently regarded as mutually exclusive concepts, whereas, as we have indicated earlier, the long-range Chinese tendency is to merge all such seeming opposites into a higher unity. On the Taoist side, Kuo Hsiang achieves this unity by simply eliminating the concept of non-being from his philosophy entirely. This he does by interpreting the term as actually meaning what it literally says: nothingness. Thus, for him, it becomes equivalent to what we would call a mathematical zero, and so, since there really is no such a thing as non-being, it follows that the only actual existence is that of being. We have already seen in Section 1 how, with this argument, Kuo Hsiang conceives of the universe as an eternal flux of being, self-caused and self-existent, which functions independently of any prior or external agent.

On the Buddhist side, the usual line of reasoning is to say that "non-being," if it really signifies the Buddhist Absolute, cannot be subject to any kind of limitation, such as that implied when it is described as the mere opposite of being. Therefore genuine non-being represents a higher kind of synthesis—one transcending, yet at the same time embracing, both being and non-being as ordinarily conceived.

Perhaps the most striking exemplification of this trend of thought is the Theory of Double Truth as propounded by Chi-tsang (549–623). According to him, there are, for the seeker of Buddhist enlightenment, three ascending levels of truth, each to be found under the two categories of mundane truth and absolute truth. The noviciate begins his spiritual cultivation by rising from mundane truth to absolute truth, as postulated on the lowest level. As his understanding deepens, however, he comes to realize that what, on the lowest level, is absolute truth is no more than mundane truth on the second level. On this higher level, therefore, he again passes from mundane truth to absolute truth, only to be confronted by yet another antithesis of the two on the third or highest level. Thus step by step he progresses in his cultivation until at last he reaches the third and final absolute truth and thereby achieves enlightenment. This process may be schematized as follows (Fung 2, p. 295):

THREE LEVELS OF DOUBLE TRUTH

Mundane	Absolute
1. Affirmation of being	1. Affirmation of non-being
2. Affirmation of either being or non-being	2. Denial of both being and non-being
3. Either affirmation or denial of both being and non-being	3. Neither affirmation nor denial of both being and non-being

Thus, in a manner reminiscent of Hegelian dialectics, being and non-being are gradually merged through a succession of negations of negation, until finally nothing remains to be either affirmed or denied.

C. MOVEMENT AND QUIESCENCE

Tung ("movement") and *ching* ("quiescence"), or their various rough equivalents, such as *wei* ("activity") and *wu wei* ("non-activity"), are antithetical terms which, like being and non-being, occur frequently in Taoism and Buddhism, especially with reference to human behavior and states of mind. And just as, in the ontological sphere, the Chinese show a strong preference for non-being as against being, so in the human sphere they emphasize the importance of quiescence as against movement. "Quiescence is the lord of movement," says Lao Tzŭ (chap. 26).[40] Therefore, he urges, "Hold fast enough to quiescence, and of the ten thousand things none but can be worked on by you" (chap. 16). Similarly, we are told by Chuang Tzŭ (chap. 13; Giles, p. 158): "Emptiness, quiescence, stillness and non-activity: these are the levels of the universe and the perfection of *Tao* and *Te* (the Power). Therefore true rulers and sages rest therein."

The same emphasis on quiescence as against movement is general in Buddhism, in which, for example, there is the following statement by Liang Su (753–93), an exponent of the T'ien-t'ai school: "What is this Reality? It is the original state of the nature. The failure of things to return to it is caused by darkness and movement. The illuminating of this darkness is called enlightenment, and the halting of this movement is called quiescence" (Fung 2, p. 423).

Both in Taoism and in Buddhism, however, there is a further tendency to merge movement and quiescence into a higher synthesis, for designating which they sometimes use a term other than "quiescence." The Neo-Taoist Wang Pi writes, for example: "The cessation of activity always means quiescence, but this quiescence is not something opposed to activity" (Fung 2, p. 181). Similarly, the Buddhist monk Seng-chao (384–414) has a famous essay, "On the Immutability of Things," in which he discusses the relationship of things past and present. Most people, he says, regard things as in a state of movement, because the events of the past do not reach into the present (they have moved away from the present). He himself, however, regards them as in a state of quiescence, precisely because events of the past do not depart from their positions in the past (they do not move into the present). But then, having thus seemingly spoken in favor of quiescence, he goes on to say that in the final analysis there is no real antithesis between it and movement, inasmuch as they may both be synthesized to form a higher state which he calls "immutability":

> In our search for immutability, we surely do not find quiescence by putting movement aside. We must seek for movement in the quiescent, just as we must seek for quiescence in movement. Therefore though (things) move, they are ever quiescent. Because we do not find quiescence by putting movement aside, therefore though (things) remain quiescent, they are ever in movement [*Book of Chao*, chap. 1; Liebenthal, p. 46].

In Neo-Confucianism we find this idea of quiescence continued among certain, though not all, thinkers—primarily they are those in whom Taoist or Buddhist influence is most apparent. Li Ao, for example, uses the Confucian term *ch'eng*, or "sincerity," to describe the state of genuine mental composure of the person who can synthesize the ordinary fluctuations of quiescence and movement. "When there is quiescence," he says, "it must be followed by movement, and when there is movement, it must be followed by quiescence. This uninterrupted (sequence of) quiescence and movement constitutes the feelings." However, "to realize that its (the mind's) original condition is that of the absence of thought; to be separated both from movement and quiescence; and to remain silently immovable: that is the state of sincerity in its utter perfection" (Fung 2, pp. 419–20).

Chou Tun-yi similarly describes the mind, in its highest state of perfection, as having two aspects: that of a quiescent "absence of thought," in which it is "silently immovable," and that of an awakened "penetrating activity of thought," in which, "becoming activated, it thereupon penetrates everywhere." The synthesis of the two is expressed by him in the words: "One's thoughts are absent, yet penetrate everywhere" (Fung 2, p. 450). Ch'eng Hao likewise emphasizes such a mental synthesis, for which, however, he uses the word *ting*, "composure": "What is termed composure is something that persists irrespective of whether there be movement or quiescence. It does not associate itself with anything, nor is there for it anything either internal or external. . . . The normality of the Sage is that his emotions accord with (the nature of) all things, yet (of himself) he has no emotion" (Fung 2, pp. 523–24).

This line of reasoning culminates in Wang Shou-jen's doctrine of the "Unity of Activity (or Movement) and Quiescence," of which he writes:

The mind may neither be said to be active nor quiescent. Its "quiescence" has reference to its (internal) substance (*t'i*), whereas its "activity" has reference to its (external) functioning (*yung*). . . . The mind is single and nothing more. Since quiescence refers to its inherent substance, to seek beyond this for yet a further basis of quiescence is to pervert this original substance. And since activity is its functioning, to be fearful of its becoming too readily active is to nullify its functioning. . . . In its state of activity it is active, but in its state of quiescence it is also active. (These two modes) rise and fall as they anticipate things; they follow one another without end [Henke, pp. 387–88].

D. THE "YIN" AND THE "YANG"

Just as in the foregoing dualisms there is a subordination of one element to another (man to nature, being to non-being, movement to quiescence), so in the interplay of the *yin* and *yang*, the former is definitely inferior to the latter. Speaking of them as cosmic forces, for example, Tung Chung-shu says that Heaven "has trust in the *yang* but not in the *yin;* it likes beneficence but not chastisement," or again that "the *yang* is Heaven's beneficent power, while the *yin* is Heaven's chastising power" (Fung 2, p. 29). Likewise, speaking of them as prototypes of the human social order, he says: "The ruler is *yang*, the subject *yin;* the father is *yang*, the son *yin;* the husband is *yang*, the wife *yin*" (Fung 2, pp. 42–43).

This inferiority of the *yin* to the *yang* is accepted—explicitly or implicitly—by all thinkers who adopt the *yin-yang* ideology. Never, however, is the suggestion made by them that the one can or should wholly displace the other. Hence there is no real analogy with the dualisms based on conflict (light vs. darkness, etc.) so familiar to us in the West. On the contrary, the *yin* and *yang* form a cosmic hierarchy of balanced inequality in which, however, each complements the other and has its own necessary function. As we have just seen, comparison is sometimes made with the existing human relationships, by which, indeed, the concept of the *yin-yang* relationship may to some extent have been inspired. Once formulated, however, this metaphysical relationship was in turn used by the Chinese to justify their existing class society. Such justification appears already, for example, in the appendixes of the *Book of Changes*, where we read in Appendix IV (Legge, p. 420): "Although the *yin* has its beauties, it keeps them under restraint in its service of the king, and does not claim success for itself. This is the way of Earth, of a wife, of a subject. The way of Earth is not to claim the merit of achievement, but on another's behalf to bring things to their proper issue."

More important than such analogies with human society, however, is the stress on the *yin* and *yang* as cosmic partners without whose joint activities the universal process would be impossible. For example, we are told in Appendix III of the *Book of Changes* (Legge, p. 395): "The *yin* and *yang* unite their forces, and the hard and the soft gain embodiment, thus giving manifestation to the phenomena of Heaven and Earth." Or, again, the same appendix (pp. 355–56) contains a famous statement which was to become basic for all Neo-Confucian cosmological speculation: "One *yin* and one *yang* (i.e., the alternation of the *yin* and *yang*) constitute what is called *Tao*. That which is perpetuated by it is good."

A noteworthy characteristic of the *yin-yang* dualism, and one distinguishing it sharply from those of the being and non-being or movement and quiescence type, is the fact that definite preference is given to the positive element, the *yang*, and not to the negative element, the *yin*. The reason for this becomes apparent as soon as we examine the ancient graphs of the two words, which, respectively, represent light rays streaming from the sun and rain clouds. Thus it is evident that they originally had to do with climatic phenomena—light and darkness, heat and cold, dryness and wetness, etc.—and that only later did they acquire such secondary connotations as activity and passivity, masculinity and femininity, hardness and softness, etc. These climatic associations are dominant in the *yin-yang* cycles of the sort we have described in Section 1, and it would be surprising indeed if the early Chinese, living in North China, with its rigorous winter climate, would have preferred the cold-bringing *yin* to the life-giving *yang*. Yet, confronted by the inexorable diurnal and annual alternation of the two, they were wise enough to see in them a pattern of movement necessary to the cosmic harmony rather than two irreconcilable warring forces.

E. "LI" AND "CH'I"

In Section 3, when discussing Chu Hsi's interpretation of the problem of evil, we touched briefly on his antithesis between the metaphysical *li*, or "Principle," which is wholly good, and the physical *ch'i* ("Ether," or matter), which is sometimes pure, sometimes turbid. Here again there is a dualism which at first sight looks like those of the West, yet on closer examination it is seen to be typically Chinese. For though Chu Hsi and his followers recognize the ontological priority of *li* over *ch'i*, as well as its precedence in dignity, they also recognize that both are equally necessary, since without either one of them there could exist no organized universe such as that in which we live. Bruce, in his study of

Chu Hsi, has admirably summed up the Sung Neo-Confucian attitude on the subject as follows:

> The Dualism, even if we call it Dualism, must be sharply differentiated from certain dualistic theories of the West. For example, in the dualism of the Sung School there is nothing antagonistic in the component elements. On the contrary, they are interdependent and complementary to each other. Law [i.e., *li*] pervades Matter [i.e., *ch'i*] as its directing principle, and Matter furnishes Law with its means of manifestation. It is true that in the dualism of Matter we have the two opposites of the *Yin* and the *Yang*. . . . But even these opposites are complementary not antagonistic. . . . However, a careful study of Chu Hsi's teaching as a whole shows that in his thought the two elements *li* and *ch'i*, coexistent and mutually dependent though they be, are not coequal; that the one is subordinate to the other, and is even derived from it. . . .
>
> To sum up, *li* and *ch'i* are coexistent and inseparable, but *ch'i* is subordinate to *li*, as the source or root from which it is derived. Here, then, we have the answer to the question with which we began. Chu Hsi asserts the essential subordination of Matter to Law as its ultimate source, Chinese Dualism resolves itself into Monism.[41]

In later times there were reactions against even this kind of dualism. The school of Wang Shou-jen, for example, attacked Chu Hsi's dichotomy from an idealistic point of view by acknowledging, with Chu, that man's nature is *li*, but then criticizing Chu's contention that man's mind is merely the physical container of the nature and therefore pertains to *ch'i* and not to *li*. On the contrary, said the Wang school, the mind itself *is* the nature. At the same time, furthermore, it actually holds within itself all the concrete physical things of the external universe. Under A of this section we have already quoted the characteristic statement of Wang's predecessor, Lu Chiu-yüan: "The universe is my mind, and my mind is the universe."

Still later, but this time from a materialistic point of view, men like Yen Yüan and Tai Chen likewise attacked Chu Hsi's dualism. Thus Yen Yüan, as we have seen, maintained that *li* is amalgamated with the *ch'i* "into a single continuum" (Fung 2, p. 637). Tai Chen went still further by saying that man's nature is a product of the physical *ch'i* and that *li*, far from being a metaphysical Principle which is ontologically prior to the *ch'i*, is in reality nothing more than the inherent orderly pattern of the physical things of *ch'i* (Fung 2, pp. 655–58).

7. *The Sage*

The *Sheng*, or "Sage," as the highest ideal for all humanity, figures prominently (sometimes under other names) in Confucianism, Taoism, and Buddhism alike. Here we shall make no attempt to give any detailed description of his many qualities, as conceived by these three schools. Very generally, however, we may say that the Sage is a being who, to a supreme degree, synthesizes in himself antitheses of the sort described in the preceding section. More specifically, he is one in whom there is a merging of "the sublime and the common, the internal and the external, the root and the branch, the refined and the coarse."[42] Unlike the ideal being venerated by some other civilizations, therefore, he does not stand aloof from the world of everyday affairs. In his state of inmost being (sometimes spoken of as quiescence) he rests in the sphere of the sublime; yet in his state of outward functioning (sometimes spoken of as movement or activity) he participates with other men in the practical affairs of daily life.

This synthesis, however, is only the final phase in a process of spiritual development by which the Sage first succeeds in rising from the sphere of the ordinary to the sphere of the sublime and then, instead of remaining in the sublime, returns once more to the world of ordinary humanity. In this process of "withdrawal and return," to use Toynbee's phrase, there thus seems to be another manifestation of that cyclical pattern of thought of which we have already seen numerous examples.

As in many of these previous examples, however, the concept is much less clearly expressed in early Chinese thought than it became later on. Thus in early Confucianism and Taoism alike the Sage is at first conceived of in comparatively narrow terms, expressive of the relative centers of interest of these two schools: man and nature, respectively.

In Confucianism, for example, we find not only the rationally minded Hsün Tzŭ but also the more mystically inclined Mencius, emphasizing the Sage as the supreme exemplar of human relationships. Indeed, for these two thinkers, the very fact that a Sage is a Sage denotes, above all, his supreme ability to formulate and participate in the institutions and relationships of human society. Mencius, for example, tells us that the Sage "is the apogee of the human relationships" (IV*a*, 2). Or again he says: "That whereby man differs from birds and beasts is but small. The mass of the people cast it away, while superior men preserve it" (IV*b*, 19). As illustration, he then cites the legendary Shun as one who "paid discriminating attention to the human relationships."[43] Similarly, Hsün Tzŭ says (chap. 21; Dubs, p. 276) that "the Sage fulfils the duties of the (human) relationships." Or again he remarks: "A ruler is one who is good at organizing society. If this doctrine of forming a social organization is carried out as it should be, . . . the people will be united, and the worthy and good will serve the ruler; it will be the rule of a Sage-king" (chap. 9; Dubs, pp. 137–38).

Among the early Taoists, on the other hand, the true Sage is not someone ever busily organizing human society but rather one who himself conforms as much as possible to the natural, and who, if he be ruler, allows his people to do likewise. Chuang Tzŭ has many sarcastic remarks (Giles, pp. 108, 113, 117, 125, etc.) about the harm done by such busybodies as Yao, Shun, and other "sages" of the Confucian type. In his first chapter (Giles, pp. 7–8) he speaks of a "spirit man" living on a distant mountain, whose flesh and skin were like ice and snow, who did not eat the five grains but inhaled wind and drank dew, and who wandered beyond the four seas, riding on the clouds and propelled by flying dragons. "Even his dust and siftings," Chuang Tzŭ concludes, "could still be fashioned and molded to form a Yao or a Shun." Lao Tzŭ, too, though less fanciful and more down to earth, stresses the mental detachment of the Sage from the seemingly vital concerns of other men. The Sage, he says, is one who "relies on actionless activity (*wu wei*), and carries on wordless teaching" (chap. 2). He "rules the people by emptying their minds" (chap. 3) and, "in his dealings with the world, cautiously dulls the wits of the world" (chap. 49). His reason for thus acting is that "man's standard is Earth, Earth's standard is Heaven, Heaven's standard is *Tao*, *Tao*'s standard is the spontaneous" (chap. 25).

In Neo-Taoism, however, the mellowing attitude toward human institutions, noted earlier, is accompanied by a corresponding change in attitude toward the Sage. "He who reaches the highest point," says Kuo Hsiang, "reverts to what is below," whereas "he who ardently reaches for a position of solitary eminence, and does not put himself on an equality with the ordinary run of men, is a hermit of the mountains and vales, but not one who is unconditioned." Thus, for Kuo, the Sage is not someone who "folds his hands in silence amidst the mountains and forests." On the contrary, he gladly "participates in the affairs of the people" and, "even when occupying the highest place at court, is mentally no different from the way he is when amidst the mountains and forests." He is one in whom "the without and the within become mutually merged. . . . Therefore the Sage constantly wanders in the without in order to enlarge what is within. . . . Though he works his body the livelong day, his essential spirit is not affected." This, says Kuo, is "the main idea in the writings" of Chuang Tzŭ, whose central purpose it is to "teach us how to ferry over to the ordinary and encompass the existing world" (Fung 2, pp. 234–36).

The return of the Sage to the ordinary mortal world is also a conspicuous theme in Chinese Buddhism. "Though Wisdom lies outside affairs, it never lacks them," says Seng-chao. "Though Spirit lies beyond the world, it stays ever within it" (*Book of Chao*, chap. 3; Liebenthal, p. 72). For this reason, "the Sage . . . dwells in the world of change and utility, yet holds himself to the realm of non-activity (*wu wei*). He rests within the walls of the namable, yet lives in the open country of what transcends speech" (*ibid*., p. 109).

In later Buddhist schools the same idea is expressed in less Taoistic language. For example, we are told by Fa-tsang (643–712), a major figure of the Hua-yen school:

> The experiencing of the Buddha-realm means the emptiness of matter, absence of a personal ego, and absence of phenomenal qualities. . . . However, having experienced entry into this realm, one may not dwell forever after in calm extinction, for this would be contrary to the teaching of the Buddhas. One should teach what is beneficial and joyous, and . . . it is in this realm that one should think about all these things [Fung 2, p. 358].

In an almost contemporary text of the T'ien-t'ai school we read similarly:

> Because of the achievement of cessation, one dwells within the great *Nirvāna*. Yet because of the achievement of contemplation, one stays within (the cycle of) life and death. Or yet again, because of the achievement of cessation, one is not polluted by the world. Yet because of the achievement of contemplation, one is not restricted to silent inactivity [Fung 2, p. 378].

Here again, as in the discussion of good and evil (see Sec. 5, end), there is a contrast between this Chinese point of view and that found in the more purely Indian Mere Ideation school. Thus the latter, while it does not explicitly deny the continued existence of the individual in the phenomenal world after he attains Buddhahood, nevertheless remains conspicuously silent on this point (Fung 2, p. 339).

However, it is in the most purely Chinese expression of Buddhism, that of *Ch'an* or *Zen*, that we find the "humanization" or secularization of the Sage carried to its greatest extent. We have already read the slogan: "In carrying water and chopping wood: therein lies the wonderful *Tao*." The ordinary man wears his clothes, eats his food, and performs other natural physical functions; but, as the Ch'anists are never tired of saying, so does the Sage. The only difference is that his state of mind is no longer the same. In the words of Huai-hai (720–814): "What the man does is no different from what he did before; it is only that the man himself is not the same as he was." The first step of leaving humanity behind and entering sagehood, says Yi-hsüan (d. 867), is that in which "both the man and his surroundings are eliminated," in other words, in which subject and object no longer exist for him. But, having made this step, he then returns from his sagehood to the mortal world, thereby achieving a final synthesis in which, for him, "neither the man nor his surroundings are eliminated." The situation is summed up by P'u-yüan (*ca*. 748–*ca*. 836) when he says: "After coming to understand the other side, you come back and live on this side."[44]

Yet if the wonderful *Tao* is to be found in carrying water and chopping wood, why should it not also be found in the mutual obligations of father and son and ruler and subject, and why should the seeker for enlightenment be obliged to abandon his family and become a monk? These are the questions that underlie many of the Neo-Confucian criticisms of Buddhism. Chang Tsai, for example, remarks of the Buddhists that "as to those who speak about *Nirvāna*, they mean by this a departure which leads to no return," whereas he describes the Confucian Sage as one who "embodies" and "completely understands" the cycle of phenomenal existence (Fung 2, p. 497).

It is not surprising, therefore, that the Neo-Confucianists, unlike the Buddhists, feel under no compulsion to stress the return of the Sage to the ordinary mortal world, since, for them, it is axiomatic that he should always remain within it. In the words of Shao Yung, the Sage is able, on the one hand, "with his mind to represent the meaning of Heaven," but at the same time he is able "to comprehend clearly the affairs of men" (Fung 2, p. 465). The following quotations further illustrate how, for the Neo-Confucianists, the Sage is thus to synthesize "the sublime and the common":[45]

"To be faithful to one's daily round, to be reverent to one's duties, and to be loyal to one's fellow-men: these words reach to the bottom of things both above and below. The Sage from the beginning has had no second way of speaking on these matters," says Ch'eng Hao.

"Men of later times have spoken about the nature and destiny (conferred on man by Heaven) as if they were very special separate matters. Yet the nature and destiny, together with filial piety and the duties of a younger brother, all actually fall into a single category. And as to sprinkling and sweeping floors, responding to demands and answering questions, these too fall into the same category as developing one's nature to the highest and making the very best of one's destiny. There is no 'more important' and 'less important,' no fine and coarse," says Ch'eng Yi.

"He keeps to the place where he is and rejoices in the daily round. . . . Yet his mind wanders freely away to be in direct contact with Heaven and Earth and all things, and in complete accord with what is above and below," says Chu Hsi.

8. *Conclusion*

At this point it is well to reiterate the warning already made at the beginning of this article, namely, that the thought patterns we have been describing, while definitely typical of Chinese thinking on a sophisticated and philosophical level, are not necessarily always equally typical of thinking on other less sophisticated levels; sometimes, indeed, cases of obvious contradiction occur.[46] With this warning in mind, let us now try to recapitulate our findings.

The universe, according to prevailing Chinese philosophical thinking, is a harmoniously functioning organism consisting of an orderly hierarchy of interrelated parts and forces, which, though unequal in their status, are all equally essential for the total process. Change is a marked feature of this process, yet in it there is nothing haphazard or casual, for it follows a fixed pattern of polar oscillation or cyclical return; in either case these is a denial of forward movement, save in proximate terms only.

This cosmic pattern is self-contained and self-operating. It unfolds itself because of its own inner necessity and not because it is ordained by any external volitional power. Not surprisingly, therefore, Chinese thinkers who have expressed themselves on the subject are unanimous in rejecting the possibility that the universe may have originated through any single act of conscious creation. Some, indeed, go still further and deny even the possibility of a more naturalistic process whereby the universe has gradually evolved from a unitary origin into the complexity it has today. For these men the universe is self-created and hence has always existed and always will exist as it does now. Such a belief that the cosmic process in its totality is eternal does not conflict with the possibility that the universe passes through alternating phases of integration and disintegration and, therefore, that our existing world may be only one in a series of such worlds, each representing one of the integrative periods.

Human history belongs to the total cosmic process and, therefore, in the eyes of many Chinese, moves according to a similar cyclical pattern. Another and probably earlier Chinese view, however, sees antiquity as a golden age and all history since that time as a steady process of human degeneration. Some thinkers combine the two theories by saying that history does indeed move in cycles but that we moderns happen to be living during the downswing of one such cycle. Regardless of which of these interpretations is accepted, it is evident that all of them reject the idea of historical progress, meaning by this a process of progressive improvement.

Though the universe is self-acting and not guided by any volitional power, it is far from being merely a mechanistic universe. Indeed, the very fact that its movements result in life is enough to show that in them must be a principle of goodness. More than this, however, even what we humans regard as evil—for example, death—is, from a higher point of view, an integral part of the total cosmic process and therefore inseparable from what we choose to call goodness. In short, whatever *is* in the universe must be good, simply because it *is*.

The vital link between the nonhuman and human worlds is man's nature, and it necessarily follows from the foregoing that this nature must be equally good for all. If, nevertheless, some men fail to actualize the potentialities of their nature, this is because of their inadequate understanding of how the universe operates. This deficiency, however, can be removed through education and self-cultivation, so that the possibility always exists in theory—though admittedly the chances of its ever being actualized in practice are remote—for all men without exception to achieve sagehood. It thus becomes clear that evil, in Chinese eyes, is not a positive force in itself. It is, from one point of view, simply an inherent factor in the universe or, from another, the result of man's temporary distortion of the universal harmony.

Human society is, or at least should be, a reflection of this harmony. Hence it too is an ordered hierarchy of unequal components, all of which, however, have their essential function to perform, so that the result is a co-operative human harmony. This means that the ideal society is one in which each individual accepts his own social position without complaint and performs to the best of his ability the obligations attached to that position. Here there seems to be a conflict between this emphasis on social stability and a belief—implied in the doctrine of the potential perfectibility of all men—in social mobility. The two are reconciled, however, by upholding the sanctity of the class structure, yet at the same time recognizing the possibility of social movement for particular individuals. The Chinese examination system was a unique, though imperfect, attempt to give substance to this compromise on the practical level.

War, as the most violent disrupter of social harmony, is, of course, opposed by all save a very few Chinese thinkers. Even those who have condoned it as a sometimes necessary instrument have never attempted to glorify it—at least on the philosophical level—as has sometimes been done in the West.

Cutting across both the human and the natural worlds there are, in Chinese thinking, many antithetical concepts, among which we have discussed those of man and nature (Heaven, or *T'ien*), being and non-being, quiescence and movement, the *yin* and the *yang*, and *li* ("Principle") and *ch'i* ("Ether"). In each of these dualisms the Chinese mind commonly shows a preference for one of the two component elements as against the other. At the same time, however, it regards both of them as complementary and necessary partners, interacting to form a higher synthesis, rather than as irreconcilable and eternally warring opposites. Thus here again there is a manifestation of the Chinese tendency to merge unequal components so as to create an organic harmony.

The Sage is the man who to the highest degree succeeds in merging these seeming opposites in himself. As portrayed by the Neo-Taoists and Buddhists, he in so doing follows a cycle-like course of withdrawal and return, leading him first from the world of the ordinary to the world of the sublime, but then back once more to the world of ordinary affairs. Among the Neo-Confucianists, owing to their intense concern for human relationships, this idea of withdrawal is not stressed. Nevertheless, they agree with the other two schools that the Sage is both this-worldly and other-worldly, both active and quiescent, so that in him the highest synthesis is achieved.

Though relatively few of these thought patterns occur equally in all the schools we have been discussing, they nevertheless seem sufficiently to complement each other as to form in their totality a homogeneous world view. This homogeneity, naturally, did not spring into being overnight. It is the product of a long evolution, in the course of which certain ideas, and with them entire schools, have been sloughed off, leaving others to interact upon one another during many centuries. Most important in this process have been Confucianism, Taoism, the *Yin-yang* and Five Elements schools, and Buddhism, all contributing to Neo-Confucianism, which thus in a very real sense may be regarded as a summation and synthesis of what had gone before.

It is significant how frequently those thinkers who diverge from one of the strands of thought we have been discussing diverge from others as well. The Legalists, for example, were exceptional in their pessimistic view of human nature, approval of warfare, indifference to any meaningful pattern of history (though as practical men they stressed the need for political change), and reliance on force rather than suasion to achieve an ordered class society. It is not surprising that as a school they totally disappeared, even though certain of their ideas were institutionally perpetuated in later times.

Hsün Tzŭ, likewise, believed that man is born evil, stressed the separateness of man from nature, and held a peculiarly static view of history. Despite his enormous immediate influence, his ideas on all three points, especially the first and second, were ultimately rejected in favor of those of Mencius.

Later on, in Buddhism, we see that the Mere Ideation school, which denied the equal possibility to all men of achieving Buddhahood, also said virtually nothing about the role of the enlightened being in the world of suffering humanity. In other aspects as well (notably its extreme subjective idealism), this was the most Indian and least Chinese of all Buddhist schools in China. Buddhism itself, for that matter, despite its enormous influence, ultimately declined in China owing to the incompatibility of some of its ideas with the prevailing Chinese intellectual pattern.

Centuries later we see that Wang Fu-chih, who believed in historical progress, also preached nationalism and the conquest of the barbarians in the name of manifest destiny. And, finally, in the second half of the nineteenth century, we find a group of men—K'ang Yu-wei, T'an Ssŭ-t'ung, and, to a lesser extent, Liao P'ing—who, under obvious Western influence, break sharply with tradition by affirming historical progress and predicting a future classless society.

As for Tung Chung-shu two thousand years earlier, he presents some curious contradictions. On the one hand, he is a firm believer in the interrelationship of man and nature and the operation in both spheres of recurring cycles. On the other, his attitude toward Heaven seems at times to be a throwback to a much earlier, personalistic conception which, though once general in China, had already by the time of Mo Tzŭ become somewhat old-fashioned.

To attempt any detailed comparison between the prevailing world view of Chinese thinkers and Western thought patterns would require far more space than is here available. Nor would it be easy in view of the enormous diversity of Western thought in different times and places, and the consequent difficulty of determining what, if any, have been its prevailing patterns. Because of this diversity, it is quite possible that Western parallels can be found for many, if not most, of the Chinese concepts we have been discussing. Chinese cyclical theories of the cosmos, for example, are reminiscent of those of Anaximander and other Greek thinkers; the Chinese approach to good and evil suggests the attitude found in Stoic pantheism; and the Confucian theory of society is curiously similar to that found in medieval European thinking.[47]

To attempt isolated comparisons of this sort, however, is a rather fruitless task, for what really counts is the impact of the two bodies of ideas—Chinese and Western—in their totality rather than in their parts. And, if we examine this total impact, two conclusions emerge. One is the much greater homogeneity and total internal consistency of the Chinese world view, as compared with the many thought systems of the West, while the other is the enormous qualitative difference between the two—a difference most pronounced, of course, in the case of modern Western thought, but which goes as far back as ancient Greece. Among the points of difference which, on the Western side, seem to be particularly significant, may be cited the belief in a divine act of creation and a divine Power who decrees laws for a universe subordinate and external to himself; antagonistic dualisms of the good-and-evil or light-and-darkness type; original sin, predestination, and personal salvation; individual and class struggle, glorification of war, and belief in historical progress.

It is worth noting, however, that Western thinking, particularly in such fields as physics, has in recent years tended to move away from some of these traditional concepts toward attitudes and techniques which superficially, at least, bear marked similarity to some of those we have seen for China. This phenomenon is noted, for example, by Lily Abegg in the recent psychological study she has made on Chinese and Japanese thinking.[48] In this work she particularly calls attention to what she calls "the 'new thought form' which is now being talked about in scientific circles," and which is described by her as "based on the complementarity principle, that is to say, on the fact that two diametrically opposed statements can be made about the same thing, both of which can be proved and are correct."

This new approach, she points out, has led some modern scientists into making such paradoxical statements as: "The world is not really finite, neither is it, on the other hand, really infinite"—a statement irresistably reminding us of Chi-tsang's postulations about being and non-being in his Theory of Double Truth (see Sec. 6, B, above). However, as also stressed by Dr. Abegg, the road followed by the West in order to reach such formulations is radically different from that taken by the ancient Chinese thinkers:

> Whereas in the first case [modern physics] it is a matter of drawing the final conclusion from formally logical premises, in the latter case [Chinese thinking] it is a question of the results of a total view of things and total thinking. Modern physics arrives at these conclusions from the outside, the East Asian from the inside. Proceeding from plurality, modern physics thus finds itself faced with an incomprehensible unity and is compelled to make paradoxical statements about it, while the East Asian, proceeding from unity, has known for a very long time that it is not possible to make other than paradoxical statements about unity.

On the social side, though Confucian political and social thought is miles removed from that of a modern democratic society, it is nevertheless interesting to note that modern Western psychology and sociology are moving away from the extreme emphasis on individualism and competition and reaching a position more akin to the Chinese ideal of an integrated social organism based on co-operation. Confucianism, despite its many glaring defects to our modern eyes, proved itself remarkably well adapted to its own agrarian society and in certain respects provided more consistent and equitable answers to the problems of human relations than, let us say, did ancient Greek thinking on the subject. Thus it is a rather curious fact that in ancient Greece, where there was democracy for the few, there was also slavery for the many, whereas in ancient China, where there was no democracy as we think of it, there was also very little slavery.

Of course, in all comparisons of this sort, we should never forget the enormous gap between ideas and practice in China—for example, it certainly did not help the Chinese peasant in his dealings with a rapacious landlord to be told that human nature is good. Similar gaps, however, have likewise always existed in our Western world. Chinese thinking provided a *modus vivendi* for its people during one of the longest spans of human history, but in the process it failed to provide for "progress," and today it is inevitable that it should be cast aside. Western thinking has given the world such progress, but it has also brought it catastrophe, from which it is too early as yet to say whether we shall finally escape.

Rather than attempting value judgments of this sort, however, it is more appropriate in a study such as this to suggest possible reasons *why* Chinese thinking developed along the lines it did. At this point the temptation is strong to make a link between such thinking and the natural, social, and institutional environment of Chinese civilization. There are, for example, the facts that Chinese civilization, though not so autochthonous as once supposed, was founded and thereafter developed in relative isolation from any other civilizations of comparable level; that this was done by a rather homogeneous people, both racially and linguistically; that their terrain was a large continental land mass, much of it plain and most of it remote from the sea, very unlike the mountainous and indented peninsulas and islands of the Mediterranean peoples; that this terrain led them very early toward a strongly monocultural way of life, based almost exclusively on the intensive growing of grain; that, according to one well-known hypothesis, in order to develop this mode of life very far in the dry North China climate, the Chinese were obliged to construct extensive irrigation works, which in turn required the establishment of organized political control over large masses of manpower, thus encouraging the formation of a strongly bureaucratic state; that, as a consequence, commerce and other nonagrarian private enterprise failed to make significant growth, so that the Chinese cities became centers of political power rather than of an independent industrial-mercantile bourgeoisie; and, finally, that the Chinese, because of their concentration on this way of life, became extraordinarily aware of the seasonal rhythm of nature, which, in North China, is marked by a remarkable clocklike regularity.

All these features distinguish China sharply from ancient Greece, as well as from later European culture as a whole. Yet here we come face to face with a consideration which should give us pause: the fact that some of the Western conceptions seemingly most antithetical to those of China—notably those of a universe created and controlled by a divine being, or of various antagonistic dualisms—are not of European origin at all but go back to the cultural complex of the ancient Near East. And yet, socially and politically speaking, this Near Eastern cultural complex, at least from the superficial view of a nonspecialist, seems to resemble more closely what is sometimes called the "oriental bureaucratic state," of which China is a prime example, than it does the patterns of Greece and Europe. How, then, on the grounds we have here postulated, are the sharp ideological differences just mentioned to be explained?

Most writers have simply ignored such problems by speaking vaguely and sometimes mystically about the "oneness of the Orient." A very few, however, notably F. S. C. Northrop, have perceived that vast ideological differences separate Eastern from Western Asia and so have chosen to group Indian with Chinese thinking, on the one hand, as against Near Eastern–European thinking, on the other. As yet almost nobody has pointed out that India and China, despite certain undoubtedly strong ideological similarities, also display differences which, in the final analysis, may be equally significant. To cite only a few examples:

Whereas India is famed for its religions and has always exalted its priestly class, China has produced no world religion, was already in early times dominated by a strongly secular trend, and possessed no important priesthood prior to the advent of Buddhism. Whereas the Indians have a rich epic literature and mythology, the Chinese have very little of either. The Chinese, on the other hand, have been meticulous recorders of historical events and undoubtedly possess the largest historical literature of any long-lived people, whereas the Indians have been notoriously unhistorical. The Chinese have shown a genius for political organization, so that they have repeatedly created durable empires often extending far beyond the borders of China proper, whereas the Indians only rarely and briefly have succeeded in uniting the Indian subcontinent. The Indian caste system has no parallel in Chinese social thinking, even though, as we have seen, Confucianism emphasizes the hierarchical structure of society. Finally, as for Indian philosophy, some of its conspicuous concepts have been reincarnation, life as suffering, *Nirvāna*, subjective idealism, and the universe as atomistic, anarchic, and unorganized; it has also produced a well-developed system of logic. All these ideas were unknown in China prior to Buddhism, and the nearest Chinese approach to a system of logic was that of the Mohists, who, however, were speedily forgotten. Can we then safely accept these many widely divergent ideological manifestations as products of essentially similar ways of thinking or of a common world outlook?

This is not the place to go into a detailed analysis of differences such as these, nor is this writer qualified to do so. What he would like to suggest, however, is that Chinese thought needs not only to be studied internally but also comparatively and that such comparative study, in order to be most fruitful, should not be limited to China and the West alone. Ideally, it should also include the thought systems of other major civilizations, as well as, possibly, some of the preliterate peoples. Furthermore, if it is to achieve its real purpose, it must study these thought systems in the full context of their institutional background (social, political, and economic) rather than merely *in vacuo*.

This, of course, is a gigantic undertaking, for which, no doubt, data on the individual systems concerned are as yet inadequate. However, as a possible first step in its direction, thought might be given to the feasibility of preparing a small list of key concepts or themes, formulated with sufficient flexibility so that they could be applied to all the thought systems concerned. By using them as a guide, it might then be possible to extract from these systems a body of data which, being grouped around a common set of themes, would be sufficiently homogeneous to lend itself readily to comparative analysis.

NOTES

* Bibliographical Note.—A few Chinese works, because of the brevity of their chapter or paragraph divisions, are cited simply according to these divisions, as follows:

Analects of Confucius	*Doctrine of the Mean*
Lao-tzŭ	*Mencius*

The following works, available in Western translations, have been cited according to these translations, whose wording, however, has often been modified by me in the interests of consistency or greater accuracy:

Book of Changes: James Legge's translation in *Sacred Books of the East*, Vol. XVI (2d ed.; Oxford, 1899)
Book of Lord Shang: J. J. L. Duyvendak, *The Book of Lord Shang* (London, 1928)
Chuang-tzŭ: H. A. Giles, *Chuang Tzŭ* (2d ed.; Shanghai, 1926)
Hsün-tzŭ: H. H. Dubs, *The Works of Hsüntze* (London, 1928)
Huai-nan-tzŭ: Evan Morgan, *Tao the Great Luminant* (Shanghai, 1934)
Lü-shih Ch'un-ch'iu: Richard Wilhelm, *Frühling und Herbst des Lü Bu We* (Jena, 1928)
Mo-tzŭ: Y. P. Mei, *The Ethical and Political Works of Motse* (London, 1929)
Seng-chao's *Chao Lun*, or *Book of Chao:* Walter Liebenthal, *The Book of Chao* (Peiping, 1948)
Wang Ch'ung's *Lun Heng*, or *Critical Essays:* Alfred Forke, *Lun Heng* (2 vols.; Berlin and London, 1907 and 1911)

Wang Shou-jen's writings and conversations: Frederick Goodrich Henke, *The Philosophy of Wang Yang-ming* (Chicago and London, 1916)

Yüeh Ling, or *Monthly Commands:* James Legge's translation in *Sacred Books of the East*, Vol. XXVII (Oxford, 1885), pp. 249–310.

Many other works, unavailable in Western translation, are, for the sake of easy reference, cited according to the quotations made from them in Fung Yu-lan, *A History of Chinese Philosophy*, translated from the Chinese by Derk Bodde (Princeton: Princeton University Press, 1952–53). The two volumes of this work are referred to as "Fung 1" and "Fung 2."

1. Joseph Needham, "Human Laws and Laws of Nature in China and the West," *Journal of the History of Ideas*, XII (1951), 3–30, 194–230.

In making this contrast between the Chinese world view and the Western concept of the "Laws of Nature," what Needham is concerned with on the Western side is, of course, the traditional body of theological belief associated with the words "Laws of Nature" and not the changed meaning assumed by this term in rather recent times. As to the theological concept, he points out (*op. cit.*, p. 3): "Without doubt one of the oldest notions of Western civilization was that just as earthly imperial lawgivers enacted codes of positive law, to be obeyed by men; so also the celestial and supreme rational creator deity had laid down a series of laws which must be obeyed by minerals, crystals, plants, animals and the stars in their courses." Elsewhere (p. 229) he stresses the fact that "in the outlook of modern science there is, of course, no residue of the notions of command and duty in the 'laws' of Nature. They are now thought of as statistical regularities."

2. Cf. the many similar quotations in Fung 1, pp. 182–85.

3. Embodiments, respectively, of light, heat, masculinity, movement, dryness, etc., and of darkness, cold, femininity, quiescence, wetness, etc.

4. *Ch'ien* and *k'un* are the names of the two primary of the sixty-four hexagrams in the *Book of Changes* and are graphic representations of the *yang* and *yin*, respectively.

5. Cf. the many similar quotations in Fung 1, pp. 384–90.

6. Hu Shih, *Development of the Logical Method in Ancient China* (Shanghai, 1928), pp. 134–36.

7. A little almanac contained both in the *Lü-shih Ch'un-ch'iu* (compiled just prior to 235 B.C.) and in the slightly later *Book of Rites*.

8. Cf. the exposition in Fung 2, chap. 2, secs. 4–5, and especially the diagram on p. 28. For the quotation see p. 24.

9. Cf. the *Lü-shih Ch'un-ch'iu* (V, 2; Wilhelm, p. 58): "Great Oneness produced the Two Forms. The Two Forms produce the *yin* and *yang*"; the *Book of Changes* (Appendix III; Legge, p. 373): "In the *Changes* there is the Supreme Ultimate, which produced the Two Forms"; the *Huai-nan-tzŭ*'s seven stages of cosmogonic evolution (chap. 2; Morgan, pp. 31–33); Tung Chun-shu's *Yüan*, or "Origin," which "existed before Heaven and Earth" (Fung 2, p. 20); Yang Hsiung's (53 B.C.–A.D. 18) *Hsüan*, or "Mystery," which underwent successive tripartite divisions whereby it evolved into the three *fang*, nine *chou*, twenty-seven *pu*, and eighty-one *chia* (Fung 2, pp. 140–42); Chou Tun-yi's (1017–73) famous *T'ai-chi T'u* ("Diagram of the Supreme Ultimate"), which graphically portrays the stages of cosmic evolution, beginning with the Supreme Ultimate, and passing through the *yin* and *yang*, the Five Elements, and thus to all

things (Fung 2, pp. 435–38); and, finally, Yen Yüan's (1635–1704) Way of Heaven, which acts through the *yin* and *yang* to produce the four powers, which, in turn, by means of their sixteen forms of transformation, produce thirty-two basic conditions or factors, as the result of which all things arise (Fung 2, pp. 636–38).

10. Cf. the conversation between the shadow and the penumbra (chap. 2; Giles, p. 32) and the difficult passage (chap. 22; Giles, p. 291) beginning: "Was what existed prior to Heaven and Earth a thing?"

11. Actually this commentary seems to have been the joint work of Kuo Hsiang and Hsiang Hsiu (*ca.* 221–*ca.* 300), but for the sake of convenience we will refer to it here simply under the former's name.

12. Note by Bodde in Fung 2, p. 237.

13. For an expression of this theory in Chinese Buddhism see Tsung-mi (780–841) as quoted in the Chinese edition (Shanghai, 1934) of Fung 2, 793–94 (revised at this point for the English edition, in which, therefore, this passage does not appear).

14. For Shao's theory see Fung 2, pp. 469–74, and for Chu Hsi's acceptance of it see Fung 2, pp. 546–47, 549–50.

15. "Pushing backward, (we see that) there has never been a time when there has not been the Ether, and turning forward, that there will never be a time when it is not here. Being contracted, it then passes from 'non-being' to 'being,' but this 'being' does not result in (permanent) being; being expanded, it then passes from 'being' to 'non-being,' but this 'non-being' does not result in (permanent) non-being" (Fung 2, p. 640).

16. "In the great process of evolutionary change there is only the single Ether, which circulates everywhere without interruption, . . . and so continues in an endless cycle. . . . The Sage, because this process of rise and fall never loses its sequence and order, refers to it as Principle (*li*)" (Fung 2, pp. 640–41).

17. There was a dispute during the Han dynasty as to whether or not the Ch'in had been a legitimate dynasty, and therefore whether or not it had really enjoyed the support of the element water. It will be noticed that the sequence of the elements here given differs from that as correlated with the seasons (see Sec. 1), in which wood (symbolizing new plant growth) goes with spring, fire (symbolizing heat) with summer, etc.

18. Fung 2, pp. 62–63. For an exposition of Tung's whole theory of cycles see Fung 2, chap. 2, sec. 1.

19. Cf. his *Lun Heng*, or *Critical Essays*, chaps. 56 and 57 (Forke, I, 471–76; II, 200).

20. *Book of Lord Shang*, chap. 1 (Duyvendak, pp. 192–73).

21. Cf. the exposition in Fung 2, pp. 82–84.

22. Cf. Hsi Wen-fu, *Ch'uan-shan Che-hsüeh* ("The Philosophy of Wang Ch'uan-shan") (Shanghai, 1936), Part II. It should be noted that though Wang's theory of historical progress makes him quite exceptional in the total range of Chinese philosophy, certain similar tendencies are discernible in a few other scholars of his and the next century, such as Ku Yen-wu (1613–82), Huang Tsung-hsi (1610–95), and Chang Hsüeh-ch'eng (1738–1801).

23. Cf. Fung 2, pp. 679–91.

24. Cf. Fung 2, pp. 710–14, esp. the table on p. 714.

25. Cf. preceding section for T'an's theory of the *yi-t'ai* or ether, and Sec. 4, near end, for his reference to "the Millennium spoken of in Western books."

26. Cf. Fung 2, pp. 657–63, and, for the comparison of Tai with Hsün Tzŭ, pp. 669–72. In his theory of the nature, Tai was anticipated in part by Ch'en Ch'üeh (1604–77). Cf. Fung 2, pp. 659–60.

27. Fung Yu-lan goes so far as to assert that "Hzün Tzŭ's Heaven . . . differs entirely from that of Mencius, inasmuch as it contains no ethical principle" (Fung 1, p. 286). This statement, however, is nowhere explicitly confirmed by Hzün Tzŭ himself, being merely inferential from his total philosophy. In fact, it seems to be contradicted by a passage in Hsün Tzŭ's nineteenth chapter (Dubs, p. 223), in which, in the course of describing the *li* (rites, rituals, rules of correct behavior, traditional mores, etc.), he gives to them a cosmic significance: "They are that whereby Heaven and Earth unite, whereby the sun and moon are bright, whereby the four seasons follow their sequence, whereby the stars move in their courses, whereby all things prosper, whereby love and hatred are tempered, whereby joy and anger keep their proper place."

The mystical tone of this passage, however, accords poorly with Hsün Taŭ's usual humanistic outlook. Indeed, at the very beginning of the same chapter in which it appears (Dubs, p. 213), Hsün Tzŭ gives an entirely rationalistic explanation for the origin of the *li*, saying that they were originally instituted by the early kings in order to put an end to human disorder. On the other hand, the passage is reminiscent of certain metaphysical interpretations of the *li* found in such Confucian compilations as the *Li Chi*, or *Book of Rites* (see Fung 1, pp. 343–44). As a matter of fact, it happens to be one of several passages in the *Hsün-tzŭ* which also appear almost verbatim either in the *Li Chi* or the closely analogous *Ta Tai Li Chi*. The thesis has already been advanced, on grounds other than those given here, that all or most of such passages do not actually come from Hsün Tzŭ's hand at all but have been incorporated at a later time into the work now bearing his name from these ritualistic texts, rather than the other way round, as traditionally assumed. See Yang Yün-ju in Lo Ken-tse (ed.), *Ku Shih Pien* ("A Symposium on Ancient Chinese History," Vol. VI [Shanghai, 1938]), pp. 138–42.

28. Cf. "On the Explanation of Retribution," by Hui-yüan (334–416), in which, after citing such acts, he concludes: "Thus the retributions of punishment or blessing depend upon what are stimulated by one's own (mental) activities. They are what they are according to these stimuli, for which reason I say that they are automatic. By automatic I mean that they result from our own influence. How then can they be the work of some other Mysterious Ruler?" (Fung 2, p. 274). Cf. also the ninth-century Ch'an (Zen) monk, Hsi-yün, who, on being asked whether certain acts were sinful or not, replied: "It cannot definitely be said that they are sinful or not sinful. Whether there is sin or not depends on the man. . . . The mind should be like a void emptiness. . . . Then to what can sin have attachment?" (Fung 2, p. 404). Cf. also Sec. C below.

29. Fung 2, pp. 644–46. In the following century a somewhat similar view was expressed by Tai Chen (cf. Fung 2, pp. 666–68). As pointed out by Fung Yu-lan, however, neither man wholly succeeded in avoiding certain logical inconsistencies in their attempts to break away from Chu Hsi's system.

30. Cf. also H. H. Dubs, *Hsüntze, the Moulder of Ancient Confucianism* (London, 1927), chap. xiv on "Inequality," which is an excellent exposition of the whole Confucian approach to the subject.

31. Cf. also Kenneth Ch'en, "Anti-Buddhist Propaganda during the Nan-ch'ao," *Harvard Journal of Asiatic Studies*, XV (1952), 166–92; Arthur F. Wright, "Fu I

and the Rejection of Buddhism," *Journal of the History of Ideas*, XII (1951), 33–47, esp. pp. 43–44.

32. Cf. Y. P. Mei, *Motse, the Neglected Rival of Confucius* (London, 1934), pp. 96–99, and Dubs, *Hsüntze*, pp. 269–70.

33. J. J. L. Duyvendak, *The Book of Lord Shang* (London, 1928), Introduction, p. 83.

34. Hsi Wen-fu, *op. cit.*, pp. 97 and 99.

35. Cf. the famous "stratagem of the empty city," recounted in C. H. Brewitt-Taylor (trans.), *San Kuo, or Romance of the Three Kingdoms* (Shanghai, 1925), II, 371–73. In this episode the sagacious leader Chu-ko Liang (181–234) finds himself, with only a handful of his troops, trapped in a city by an opponent commanding a huge army. He meets the situation by throwing open the gates of the city and calmly sitting on top of the city wall, where he plays his lute in full sight of the enemy. His opponent, convinced that this is a trick and that within the city must be concealed a large force of soldiers, thereupon marches his soldiers away without even venturing an attack.

36. Abstracted from quotations in Fung 2, pp. 30–32, 47–51. For innumerable similar correlations see the *Po Hu T'ung*, attributed to Pan Ku (A.D. 32–92), and translated by Tjan Tjoe Som as *Po Hu T'ung: The Comprehensive Discussions in the White Tiger Hall* (2 vols.; Leyden, 1949, 1952).

37. For these quotations see Fung 2, pp. 393, 396, 402.

38. Quoted in J. Percy Bruce (trans.), *The Philosophy of Human Nature, by Chu Hsi* (London, 1922), p. 68.

39. Fung Yu-lan, *A Short History of Chinese Philosophy*, ed. D. Bodde (New York, 1948), p. 24.

40. The word here used for "movement" is not *tung* but *tsao*, "hasty or impetuous movement" (Mathews' *Chinese-English Dictionary*, No. 6729). It appears again in chap. 45 in apposition to *ching* but did not succeed in establishing itself as a technical term in later Taoist literature.

41. J. Percy Bruce, *Chu Hsi and His Masters* (London, 1923), pp. 121–24.

42. Fung Yu-lan, *The Spirit of Chinese Philosophy*, trans. E. R. Hughes (London, 1947), p. 200.

43. Cf. also VI*b*, 2, where Mencius says of Shun and of another Sage, Yao, that "their course was simply one of filial piety and fraternal duty."

44. Cf. the quotations in Fung 2, pp. 396, 403, 405; also Sec. 6, A, above.

45. Quoted in Fung, *Spirit of Chinese Philosophy*, p. 200 (translation slightly modified by me). Cf. also *ibid*., p. 201, for a Taoist-like poem by Ch'eng Hao, as well as Fung, *Short History of Chinese Philosophy*, pp. 291–93, for the same poem and a similar one by Shao Yung.

46. These emerge clearly, for example, when we compare Taoism as a philosophy (the kind of Taoism we have been discussing here) with Taoism as a popular organized religion. Thus in philosophical Taoism the emphasis is on the subordination of man to nature, whereas in religious Taoism the goal is the acquisition of human immortality through magical means, in other words, the gaining by man of control over natural forces; likewise in philosophical Taoism any idea of divine causation is rigidly excluded, whereas in religious Taoism the universe is peopled by a vast host of anthropomorphic deities.

47. On this last point, cf. Tawney's description of European medieval social theory, which reads almost as if it might have been written by a Confucian scholar: "The facts of class status and inequality were rationalized in the Middle Ages by a functional theory of society. . . . Society, like the human body, is an organism composed of different members. Each member has its own function. . . . Each must receive the means suited to its station, and must claim no more. Within classes there must be equality. . . . Between classes there must be inequality. . . . Peasants must not encroach on those above them. Lords must not despoil peasants. Craftsmen and merchants must receive what will maintain them in their calling, and no more" (R. H. Tawney, *Religion and the Rise of Capitalism* [London, 1926], pp. 22–23).

48. Lily Abegg, *The Mind of East Asia*, trans. from the German by A. J. Crick and E. E. Thomas (London and New York, 1952). The quotations that follow are taken from pp. 36, 39, and 40.

A REAPPRAISAL OF NEO-CONFUCIANISM

W. THEODORE DE BARY

FROM THE earliest times Confucianism has been concerned primarily with the problems of men living together. Even questions of individual ethics, upon which it has said much, have been approached largely with a view to political and social requirements. This is because its spokesmen in classical times directed their teachings to prospective officials and because Confucianism in various forms has represented a state creed or cult for centuries. Yet study of the Confucian tradition after the classical period has tended to overlook the development of its political and social doctrines and their relation to those teachings which became the official orthodoxy through incorporation into the civil service examination system. This has been especially true of that vast intellectual movement which was launched in the early years of the Sung dynasty, during the eleventh century A.D., and which continued to exert a preponderant influence in China down to modern times.

There are several reasons for such neglect of this important aspect of Chinese thought in later centuries. The new metaphysical, psychological, and ethical theories of the Sung period, together forming the basis of what we now call "Neo-Confucianism," have been of more lasting significance, since they transcend the time and place of their creation. That Western students of Chinese thought should have been attracted first to this aspect of the revival was natural. Centuries ago the Japanese and Koreans were similarly attracted to the philosophical writings of Chu Hsi and his school and were deeply influenced by them.

Another reason for the greater interest in Neo-Confucianism has been the tendency to attach special importance to whatever seemed new in the thought of a given period. Neo-Confucianism was clearly a new development, borrowing much from Buddhism and Taoism in order to supplement and expand the teachings received from the classical exponents of this school, whereas the more practical thought of the Sung school seemed, on the surface at least, to follow traditional lines, dealing with age-old Chinese institutions and with social problems which had been often met and handled in the same way before.

The study of Confucian political thought has also suffered from the general disfavor in which this school has been held recently by those who have attributed to it all the evils and weaknesses of the old order in China. A reflection of this is the view that Confucianism was inherently reactionary and sterile, so that little of importance was thought or done in the political and social spheres. Unfortunately this impression has too often been confirmed by the few modern students who have sought to dispel it, since they have been prone, especially in writing for a Western audience, to think of Chinese political thinkers as something of a marvel if only they approximated the ideas of an influential Western writer. Such attempts to rehabilitate Chinese thought have usually been self-defeating. On close examination the thinker in question has proved to be more deeply immersed in his own tradition than was originally supposed, so that the resemblance to Western writers was largely superficial, or else his originality could not be seen in its true proportions so long as the traditions from which he departed remained poorly understood.

Even a cursory study of the Confucian revival in the Sung, however, shows that its leading spokesmen were as vitally concerned with the immediate problems of Chinese society as with the ultimate problems of human life. Moreover, since some of the major problems and institutions of Chinese society have persisted in the same form for centuries and even today have by no means wholly changed, such a study helps to explain why Confucian tradition should have a continued relevance to the understanding of Chinese society. In particular the early Sung Confucianists gave their attention to the validity of the basic ethical doctrines and ideals of their school when applied to the social and political situation confronting them. The answers they gave to some of the questions which arose reveal that a close relationship existed between Neo-Confucian doctrine and important political developments of the Sung period, such as the reforms of Wang An-shih.

In this respect the Sung may be unique, for the scope and diversity of its intellectual life is wider than in some other periods of Chinese history. Yet, despite the Neo-Confucian tendency in later dynasties to regard ethical and metaphysical questions as alone worthy of consideration, the fact remains that Confucianists in office went on grappling with the problems of government, and individual writers of great stature still appeared to take up the challenge which these problems presented. Among the latter Huang Tsung-hsi and Ku Yen-wu may be cited as outstanding examples in the seventeenth century. To study Confucian thought in this sphere involves special difficulties, since in the West particularly we have only begun to study some of the key institutions which were the subject of their discussions, and without such background studies it is difficult to appreciate the significance of their work. But, as we progress along both fronts, institutional and intellectual history can contribute much to each other and in the process enlighten us as to the true range, depth, and vitality of traditional Chinese thought.

In the future, studies of this type should be of increasing importance. For one thing they would throw new light on the original deposit of Confucian teaching, showing how the Classics were interpreted and their doctrines applied in radically different circumstances from those of Confucius and Mencius. Furthermore, in their application to the historical scene in China there may be some lessons which have an indirect bearing on the problems of our own society. For instance, as our own government has expanded its functions in recent decades, it has encountered problems involving civil service, standards of competence and loyalty, corruption and factionalism in office, economic controls and red tape—problems which are not new but have become far more acute in a vast and unwieldy bureaucracy. On these questions the Confucianists are better qualified to speak than many other writers in the past, since they have had to face them for centuries in their own highly centralized, bureaucratic government. Finally, study of the more practical aspects of Chinese thought should be of value as a basis for studies in comparative thought. The same Confucian ideas take on new meaning and significance when adapted to different social requirements in the later Chinese dynasties, in Japan during the Tokugawa period, and in Korea under the Yi dynasty. Only when these divergent experiences are assessed can the social implications of Confucian doctrine be formulated in sufficiently general terms to be of use for broader comparative studies.

The present survey of Sung thought is not the fruit of as close an acquaintance with the period as would be desirable in anyone attempting such an ambitious project. The writer has been led back to this period through his studies in the work of Huang Tsung-hsi, whose history of Confucian philosophy in the Sung and Yüan dynasties (*Sung Yüan Hsüeh-an*) served as the starting point for this investigation. It is to be hoped that others better qualified will pursue the subject to greater advantage.

1. Han Yü and the Confucian Inheritance of the Sung School

No account of the early Sung school can begin without some mention of the late T'ang writer, Han Yü (786–824), who became the patriarch of this school. Today the influence of Han Yü on Chinese thought is not always appreciated. Often he is regarded as merely a great prose stylist, and in histories of Chinese philosophy his importance is apt to be overlooked because he made no original contribution to the speculative thought which flowered in the metaphysical systems of the Neo-Confucian masters in the Sung. There is some truth in what Fung Yu-lan says about Han Yü's intellectual manifesto, *On the Origin of the Way* (*Yüan Tao*): "Han Yü is primarily famous as one of China's great prose stylists, and there is little of purely philosophical interest in what he says here."[1] Nevertheless, it should be recognized that as an essayist Han Yü was far more concerned with content than with elegance of language and adopted the classical prose style (*ku-wen*) precisely because it enabled him to state his convictions with greater clarity and force than did the elaborate parallel prose style of his day.[2] These convictions may not be of "purely philosophical interest," since they have to do with immediate ethical and political problems, nor are they original with Han Yü. And yet the forceful manner in which he advocated them made an indelible impression on generations of scholars and officials who followed in the main stream of Confucian thought, including many thinkers whose philosophical views differed widely in other respects and many men of affairs who were largely unconcerned with philosophical issues. Among these articles of belief which formed a common legacy for most later Confucianists, the following may be cited in particular:

1. Uncompromising rejection of Buddhism and Taoism as subversive of public morality.
2. Reassertion of Confucian ethics as essential to political stability and social welfare.
3. Confucian ethnocentrism—the rejection of certain ideas as inherently evil because they are foreign.
4. Formulation of Confucian orthodoxy in regard to texts and transmission.
5. The importance of energetically upholding this orthodox tradition and asserting its validity for later times, even against opposition from the court and hostile public opinion.

Of these characteristic features of Han Yü's thought, perhaps only the last requires some explanation here.[3] His role as a defender and definer of Confucian orthodoxy is fairly well known, but it is not usually recognized that in his time to take up this role also put him in the position of a reformer and nonconformist. During the T'ang dynasty Buddhism and Taoism, though to him insidious heresies, had frequently enjoyed the patronage of the court and had also won favor with many intellectuals. To oppose them as Han Yü did sometimes involved paying a heavy price. When, for instance, he remonstrated with the emperor against the latter's intention to venerate publicly a supposed relic of the

Buddha, Han Yü narrowly escaped execution for his forthrightness and was subsequently banished from the court.[4]

On the other hand, Confucian orthodoxy as he understood it was by no means generally accepted even by those classed as Confucian scholars. Supposedly the imperial bureaucracy remained a stronghold of Confucianism even during the years when Buddhism and Taoism attained their greatest popularity, since entrance to the civil service was generally limited to those who qualified through the Confucian-style examinations. Yet in actuality the civil service examinations, despite their Confucian provenance, did little to perpetuate the more vital teachings of this school. It is true that one of the many types of examination which candidates might elect to take in the T'ang dynasty was devoted exclusively to the Confucian Classics (that for the *ming-ching* degree), but it stressed memorization of the texts and their commentaries, not an understanding of their teachings.[5] Toward the end of the dynasty scholars naturally enough looked upon this kind of "learning" with some contempt and preferred to seek the degree awarded to those proficient in the composition of prose and poetry (the *chin-shih* degree). The effect of this was to fill the ranks of Chinese officialdom with men skilled at writing the prescribed forms of prose and poetry but not necessarily with able exponents of Confucian doctrine in the political sphere. Other writers in Han Yü's time strenuously criticized this state of affairs and called for a change in the examining procedure so that less emphasis would be put upon memorization or literary skill and greater stress laid on comprehension of the general meaning of the Classics and an appreciation of the Way of the sage-kings—that is, Confucianism as a way of life and a guide to good government.[6]

Han Yü too regarded Confucianism as more a way of life than an academic discipline. Initially he had suffered repeated setbacks in his attempt to win the coveted *chin-shih* degree, which he achieved only after failing three times. Even then he obtained official appointment only long after taking three supplementary examinations, an experience not unusual among candidates for office in the T'ang dynasty. But while his progress in an official career was thus held up, Han Yü devoted himself to writing and teaching, and this was unusual inasmuch as he conceived of himself as more than a mere tutor of reading and writing, being convinced that the business of a teacher was to inculcate the principles of Confucianism as the great classical philosophers had done.[7]

In this way Han Yü established himself as the exponent and exemplar of a new ideal, a new *tao* as it were: the scholar whose worth was not measured in terms of his success in achieving high office and a big salary but rather in terms of his devotion to reviving and reasserting Confucian teachings in a decadent age. At one point he openly declared that pursuit of an official career through the examinations was incompatible with true scholarship.[8] By this he certainly did not mean to rule out government service altogether, for the ultimate aim of any true Confucianist must be to exert some influence on the conduct of government, and eventually Han Yü himself won high honors as an official. But, like his idol Mencius, Han Yü insisted that official employment is not an end in itself. Steadfast devotion to principle, which for Han Yü meant adherence to Confucian tradition, must be the true end of the scholar, and acceptability to the court is no measure of orthodoxy. Regardless of either official disfavor or unpopularity with the general public, the genuine scholar must adhere to the Confucian code and strive to spread it.

In this respect Han Yü's ideal contrasts with another way of life which appealed to men of his time: the monastic ideal of Buddhism and the Taoist ideal of the recluse.[9] These called upon men to "leave the world," withdraw from society and abandon the worldly cares of men. But to a thoroughgoing Confucianist like Han Yü the disappointments of political life and the burdens of one's social obligations could never justify retiring from the field of struggle. Han Yü was a crusader and thought of himself as almost a martyr to his cause. In the past both Mencius and Hsün Tzŭ had exemplified this ideal, standing fast against the evil tendencies of their times. Han Yü obviously sees himself as their successor in his own day, who is ridiculed or persecuted for his independence of mind and devotion to an ideal. His writings, particularly since his style was so expressive of his inmost personal feelings, eloquently impart this sense of his mission (which was nearly an obsession with him) as a lone defender of the True Way.[10]

Han Yü's biography in the *New T'ang History*, written two centuries later by leaders of the Sung school who regarded him as something of a patron saint,[11] portrays him in this same light:

> From the Chin dynasty (A.D. 265–420) through the Sui (590–618), while Taoism and Buddhism were widely practiced, the Way of the Sages (i.e., Confucianism) was carried on without interruption, but the Confucian scholars utilized the orthodox ideas in the world (of Confucianism) to give support to the strange and supernatural. Han Yü alone grievingly quoted the Sages to combat the errors of the world, and, although mocked at by others, he met rebuffs with renewed ardor. In the beginning nobody believed in him, but finally he gained great renown among the people of his generation. Of old, Mencius, who was removed from Confucius by only two hundred years, had refuted Yang Chu and Mo Ti. But Han Yü, who attacked these two schools (of Buddhism and Taoism), came more than one thousand years after (Confucius). In destroy-

ing confusion and reviving orthodoxy, his merit is equal to and his energy double (that of Mencius). . . . Since the death of Han Yü, his words have gained wide currency, so that scholars now look up to him as if he were Mount T'ai or the Great Dipper.[12]

In view of the tendency in some recent works on China to stress the stereotyped character of Neo-Confucian thought, as if to suggest that later scholars were motivated exclusively by a concern for strict orthodoxy and blind conformity to whatever was sanctioned by the state, it is worth drawing attention to Han Yü as a symbol in this earlier period of the two-sided nature—at once traditionalist and nonconformist—of much Confucian thought in later centuries. No one will deny that there were powerful forces working to compel conformity to the established order or that through the examination system and imperial patronage generations of educated Chinese were wedded to a sterile scholarship. But alongside those whose Confucianism was only a means to office, or a guaranty of their political and intellectual reliability, stood others who took up the challenge of their times and did more with their Confucian inheritance than simply pass it along untouched to others. Among the intellectual pioneers and political reformers were many who withstood the opposition or condemnation of the state. Long before Chu Hsi's commentaries became standard texts in the examination halls of the Ming and Ch'ing dynasties, Chu Hsi himself suffered at the hands of the government for his independence of mind and, when he died, was subjected to further abuse by an annalist of the existing regime who described his funeral as a "gathering of heretics from all over the empire to follow the arch-heretic to the grave."[13] Again, after Chu Hsi's own interpretation of the scriptures was accepted as orthodox by the Ming, others like Wang Yang-ming rejected it and established their own schools, which were likewise subjected to official persecution. Later still, the Tung-lin school, Huang Tsung-hsi, and Ku Yen-wu—to name only a few—carried on this tradition of independent thought and scholarship by standing in opposition to the court, or aloof from it, and by protesting in the name of true orthodoxy against that debased form of Confucian "learning" which had the seal of state approval. That they were dissenters means, of course, that they were not representative of their times. In their own lifetimes they influenced only a few compared to the great number who followed the established pattern and sought their success in serving the ruling power. But it is also true that from these few dissenters came the outstanding contributions to the development of Chinese thought. It was to them that later ages looked for guidance, and it is to them that Confucianism owes its survival as a living tradition instead of simply as a state cult.

Han Yü was not a scholar or classicist in the usual sense. He did not devote himself to the exegetical study of Confucian scripture, as so many commentators did before and after him.[14] What concerned him were the essential teachings of the Classics, reduced to their simplest terms. These were the ethical precepts which underlay good government and social harmony: chiefly the Five Human Relations or Obligations between ruler and subject, father and child, husband and wife, elder and younger brother, and friend and friend, together with the personal virtues proper to each. For Han Yü a return to the Ancient Way involved primarily moral reform and not political reform as we understood it. The reformers of the Sung school, however, pursuing the same ideal of Confucianism as a living faith, extended it to almost every sphere of life and especially to political and social institutions. Thus conservatism and reform were to be united under the banner which proclaimed "Restoration of the Ancient Order" (*fu-ku*).[15]

2. *Origins and General Character of the Sung School*

A. HU YÜAN

The development of Neo-Confucianism in the Sung dynasty is generally traced down through those who contributed most to the impressive synthesis of Chu Hsi, which, to judge only from its lasting influence in Japan and Korea as well as China, must be accounted the crowning achievement of Sung thought. With Chu Hsi as a reference point, it has been customary to work back through the intellectual genealogy of the Ch'êng-Chu school to Shao Yung and Chou Tun-i, who in the early years of the dynasty formulated some of the basic principles embodied in this synthesis.

This line of transmission starting with Chou Tun-i is followed, for example, in the biographical section of the *Sung History*, where contributors to the new Ch'êng-Chu orthodoxy are classified under the special designation of *Tao-hsüeh-chia* (roughly: "followers of the True Way"), while other important thinkers of the period are classed simply as *Ju-lin*, "Confucian scholars."[16] It is principally to the teachings of the former group, the *Tao-hsüeh-chia*, that the term "Neo-Confucian" has been applied in the West.[17]

Other intellectual historians of the period, however, have traced the origins of the Sung school in general back to other sources. In their monumental *Survey of Confucian Philosophers in the Sung and Yüan Dynasties* (*Sung Yüan Hsüeh-an*)[18] the great Ch'ing scholars, Huang Tsung-hsi and Ch'uan Tsu-wang, dispel at the outset the notion that Chou Tun-i was the chief progenitor of the Confucian revival in the

Sung.[19] This honor must go instead to Hu Yüan (993–1059) and Sun Fu (992–1057). More than twenty years the senior of Chou Tun-i, Hu Yüan[20] was recognized in his own time as the leader of the Confucian renaissance, presiding over one of the outstanding private academies of his time, where he taught the Confucian Classics as guides to the ethical life rather than as mere texts to be studied for the civil service examinations. In this respect Hu Yüan may be taken as one of the earliest in a long line of teachers who made private academies, in contrast to official schools, the leading intellectual centers of China from the eleventh to the seventeenth centuries. So important was the contribution of these academies to creative thought and independent scholarship that, according to the Ming historian, Wang Ch'i, it is through them that the origins and development of Neo-Confucianism can be traced.[21]

Hu Yüan was above all a teacher who took seriously his duties as a moral preceptor of youth and stressed an appreciation of the teacher-disciple relationship as essential to genuine education. Thus it was regarded as noteworthy in his time that Hu Yüan "adhered strictly to the traditional concept of the master-disciple relationship, treating his students as if they were sons or younger brothers, and being trusted and loved by them as if he were their father or elder brother."[22]

The philosopher Ch'eng Yi, though a student of Chou Tun-i, was himself a protégé and devoted disciple of Hu Yüan[23] and testified to the latter's remarkable moral influence over his students: "You can recognize at a glance anyone who has studied under the Master of An-ting by his purity and sincerity and his calm, amicable disposition."[24]

Hu Yüan's effectiveness as a teacher was also affirmed after his death by one of his leading disciples who, when questioned by the emperor Shên-tsung as to who was superior, Wang An-shih or Hu Yüan, replied:

My master was teaching students in the Southeast about the Way and Virtue, Benevolence and Justice, when Wang An-shih was still busy in the examination halls working for the *chin-shih* degree. It is said that the Way of the Sages has three forms, Principle (*t'i*), Practice (*yung*), and Literary Expression (*wên*). The bond between prince and minister and between father and son, Benevolence, Justice, Rites and Music—these are things which do not change through the ages; they are Principles. The Books of Poetry and History, the dynastic histories, and the writings of the philosophers—these perpetuate the right example down through the ages; they are its Literary Expression. To initiate these principles and put them into practice throughout the Empire, enriching the life of the people and ordering all things to imperial perfection—this is Practice.

Our dynasty has not through its successive reigns made Principle and Practice the basis for the selection of officials. Instead we have prized the embellishments of conventional versification, and thus have corrupted the standards of contemporary scholarship. My teacher (Hu Yüan), from the Ming-tao through the Pao-yüan periods (1032–

40), was greatly distressed over this evil and expounded to his students the teaching which aims at clarifying Principle and carrying it out in Practice. Tirelessly and with undaunted zeal, for over twenty years he devoted himself wholly to school-teaching, first in the Soochow region and finally at the Imperial Academy (*T'ai-hsüeh*). Those who have come from his school number at least several thousands. The fact that today scholars recognize the basic importance to government and education of the Principle and Practice of the Sages is all due to the efforts of my Master. Wang An-shih cannot even be compared to him![24a]

This tribute to Hu Yüan suggests several characteristic features of the Confucian revival in the early Sung. Hu Yüan is both a traditionalist and a reformer. He is a moralist, not a metaphysician, and his primary interest is in the application of Confucian ethics to the problems of government and everyday life. Hu Yüan is also an independent scholar, one whose success came through years of private study and teaching, and who gained official recognition only late in life. Echoing criticism of late T'ang writers of the literary examination system, he condemns it as a perverter of scholarship and as productive of a mediocre officialdom. Finally in the threefold conception of the *Tao* as Principle, Practice, and Literary Expression, which Hu Yüan expounded so effectively among early Sung scholars, we have a concise statement of the aims of the Sung school in their most general terms, amplifying Han Yü's initial reassertion of the Confucian Way and suggesting the broad lines along which it was to be developed by the manifold activities of Sung scholars.

According to this view, the Classics were to be studied as deposits of eternal truth rather than as antiquarian repositories, and the true aim of classical studies was to bring these enduring principles, valid for any place or time, to bear upon both the conduct of life and the solution of contemporary problems. Conversely, no attempt to solve such problems could hope to succeed unless it were grounded on these enduring principles and undertaken by men dedicated to them. Yet neither classical teaching nor a practical program of reform could be furthered except through the mastery of literature and writing—not the intricacies of form and style with which the literary examinations were concerned but literature as a medium for preserving and communicating the truth in all its forms. Therefore these three concepts, Principle, Practice, and Literary Expression, were seen as essential and inseparable constituents of the Way, which, as the Sung school exemplified it, embraced every aspect of life. In a sense they may be called the Three Treasures of Confucianism, just as Buddha (Truth), Dharma (Law or Scripture), and Sangha (Monastic Discipline) are the Three Treasures of Buddhism which the Sung Confucianists sought to displace.

With this in mind we should be prepared to recognize the many-sided character of both the Confucian revival in the Sung and its individual representatives in this period. The broad current of political reform, most conspicuously promoted by Wang An-shih, and the work of the great Sung historians, such as Sung Ch'i, Ou-yang Hsiu, Ssu-ma Kuang, and Ma Tuan-lin, are as much the products of this revival as Chou Tun-i's Diagram of the Supreme Ultimate or the commentaries of Chu Hsi. And the work of Chu Hsi himself must be appreciated as an expression of the Sung spirit in the fields of history and politics as well as in classical scholarship and metaphysics. The Sung, indeed, has been known for its versatile intellects: Wang An-shih, whose reputation as an outstanding classical scholar in his day has been overshadowed by his fame as a statesman; Ssu-ma Kuang, his chief political antagonist, who is better known today as one of China's great historians; and Su Tung-p'o, perhaps the outstanding literary figure of his time, who was also a man of affairs and played a leading part in the political struggles of that memorable era. These men—to name just a few—are all beneficiaries of the creative and wide-spreading energy of the Sung revival, and their individual accomplishments, spectacular though they may be, should not be seen in isolation. Their several contributions may have been most significant in one particular sphere of activity, either that of Principle, Practice, or Literary Expression, but both alone and together they exemplify the ideal of unity and universality which the Sung school strove to fulfil.[25]

Especially in its emphasis upon the practical application of Confucian principles to problems of the day, Hu Yüan's threefold formulation points to the fact that political, economic, and social thought were to be as integral a part of the Confucian revival as were classical studies and philosophical inquiry. In his own teaching Hu Yüan exemplified this by his insistence upon practical measures to improve the people's livelihood, to strengthen military defenses against the barbarian menace, to expand irrigation projects in order to increase agricultural production, and also to promote mathematical and astronomical studies.[26] But Hu Yüan never became a practicing politician and cannot himself be called a political reformer. For him a career devoted to teaching was the most effective way of putting classical principles into practice, since the training of able men was a prerequisite to any program of general reform.

B. SUN FU AND SHIH CHIEH

Another scholar of the time who distinguished himself as a teacher and must be acknowledged as one of the founding fathers of the Sung school is Sun Fu (992–1057).[27] Like Han Yü and Hu Yüan, he had failed to win recognition in the literary examinations. Retiring to T'ai-shan in Shantung, Sun dedicated himself to the study and teaching of the Classics. In the school he opened there, which became one of the most famous private academies of the time, he affirmed the need for a new appreciation of the Classics and for a return to true orthodoxy. Among the Classics, Sun gave special attention to the *Book of Changes* and the *Spring and Autumn Annals*. Of his studies on the latter, Ou-yang Hsiu wrote that Sun sought to express its essential meaning in the simplest terms, without regard to the diverse and confusing commentaries on the work, so as to clarify its ethical implications and the application of the Way of the sage-kings to the problems of his time.[28]

Sun's repudiation of the degenerate intellectual tendencies of the time is reflected in a work by one of his outstanding disciples, Shih Chieh (1005–45),[29] entitled *Strange Teachings* (*Kuai Shuo*). Here the Way of the ancient sage-kings and Confucius is upheld as the only true and immutable teaching down through the ages. Specifically condemned as one of three unorthodox paths to learning, along with Buddhism and Taoism, is the mastery of conventional literary forms for the state examinations.[30] Thus, again, a reform in the civil service examinations is pointed to as a first step in the direction of general reform, and it was to become a burning issue in the political debates of the time. Without a change in the examination system, men of character and true learning could find their way into the government only with difficulty. Officials whose accomplishments were purely literary—and that only in a narrow and superficial sense—could not be depended upon to promote the general welfare, to adopt policies based on Confucian principles, or conscientiously to implement such policies if it entailed sacrificing their own interests.

Unfortunately this attempt to rally the serious scholars of the land in support of a new political program, with the aim of bringing into the government a corps of competent officials sympathetic to these objectives, necessarily involved the creation of an organization much like a political party committed to the formation of a government composed of like-minded individuals. Chinese political traditions did not allow for such a development, however. Rulers had always looked with suspicion on any political alignment which might bring pressure upon the throne or threaten its security. Moreover, those in power at court were prone to regard any organized opposition as "factions" or "cliques," bent on serving their own interests rather than those of the state, and therefore potentially subversive.[31] One of the main objectives of the civil service examination system was to prevent "packing" of offices with representatives of any single group or faction through favoritism in the recruitment of officials, and this was in part the reason why the reformers of this period considered the examination system such an obstacle to their plans. Thus the political movements associated with the Confucian revival, in so far as they were aggressive and well organized, were bound to stir up contention and become involved in bitter "factional" struggles. Consequently, the Northern Sung period was torn by intense party strife, which increased rather than abated as the dynasty wore on. Also for this reason many of the reforms attempted in this age of great political activity came to nothing in the end, because each faction, on coming to power, tended to make a clean sweep of policies and personnel associated with the displaced regime.[32]

3. *Proponents of the New Order*

A. FAN CHUNG-YEN

The first steps taken in the government itself to implement a broad program of reform were sponsored by Fan Chung-yen (989–1052),[33] the statesman and general whose patronage of Hu Yüan and Sun Fu had brought them to the capital as lecturers in the Imperial Academy. Something of a self-made man, who had been orphaned at the age of two, Fan was a deep student of the Classics, especially the *Book of Changes* and the *Mean*. He was also known as a staunch defender of the Confucian Way and a vigorous opponent of Buddhism. As a young man he had adopted for himself the maxim, "Before the rest of the world starts worrying, the scholar worries; after the rest of the world rejoices, he rejoices."[34] During the reign of Jen-tsung (1023–56) Fan tried as a prime minister to implement a ten-point program including administrative reforms to eliminate intrenched bureaucrats, official favoritism, and nepotism; examination reform; equalization of official landholdings to insure a sufficient income for territorial officials and to lessen the temptation toward bribery and squeeze; land reclamation and dike repair to increase agricultural production and facilitate grain transport; creation of local militia to strengthen national defense; and reduction of the labor service required of the people by the state.[35]

Of Fan's policies those dealing with education and the examination system had the most significant effect. In his memorial he called for the establishment of a national school system, through which worthy men could be trained and selected for the civil service. Though this would represent a departure from dynastic precedent,[36] Fan justified it as a return to the system set forth in the Classics as obtaining under the benevolent rule of the early Chou kings. He also asked that in the examinations for the *chin-shih* degree more importance be attached to an understanding of the Classics and of political problems than to the composition of poetry. One of his most revealing proposals was to abolish the pasting of a piece of paper over the candidate's name on an examination paper, a practice designed to insure impartial judgment by the examiner. The reasoning behind this suggestion follows from the importance Fan always attached in both teaching and politics to a man's personal integrity. It was just as vital to know the candidate's moral character as his literary and intellectual capacities, which it was impossible to judge except from personal knowledge.

Prompted by Fan's memorial, the emperor called for a general discussion of these questions at court. Fan's proposals were supported by Sung Ch'i and others, who expostulated against the evils of the existing system and urged a "return" to the ancient ideal. As a result a national school system was promulgated by Jen-tsung in 1044, calling for the establishment of a school in each department and district to be maintained and staffed by the local magistrate. At the same time the civil service system was reformed so that the examinations were divided into three parts, with priority given to problems of history and politics, then to interpretation of the Classics, and last to poetry composition.[37] Subsequently instruction in the Imperial Academy was also revamped by Hu Yüan to conform to the methods he had used in his private academy, which Fan had indorsed.[38]

Thus, as the recent historian Ch'ien Mu has put it, "with Fan Chung-yen at court and Hu Yüan in the schools, the whole pattern of the Sung school was laid out."[39]

B. OU-YANG HSIU

Few of Fan's reforms survived when he fell from power as a result of bitter factional struggles. But his influence, and that of Hu Yüan, remained among a number of men who were to dominate the intellectual and political scene for decades to come. First among these stands Ou-yang Hsiu (1007–72), the master of prose and poetry, the historian and statesman whom the brilliant and versatile Su Tung-p'o ranked with the greatest of Chinese writers. "In the discussion of great principles he resembled Han Yü; in the discussion of public questions he resembled Lu Chih; in narrative writing he resembled Ssŭ-ma Ch'ien; and in the writing of poetry (*shih* and *fu*) he resembled Li Po."[40]

The terms in which Su pays tribute to the extraordinary genius of his master have special significance here. Ou-yang Hsiu has probably been best known as the writer who rediscovered Han Yü and made his "classical prose style" (*ku-wen*) the standard for centuries. But Su says that it is in the "discussion of great principles" (*lun ta tao*) that they resemble each other—that is, as writers on philosophical and moral questions. Ou-yang Hsiu's fame as a historian is well established by virtue of the leading part he took in compiling the *New History of the T'ang Dynasty* and the *New History of the Five Dynasties*, and so the resemblance between him and the great classical historian, Ssŭ-ma Ch'ien, is understandable. In his own time, however, Ou-yang was equally well known as a writer on public questions and as the statesman who shared with Fan Chung-yen leadership of the Sung school in official circles.

Between these latter activities and his historical studies there was in fact a close connection. Hu Yüan, Sun Fu, and Fan Chung-yen had devoted themselves especially to study of the *Book of Changes* and the *Mean*, as containing the most important truths of the Confucian teaching; and in this way they had opened up the field of classical study which Chou Tun-i and the Ch'êng brothers were later to develop so spectacularly.[41] Ou-yang Hsiu, though an admirer of these earlier scholars and a political ally of Fan Chung-yen, had little interest in the *Book of Changes*, to which he considered the appendixes of dubious authenticity, and he thought the *Mean* much too abstruse and impractical. For him study of the *Spring and Autumn Annals* was of the first importance, since in this history were embodied the essential teachings of Confucius as applied to events in the practical order. The three early commentaries on this work he rejected precisely because they obscured its original ethical import.[42] Thus as a historian and statesman who found in history lessons of practical significance for his own time, Ou-yang Hsiu appears in a role which prefigures that of Ssŭ-ma Kuang, perhaps the most eminent historian of the period and the great political opponent of Wang An-shih.

As the intellectual heir of Han Yü, Ou-yang Hsiu proved himself a mighty champion of Confucian orthodoxy, who carried on Han Yü's struggle against the twin evils of Buddhist escapism and literary dilettantism.[43] He insisted that "literary activity just benefits oneself, while political activity can affect the situation around us."[44] In him also the Sung school found a vigorous defender of the scholars' right to organize politically for the advancement of common principles,[45] and in him many of the leading figures of the next generation, such as Wang An-shih, Ssŭ-ma Kuang, and Su Tung-p'o, discovered a patron and sponsor.

C. WANG AN-SHIH

Wang An-shih himself, though in his later years the archenemy of those in the main line of Neo-Confucian succession, was in his early years the protégé of several leaders of the Sung school. He called Fan Chung-yen "a teacher for the whole world"[46] and wrote a poem to Hu Yüan praising him for his steadfast devotion to scholarship.[47] Wang's debt to Ou-yang Hsiu, who helped him to gain recognition at the capital, was such that he has been numbered among the disciples of this great scholar.[48] Han Ch'i (1008–75),[49] another protégé of Fan Chung-yen who was a powerful confederate of Ou-yang Hsiu in the councils of three successive emperors, was Wang's superior during his novitiate in public office, and, though the two later differed sharply on political questions, Wang retained a high personal regard for his former mentor.[50]

Moreover, Wang's relation to the Confucian revival was one which went beyond purely circumstantial associations and acquaintances. His personal outlook too—his approach to classical scholarship, his view of history, and even much of his political philosophy—was strongly influenced by the intellectual climate which the early Sung school produced. This fact has been somewhat obscured by the subsequent course of the Neo-Confucian movement, inasmuch as tradition has followed Wang's opponents in condemning him as unorthodox. In more recent times, owing to the general unpopularity of traditional Confucianism, few have cared to re-examine this judgment; the tendency has been to glorify Wang as a reformer who boldly broke with established tradition. Yet in Wang's own time tradition was by no means so well established, and only when the underlying tendencies of the Sung school are examined can the true relation of Wang's reforms to the Confucian tradition be understood. Only then can we appreciate the extent to which his program was inspired by the same ideal which had stimulated many of his predecessors and how in the end the controversies provoked by his policies served to define more sharply the orthodox tradition.

4. The Confucian Program for the Sung

It has already been shown that the spread of Buddhism from the fourth to the tenth centuries presented Confucianists with a special problem and a specific occasion for urging a revival of their doctrines. It is also true that the early Sung Confucianists attacked certain established institutions as falling far short of the ancient ideal. This implied, in effect, a conflict between traditions, or perhaps more accurately a conflict between accepted institutions, on the one hand, and, on the other, hallowed ideals never actually established or attained in historical times.

Thus in the Sung dynasty those who advocated a return to the classical order implicitly, and often explicitly, rejected a tradition which had become established through more than twelve centuries of social development and which was in some respects supported by the prestige of the greatest imperial dynasties. It was only natural for later conquerors and statesmen to hope that they might themselves achieve the power and magnificence of the Han and T'ang dynasties and to see in the institutions they had established the key to dynastic success. Yet the Neo-Confucianists could not accept such a view. To follow the Han and T'ang was not enough; indeed, it might be fatal, for both the Han and the T'ang had eventually succumbed to corruption and decay and had left to posterity as vivid an impression of final weakness as of initial strength. Hence the necessity for a complete reappraisal of institutions inherited by the Sung, if it were to avoid their fate. To this was added a special sense of urgency arising from the threat of foreign conquest, an almost constant danger to the life of the dynasty.

As an expression of this view we may cite a memorial on the state of the nation submitted to the emperor Jen-tsung in 1050 by the philosopher Ch'êng Yi (1033–1107)[51] when this disciple of Hu Yüan was only seventeen years of age:

> In the Three Dynasties (the era of the Sage Kings) the Way was always followed; after the Ch'in (221–207 B.C.) it declined and did not flourish. Dynasties like the Wei and Chin indeed departed far from it. The Han and T'ang achieved a limited prosperity, but in practicing the Way they adulterated it. . . .[52]
>
> [Thus] for two thousand years the Way has not been practiced. Foolish persons of recent times have all declared that times are different and things have changed, so that it can no longer be practiced. This only shows how deep their ignorance is, and yet time and again the rulers of men have been deceived by their talk. . . . But I see that Your Majesty's heart is filled with solicitude for the people, and if Your Majesty practices the Way of the Sage Kings with such solicitude for the people, how can any difficulties stand in the way?[53]
>
> Of old the Emperor Wu of Han laughed at the failure of Duke Hsüan of Ch'i to heed the counsel of Mencius. But he himself did not act as a true King and failed to adopt the recommendations of Tung Chung-shu.[54] Emperor Wên of the Sui dynasty laughed at Emperor Wu's failure to adopt the recommendations of Tung Chung-shu but he himself did not listen to the advice of Wang T'ung.[55] The folly of these two rulers—I wonder if Your Majesty has not laughed at it sometime. Though Your humble servant cannot pretend to the wisdom of these three masters, nevertheless what he studies is the Way of these three masters. Would that Your Majesty could see the present as future generations will, just as we now see the past![56]

This same view is reiterated and expanded by Ch'êng Yi's elder brother Ch'êng Hao (1032–85)[57] in a memorial to the emperor Shên-tsung (1068–85) which provides a classic exposition of the Principle-and-Practice concept of Hu Yüan:

The laws established by the Sage Kings were all based on human nature and were in keeping with the order of nature. In the great reigns of the Two Emperors and Three Kings, how could these laws not but change according to the times and be embodied in systems which suited the conditions obtaining in each? However, in regard to the underlying principles of government and to the basic doctrines by which the people may be shepherded, these remain forever unalterable in the order of nature, and on them the people depend for their very existence, so that on such points there has been no divergence but rather common agreement among the Sages of all times, early or late. Only if what we call human life should come to an end could the laws of the Sage Kings ever be changed.[58]

Therefore, he explains, "those in later times who practice this Way to the fullest may achieve Ideal Rule, while those who practice only a part will achieve limited success." The T'ang dynasty, for example, achieved such limited success, because it retained some residue of good government as embodied in its administrative codes and attempted to maintain a system of land distribution based on the size of the family. But if the Sung is to succeed where the T'ang failed, it must attempt a general re-establishment of ancient institutions, including a gradual return to the well-field system of equal land distribution, as described by Mencius,[59] a militia of soldier-cultivators to replace the mercenaries of the Sung, and a universal school system, toward which Fan Chung-yen had made an abortive first step. Moreover, since the cost of government has increased enormously over ancient times, expenses must be reduced in order to lighten the tax burden on the people. As it is, the government draws all surplus from the land. "Even the rich and powerful families rarely have a surplus; how much worse off are the poor! Just one bad year and they starve or turn to banditry. In some unfortunate cases the calamity affects thousands of miles of territory or extends over a period of several years." Under such conditions cultivators abandon their land, and the consumers of food far outnumber the producers of it. "In ancient times the four classes of people each had fixed occupations, and eight or nine out of ten were farmers. Therefore food and clothing was provided with no difficulty, and the people knew no want. But today the capital has a floating population of over a million, who are idlers, vagrants or beggars."[60] To correct this, not only must the occupations of the people be fixed and the resources of the land conserved, but the ancient ceremonial regulations, set forth in the *Books of Rites*, must be restored so that people do not waste their substance through competitive extravagance in the satisfaction of their meaner desires.

These recommendations of Ch'êng Hao also reflect the political views of his uncle Chang Tsai (1020–77),[61] known for his insistence upon the adoption of the institutions described in the *Books of Rites*. Chang long cherished the dream of purchasing some land for himself and his disciples and of dividing it up into well-fields in order to demonstrate the feasibility of restoring the system which the early sage-kings had left to posterity, but he died without accomplishing his objective.[62] "If the government of the Empire is not based on the well-field system," he said, "there will never be peace. The Way of Chou is simply this: to equalize."[63] So convinced was he that this system could be re-established in his own time that he asserted, "All the government has to do is issue an order and it can be established without having to resort to flogging even once (the Confucianist's criterion of practicability being whether or not a given measure required coercion for its enforcement)."[64] Chang further looked upon the well-field system as the first step in the gradual restoration of the feudal system which had obtained under the Chou dynasty but had been destroyed by the Ch'in in the third century B.C. "The reason a feudal system must be established is that the administration of the Empire must be simplified through delegation of power before things can be well-managed. If the administration is not simplified [through decentralization], then it will be impossible to govern well. Therefore the Sages insisted on sharing the affairs of the Empire with other men. It was thus that everything was well-administered in their times."[65] "For the government to follow any other way than that of the Three Dynasties will simply mean following the way of expediency."[66]

These two alternatives, the Way of the Sages and the way of expediency, were summed up by Sung writers under the terms *wang* and *pa*, which Mencius had applied to those who were True Kings (*wang*) and those who merely sought power (*pa*).[67] Thus Wang An-shih, like the Ch'êng brothers,[68] emphasized the difference between the ruler who is motivated by a genuine desire to do what is right (*i*) and he who, while making a great display of those virtues expected in a king, is actually motivated by a desire for personal gain (*li*). Despite this pretense the despot or dynast can always be recognized for what he is; he cannot exert that moral influence over his people by which the True King maintains peace and order, and this inner weakness reveals itself in a reliance upon expedient and coercive devices which ultimately fail to achieve the desired end.[69]

At their best the Han and T'ang only achieved the successful overlordship associated with the term *pa*. Lacking the inherent moral power of True Kings, the scions of these dynasties were unable to hold the empire together. This view finds expression, not only in the moral or political essays of the time, but also in historical writings such as Ouyang Hsiu's *New History of the T'ang Dynasty*. In the prolegomena to his *Treatise on the Army* he writes:

> In ancient times it was the moral strength of those who possessed the Empire which determined whether they rose or fell, ruled in peace or gave way to disorder. But since the period of the Warring States, since the Ch'in and Han dynasties, this has been determined almost always by military power. Such being the case we cannot help but recognize how important armies have become.
>
> But military organization has changed with the times, being adopted to obtain some momentary advantage or make the most of an opportune situation, to such an extent that any and all means have been resorted to. And so when we study the systems and regulations adopted in the past, we find many which proved useful at a given time but are not worthy of perpetuation in the present.
>
> However, the T'ang did create a militia system which is worthy of praise. In antiquity the military system was based on the well-fields, but since the decline of Chou, the institutions of the Sage Kings were destroyed and never restored. Only with the T'ang militia did soldiers once again become farmers. Their domiciles, their education, their training, their functions and their employment were all governed by regulations, and though it was not possible to conform in all respects to the ancient model, this system did embody the general spirit of the ancient one. For this reason the reigns of Emperors Kao-tsu and T'ai-tsung were glorious ones.
>
> But their descendants in later times were vain and weak; they could not preserve the system and instead changed it repeatedly. Armies are maintained to prevent disorder, but when allowed to deteriorate, they themselves can cause disorder. At their worst they impoverish the Empire by forcing it to feed the forces of disorder, which bring it in the end to utter ruin.[70]

5. Wang An-shih's "New Deal" as a Restoration of the Ancient Order

In general, then, it may be said that the men of the Sung school, whether they became known as statesmen, historians, poets, or philosophers in the narrow sense, were mindful of the failure of the Han and T'ang to achieve political stability and desirous of inaugurating a new order based on the ancient ideal of the sage-kings. Even Su Tung-p'o, who took some exception to this view, testified to its prevalence: "Everyone who serves in the government chatters about the Way of the Ancient Kings and holds forth on Rites and Music. They all want to restore [the social order of] the Three Dynasties, to follow the ways of Yao and Shun."[71] Wang An-shih, the most determined and perhaps the most dedicated statesman of his time, was no exception to this. In his first audience with the emperor Shên-tsung in 1068 Wang presented his case for reform in these terms:

> "What is the most important thing to do in a government?" asked the Emperor.
>
> "To choose the right policy," answered Wang.

"What do you think of the Emperor T'ai-tsung of T'ang?" asked the Emperor again, referring to the most beloved emperor of that dynasty.

"Your Majesty should take the Emperors Yao and Shun as your standard. The principles of Yao and Shun are really very easy to put into practice. Because the scholars of the latter days do not really understand them, they think that the standards of such a government are unattainable."[71a]

In an earlier memorial to the emperor Jen-tsung, Wang had explained how these principles were to be understood and put into practice:

I am not arguing that we should revive the ancient system of government in every detail. The most ignorant can see that a great interval of time separates us from those days, and our country has passed through so many vicissitudes since then that present conditions differ greatly. So a complete revival is practically impossible. I suggest that we should just follow the main ideas and general principles of these ancient rulers.

Let us recall the fact that we are separated from the rule of these great men by over a thousand years of history; that they had their periods of progress and decline; that their difficulties and circumstances differed greatly. But although the measures they devised and adopted to meet their various circumstances varied in character, they were at one in the motives which actuated them, and in their conception of what was fundamental.

Therefore I contend that we need only follow their principles. I believe that if that could be done, the changes and reforms that would ensue would not unduly alarm the people, or excite undue opposition, but would in the end bring the government of our day into line with that of the Golden Age.[72]

Ever since Wang An-shih's time it has been debated whether or not the measures he enacted were truly in keeping with the basic teachings of the Confucian tradition. But, in spite of his obvious debt to earlier, Legalist-inspired experiments in state capitalism,[73] there is no doubt that Wang himself was inspired by what he considered to be the essential spirit of the Confucian Classics and that the benevolent paternalism ascribed to the sage-kings could easily be construed to justify a vigorous exercise of state power to promote the general welfare. Not only was each of his major reforms prefaced by an appeal to the authority of some classical precedent or principle, but, lest this be regarded as merely conforming to an established convention,[74] it must be said that his entire career, his writings, and the testimony of his contemporaries confirm the deep seriousness—amounting almost to a self-righteous fanaticism—with which he held to his mission of putting Confucian principles into practice in politics.[75]

The close tie between Wang's reforms and classical authority is best shown by his project to bring out a complete revision of the Classics with a modernized commentary, clearly establishing the unity of his policies with the classical teaching.[76] Of these revisions, the most famous was the *New Interpretation of the Institutes of Chou* (*Chou Kuan Hsin-i*), from Wang's own hand, which became a virtual Bible of his political philosophy. For this classical text[77] Wang made the strongest claims in his personal Preface:

> When moral principles are applied to the affairs of government . . . the form they take and the use they are put to depend upon laws, but their promotion and execution depend upon individuals. In the worthiness of its individual officials to discharge the duties of office, and in the effectiveness with which its institutions administered the law, no dynasty has surpassed the early Chou. Likewise, in the suitability of its laws for perpetuation in later ages, and in the expression given them in literary form, no book is so perfect as the *Institutes of Chou* (*Chou-kuan*).[78]

So effectively did Wang use this book to justify his reforms that his edition of it became one of the most influential and controversial books in all Chinese literature. To deny Wang the support he derived from it, his opponents alleged that the *Institutes of Chou* was itself a comparatively recent forgery.[79] In later times writers commonly attributed the fall of the Northern Sung dynasty to Wang's adoption of this text as a political guide.[80]

Thus Wang's espousal of the *Institutes of Chou* represents the culmination in the political sphere of the long debate in Confucian circles over the applicability of classical institutions, as described in the *Books of Rites*, to conditions obtaining in the Sung dynasty. At the same time, Wang's effort to reinterpret these texts—to discard the Han and T'ang commentaries—and to use a modernized version as the basis for a reformed civil service examination system, stressing the general meaning of the Classics instead of a literal knowledge of them, represents the culmination of the Confucian campaign to cast out the corruptions of the Han and T'ang dynasties, both in the field of classical scholarship and in the form of civil service examinations, in order to return to the essential purity of the classic order.[81] In this respect Wang stands together with the Ch'êng brothers, Chu Hsi, and a host of other Sung scholars in their determination to set aside accepted interpretations and find new meaning in their Confucian inheritance, just as subsequent scholars of a creative or scientific temper were some day to reject the Sung interpretations and press anew their inquiry into the meaning and validity of the Classics.

Finally, in spite of Wang's general condemnation by later Neo-Confucianists, it must be acknowledged that many of the leading scholars of his day were at first sympathetic to his policies, sharing the common outlook of the Sung school. On this point no testimony could be more conclusive than that of Chu Hsi, the final arbiter of Neo-Confucian opinion in the Sung:

> When the New Laws of Wang An-shih were first promulgated, many worthy men were sincerely desirous of cooperating in their promotion, even Ch'êng Hao thinking it right to do so. For in those times such reforms were called for by the circumstances obtaining. Later, however, they found these measures contrary to the general desire, and Ch'êng Hao attempted to remonstrate with Wang on the ground that they could not be made to work in the face of general opposition. But Wang spurned the opinion of the majority and pressed his reforms with greater determination than ever. Only then did these worthy men desert him.[82]

That so many "worthy men" initially should have been sympathetic to the objectives of Wang's reform program is understandable in view of the wide acceptance won for these aims by the earlier reformers and leaders of the Sung school. Kracke testifies to this in concluding his study of civil service reforms during the period:

> Equally noteworthy was the remarkable number of influential officials that in the mid-eleventh century showed a zeal for the improvement of government according to Confucian standards, and a dedication to their task that often courted political eclipse and adversity rather than yield a principle. We need only to think of such men as Fan Chung-yen, Pao Ch'êng, Ou-yang Hsiu, Han Ch'i, Ssŭ-ma Kuang, Wang An-shih, or (somewhat later) Su Shih. These men differed and sometimes conflicted, but rather through temperament and in questions of immediate method than through any basic disagreement in their ultimate objectives.[83]

In this case the ground upon which many of his earlier supporters eventually broke with Wang—that his measures were contrary to the general desire—had considerable bearing on the subsequent course of Neo-Confucian political thought. Even before the break with Wang this issue had been touched upon in a colloquy among the Ch'êng brothers and Chang Tsai on the feasibility of restoring the ancient well-field system. Ch'êng Hao expressed the opinion that "if land of the people were taken and redistributed so that rich and poor shared alike, then there would be a great majority in favor of the step and only a few against it." Ch'êng Yi dissented: "It is not a question of how much opposition would be put up by the people, but of whether the thing ought to be done or not. Only when everyone, high and low, comes to accept it without nurturing any resentment, can the well-field system be put into effect." Ch'êng Yi accepted the fact that it might take some time to prepare the people for such a big step. "It makes no difference if one's ideas are not carried out in one's own lifetime, so long as they are put into effect by later generations." Chang Tsai, however, insisted upon the necessity for early adoption of the well-fields. Quoting Mencius, he said: " 'Virtue alone is not sufficient for the exercise of government; laws alone cannot put themselves into effect.' . . . Again 'there are those who have benevolent hearts and a reputation for benevolence,' yet they do not achieve good government—'all because they do not practice the ways of the Sage Kings' (*Mencius*, IV*a*, 1). We must follow the practices of the Sage Kings."[84]

Chang Tsai's attitude is doctrinaire and uncompromising: if the sage-kings maintained a system of well-fields, such a system must also be appropriate for his own time and should be instituted without regard to opposition. Ch'êng Hao, on the other hand, implies that this step should not be taken unless opposition to it is negligible, while Ch'êng Yi stands on principle by maintaining that any opposition at all renders the plan unacceptable, although it might ultimately be achieved if the people as a whole could be educated in its favor. Thus at one extreme Ch'êng Yi holds to the hallowed Confucian doctrine that no act can be justified which involves any coercion, however slight, since it violates the strict standard of virtue as defined by Mencius.[85] At the other extreme Chang Tsai steadfastly maintains that inward virtue alone is not enough, that it must be expressed in political action by adopting the institutions of the sage-kings. And he, too, is backed by the authority of Mencius.

Wang An-shih, though a believer in the well-field system, never went so far as to force its adoption but took other measures in the field of taxation, farm credit, and marketing controls which were designed to advance the same ideal of economic equality.[86] Yet, when Wang's reforms encountered strong opposition, this was enough to cause men like Ch'êng Hao to back down,[87] in keeping with the attitude expressed in his discussion of the well-fields. Meanwhile Wang's position was much like that of the doctrinaire and uncompromising Chang Tsai. Convinced of the rightness of his policies, he overrode all criticism and pressed his program with greater determination than ever. In this light it is not easy to say which party, at that critical juncture in Chinese history, abandoned its Confucian ideals. Indeed, it would be more accurate to say that each party was forced to abandon certain of its ideals in order to remain true to others. Both sides had to face the fact that it was proving far more difficult to "Restore the Ancient Order" than they had originally supposed. Wang held fast to his program, abandoning the strict ethical precepts of Confucius and Mencius in the vain hope that he could still achieve the political ideals of Mencius and the *Chou Li*. His opponents, who balked at coercive methods which violated the ideals of Benevolence and Justice, were thereby compelled to abandon, or rather to postpone indefinitely, achievement of those ends which tradition likewise had led them to accept.

It is more in the light of subsequent, than of earlier, tradition that this question has generally been settled in favor of the Ch'êng brothers, and

Wang ostracized from the company of orthodox Confucians. His policies themselves outlasted Wang's tenure of office and, when abolished by Ssŭ-ma Kuang, were afterward revived for a time, some even enduring into later dynasties. But the fate of his policies had little to do with his standing among later Confucians. After the fall of the Northern Sung the cleavage which had developed in the Sung school over Wang's reforms widened still further, to the point where a great gulf separated those who retained an active interest in political reform and those who had retired to the quiet groves of classical scholarship and metaphysical speculation. The line was now clearly drawn between men like Ch'ên Liang (1143–94), who still believed in the possibility and necessity of effecting immediate reforms, and the great Chu Hsi, whose attitude toward politics reflected the disillusionment of his master, Ch'êng Yi.[88] This is not to say that Chu Hsi had lost all interest in politics. He still adhered to the political ideal of the sage-kings and regarded the well-field system as indispensable to the people's welfare. But these ideals were now far more distant. The failure of Wang An-shih had demonstrated that they could only be approached through a long process of education and moral reform, which would prepare the people to accept such changes and bring about a personal reformation in their rulers, since the earlier debacle was seen as due in great measure to Wang's own defects of character. Therefore among the immediate reforms advocated by Chu those in the field of education took priority, while in the philosophical realm he and his school were led back to the central problems of Confucianism: the problems of human nature, personal cultivation, and man's place in the universe.

A letter to Chu Hsi from his friend Lü Tsu-ch'ien illustrates the prevailing opinion among scholars of the Southern Sung toward political reform. Noting that Chu had written on political questions, urging restoration of the well-fields and making detailed recommendations in regard to taxation and finance, Lü agrees that these are all essential to good government.

> But the execution of them involves a step-by-step process. Today the first requirement is to awaken the mind of the ruler. If the ruler possesses that sincerity which leads him to respect virtue and delight in the True Way, then good men will come in great numbers to assist him. Only when everyone, high and low, has full confidence in them, can the necessary steps toward good government be taken in their proper order. But if the people do not have confidence in this program and it is enacted suddenly, then there will be a great furore and it will ultimately fail.[89]

It is this attitude, which reflects Chu Hsi's own point of view, that became dominant in Neo-Confucian circles thereafter and was accepted as orthodox when later dynasties installed Chu Hsi as the official philosopher. It is therefore the point of view from which Wang An-shih has been adjudged a renegade from Confucian tradition. Nevertheless, we should keep in mind that Wang An-shih himself played a leading part in the debates which shaped that tradition and that Neo-Confucian orthodoxy is as much the product of political controversy and experiment in the Sung as it is the fruit of study and speculation in the sanctuaries of Confucian learning.

6. *Conclusion*

The purpose of the foregoing discussion has been to bring out some of the main features of the Confucian revival in the Sung in order to show what its adherents originally held in common and on what basic issues they ultimately diverged. Little attention has been given to the considerable diversity of opinion which existed in regard to specific problems of political, economic, and social reform. But it is worth noting that, quite apart from partisan differences involving controversial figures like Wang An-shih, those who subscribed to the same Confucian ideals often differed on their precise applications to conditions obtaining in their own time. Just as one instance we might cite the opinions of Su Hsün, the father of Su Tung-p'o, on the land problem. As we have seen, many scholars of his day had complained about high taxes and demanded a return to the well-field system of feudal times. Su, while asserting that a return to the ancient order was necessary, attempted to show that land taxes in the Sung were not actually much greater than those of the Chou but that they were more oppressive when added to the high rent most cultivators had to pay. Landlordism was the big evil, but the well-field system was not a practical remedy, since the Chinese people would probably perish in the attempt to re-establish so meticulous a system. Instead he urged a simple limitation on landownership to achieve the more equitable distribution which was the essence of the classic order. In the same way, other writers, proceeding from the same general principles, arrived at different practical conclusions on many current problems. It is essential to explore these differences further and to examine Confucian thought more closely in relation to the perennial problems and characteristic institutions of Chinese society if we are to obtain a clear and balanced picture of intellectual life in the Sung or in any other period.

NOTES

1. Fung Yu-lan, "The Rise of Neo-Confucianism and Its Borrowings from Buddhism and Taoism," translated by Derk Bodde, *Harvard Journal of Asiatic Studies*, VII, No. 2 (July, 1942), 96.

2. Cf. J. R. Hightower, *Topics in Chinese Literature* (Cambridge, Mass., 1950), p. 68.

3. On these aspects of Han Yü's thought see Fung and Bodde, *op. cit.*, pp. 89–99; H. H. Dubs, "Han Yü and the Buddha's Relic: An Episode in Medieval Chinese Religion," *Review of Religion*, XI, No. 1 (November, 1946), 5–17; J. K. Rideout, "The Context of the *Yüan Tao* and *Yüan Hsing*," *Bulletin of the School of Oriental and African Studies* (London University), XII, No. 2, 403–8. The most important of Han Yü's general essays on these subjects are the "Yüan Tao," "Yüan Hsing," "Yüan Jen" (*Chu wên-kung Chiao Ch'ang-li Hsien-shêng Chi* [*Ssŭ-pu Ts'ung-k'an* ed. (hereafter cited as "SPTK"), 1st ser.], chap. 11, pp. 1*a*–7*a*), and "Shih-shuo" (*ibid.*, chap. 12, pp. 1*b*–2*b*).

4. Dubs, *op. cit.*, p. 14.

5. This was one result of the attempt to give the examinations in as objective and impartial a manner as possible. In order to rule out arbitrary judgment or favoritism which might enter into questions of interpretation, literal knowledge of the texts and their commentaries was stressed.

6. See the exchange of letters on this question between Liu Mien and Ch'üan Tê-yü (759–818) in *Ch'üan Ts'ai-chih Wên-chi* (SPTK, 1st ser.), chap. 41, pp. 1*a*–2*b*.

7. Hightower, *op. cit.*, pp. 68–69.

8. Rideout, *op. cit.*, p. 406.

9. Ch'ien Mu, *Chung-kuo Chin San-pai-nien Hsüeh-shu Shih* (Shanghai: Commercial Press, 1937), pp. 1–2.

10. *Ch'ang-li Hsien-shêng Chi*, chap. 12, pp. 1*a*–4*b*; G. Margoulies, *Le Kou-wen chinois* (Paris, 1926), pp. 183–88.

11. This history, the *Hsin T'ang-shu*, was edited chiefly by Ou-yang Hsiu and Sung Ch'i, the biographical section being attributed to the latter. Cf. Robert des Rotours, *Le Traité des examens* (Paris, 1932), p. 57.

12. *Hsin T'ang-shu* (*Han-fên lou* facsimile of Palace ed. of 1739), chap. 176, p. 15*a*; translation adapted and revised from that of Bodde in Fung, *op. cit.*, pp. 93–94.

13. J. P. Bruce, *Chu Hsi and His Masters* (London, 1923), pp. 85–88, 91.

14. Cf. Takeuchi Yoshio, "Sōgaku No Yurai Oyobi Sono Tokushusei" ("The Origins and Special Character of the Sung School"), *Tōyō Shichō, Iwamani kōza* (Tokyo, 1934), pp. 5–12.

15. Since this paper is primarily concerned with the Sung school as a general movement toward intellectual and social reform, no mention is made here of Li Ao, the other important forerunner in the T'ang of this school. In contrast to Han Yü, Li Ao attempted to assimilate Buddhist concepts into Confucianism and synthesize the two. By so doing, he contributed more to the metaphysical speculations of the Ch'êng-Chu school than to the initial phase of practical reform. On Li Ao see Fung and Bodde, *op. cit.*, pp. 99–113; Rideout, *op. cit.*, p. 406; and Takeuchi Yoshio, *op. cit.*, pp. 10–12.

16. Unless they were better known as state officials, literary men, etc. (cf. *Sung Shih*, chaps. 427 ff.). This history was written, of course, well after the period in question, from 1341 to 1345, by which time the limits of orthodoxy had become more clearly defined and Chu Hsi's commentaries on the Four Books had been adopted as standard for the civil service examinations (1313). Cf. Fung Yu-lan, *A Short History of Chinese Philosophy*, trans. D. Bodde (New York, 1948), p. 268.

17. Actually "Neo-Confucianism" is not used as an exact equivalent for *Tao-hsüeh* as found in the *Sung Shih*. It implies broader criteria of classification such as to include philosophers like the unorthodox Lu Chiu-yuan, and those who followed in his school, whereas in the *Sung Shih* he is placed among the *Ju-lin* (*Sung Shih*, chap. 434, p. 9*b*; Fung, *op. cit.*, chap. 26). Thus the term "Neo-Confucian" now is used to cover any new developments in Confucian thought which derive from the metaphysical speculations of the early Sung. Even this interpretation is not strictly adhered to, however; Bodde, for instance, describes as "Neo-Confucian" the school of Ch'ên Liang in the Southern Sung, although it was noted chiefly for political thought and action and was openly opposed to the metaphysical speculations of the Ch'êng-Chu school (Fung and Bodde, "The Philosophy of Chu Hsi," *Harvard Journal of Asiatic Studies*, VII [1942], 45). The term "Neo-Confucian" here is an interpolation of the translator, not in the original text. Cf. Fung Yu-lan, *Chung-kuo Chê-hsüeh Shih* (Shanghai: Commercial Press, 1941), p. 923.

The difficulty of isolating one orthodox school from among others sharing a common tradition was probably recognized when the *Tao-hsüeh* classification was abandoned in subsequent dynastic histories (*Yüan Shih*, chap. 189, p. 1*a*; *Ming Shih*, chap. 282, p. 1*a*). Meanwhile this term acquired the derogatory connotation of "pompous moralist" or "pedant."

18. Started by Huang Tsung-hsi (1610–95) as an extension into these earlier periods of his famous *Ming-ju Hsüeh-an*, this work was continued after Huang's death by his son Po-chia and largely completed by Ch'üan Tsu-wang (1705–55).

19. *Sung Yüan Hsüeh-an* (*Shih-chieh Shu-chü* ed.), chap. 1, pp. 17–18, chap. 2, p. 43; Ch'üan Tsu-wang, "Ch'ing-li Wu Hsien-shêng Shu-yüan Chi," in *Chi-ch'i-t'ing Chi, Wai-pien* (Commercial Press ed.), chap. 5, p. 865. This account is followed by such modern historians as Ch'ien Mu, *op. cit.*, pp. 2–3, and Takeuchi Yoshio, *op. cit.*, p. 13.

20. Biography in *Sung Shih*, chap. 432, p. 10*a*; *Sung Yüan Hsüeh-an*, chap. 1, p. 17; Herbert Giles, *A Chinese Biographical Dictionary* (London, 1898), No. 827 (hereafter cited as "Giles").

21. *Hsü T'ung-k'ao* (1603 ed.), fan-lei, chap. 2*a*, chap. 61, pp. 1 ff.; *Ch'in-ting Hsü T'ung-k'ao* (Commercial Press ed.), chap. 47, p. 3209*a*.

22. *Sung Shih*, chap. 432, p. 10*b*.

23. He usually referred to Chou Tun-i by his literary name (*tzŭ*) but always to Hu Yüan by his honorific, *An-ting hsien-sheng*. Cf. the note of Huang Po-chia in *Sung Yüan Hsüeh-an*, chap. 1, pp. 17–18; and Chu I-tsun, *P'u-shu-t'ing Chi* (SPTK, 1st ser.), chap. 58, pp. 1*b*–2*b*.

24. *Sung Yüan Hsüeh-an*, chap. 1, pp. 17–18.

24a. *Ibid.*, p. 17.

25. Cf. E. A. Kracke, *Civil Service in Early Sung China* (Cambridge, Mass., 1953), p. 197, where, in summing up the effects of examination reforms and the practice of sponsorship in the civil service, he states: "Nearly all the great statesmen were also famous as writers and scholars. They were men in the humanist tradition, whose interests extended to the whole culture of their time. Practically none of them were really specialists in a single narrow aspect of government activity, such as finance or water control. In this attainment, and this limitation, they displayed not merely the influence of the examination system, but the generally accepted values of their time, which guided the operation of sponsorship as well."

26. *Sung Yüan Hsüeh-an*, chap. 1, p. 17.

27. Cf. *Sung Shih*, chap. 432, p. 6*a*; *Sung Yüan Hsüeh-an*, chap. 2, p. 43.
28. "Sun Ming-fu Mu-chih-ming," in *Ou-yang Wên-chung Kung Chi* (SPTK, 1st ser.), chap 27, p. 12*a*.
29. Cf. *Sung Shih*, chap. 432, p. 7*a*; *Sung Yüan Hsüeh-an*, chap. 2, pp. 61–62.
30. *Sung Shih*, chap. 432, p. 7*a*.
31. On this characteristic of Chinese politics see Lin Yutang, *The Gay Genius* (New York, 1947), p. 100.
32. See J. C. Ferguson, "Political Parties of the Northern Sung," *Journal of the North China Branch of the Royal Asiatic Society*, LVIII (1927), 35–56.
33. Cf. *Sung Shih*, chap. 314, p. 1*a*; *Sung Yüan Hsüeh-an*, chap. 3, pp. 78–79; Giles, No. 535.
34. *Sung Yüan Hsüeh-an*, chap. 3, p. 79. Needless to say, the translation does not do justice to the simplicity and force of the original. This maxim is so famous and often repeated that a learned Chinese friend assured the writer it must be a quotation from the Classics. Indexes to the Classics do not bear this out, however.
35. *Sung Shih*, chap. 314, pp. 7*b*–8*b*.
36. Cf. Kracke (*op. cit*., pp. 18–19): "During the earlier Sung, advanced education was provided almost entirely by private academies. . . . The government had merely provided limited educational facilities at the capital for children of officials. During the eleventh century, however—particularly after 1030—the state undertook the responsibility of supplying schools for private citizens as well, at the capital, and in the prefectures and more important sub-prefectures. While the implementation of this measure seems to have progressed rather slowly, it must have meant from the beginning a considerable widening of educational opportunity." The period during which the state undertook this responsibility was that of Fan's administration. In a further note on this passage Kracke indicates that the founder of the Sung dynasty "had shown an interest in local education by donating books to the private academies"—a far cry from the universal public education ascribed to the Chou dynasty by the Classics.
37. An examination of this type was given by Ou-yang Hsiu to Su Tung-p'o in 1057 (see Lin Yutang, *op. cit*., p. 39).
38. On this debate and consequent reforms see *T'ung-k'ao* (Commercial Press ed.), chap. 31, p. 290*bc*; *Sung Shih*, chap. 11, p. 6*b*, chap. 155, p. 11*b*, chap. 157, p. 3*a*.
39. Ch'ien Mu, *op. cit*., p. 3.
40. *Sung Yüan Hsüeh-an*, chap. 4, p. 105.
41. Takeuchi Yoshio, *op. cit*., pp. 13–15.
42. *Ibid*., p. 14.
43. See his "Essay on True Orthodoxy" ("Cheng-t'ung Lun") and "Essay on Fundamentals" ("Pen Lun"), in *Ou-yang Wên-chung Kung Chi* (SPTK, 1st ser.), chap. 16, p. 1*a*, chap. 17, p. 1*a*; also L. Weiger, *Textes historiques* (Ho-chien, 1905), pp. 1860–62.
44. *Sung Yüan Hsüeh-an*, chap. 4, pp. 105, 115.
45. See his "Essay on Societies and Cliques" ("P'eng-tang Lun"), in *Ou-yang Wên-chung Kung Chi*, chap. 17, p. 6*b*. (French translation in G. Margoulies, *Anthologie raisonnée de la littérature chinoise* [Paris, 1931], p. 145.)
46. Ch'ien Mu, *op. cit*., p. 4.
47. Wang An-shih, *Lin-ch'uan Hsien-sheng Wên-chi* (SPTK, 1st ser.), chap. 13, p. 7*b*.
48. *Sung Yüan Hsüeh-an*, chap. 4, p. 103, chap. 97, p. 1831; *Lin-ch'uan Hsien-shêng Wên-chi*, Preface of Huang Tz'ŭ-shan, p. 1*b*; Ch'ien Mu, *op. cit*., p. 4.

49. Cf. *Sung Shih*, chap. 312, p. 1*a; Sung Yüan Hsüeh-an*, chap. 3, p. 81; Giles, No. 610.

50. H. R. Williamson, *Wang An-shih* (2 vols.; London, 1935–37), I, 14.

51. Giles, No. 280; J. P. Bruce, *Chu Hsi and His Masters*, p. 45.

52. Ch'êng Yi, *Erh-Ch'êng Wên-chi*, chap. 4, p. 43.

53. *Ibid.*, p. 46.

54. Leading Confucian philosopher of the former Han dynasty (see Giles, No. 2092).

55. Confucian scholar of the Sui dynasty (590–618) also known as Wên-chung Tzŭ (see Giles, No. 2239).

56. *Erh-Ch'êng Wên-chi*, chap. 4, p. 47.

57. Cf. Giles, No. 278; Bruce, *op. cit.*, p. 41.

58. Ch'êng Hao, *Lun Shih Shih Ta-tzŭ*, *Erh-Ch'êng Ch'üan-shu* (*Ssŭ-pu Pei-yao* ed.), *Ming-tao Wên-chi*, chap. 2, p. 6*a;* also in *Sung Yüan Hsüeh-an*, chap. 14, p. 332, as *Ch'ên Chih-fa Shih-shih.*

59. A square plot divided into nine equal squares, the one in the center being cultivated in common by those occupying the eight surrounding ones. Cf. *Mencius*, III*a*, 3.

60. Ch'êng Hao, *op. cit.*, chap. 2, p. 7*a*.

61. Cf. Giles, No. 117; Bruce, *op. cit.*, p. 50.

62. *Sung Yüan Hsüeh-an*, chap. 17, p. 383.

63. *Chang Tzŭ Ch'üan-shu*, *Kuo-hsüeh Chi-pên T'sung-shu*, chap. 4, p. 83.

64. *Ibid.*, p. 84.

65. *Ibid.*, p. 85.

66. *Sung Yüan Hsüeh-an*, chap. 17, p. 383.

67. *Mencius*, II*a*, 3.

68. Cf. *Erh-ch'êng Wên-chi*, chap. 1, p. 4; Ch'ien Mu, *op. cit.*, p. 5.

69. Wang An-shih, *Lin-ch'uan Wên-chi* (SPTK, 1st ser.), chap. 67, p. 6*a*, *Wang-pa Lun*. On this point Wang's views are much closer to those of Chu Hsi than they are to those of Li Kou (1009–59) and Ch'ên Liang (1143–94), who saw the rule of later dynasties as not essentially different from that of the sage-kings, but with whom Wang is sometimes classed as a proponent of radical reforms. Cf. Hsiao Kung-ch'üan, *Chung-kuo Chêng-chih Ssŭ-hsiang Shih* (Shanghai: Commercial Press, 1947), pp. 147, 154–55.

70. *Hsin T'ang-shu*, chap. 50, p. 1*ab*. (French translation in Robert des Rotours, *Traité des fonctionnaires et traité de l'armée* [Leyden, 1948], pp. 747–50).

71. *Ching-chin Tung-p'o Wên-chi* (SPTK, 1st ser.), chap. 42, p. 4*a*.

71a. As rendered by Lin Yutang, *op. cit.*, p. 83; also in Williamson, *op. cit.*, I, 102.

72. *Lin-ch'uan Hsien-shêng Wên-chi*, chap. 39, pp. 1*a*–2*b*, *Shang Jen-tsung Huang-ti Yen-shih Shu* (translation adapted from Williamson, *op. cit.*, I, 50).

73. See Williamson, *op. cit.*, I, 136, 144, 300–301; II, 233–39; Lin Yutang, *op. cit.*, p. 75.

74. In summarizing the contents of the memorial to Jen-tsung just cited, Lin Yutang (*op. cit.*, p. 81) states: "He cleverly pointed out that in making radical reforms, one should connect them with the practices of the ancient sage kings so that people would not regard them as a radical departure from the past." I can find nothing in the text of the memorial to support this imputation of a calcuated attempt to play on common prejudices by dressing up unpalatable reforms in antique disguise.

75. Cf. Hsiao Kung-ch'üan, *op. cit.*, pp. 149–50. Though many passages in his writings could be cited in this connection, the following excerpt from one of his essays

succinctly expresses his basic intent: "Nowadays Confucian scholars are zealous enough for the doctrines of the Sages, but they have the idea that the quicker they sell their principles, the quicker will be their progress. If they get a good price they will serve their master, but if not, they cast off their Confucian robes and engage in business. . . . There are very few indeed who, having gained their desire for high office, continue to practice the teachings of the Sages without wavering" (*Lin-ch'uan Wên-chi*, chap. 66, pp. *6b–7a;* translation by Williamson, *op. cit.*, II, 364–65).

76. See Williamson, *op. cit.*, Vol. I, chap. 22; Vol. II, chap. 18.

77. The *Institutes of Chou* (*Chou Kuan*) is another name for the *Rites of Chou* (*Chou Li*).

78. *Chou-kuan Hsin-i*, Personal Preface of Wang An-shih.

79. A. Wylie, *Notes on Chinese Literature* (Peking reprint, 1939), p. 4; Williamson, *op. cit.*, II, 300.

80. *Ssu-k'u Ch'üan-shu Tsung-mu*, chap. 19, p. *1b*.

81. The type of examination instituted by Wang (as distinct from the particular interpretations of the Classics adopted by him) was not a new idea. Liu Mien had made essentially the same proposal in the late T'ang, as shown above, and during the era of reform led by Fan Chung-yen similar recommendations were offered by Sung Ch'i. Shortly thereafter Wang Kuei, later to become one of Wang An-shih's closest supporters and co-workers, again advocated examinations which required an understanding of the general principles of the Classics rather than memorization of the texts and their commentaries. Other reforms of Wang An-shih, such as his universal school system and the "square fields" system of taxation, were also anticipated by reforms attempted in Fan Chung-yen's time. Cf. *Yü-hai* (*Chekiang Shu-chü* 1883 ed.), chap. 116, p. *21b; Sung Shih*, chap. 155, pp. *11b–12b*, chap. 284, p. *13b*, chap. 312, p. *21a;* Hsiung Kung-chê, *Wang An-shih Chêng-lüeh* (Shanghai: Commercial Press, 1937), pp. 113, 120, 129.

82. *Chu-tzŭ Ch'üan-shu* (*K'ang-hsi* ed. 1714), chap. 62, p. *32a*.

83. *Op. cit.*, pp. 197–98.

84. *Ch'êng Shih I-shu* (*Erh-Ch'êng Ch'üan-shu*), chap. 10, pp. *1b–2a;* T'ao Hsi-shêng, "Pei-Sung Chi-ko Ta Ssŭ-hsiang-chia Ti Ching-t'ien Lun," *Shih-huo*, II, No. 6, 37–38.

85. Cf. *Mencius*, II*a*, 2, where it is asserted that Confucius would not, in order to obtain power, "commit a single act of unrighteousness or put one innocent person to death."

86. T'ao Hsi-shêng, *op. cit.*, pp. 35–36.

87. Williamson, *op. cit.*, I, 126, 167. Of course the objections to Wang's measures took many forms, but most of them were based on the complaint that he was forcing upon the people what they did not find it in their interest to accept. When, instead of listening to those objections, Wang attempted to silence his critics, many others withdrew from the government.

88. Cf. Hsiao Kung-ch'üan, *op. cit.*, pp. 154, 186–87; Fung and Bodde, "The Philosophy of Chu Hsi," *op. cit.*, pp. 41–45.

89. *Lü Tung-lai Wên-chi*, chap. 3, p. 53; Ch'ien Mu, *op. cit.*, p. 5.

THE PROBLEM OF "KNOWLEDGE" AND "ACTION" IN CHINESE THOUGHT SINCE WANG YANG-MING

DAVID S. NIVISON

WHAT I SHALL have to say in the following pages is the combined product of three interests I have had in the history of Chinese thought: first, an interest, which can scarcely be wholly absent in anyone seriously concerned with China, in contemporary politics and the recent history of political opinion; second, a general interest in the later part of Chinese intellectual history, the so-called Neo-Confucian period, usually considered to have started in the Sung (960–1280); and, third, a special interest in the seventeenth and eighteenth centuries and in particular in the eighteenth-century essayist and historian Chang Hsüeh-ch'eng (1738–1801), whose writings I have been reading for several years past. I believe this particular enterprise has a value considerably greater than its mere curiosity, and, in pretending here to consider the "problem of 'knowledge' and 'action' " during the last four or five centuries, I am in effect stating and holding up for scrutiny certain assumptions about the recent history of Chinese thought to which my study of Chang's ideas has led me. If these assumptions turn out to be approximately correct, they point to one important way in which the history of Chinese thought shows a continuous development, which has been modified, but not broken, by the "impact of the West."

1. Some Traditional Habits of Thinking

A Chinese of the sixteenth century had behind him a civilization as rich and as varied, in its own way, as our own. For any idea we may find him entertaining, for any thesis he enunciates, we can construct out of this background an indefinite set of precedents, suggestions, approximations, sources—which will, in fact, be limited only by our conception of what is relevant. When Wang Yang-ming (1472–1528)[1] states, and insists repeatedly, that there is no knowing, to be recognized as such, which does not involve some kind of doing, or perhaps that knowing must actually be doing, what may we take him to mean? Part of what he means may be discovered by looking into the traditional background of his words—a background which is for him timeless, since, as he apprehends it, its availability to him is not related to its historical extension. It is not, therefore, a history of his idea, though it is part of the set of data out of which we could construct such a history. It is important to take note of this set of data. It is important, first, because this traditional fund supplies the stuff out of which his habits of thinking could form and out of which his beliefs could be selected; and, second, because we have notions of our own, drawn from the history—and the recent history—of our own thought which are suggested by the words we use to translate him and which we cannot afford to assume are his.

But we do not, by taking note of this background, explain why he had this habit and not a different one, why he held this belief and not another. We are on the way to an adequate explanation of Hobbes's theory of the state if we consider the religious thought which preceded and surrounded him, the political facts of seventeenth-century England, and the new mechanistic hypotheses in science. We do not explain him by referring to the notions of a shadowy fellow student of Plato named Glaucon, though we might argue that we establish thereby a possibility in his tradition. For the student of Western thought this will seem trite, but the student of China must remind himself of it, because in the writers he examines the authority of tradition is constantly acknowledged, and the sanction of classical text constantly appealed to. Consequently, while this background is important, it must not be taken as a substitute for relating a man to the intellectual history of his own time—in Wang Yang-ming's case, the development of Neo-Confucianism.

In earlier attitudes and ways of thinking which make up the background of the recent history of thought about "knowledge" and "action," a marked characteristic is the constant Chinese habit of dualizing in forming their concepts. "Knowledge" (*chih*) and "action" (*hsing*) are one such dualism and are closely related to certain others. I suggest that the traditional stock of ideas, attitudes, and habits of thought relating to "knowledge" and "action," as these were available to Wang Yang-ming, may be described under the following generalizations.

1. There is observable since earliest times a habit of categorizing problems and situations as involving knowledge or involving action, of distinguishing principles from practice. In the *Shang Shu*, a classical source of great prestige, Fu Yüeh, minister to the Shang sovereign Kao-tsung (i.e., Wu-ting), advises his majesty as to the guiding principles of the conduct of government. His advice is "knowledge"; the king's subsequent behavior, if he sincerely attends to his minister's instruction and his virtue is thereby perfected, will be appropriate "action." And, his minister cautions, "It is not knowing but *acting* which is difficult."[2] As this example suggests, the classification of knowledge and action often

implies a classification of persons into knowers and doers. Thus, Han Yü (768–824) classifies the Confucian sages into two groups: those who were in authority and hence could act (viz., govern) and those who lacked authority and who were important for what they said and wrote.[3] This suggests a further distinction of attributes of persons; some have "virtue" (*te*), innate goodness, and direct insight into what ought to be done; and some have "authority" (*wei*), power to make their ideas visible in action. The *Chung Yung*, possibly representing the influence of Legalism on early imperial Confucianism, argues that a ruler must have both and that a Sage may not propose changes in government unless he has "authority."[4] The classification can even, in effect, be extended to books: there are those which set out principles, theories, and opinions and those which relate actions. Thus Confucius, in defending the *Ch'un-ch'iu* (which he was traditionally supposed to have written), is made by Ssŭ-ma Ch'ien (145–86 B.C.) to say, "Though I should wish to express [my judgments] in 'empty words' (viz., general statements), they would not be as sharp and clear as they will if I illustrate them in [a record of] actions."[5]

2. As these examples illustrate, the use of "knowledge" and "action" or related concepts as categories raises the problem of relating the one to the other, of evaluating one relatively to the other. It is usually "action" which is regarded as more important, more trustworthy, more easily grasped, or more difficult and hence of greater concern. There are, of course, exceptions. Confucius, in what is an important statement in the developing philosophy of early gentry society, could say: "The people may be made to follow [the 'Way'] but cannot be brought to understand it,"[6] this being the proper business of their betters. And in the third century A.D., Hsü Kan (171–218), in an essay on "Knowledge and Action," argues that a life of learning and the attainment of perfect understanding is more valuable than a life of action and the perfection of one's conduct.[7] "Study" is the Sage's highest duty, he held; it is the "bright sun" of the mind, dispelling human ignorance.[8] The attainment of the Sage is not limited to "empty deeds."[9] Hsü was perhaps trying to justify the scholar confronted with the rising prestige of military men at the end of the Han. But his position was always a possible one.

3. With a dualistic habit of thought there is likely to develop a compulsion to overcome the dualism. Wang Yang-ming, in attempting to overcome the opposition of "knowledge" and "action," was able to draw upon an ancient moral conception of a peculiar structure. Failure to make one's deeds correspond to one's words, it was felt, is morally reprehensible. The *Ta Hsüeh* and the *Chung Yung* present a yet stricter

view: to profess to accept a standard of goodness, and to conform to it, merely in order to gain approval, profits a man nothing. "There is no evil to which the mean man, dwelling retired, will not proceed, but when he sees a superior man, he will instantly try to disguise himself, concealing his evil, and displaying what is good." But he deceives no one; the man of virtue sees through his pretense. "This is an instance of the saying, 'What truly is within will be manifested without.' Therefore the superior man must watch over himself when he is alone."[10] He should watch both his unobserved actions and his private feelings, lest secret motives intervene between his behavior and his professions. This is the source of the concept of "sincerity," which became of fundamental importance in Neo-Confucian thought. But in early imperial mysticism it is a magical force; he who attains it has tapped a mysterious power, giving him influence over all things and all men; he becomes omniscient, with the ability to foresee the future.[11]

4. With this moral attitude is involved a feeling that there is something unsatisfactory about a knowledge *claim*. In ancient times this uneasiness was intimately related to a fascinated puzzling over the nature of language, which became for a short time highly sophisticated; much of this reflected a primitive and persisting belief in the magical properties of words: words properly used and combined had the power to compel action. But the interest in language was very largely a moral concern. The question how language refers to things and processes could be to ask whether a thing or moral agent merits the characterization it pretends to; hence Confucius' supposed indignation at the "cornered vessel" which actually had no corners,[12] and the Legalist obsession with the idea that a ruler's power over his officials is secured if he holds them responsible in their actions for precisely what is implied in their titles or for what they claim they know how to do. This was to make the impossible demand that reality conform to language, and another sort of question was prompted—How can "mere words" be adequate to express the richness of existence or the infinite variety of human thought?[13]—a question containing the suspicion that the man who claims to know a truth knows nothing; he would do better to remain silent or to demonstrate his understanding in some visible way. In such a way, words as used came under skeptical review. It was one of the effects of the philosophy of Wang Yang-ming to raise again this suspicion of language in a new and acute form.

5. What is meant by "knowledge" in early writing is a twofold problem. The inevitability of thinking of "knowledge" as opposed and related to "action" made it natural that what knowledge is about should

be action, or rules of behavior, or government. Some, such as the Mohists and Legalists, went so far as to hold that a man should be concerned with no learning which is not of practical use. The suspicion of knowledge claims just suggested consequently was less likely to lead to a criticism of the truth of statements than to a feeling that one should get beyond words to action or to genuine conviction. What knowing as a mental process is conceived to be is more difficult. The difficulty of pinning down what is meant by "knowing," even in a single context, is brought out by a passage from Hsün-tzŭ: "Not to hear of something is not as good as to hear about it; to hear about it is not as good as to witness it; to witness it is not as good as to 'know' it; and to 'know' it is not as good as to act upon it: the end of learning is action."[14] Hsün-tzŭ seems here to be arranging modes of moral knowing by their degree, so to speak, of epistemological intensity. But we could fill in the sequence "hearing, seeing, . . . , doing" equally well by "really understanding" or by "knowing full well" (viz., "believing," "accepting wholly"). Hsün-tzŭ may well have meant both. In fact, a noticeable feature of much of Chinese thought about knowledge seems to be the absence of a radical distinction between having an understanding of a thing or situation and comprehending the meaning of a statement, and, in turn, between such comprehension and acceptance of an assertion by conviction. Believing often seems to be an intense or perfect sort of knowing. This may partly account for the ancient Mohists' curious conception of argument. Their assumption was that if one could, by constructing an argument perfectly, make one's adversary follow the force of one's reasoning, he would be powerless to resist it and would automatically be governed by it in his actions and feelings, so that "word and deed" would fit together "like the two halves of a tally."[15] The Mohist treatment of "universal love" as a rational matter seems to betray the assumption that really knowing something amounts to a conviction the evidence of which is appropriate behavior. This is at least an important attitude in later Neo-Confucian thinking. In Neo-Confucian times, however, the concept of "knowledge" ranges very widely, from sense perception to abstract thought; and "action" has a similar indeterminacy.

6. A final point to be noted in the background of the Neo-Confucian thought Wang Yang-ming expressed is the extraordinarily fluid way in which Chinese dualisms functioned: "knowledge" and "action" suggest "words" and "deeds," "principles" and "events" (or "things"), "virtue" and "authority," and these pairs of concepts in turn have further associations. In Neo-Confucian thought this looseness of conception is much more easily observed. In view of this fluidity of meaning, the

study of ideas of knowledge and action cannot be strictly limited to a particular pair of symbols; for what Chinese writers say about "knowledge" and "action" may reflect, or be reflected in, what they say in other words.[16]

2. *The Neo-Confucian View of Mind and the "Unity of Knowledge and Action" in Wang Yang-ming*

These ideas developed and changed but were from fairly early times always available. For them to come together in an explicit, co-ordinated conception of "knowledge" and "action" and thus to exert a concerted influence at a later stage in time, they had to be brought into some sort of focus by the intervening history of thought. This focusing was accomplished by the Neo-Confucian response to Buddhism, and, while the analysis of Neo-Confucian thought as a whole is not within the scope of this inquiry, some relevant features of that new philosophy must be noted.

Ch'an Buddhism gave to the Confucian of the Sung the object of his intellectual endeavor, an experience of understanding or realization which, when reached, would knit together his knowledge into a meaningful whole. In giving him this goal of enlightenment, it gave him a problem associated with it in Buddhism itself: Is this enlightenment to be reached after long-disciplined effort, or is it to be attained suddenly, by some mystical event the occurrence of which may actually be impeded by such effort? A second legacy of Buddhism to Confucian thought, apparent in the Ming period, was the tendency more and more to conceive of reality in terms of consciousness, perception, or "feeling." Yet another Buddhist influence was a tendency in later Neo-Confucianism to think of enlghtenment as a mystical discovery of ultimate reality in one's "real self"; and, as in Ch'an, this discovery is a discovery of something inexpressible in words.

The core of the new Confucianism was a much more sophisticated concept of mind than had earlier been available, put together of new and old elements. This concept was rather loose, for it was probably nowhere worked out fully and consistently, but in the main it was built around suggestions drawn from the *Chung Yung*. There is in each man a "nature" and "feelings," the latter including emotion and judgment; perception of external objects is passive and apparently to be identified with "nature." "Nature" and "feeling" are, respectively, the mind, or self, as "quiescent" and the mind as "active." The mind is *tao*—ultimate reality—itself: "All things in the world are basically our own single essence; when our mind is correct, then the world mind is correct."

Consequently, the quiet mind and the active mind are identified, respectively, as the *tao* in its "essence" (*t'i*) and the *tao* as it "functions" (*yung*). The "nature" or *tao* essence is that "through which the principles of everything come." The *tao* in "function" is "the way universally followed in past times and present."[17]

These "principles" include both norms for human behavior in various types of situations, and determining essences or purposes of material objects. All minds contain these principles, at least to some extent, and hence have natural "knowledge." But a number of disagreements were possible. One point of view, identified with Chu Hsi (1130–1200), held that the knowledge naturally in the mind is incomplete and that enlightenment is the end result of long study—of filling out the mind's knowledge by acquiring that knowledge of the "principles" of things which it lacks.[18] Another view, exemplified by Wang Yang-ming, was interested not in the "principles" of things in themselves but in personal ethical behavior and held that the "principles" for conduct are completely available in the mind. Enlightenment in this view is attained by ridding the mind of confusion and selfishness which prevent innate moral knowledge from expressing itself naturally in action and in the spontaneous movement of feeling. On either view, the end of intellectual life is self-perfection, a state of affairs which made "learning" a very personal problem, even for the scholar. Its object was the cultivation of one's moral nature and the gaining of an understanding which was necessarily private. But, roughly speaking, Chu Hsi's school of thought was interested in the acquisition of knowledge of matters of fact, particularly in classical scholarship, while the Wang school identified "knowledge" with perfect "action."[19]

There is another way in which the knowledge-action antithesis appears in Neo-Confucian thought. In the Sung analysis of mind there seems to be a tendency to identify "knowledge" with the "nature" and with abstraction, and "action" with the feelings and emotions. The study of mind, of one's "basic essence," is, in Ming thought especially, what moral self-cultivation involves. But a problem arises: Is the mind really separable, so to speak, into two halves? If it is, then it seems it is the "nature" one is after, and one must grasp it by isolating it, by long exercise in "quieting" the mind. If it is not, then *tao* is known directly, apprehended suddenly, in the movement of "feeling."[20] This was a problem which became important in late Ming Confucianism, and here again Wang Yang-ming's position was most consistent with the latter view. In either case, what the adept is after is a self-realization which will resolve the division in himself and which will have the effect of a mystical release of spiritual force. This is the "sincerity" of earlier Confucianism, whose possessor can "transform" all things. "The more one gathers [one's self] together, the more [one's power] is extended."[21]

It can be seen how earlier ideas and tendencies are here brought into correlation. The dualistic habit of forming concepts is reinforced in an explicit theory of mind and (it could be shown) in a metaphysical system. The problem of relative emphasis appears in the problem of "gradual attainment" as against "sudden enlightenment," viz., whether the adept's attention should be focused on his "nature" or its activity or whether he should cultivate himself by learning—acquiring information—or by perfecting his conduct. The attempt to resolve the Neo-Confucian dualisms and an attitude of suspicion toward abstract statement are basic characteristics of Wang Yang-ming's philosophy; they are preoccupations to which he is led by the structure of ideas within which he works—a structure in which there is always some sense in which any concept is identical with any other, and which implies that perfect understanding is subjective and inexpressible. Finally, Neo-Confucianism exploits the fluidity of Chinese philosophical language to the utmost. A large class of new dualistic terms becomes current, no two pairs identical in meaning, but each easily suggesting another. This tricky set of mystical concepts accounts for the way in which Wang Yang-ming talks about "knowledge" and "action" and supplies the attitudes which underlie much of later talk on the subject.

In the self-cultivation of the would-be Sage, Wang taught, "knowledge" and "action" should develop simultaneously. "Knowledge" he tends to think of as at once moral and practical; study is a learning to affirm moral laws, to make them genuinely part of one's own emotional constitution; it further implies studying how to act, becoming able to do something. But there seems scarcely to be a distinction in Wang between an action and a disposition to act. The genuine affirmation of a moral law is the practicing of it, and a knowledge of how to do something is the doing of it: only experience is real knowledge. This attitude yields a reconstruction of Chu Hsi's idea of the nature and end of learning: at the point at which knowledge is perfectly genuine and "sincere," it passes over into and includes practice. The unity of knowing and doing is, in short, the realization the student seeks. To suppose that one can develop and perfect knowledge in advance of acting is incorrect, for such knowledge would be "insincere." The attempt is evidence of a moral fault. It is a failure to understand the true self, one's "basic essence," splitting it apart. It is evidence that selfish hesitation is intervening to prevent the moral nature from expressing itself. Wang's manipulation of the Neo-Confucian concept of mind was to make the problem of knowledge and action explicitly one of moral and psychological health; failure to identify one with the other is a failure to be effective. The source of moral knowledge or moral laws for Wang is the mind, and the mind is known in its movement: "To seek for (moral) principles in things outside the mind implies separating knowledge and action," for this would be to seek a knowledge preceding action. Elsewhere Wang tries to explain knowledge and action not as literally identical but as two aspects of a single process. Thoughts are incipient acts: "Knowledge is the beginning of practice; doing is the completion of knowing," he says, though we are not, perhaps, to think of the "beginning" and the "completion" as separated in time. "Evil thoughts," consequently, can never be dismissed as harmless.[22]

Certain common distinctions either are denied or are simply absent in Wang's thought. There is, first, no distinction between *what* is known and the *process* of knowing. Wang is almost clear about this: "The mind originates a 'thought,' and the essence of the 'thought' is knowledge." This "knowledge" is not an abstraction or a generalization *about* something; it is both the thing and the focusing of attention upon it: "Wherever the 'thought' is we have an 'object.' "[23] In close relation to this, another distinction which is, explicitly, ruled out is that between acts and things; both are mental acts or states. An object which appears to be outside the mind is simply an act of perception.[24]

A distinction which is simply absent is that between act and judging or feeling, a situation which is hardly surprising in view of the Neo-Confucian assumption that "feeling" is the mind in activity. The range of meaning of activity in this sense could be, and is in Wang, very wide; it includes ideas (considered as acts of mind and not as assertions of truths), feelings, moral judgments, and convictions and the behavior which is their spontaneous expression. As examples of the unity of knowledge and action we are given these statements: "Smelling a bad odor involves knowledge; hating the odor involves action. Nevertheless when one perceives the bad odor one already hates it. One does not determine to hate it after one has smelt it."[25] And, as another example, Wang gives "to understand cold, one must first have endured cold."[26] This, if taken seriously, can only mean that a statement *about* cold, in so far as it pretends to convey information, is, without an accompanying experience, fundamentally incomprehensible. A possible result is that epistemology and ethics after Wang Yang-ming are aesthetic; knowledge is personal experience; "virtue" is closely associated with states of feeling. The sort of understanding Wang and his followers were after is almost kinesthetic. Thus, Wang's disciple Hsü Ai (1487–1517), relating his progress on the path of learning, admits being puzzled by his master's teachings at first, "but after one has thought about them for a long time one spontaneously gesticulates with hands and feet."[27]

The ability to use words about some matter is not knowledge of it. "Knowing how to converse about filial piety and respectfulness is not sufficient to warrant anybody's being described as understanding them." Otherwise the identity of knowing and known would be lost. There are no valid abstractions: "*Tao* is simply events; events are *tao*."[28] Wang finds most writing useless and misleading and condemns Ch'in Shih Huang for the Burning of the Books only because he burned the wrong ones.[29] In short, there is in Wang, and in thought after him throughout the Ch'ing, a general suspicion of "words." Sometimes this suspicion is critical and fruitful; sometimes it leads to confusion in thought; but in every department of intellectual activity it has great importance. Kinds of writing which are valued are those in which there is no attempt to state ideas: poetry and the expression of feeling, and scholarly writing in which the writing is completely absorbed into the data of the subject matter. This denial of the value of abstraction and general statement to which Wang's thought tends both prompts and is prompted by his constant attempt to overcome Neo-Confucian dualisms—not only the dualism of "knowledge" and "action" but likewise that of "essence" and "function," "principle" and "matter," mind and body, the observer and the observed. Any attempt to break the world up into categories, he implies, is to distort it.

3. Changing Meanings of "Learning" in the Early Ch'ing

For a century or more after Wang, ethical and psychological speculation seems to have been the major intellectual interest, but a gradual change is detectable. One can see signs of a covert development of attitudes resembling ancient Legalism, such as the notion that knowledge should be "practical." After the Manchu conquest, many who had been active in the state were reduced to the activity of the pen. Interest turned somewhat away from ethical thought toward history, research into ancient science, and a classical scholarship interested less in the ethical meaning of the Classics than in a criticism of their language and their character as historical documents. But earlier habits of thought governed the mode of approach to new subjects. A man of Wang Yang-ming's age, for example, interested in moral behavior, would have felt that if a person knows, or says he knows, that he ought to act in a certain way, but still does not, selfishness is interfering to stop the practice which is the natural completion of knowledge. He should either act or stop claiming to be moral. In the eighteenth century a man interested in some problem of scholarly, literary, or pedagogical method would have given this attitude a different twist. He might say, "If I have a theory about how my subject should be ordered (perhaps a rather dubious thing to admit having), I should at least have the ability and make the effort to act it out, if I am to expect anyone to take me seriously." Philology, moreover, was not wholly different, as an intellectual way of life, from "studying to be a Sage." The interest of the scholar in his work was likely to be personal, in somewhat the same way as had been the interest of the disciple of some Confucian moral teacher. The intensity with which one could concentrate on philological problems was perhaps more the source of their appeal than the hope that by solving them one might contribute to the eventual extension of man's understanding, and great scholars could command the same sort of respect as in earlier times was paid to teachers famed for their virtue.

But why should the content of what was meant by "learning" have changed? In part, the change seems to have been the outcome of Wang Yang-ming's type of thinking. Wang had criticized his opponents for holding moral "principles" to be isolable from the action of one's own mind in particular situations. Moral truths could only be grasped intuitively; they could not be stated, for to state is to abstract the "principle" from the situation. This force of Wang's philosophy was that which had lasting effect upon Chinese thought. But Wang's views had never been orthodox. The state had always supported the rival earlier philosophy of the Sung. What appears to have happened at the end of the Ming was a synthesis of the two. Wang's assumptions served eventually to kill off interest in philosophical speculation, which came to be termed, opprobriously, "empty words," and regarded as dangerously distant from "actual facts," preferably handled with a minimum of generalization. What remained, therefore, of Chu Hsi's real influence was his stress on classical scholarship. A case of this synthesis at possibly an intermediate stage is found in the thought of the Ming patriot and Ch'ing scholar Huang Tsung-hsi (1610–95), who was an admirer both of Wang Yang-ming and of the Sung philosophers. The life of learning, he held, must include both solid scholarship and reflection. "Unless you read history extensively," said Huang, "you will be unable to grasp concretely the development of *li* ('principles'); and even if you do this, but do not seek for understanding within your own mind, you will be a crude pedant."[30] Huang's study of history, it might be noted, was a study of events and actions. But Huang, like Wang Yang-ming, believed that mind comprises all that exists; this belief indicated for him that the proper object of study is not only one's own mind but also the observable movement of mind in the history of thought.[31] "Thought" (reflection) and "learning" (the study of history), upon which Huang's moral is organized, is another common pair of categories in Neo-Confucian "discussion about learning," which is loosely related to "knowledge" and "action." A curious proportion seems to exist among the four concepts: to attempt to *know* without working with things or *acting* out what one is learning is to try to advance by the means of *thought* alone; to *learn*, on the other hand, as distinct from meditating, is to move outside one's mind, to come into contact with objective facts. I suspect this association of dualisms was a commonplace.[32]

The events of the middle of the seventeenth century shaped and concentrated the impact these ideas had upon subsequent thought. With the victory of the Ch'ing armies in 1644 and the successive collapse of Ming pretenders in the south, the literati had been in a position of desperation, torn between inaction in the face of foreign invasion and support of a corrupt court, no longer representing their interests and philosophy and dominated by military opportunists. Some had continued a futile local resistance; many were driven by their dilemma to suicide. In the end, however, most had had to accept the fact of defeat, continuing their resistance not actively but in a devotion to the fallen dynasty and in a refusal to take office or to co-operate with the new government.[33] There ensued a period of veiled intellectual struggle. Different philosophies prevailed in the court and in the provinces. Among the defeated, effectiveness in service to family, society, and civilization acquired a value enhanced in compensation for failure in loyalty to a fallen state and nation. But at length the wounds of conscience began to heal. The conquerors offered the greatest attractions to lure the scholars to the capital; the special degree of *po-hsüeh hung-tz'u*, scorned at first, became with the newer generation a coveted prize. Finally, the last recurrences of military opposition were overcome. The court bestowed posthumous honors on the heroes of the resistance and became the patron of Chinese arts and letters. The literati were reconciled and became firm, even ardent, supporters of the dynasty. But the moral struggle they had undergone left a permanent mark on the Ch'ing. The distress of the learned class had been its inability to act upon its convictions.

In their activity, which was their learning, their scholarship and writing, these men felt a need to do something effective and valuable, a need which could no longer be satisfied by toying with Sung philosophical concepts. An example of one direction in which attention was turned is provided by the pedagogical thought of Yen Yüan (1635–1704), which is perhaps the most familiar and obvious example in the Ch'ing of the idea that knowing is doing or that knowledge is experience. Yen Yüan did not create a great commotion in Ch'ing thought. Beyond Li Kung 李塨 (1659–1733) and such relatively little-known persons as Kuo Chin-ch'eng 郭金城 (1660–1700) and, in the eighteenth century, Ch'eng T'ing-tso 程廷祚 (1691–1767), the influence directly traceable to him is a matter of dispute.[34] But I suspect research will disclose the attitudes found in him were, in less angular form, not uncommon in local schools. The local "academy" (*shu yüan*) was a basic social institution of the Ch'ing. The teaching position it offered was a standard, if temporary, means of subsistence for the ubiquitous petty scholar, and, as population increased and official positions became relatively scarcer, his assimilation into the social scheme was increasingly less satisfactory. The fixed demands of the examination system could be frustrating to a teacher or student of independent mind, and the sort of protest found in extreme form in Yen Yüan would be natural to such people. Education, it was felt, should be of practical use; the requirements upon the curriculum imposed by the examinations seemed artificial; the reading and memorizing of which educational method consisted, pointless; and the sort of philosophical discussion for which the local academies had earlier been centers, devoid of meaning.

"The 'principles' of the 'nature' and of 'endowment,' " says Yen, "cannot be discussed; if they are, people will still not be able to listen; and if they listen, they still will be unable really to understand; and even should they understand, they will be unable to practice what they hear."[35] Li Kung explained the point of view to Kuo Chin-ch'eng simply and directly:

> The mere reading of books is not learning. People who read books in these times merely value the elucidation of unreal "principles" and the memorization of "empty words." On this account their spirits are dissipated; on this account their years of life slip uselessly away. When a time arrives for them to exert themselves and engage in the affairs of the world, they are as though blind. Surely, learning as practiced by the ancient sages was never of this sort! The studies of the ancients—rites, music, military arts and agriculture—served both for the cultivation of the self and for practical application. The proper methods of governing the world and assisting the people were all to be found therein. This is what "learning" really means. Books should merely be used for investigation into these matters. Making memorizing and reading one's only endeavor is not learning—nay rather, it is a detriment to learning.[36]

The Classics, however, retain their status. They not only are useful as a guide to action but partake in themselves of the metaphysical character of activity. They are, in Yen's words, the "concrete operation of the 'nature' and of 'endowment.' "[37]

It should be observed that Yen's thought is still much concerned with moral self-cultivation. He has, for example, a series of essays "on the 'nature,' " accompanied by a collection of self-improvised edifying metaphysical charts in the best tradition of Neo-Confucian moral speculation.[38] Activity he values at least as much as a moral-aesthetic experience as for its social usefulness. The correct way to "investigate things" for him is to work with them and use them, but the purpose of the investigation is a transcendent enlightening experience. To learn the lute, for example, one must actually play it; and true ability will be attained "when poem and song come according to desire, when the connection of heart and hand is forgotten and the connection of hand and string, when . . . secret desires are not working in the heart and great peace is constantly in the home, when the feelings respond to the *yang* and *yin*, changing things and reaching to heaven."[39] This attitude, we shall see, is closely related to contemporary ideas about literary art. In view of this aesthetic cast of his thinking, Yen cannot, I think, be said to have an experimental concept of truth. He is interested in understanding or feeling things known beyond all doubt to be real rather than in testing assumptions.

Interesting as Yen Yüan is, a man more typical of the Ch'ing, at least in the opinion of its later scholars, was Ku Yen-wu (1613–82). Like Yen, Ku seriously believed that what the man of learning does should be of practical social or political use; but he had a love of classical scholarship for its own sake and was content to hope, humbly, that at some future time his writing might be instructive to a ruler of men.[40] Later in the Ch'ing, however, the utilitarian ideal of knowledge was submerged. Ku's significance was in introducing principles of philological evidence and in being able to show that a classical scholarship dealing with particular facts and details could attain interesting results without resorting to unsteady generalizations. But, though classical scholarship was the main preoccupation of the Ch'ing, Sung and Ming philosophical thought out of which the new philology had grown was not eliminated. Its concepts and categories continued to serve as the basic instruments of thinking; they had become infused into the very language of ordinary intellectual discourse, and continued familiarity with them was insured by the necessity of learning the Sung philosophy to pass the examinations. In particular, the ideas about knowledge and action which Wang Yang-ming had expressed, or attitudes closely related to them, seem to have remained an important undercurrent, molding men's assumptions in a very wide range of matters, from history and literature to politics.

4. *The Thought of Chang Hsüeh-ch'eng*

While the extent of the influence of this part of late Neo-Confucian thought in the middle Ch'ing is uncertain, its importance is strongly suggested by the writing of Chang Hsüeh-ch'eng—both by the interrelationship of the ideas Chang himself worked out and by the close relationship often discoverable between his ideas and those of others. I shall analyze some of this material with a double purpose: (1) to suggest the extent to which Wang Yang-ming's ideas, or ideas similar to his, permeated the thinking of the literati and (2) to point out that the "unity of knowledge and action" as it appears in Ch'ing thought has political implications which call for the closest examination. It must be admitted at the outset that Chang Hsüeh-ch'eng was not an ordinary man, either in his own estimation or by the appraisal of others.[41] Furthermore, although he professed to adhere to the philosophy of Chu Hsi, he was quite tolerant of Wang Yang-ming and obviously thought himself unusually broad-minded in this respect.[42] With these caveats as to Chang's possible significance, I shall let the reader appraise him for himself.

A fundamental part of Chang's thought was a conception of the history of the state (viz., of civilization) from the beginning of mankind to the age of Confucius. In this conception, *tao* is an inexpressible principle informing all of society, which virtually grows with history. Chang's object was to establish a view of the Classics.

> In the most ancient times there were no written words; then government, at first conducted by the knotting of cords, changed to the use of written signs. The sage, in explaining their use, says, "The many officials were thereby governed, and the people were thereby scrutinized." . . . But principles became more involved and problems more extended, so that they could not be completely dealt with. On this account, the sages established offices and divided responsibilities, and written language came to be organized accordingly. There being offices, hence there were laws, and so the laws were embodied in the offices. There being laws, hence there were books, and so each office preserved its own books. There being books, hence there was learning, and so teachers perpetuated this learning. There being learning, hence there were professional traditions, and so disciples practiced these professions. The office, its special responsibility, the learning and the profession all proceeded from a single source, and government in the world consisted in a unity of culture; hence there were no writings of private schools of thought.[43]

In this series of conjectures Chang described the course of history down to the Western Chou. Each successive ruler and dynasty added to the fund of institutions and methods of conducting affairs as need arose. At any stage in this "golden age," all of man's knowledge was a working part of the daily business of society and the operation of government. This is what Chang means by saying, as he does repeatedly, that in antiquity there was a unity of "government and doctrine" and an identity of the "official and the teacher." This situation was, he suggests, simply a unity of "knowledge" and "action" in historical fact. But, with the end of the Western Chou, traditions of learning were separated from government offices. This split between learning and government caused a long and progressive decline in writing, an inevitable development of "private schools" of thought whose ideas were without foundation, and the distortion of true scholarship and good writing by intellectual "fashions," the desire for fame, and by the preconceptions of writers who no longer had a firm grip on reality.[44] Confucius, seeing at the beginning of this process that civilization was breaking apart and that the wisdom it embodied would be lost, edited a selection of the documents of the Chou feudal order to serve as a permanent illustration of the *tao* of the classical age. The Classics, excluding those which Chang would call early commentaries, are consequently simply the observable remains of the experiences of the ancients.[45] This is what Chang intended to convey by his famous dictum that the Classics are really "history"[46] (a statement which Wang Yang-ming had made, however, and which seems to have been familiar to some of Chang's contemporaries). The prestige they have as guides to modern behavior and modern writing must be squared with this view of them, which is pointedly that they are not "empty words." They do not *tell* what *tao* is but simply illustrate it by being what they are.

Related to this view, Chang had definite ideas about education and about the business of the scholar. As to the latter, Chang argued that the scholar's work should be of practical use (viz., to society and to the state) and that it can be of use only if he studies documents—illustrating the working of government—and the actual conduct of men in society. A classical scholarship which concentrates on the past to the exclusion of the present is as bad as trying to isolate *tao* from things and events,[47] all of which is to say that learning should not be separated from the context of practice. In taking such a position, Chang obviously not only was not typical of his intellectual milieu but was consciously attacking it. As might be expected from this, Chang sharply criticized the examination system and proposed, as an alternative to its standard requirements of classical learning and the mastery of poetic and prose styles, that examinees be allowed to specialize in various historical subjects, so that "solid learning" would be advanced.[48] History, he felt, had the peculiar value that it is as close as one can get, in scholarship, to actual happenings and deeds. In evaluating the historical school of Huang Tsung-hsi, which he regarded as his own and which he considered to have included Wang Yang-ming and earlier philosophers, he said:

> If it should be asked, can practical achievement and disciplined rectitude (attributes of, respectively, Wang Yang-ming and Liu Tsung-chou 劉宗周 [1578–1643], a Southern Ming patriot) really be discussed on the same plane with writings, I would say that historical scholarship shows the proper practice of statecraft, and is assuredly not writing which can be called "empty words." I would further observe that the Six Classics all came from Confucius, yet scholars of old held that none was as great as the *Ch'un-ch'iu* in value; this was precisely because that Classic was closely concerned with the contemporary affairs of men.[49]

The argument had the additional point that it is current or recent history that the historian should deal with. Chang's criticism of the examination system, it should be observed, was scarcely new; and the idea of the moral and political utility of historical knowledge was of very ancient standing. It had been reasserted by Ku Yen-wu: noting that special examinations in historical subjects had been a part of the examination system in the T'ang, he proposed to improve historical scholarship, and with it the civil service, by reviving T'ang practice. "If we could follow this system and employ it for ten years," Ku wrote, "we would obtain men with a thorough understanding of the essence of government; this would surely be of advantage to the state."[50]

If this criticism of scholarship echoes Ku, it is equally suggestive of Yen Yüan's ideas. So, in some respects, are certain of Chang's ideas about education. In an essay on "learning," he asserted the value of studying the "words and deeds" of great men of history. But one has not really learned from them until one has grasped intuitively what is the right course in one's own situation; study is complete only in practice, and the reading of books is only a means to the end.[51] This view approaches Yen's, and Wang Yang-ming's, theory of understanding in another way. To say that the student must apprehend the significance of what he reads for himself and in terms of his own situation is to say that he cannot be told what it is. Explanation is not a substitute for experience. This assumption comes out strongly in Chang's analysis of the learning process of the student of literature and literary composition. The teacher cannot tell the student what is good about a piece of writing; he can only present it to the student to read and let him grasp its goodness for himself:

The excellence of good writing essentially requires the reader to apprehend it for himself, like the flavor of food and drink, or the warmth and lightness of clothing. The person who eats the food or wears the clothing understands it for himself, but it is hard for him to explain it to others. If you want to explain to a person the nature of clothing and food, you must show him a piece of roast meat and let him taste it for himself, and then he may appreciate its flavor; or show him a fur garment and let him try it on, so that he may appreciate its warmth and lightness, and then you have the right idea. But you are making a mistake if you try to convey the flavor of the food by spitting it out of your mouth into his, or if you try to convey the warmth by grabbing him and enfolding him in the garment you are wearing.[52]

The literary critic, for his part, cannot say explicitly what the value of a piece of writing is but can merely suggest.[53] No more can the teacher tell the student how to write, beyond explaining to him certain purely formal rules. What the student must do is to build up his own understanding of good writing. He must "read books to nourish his spirit," as Han Yü would have argued.[54] When he has succeeded, his writing will be naturally good. "His mind" will be "fitted to 'principle' (*li*), his hand doing the bidding of his mind as though it could not help but write."[55] If his writing is of the scholarly sort, he is led entirely by the problem which calls it forth and by his own natural compulsion to deal with it; if he is writing a poem, the poem occurs unforced, as the result of the movement of his feeling, without the interference or prompting of any ulterior motivation. Beauty of style is not an end in itself. Learning to write is actually a species of Neo-Confucian moral self-cultivation.

This character of the learner's problem in studying writing is partly due, it is obvious, to the nature of literary creation itself. A literary piece is nothing one can say anything *about*, because what it *is* (except for formal properties in which Chang is not interested) is simply what happened when the writer had a particular experience or felt something, and any statement or other device of exposition you resort to, to convey what it is, is itself something else. You would be conveying your apprehension of the writing but not the writing itself. The notion that literature must be directly experienced to be understood and appraised thus itself follows from a view of literature as the spontaneous expression of feeling. This view of literature is tied to Chang's concept of the Classics. The ancient sages governed, he speculates, by "rites" and "music." This in itself is a common notion. But, Chang argues, the poems of the *Shih Ching* represent the "music" of ancient government; they are the product of movements of feeling, whereas the other Classics (representing "rites") document the daily activity and practical experience of government officials. Later literature "derives" from the *Shih Ching*, and is, or ought to be, essentially like it.[56] As a consequence, literature and the Classics are alike in being the perceptible part of particular experiences, and what is to be learned from each is not statable or abstractable but must be intuited and felt. For the same reason, each piece of writing is unique; you cannot, in writing a book, imitate a Classic (and to try to do so is morally objectionable); neither may you imitate a poem or a poetic device, for a feeling cannot be copied.[57] What Chang implies is what Wang Yang-ming had held: you cannot know what it is to feel something unless your feelings move in response to it, and you cannot safely separate your judgment or conceiving of something from the perceiving of it. To imitate a piece of writing, Chang feels, or bluntly to assert a judgment of something (or of some famous man in history), is not merely silly; it is pretense: it is to reveal a desire for reputation, or the secret working of an impurity of mind; and it is to claim an understanding which one cannot claim on the basis of one's own experience, and to reveal thereby a lack of "real knowledge."[58]

Similar, if not identical, attitudes are found in other Ch'ing writers. The pointlessness of imitating other writers' poems is affirmed by a line of Ch'ing poets and critics. The list includes a certain Yeh Hsieh 葉燮 (1627–1703), of whom the poet Wang Shih-chen 王士禎 (1634–1711) said that "in his poetry and artistic prose he assimilated the best of the past and achieved an individuality of his own."[59] And early in the eighteenth century the poet-historian Li E 厲鶚 (1692–1752) argued that a poem should have "essential character" (*t'i*), by which he meant that it should not be imitative but should reflect the writer's own nature and situation.[60] Still later, Yüan Mei 袁枚 (1716–98), a contemporary of Chang (the two were spirited enemies) and the best-known representative of this school of critical thought, held that a poem should be an expression of the poet's own feeling and should not attempt to re-express the feelings of others. "If a poem deals with other persons but does not have in it one's own self, it is merely playing with puppets."[61] If one cannot separate a feeling response from experience, a fortiori one cannot preconceive a feeling or its expression. "There is no gaiety in forced laughter; there is no sadness in forced tears," wrote Chang.[62] Some such notion had occurred to Ku Yen-wu. The poems in the *Shih Ching*, he noted, are almost entirely without titles (the titles in use being simply their first words or first lines). Such poems are the best: "In the poetic writing of the ancients, the poem comes first and then the title; in modern poetry the title is first set and then the poem is written. When the poem is written before the title is chosen, the poem will be rooted in feeling; when the title is chosen before the poem is written, the poem will follow external objects."[63] Yüan Mei agrees; a poem should have no set title, for, if it has, it is not genuine—it is an attempt to move the emotions upon preconception. "A poem without a title is 'heavenly' (i.e., natural) music; a poem with a title is 'human' (i.e., artificial) music." The poetry of antiquity is in this respect superior to later art. As the practice of writing poems to set themes is introduced in Han and Wei, "feeling" diminishes. The nadir of this progress of the creeping vice of artificiality is reached in the T'ang examination system, which demanded the composition of "regular" poems on lines extracted from older poets.[64]

Curiously, Yüan's conception of the history of poetry reappears in Chang Hsüeh-ch'eng's view of the history of historiography. Chang tends to think that no writing should be guided by formal concepts which would in any way force its content, whether this content be feeling, as in belles-lettres, or facts, as in history. The earliest history (i.e., the *Shang Shu*), he notes, had no fixed or consistent form; "its chapters are named for their content." But, as historiography developed, there came to be more and more precise notions of the form in which a history should be cast; thus a history might be an "annalistic" history of one particular dynasty or a "standard" history of another. This formal development was ultimately—in the T'ang and Sung—the ruination of history. Mediocre compilers would simply use a standard form as a set of pigeonholes and fill it up with facts, much as the civil service examinee would use the forms of composition prescribed by the examinations. In so doing, they were imposing their own preconceptions upon historical events.[65] One such formal notion to which Chang particularly objected was the idea that a compiler should carefully separate historical events from important historical utterances. There had been, in Chinese historiographical thought, an ingrained habit of thinking of "words" and "acts" antithetically. There is, as early as the *Li Chi*, the theory that in the ancient Chou government the "historiographer of the right" recorded the "words" of the sovereign, while the "historiographer of the left" recorded his "acts."[66] "Records of words and deeds" of great men form a standard category of traditional historical writing. But the sort of interest that "words" (i.e., edicts, political proposals, philosophical opinions) would have to the late Neo-Confucian viewpoint which Chang represented (with its suspicion of the expositive uses and formal properties of language) would be not their truth value as statements or their stylistic beauty but their character as events in time and historical circumstance. Chang accordingly argues that "words" should be treated as historical "acts" and that it should be recognized that historical events are complexes in which the making of statements, verbally or in writing, always enters.[67] This attitude leads Chang to the realization that all written utterance, including belles-lettres, has historical interest.[68]

The foregoing has aimed to suggest that the late Neo-Confucian ideas Wang Yang-ming had expressed in his views of "knowledge" and "action" underlay a considerable part of Ch'ing thinking—especially what Ch'ing intellectuals were thinking about the activities they were constantly engaged in: teaching, scholarship, and writing. Chang's ideas about historiography, however, lead back to a tendency in his thought which is of double interest. From Chang's view that the form of a history should be fluid and should fit its matter, we would expect him to hold, and he does, that it is the business of the practicing historian and of him alone to *say how* history is to be written. This is an important point in his personal psychological history. All his life he was keenly interested in theories about writing, particularly historical writing. But theory is "empty words"; it cannot be valid unless it is applied, practiced; it is not otherwise comprehensible, and so Chang felt that he had no business talking about historiography unless he also wrote history. In this attitude toward his work, Chang shows how the old way of thinking about "learning" (viz., moral self-cultivation) carried over to non-ethical senses of the word. For Wang Yang-ming and Yen Yüan, to be able to talk about moral rules is not moral knowledge. One must practice; if one does not, one is morally at fault, either pretending to know what one does not or being selfish in not doing what one admits to be right. Chang, like his contemporaries, was much less interested in ethics than were the earlier Neo-Confucianists, but he too feels he should either practice what he preaches or stop preaching.[69] This is all to say, as did Wang,[70] that what is difficult, what is crucial, is to act. Merely knowing or working out a theory is not enough to justify a person's existence.

Chang was an innovator. The force of this kind of thinking could be that the expression of *new* ideas is the privilege of the man who is able to act upon them or cause them to be realized in practice. What would be the result if this attitude were extended to ideas about government—about matters of concern to the state? The answer is more than suggested in Chang's picture of the golden age of Chou. I have no reason to suppose that this particular view of an idealized antiquity, in which "government and learning" were united, was a common one; but it was not unique in Chang. Yen Yüan himself had said that "for the sages, study, doctrine, and government were all part of one whole."[71] In the

K'ang-hsi reign of the early Ch'ing, the scholar-official Li Kuang-ti 李光地 (1642–1718), who stood very close to the emperor, had eulogized him as a modern sage-ruler: "In your servant's view, the relation between *tao* and government is this: in ancient times they proceeded from one single source, but in later times they proceeded from two separate sources." The greatest of the ancient sages appeared at five-hundred-year intervals; down to King Wen, the founder of the Chou, they were rulers, and accordingly until the end of Western Chou "centralized unity was continued." But "when Confucius appeared during the Eastern Chou, and when Chu Hsi appeared during the Southern Sung, Heaven found it expedient to entrust them with the true *tao*, but their times rejected them, and thus *tao* and government proceeded from two separate sources. From Chu Hsi to our present sovereign has also been a period of five hundred years; our sovereign has fulfilled the expectations of a true ruler, and has personally displayed the learning of sages and worthy men. Surely, Heaven is about to recommence the succession [of the ancient sage-rulers], and the authoritative lines of *tao* and of government will again be united."[72] Li's encomium shows rather clearly the political force the "unity of knowledge and action" could have. Chang, for his part, thought that in the present age, as in antiquity, all learning and writing should be the concern of the state. This view led him to formulate what appears to be a philosophical justification of the emperor Kao Tsung's interest in book-collecting *and* of the Ch'ien-lung literary inquisition which had been conducted concurrently with the compilation of the imperial manuscript library, the *Ssu-k'u Ch'üan-shu*. The government, Chang held, should cause the teachers in local schools to make a census of all books, "after the fashion of census registers for population," which would be kept for use as need arose by the local officials. This scheme would facilitate the collection of books into public libraries and would also make easier the elimination of those which are undesirable or prohibited. Such a procedure would restore the "unity of culture" of antiquity. "To have books in the charge of officials, and not to allow private parties to conceal writings," Chang asserted, "is very much in accord with ancient practice."[73]

But let us not hold Chang too closely responsible for a single unfortunate opinion and attend rather to the mechanics of his thinking. A man may have the insight of a Sage, he says—in the language of the *Chung Yung*, he may have "virtue"—but, if he does not have "position" (i.e., authority), he cannot propose new ways of doing things, new political practices, new institutions, for his proposals would be unintelligible. "One cannot teach others by 'empty words.' " One must be able to illustrate what one is after in ways that are directly perceptible, by "creating institutions," viz., by fiat. It was for this reason, Chang insists, that Confucius, who "had virtue but lacked position," was, in the Sage's own words, a "transmitter and not a creator" (i.e., simply passed on the wisdom of the past and did not write anything new or express any new ideas of his own). His function was to gather together the wisdom of Chou Kung—in other words, the basic documents of the government Chou Kung put into practice—and to transmit this material to posterity in the form of the Classics. Echoing Han Yü, Chang regarded Chou Kung as the last and greatest of those sages who governed—who had power to act. Confucius was the first and greatest of those whose business was the preservation of true doctrine in later times, when "government and doctrine" had been separated. In holding this view, Chang shows his conception of the history of *tao* to be much like that of Li Kuang-ti. A correct appraisal of Confucius, as the ideal of the man of letters, seems to be of the greatest importance for Chang. It is essential, he emphasizes, to grasp the relation of Chou Kung to Confucius. "To understand the *tao* is to understand why Chou Kung and Confucius were what they were."[74]

5. *The Reformers of the Late Ch'ing*

Chang's preoccupation with the question of the relative positions of Confucius and Chou Kung is interesting not alone because it reflects the knowledge-action conceptual scheme behind his thinking but for the additional reason that just this question was one of the most important issues between the Old Text (*ku-wen*) and New Text (*chin-wen*) scholars in the late nineteenth century. Chang's concentration upon it strongly suggests that it was in his time already an important intellectual problem. His position was the conservative one, upheld by the Old Text school. Their opponents were interested in political reform, in the introduction of Western technology, and in gaining acceptance for a body of new ideals which would move the state forward. They adopted views which were almost exactly antithetical to Chang's in surprising ways. Thus, K'ang Yu-wei (1858–1927) and his friends regarded Liu Hsin (d. 23 B.C.), the Han bibliographer, as a master-forger and as almost the archfiend of Chinese civilization. Chang, on the contrary, had paid Liu the greatest reverence and did so because he saw in Liu's comments on the Classics and the ancient philosophers his own thesis that the Chou state had been a "unity of government and doctrine" and that later learning and writing is defective because it is not directly connected with practice and experience or with the state.[75] In particular, Chang's way of dealing with Chou Kung and Confucius suggests what this part of the controversy was really about. The reformers wanted Confucius elevated above Chou Kung and actually worshiped as a divine being. In this way, they wanted to counter the ideological force of Western religion.[76] This, however, was only part of the matter.

What the reformers were after was put explicitly by T'an Ssu-t'ung (1865–98). The reason for making Confucius the founder of a "religion" was to guarantee the priority of "knowledge" *over* "action," that is, of the man of vision, who constructs an ideal, a blueprint for the future, over the defenders of traditional experience and practices actually in use. At the end of his *Treatise on Benevolence* (*Jen Hsüeh*), which included a defense of the reformist view of Confucius as the founder of an ideology, a man who though without authority proposed "changes in the law" without reference to the past,[77] T'an posed a possible objection to his own book: is it not, after all, mere theory, mere "empty words," and a useless waste of time, as long as T'an himself is unable to *act?* To which T'an replies, "What I value most highly is knowledge, not action. Knowledge is the business of the mind, whereas action is the business of the body. . . . Whereas action is limited, knowledge is unlimited; whereas action is exhaustible, knowledge is inexhaustible."[78] The dualism of mind and body, which later Neo-Confucian thought tended to reject, is strongly asserted throughout the treatise, and in this and in other ways T'an perhaps shows the influence of Christianity (though he appears to have been more impressed by Buddhism).[79] His loose conception of Western thought, compounded with his traditional background, had a strange result. "Knowledge" he seems to conceive indifferently both as scientific theory, with its positivistic promise of social progress, and as religious belief. "Religion is the means of pursuing knowledge." The vitally important task of great "founders of religions" has been to set up a body of doctrine and to pass it on to their disciples; they have had no time to put their doctrines into practice themselves. T'an, it would seem, thought of a "religion" as essentially a formula for a millennial state, leading to an earthly paradise, an inspired vision of the sort imputed to Confucius. Knowledge is what the Sage, in founding a religion, enables man to possess. It is, in effect, faith in a doctrine, a faith which will make possible any accomplishment. "The difficulty pedantic scholars have in being able to 'know' but not to 'act' is due to the fact that their knowledge is not 'real' knowledge. When one's knowledge is 'real,' there is nothing one cannot do."[80] This seems very close to Wang Yang-ming's knowledge (which when perfectly genuine naturally passes over into practice) and recalls the Neo-Confucian concept of "sincerity" as a release of mystical power.

T'an's religious leader was at once a justification for the man of ideas and for the prophetic founder of an ideology. Another New Text intellectual who, like T'an and K'ang Yu-wei, tried to twist traditional Confucianism to justify change and new ideas, and to accommodate a vision of progress, was Liao P'ing (1852–1932). In order to capture the prestige of Confucius and make of the Sage what he wished, Liao persuaded himself that the Classics have a hidden meaning; whereas they seem to present a picture of civilization as declining from an ancient golden age, this picture actually is a fiction, hiding in reverse image a prophetic vision of the future.[81] To demonstrate this thesis, Liao devised an esoteric chart—a device which has always been a favorite of Chinese philosophers—"illustrating progress and decline in successive ages as revealed in the Classics." This chart appeared in 1898, at the time of the reformers' brief moment of power. In it, Liao characterized the Classics in the very language of Chang Hsüeh-ch'eng, the positions and the values of the words reversed: "The Classics are all 'empty words' [i.e., the product of a Sage's vision]; they are not history."[82] This surprising statement leads one to ask how closely the reformers had read Chang's writings, or whether, on the other hand, Chang's views simply reflected common attitudes to which the reformers objected. These are questions which at present I cannot answer.

It would seem, at any rate, that the reformers saw precisely what the force of their tradition was and, staying within this tradition (and in so far as they could free their thinking from it), tried to turn it completely about. In this they failed utterly. Their political failure was the debacle of the Hundred Days and the martyrdom of T'an. And, in the years that followed, the Confucian tradition which they had tried to preserve disintegrated, while the new attitude toward "knowledge" which they had tried to establish turned out to be an old one in disguise. For, in justifying new ideas and a concept of progress, they were not just affirming the claim of the thinker to be heard. It was their ideas and their program they wanted, as a new unifying faith which would absorb and direct society. Even in their moment of temporary success, their only practical course had been to get possession of the emperor and to try to impose their program from the top down. If there is to be a unity of *tao* and government, it is perhaps not of prime importance which absorbs which.

6. *"Knowledge" and "Action" in Republican China*

The reformers' conception of "religion" as a political program, a promise of a golden age, may have been one of the most important intellectual developments in modern China. It was natural for Sun Yat-sen, framing his own political ideas within the next twenty years, to claim for them the force of an ideology which, to succeed, need only be believed. In 1918, after seven years of frustration from seeing the republic divided up among cliques of rival warlords, and having his own ideas for the development of China dismissed by his military opponents and his followers alike as a "mere mass of words," Sun wrote a book of his political plans and theories, in the Preface to which he defended the thesis that "action is easy and knowledge is difficult." He intended his dictum as a contradiction of the words of the *Shang Shu*—that "knowledge is easy but action difficult"—and felt that he was thereby attacking the most undesirable single habit of thinking in Chinese tradition.[83] But what, exactly, did Sun mean? He would seem to be agreeing with T'an Ssu-t'ung that knowledge is more to be valued than action; since the part of the man who makes plans and ascertains what is to be done is more difficult, and so more crucial, than that of those who simply carry out a program, the theorist (i.e., Sun himself) should be deserving of honor and should be taken seriously.

But, by saying "knowledge is difficult," Sun was not saying simply that he had found the working-out of his political ideas a formidable task. He was arguing that "knowledge" is that element in a situation which is hardest to come by, and the element the absence of which explains failure to act. Sun's complaint was that his followers were inert. "They take my projects for useless verbiage and abandon the task of reconstruction. Seven years have passed and no progress in reconstruction has been made. . . . Oh! People! What do you hesitate for?"[84] Sun's real concern was with the curing of *inaction*, which he thought was due to a confusion of the mind and was a moral defect. The idea that "action is difficult" had "caused a decadent China, reluctant to face difficulties. . . . As a result, those who had no knowledge naturally would not act, and even those who had knowledge still did not dare to act."[85] The overthrowing of the Ch'ing had succeeded simply because the heroes of the revolution had realized the necessity for it (and not, as we might have assumed, because of the opportune defection of Yüan Shih-k'ai); constructing the republic had failed because the followers did not know what to do, did not realize the need for acting, and had no faith in the revolutionary cause.[86] It was Sun's business to provide the "knowledge" they lacked, and theirs to accept it wholeheartedly. Sun's stress upon faith perhaps shows his Christian background: "Whether we succeed or fail," he wrote, "depends largely upon whether we think we can succeed or not. If we have faith in what we do, we can move mountains and level seas. If we have no faith, we cannot even raise our hands and break a twig."[87] What Sun is asking is that the people take as the substance of their genuine convictions a program of action given to them and assumed in advance to be desirable. In this context, the power of "faith," like that of T'an Ssu-t'ung's "real knowledge," is close to the Neo-Confucian notion of effectiveness resulting from "sincerity."

It has been this traditional ethical possibility in Sun's thought that subsequent Kuomintang doctrine has developed. His concept of "knowledge" was a useful support for party ideology and for the claim of party leaders that they understood what must be done and why and that they should accordingly be obeyed and followed; for Sun's view could imply that to criticize or hesitate is to be "insincere." It is to the credit of Hu Shih that he saw the dubious assumptions behind such moralistic talk, expressing himself in an essay "On Knowledge and Action," which appeared after Chiang Kai-shek's unification of the country in 1927. Hu himself, since his student years in the United States, had been keenly interested in the philosophical problem of the relation of knowledge to action as it is considered in American pragmatic thought. Characteristically and adroitly, however, he couched his criticism in a form appealing to a traditionally approved idea: Sun Yat-sen and the party were committing the error of *separating* knowledge and action. They fail, he argued, to realize the value and the justice of criticism from the ranks; for, "as one knows, one acts a little better, and as one acts, one knows a little more."[88] Hu stated his case plainly: "Dr. Sun's theory, 'Action is easy, knowledge is difficult,' teaches us that everybody can act and only a small number of people are charged with the task of knowing and discovering. The great number of people ought to look up to intelligence and knowledge, obey their leaders and follow their plans."[89] If this does credit to Hu's courage, it is evidence of the fundamental importance of the issue that the Kuomintang reacted with vigor. It was officially charged that Hu had "overstepped the limit of scholarly discussion and indulged in meaningless quibbling," and it was recommended that he be "duly punished."[90] His criticism of the authoritarianism of party ideology apparently came to nothing.

Party philosophy continued to lay stress on the knowledge-action theme. An essay by Chiang Kai-shek entitled *A Philosophy of Action* appeared in official English translation in 1940. In it, Chiang interpreted

Sun Yat-sen's idea as a "principle of action as the natural product of knowledge"[91] and worked this notion into an appeal for a rededication of party workers to the revolutionary cause. "We need . . . only to assert our wills," he concluded, "inflame our hearts with a fresh sincerity and faith, and give ourselves up to positive action."[92] Chiang's emphasis was upon the individual's proper frame of mind and consequent effectiveness. "We must model ourselves on the activity of nature, on its spontaneous and unremitting flow of energy."[93] In developing his argument, he stressed Neo-Confucian virtues and made constant use of traditional philosophical vocabulary and hallowed text. In this essay, as in *China's Destiny*, first published in Chinese in 1943,[94] Chiang dwells upon "sincerity." Its power is the same as Sun's power of faith: "Without sincerity, nothing in the world can be accomplished, while with absolute sincerity, there is nothing in the world that cannot be accomplished." The leaders and the party have supplied the knowledge and the directives necessary for action; the gift of the government to the people is to enable them to understand; it is the duty of the people only to follow sincerely. "The principles of the revolution are as clear as the sun and the moon in the sky. . . . Citizens of the country need only adhere to these principles, methods and strategy, follow the road of accomplishment; . . . and put their knowledge into concrete practice through energetic endeavor." Not to do so is to fail morally: "Thorough understanding and active endeavor must be based on absolute sincerity, free from any falsehood or dishonest conduct as well as from the slightest opportunistic motive." " 'Sincerity,' " Chiang asserts, "is the motivating force for all our activity. . . . This is precisely what our Leader's theory of 'to know is hard, but to act is easy' means when applied to the revolutionary movement."[95]

It would be strange indeed if such a powerful traditional sanction for inspired acceptance of authority were neglected by Chiang's rivals, the Chinese Communists. Mao Tsê-tung himself has a philosophy of "action" presented in a pamphlet *On Practice*. The purpose of Mao's argument is to give revolutionary theory a value in curbing the errors of individual judgment, such as to justify the party's authority in dogma, while giving expediency an importance that would prevent "know-it-alls" and "die-hards" from quoting the Marxist saints against present leaders.[96] Accordingly, knowledge is of two kinds, "perceptual" and "rational." All knowledge begins as perceptual knowledge; it must be developed by trial and error in the party's revolutionary activity, until through "scientific abstraction" it becomes rational knowledge, which alone is a reliable guide for action.[97] It follows that the revolutionary theory which is to guide revolutionary practice in a given stage of the revolution's historical course cannot be perfected until that stage in action is reached.[98] Mao's epistemology of dialectical materialism itself owes nothing to Chinese tradition, but his emphasis, like the traditional attitude toward knowledge, is not on arriving at true scientific propositions about the world but on acting out one's knowledge: "What Marxist philosophy considers most important is not understanding the laws of the external world and thereby explaining it, but actively changing the world by applying the knowledge of objective laws."[99]

In so far as Mao is concerned with the attitude of the party member toward authority, his essay is related to a large body of recent Communist writing which does make constant appeal to traditional ethical ideas. It is noteworthy that Marxism, which in general has not been very productive of ethical thought, is apparently following a different course in China. In recent years, essays and pamphlets on "cultivation" (*hsiu-yang*) have become almost a fad in party circles. These writings explore in detail the ethical nuances of the party member's attitude toward his work, toward party authority and ideology, and the relation of his attitude to his effectiveness in revolutionary service. One of the most important of the writers who deal with these subjects is the leading theoretician Liu Shao-ch'i. Liu has proposed a "Communist ethics," which is bulwarked at every step by references to classical texts and traditional virtues.[100] Liu and writers who take their lead from him argue that the mastering of revolutionary theory means for the good Communist taking the party's interest as his own so genuinely that he will work without thought of himself, even when observed by no one. The Confucian moral ideas of "self-examination" and "self-watchfulness" are appropriated for their obvious utility. How this tendency in Communist thought is to be interpreted—whether it means native habits of thinking are making their mark upon Marxism in China or simply that Communist leaders are astute enough to use what they find in the tradition of an area in which they happen to work—is a question I merely raise. Its answer must be provided by those whose acquaintance with Communist thought and history is wider than mine.

This inquiry has dealt with the past and, tentatively, the present; it cannot safely go further. The analysis of what has been said about "knowledge" and "action" by modern leaders, by nineteenth-century reformers, by Chang Hsüeh-ch'eng and early Ch'ing philosophers, and by Wang Yang-ming and by ancient writers has led to what seem to be fundamental characteristics of Confucian mystical and ethical thought. If my assumptions are defensible, the problem of the relation of "knowledge" to "action," in the form in which Wang Yang-ming had cast it, has had much to do with determining the aesthetics of the Ch'ing, its political thought, and its attitudes toward learning. Throughout the period studied the problem of "knowledge" and "action" appears to involve twin tendencies of thinking. One is a tendency to assume that performance is the evidence or natural result of knowledge, if knowledge is genuine or "sincere." The other is a tendency to a set of assumptions: that only those who have experience, or who do act, or who can act, or have power to act, or have authority, can claim to "know." These tendencies appear in many ways, but their political force, from what can be observed, seems to be authoritarian. In view of this result, it may be well to forestall one possible misconception. This account of the problem of "knowledge" and "action" has been a description not of Chinese civilization but only of a limited group of ideas within it. Most of the men whose ideas have been analyzed have both intellectual and moral qualities which could be admired. And if this inquiry has pointed to habits of thought which reinforce authority, there has also been a tradition in China of protest against authority which is equally interesting and complex and in which, in fact, some of the men discussed in the early Ch'ing are particularly important. But this would have to be the subject of another investigation.

NOTES

1. I.e., Wang Shou-jen. Throughout this article I have used, because of its familiarity, the name by which Wang was known among his followers.

2. James Legge, *The Chinese Classics* (2d ed.) (hereafter cited as "Legge"), III, 258.

3. See Han's essay "Yüan Tao," *Chu Wen-kung Chiao Han Ch'ang-li Hsien-sheng Chi* 朱文公校韓昌黎先生集 (*Ssŭ-pu Ts'ung-k'an* ed. [hereafter cited as "SPTK"]), chap. 11, p. 3*b*. Another obvious related example of classification is that of "military" (*wu*) men and men of "culture" (*wen*).

4. Legge, I, 424.

5. *Shih Chi*, *T'ung-wen Shu-chü* (photolithographic ed.; Shanghai, 1894), chap. 130, p. 9*b*.

6. Legge, I, 211.

7. Hsü Kan, *Chung-lun* 中論 (SPTK ed.), chap. 1, p. 22*a*.

8. *Ibid*., chap. 1, p. 1*a*.

9. *Ibid*., p. 22*b*.

10. Legge, I, 366–67.

11. For the mysteries of "sincerity" see Legge, I, 414–19.

12. Legge, I, 192.

13. Cf. *I Ching* (Harvard-Yenching Index Series Supplement No. 10), p. 44: "Writing does not completely express language and language does not completely express thought." Taoist mysticism exhibits this suspicion of language more conspicuously.

14. *Hsün-tzŭ* (SPTK ed.), chap. 4, p. 18*b*. There is more of this passage that is instructive. "To act out one's knowledge," Hsün-tzŭ continues, "is to be 'clear' (*ming*), about it, and to be 'clear' is to become a Sage. A Sage is one who . . . equalizes 'words' and 'actions.' . . . His *tao* is simply this: his objective is 'action.' " For the connection between *ming* and "sincerity" cf. *Chung Yung*, chap. 21; Legge, I, 414-415.

15. Mei Yi-pao, *The Ethical and Political Works of Motse* (London, 1929), p. 90 and *passism*.

16. This fluidity of association is well illustrated by a passage from T'an Ssŭ-t'ung (whose ideas will be examined in due course). T'an argues, like Hsü Kan, that "knowledge" is superior to "action"; and to show how obvious is the truth of his contention he gives several examples: "It is a matter of necessity that 'action' cannot equal 'knowledge'; what the hand or foot can touch is necessarily less than the range of the eyes and ears; the scope of memory is necessarily less than that of intuition; measurement possible by scales or a foot rule can hardly equal the definiteness of appraisal [by the mind]; the beauty of physical reality (*shih shih* 實事) can hardly approach the purity of abstract principle (*k'ung li* 空理)." From *Jen Hsüeh* 仁學 (in *Ch'ing I Pao Ch'üan Pien* 清議報全編, Vol. III), p. 91.

17. *Ssu-shu Wu Ching Tu Pen* 四書五經讀本 (*Shih-chieh Shu-chü* ed.), *Chung Yung Chang Chü* 中庸章句, p. 1. The commentary is that of Chu Hsi, but it is closer to the later "mind" school than most of Chu's thought and seems to express ideas rather generally encountered.

18. *Ssu-shu Wu Ching Tu Pen*, *Ta Hsüeh Chang Chü*, p. 3.

19. Wang himself, it might be noted, was a military commander.

20. Cf. Miao T'ien-shou 繆天綬 (ed.), *Ming Ju Hsüeh-an* 明儒學案 (*Hsüeh-sheng Kuo-hsüeh Ts'ung-shu* ed.), Editor's Preface, pp. 25–26.

21. *Ibid*., p. 285.

22. Frederick G. Henke, *The Philosophy of Wang Yang-ming* (Chicago, 1916), pp. 53–56, 155, 179–81, 298-99. Also *Wang Wen-ch'eng Kung Ch'üan-shu* 王文成公全書 (SPTK ed.), esp. chap. 1, pp. 5*b*–10*a*.

23. *Wang . . . Ch'üan-shu*, chap. 1, p. 9*b*.

24. Henke, *op. cit*., p. 169.

25. *Ibid*., p. 54. Wang's example is taken from the definition of "sincerity" in the *Ta Hsüeh* (Legge, I, 366).

26. Henke, *op. cit*., p. 54.

27. *Ibid*., p. 72.

28. *Ibid*., pp. 69–70. This view leads Wang to say, as Chang Hsüeh-ch'eng did later, that the Classics are really "history."

29. *Ibid*., p. 65.

30. Chin Yü-fu, *Chung-kuo Shih-hsüeh Shih* ("History of Chinese Historiography") (Shanghai, 1946), p. 256.

31. Cf. Huang's Preface to his history of Ming philosophy, *Ming Ju Hsüeh-an*.

32. My interpretation here is suggested by Chang Hsüeh-ch'eng's second essay on "learning." "Yüan Hsüeh" 原學.

33. Huang Tsung-hsi affords a curious example of this state of mind. After the conquest he refused to take office; but he had an unrivaled knowledge of Ming history and apparently felt the official compilation of the history of the Ming to be an enterprise in

which, out of devotion to the dynasty, he ought to take part. This he succeeded in doing through his student, Wan Ssu-t'ung, who worked on the *Ming Shih* unofficially in the capital. In a piece of writing addressed to Wan, Huang compared his student (and vicariously himself) to a historian of the Yüan: "When the Yüan fell, Wei Su fled into the Pao-en temple, and was on the point of throwing himself into a well, when the monk Ta-tzu said to him, 'No one knows the dynastic history save yourself; if you die, it will be the death of the history of the dynasty.' Wei Su thereupon did not kill himself and later assisted in compiling the *Yuan Shih*" (Chin Yü-fu, *op. cit.*, p. 256). This is but one instance of the compulsion the sincere loyalist felt to justify himself by doing something worth while; the alternative was suicide.

34. Other speculative additions to this list are Yüan Mei and Tai Chen; on the former, cf. Kuo Shao-yü 郭紹虞 in *Hsüeh-lin* 學林, VIII (June, 1941), 60 ff.; on the latter, A. Hummel (ed.), *Eminent Chinese of the Ch'ing Period (1644–1912)* (Washington: Government Printing Office, 1943–44), p. 915.

35. Yen Yüan, *Ts'un Hsüeh* 存學 (*Chi-fu Ts'ung-shu* ed.), chap. 1, pp. 3*a*–4*b*.

36. Quoted by Kuo Chin-ch'eng in his Preface to Yen's *Ts'un Hsüeh*.

37. *Ts'un Hsüeh*, chap. 1, p. 3*a*.

38. Fung Yu-lan, *Chung-kuo Che-hsüeh Shih* ("History of Chinese Philosophy") (Shanghai, 1934) (hereafter cited as "Fung"), pp. 978–79.

39. Mansfield Freeman, "Yen Hsi Chai, a Seventeenth Century Philosopher," *Journal of the North China Branch of the Royal Asiatic Society*, LVII (1926), 79.

40. This idea appears in selections from Ku's letters quoted at the beginning of his *Jih-chih Lu* (*Kuang-chou Shu-ku-t'ang* ed.).

41. Cf. Hu Shih and Yao Ming-ta, *Chang Shih-chai Nien-p'u* 章實齋年譜 (Shanghai, 1929) (hereafter cited as "*Nien-p'u*"), pp. 81–82, where one of Chang's "family letters," written in 1790, is quoted.

42. *Chang-shih I-shu* 章氏遺書 (*Chia-yeh-t'ang* ed., 1922) (hereafter cited as "*I-shu*"), chap. 2, p. 22*a*.

43. *I-shu*, chap. 10, p. 2*a*. Compare with this *I-shu*, chap. 2, pp. 1*a* ff.

44. These ideas are constantly encountered in Chang; one might, however, look especially at *I-shu*, chap. 2, pp. 16*a*–*b*, 25*a*, and chap. 9, pp. 35*a* ff.

45. E.g., *I-shu*, chap. 2, pp. 7*b*–8*a*.

46. *I-shu*, chap. 1, p. 1*a*; chap. 4, pp. 44*b*–45*a*.

47. *I-shu*, chap. 5, pp. 6*a*–7*a*.

48. *Nien-p'u*, pp. 143–44.

49. *I-shu*, chap. 2, p. 24*b*.

50. *Jih-chih Lu*, chap. 16, p. 25*b*.

51. *I-shu*, chap. 2, pp. 14*b*–15*a*.

52. *I-shu*, chap. 2, p. 37*a*.

53. *I-shu*, chap. 2, pp. 37*b*–38*a*.

54. *I-shu*, chap. 2, p. 37*b*; I refer, of course, to Han Yü's "Reply to Li I 李翊," *Han Ch'ang-li Chi*, chap. 16, pp. 9*a* ff.

55. *Nien-p'u*, p. 54.

56. *I-shu*, chap. 1, pp. 24*a* ff.; also chap. 1, pp. 20*a* ff.

57. *I-shu*, chap. 1, p. 3*a*; chap. 2, p. 36*b*.

58. *I-shu*, chap. 5, p. 15*a*–*b*.

59. Aoki Masaru 青木正兒, *Shina Bungaku Shisō Shi* ("History of Chinese Literary Thought") (Tokyo, 1943), p. 183.
60. *Ibid.*, p. 184.
61. *Ibid.*, p. 188.
62. *Nien-p'u*, p. 57.
63. *Jih-chih Lu*, chap. 21, p. 3*a*.
64. Aoki, *op. cit.*, pp. 187–88.
65. E.g., *I-shu*, chap. 1, p. 9*a;* chap. 1, pp. 15*a*–16*b*.
66. *Li Chi* (SPTK ed.), chap. 9, p. 1*b*.
67. *I-shu*, chap. 1, p. 10*b*.
68. *Nien-p'u*, pp. 64 and 137.
69. An example of this attitude appears in a letter Chang wrote to Shao Chin-han 邵晉涵 (1743–96), discussing an essay Chang was writing on the method of organizing and writing history, and a revision of the *Sung Shih* he proposed to undertake (*Nien-p'u*, p. 99): "But the ancients have said that setting an idea down in 'empty words' is not as good as to exhibit it in actual deeds; I have thought that I might myself write a book according to my own principles, in order to show clearly that what I propose is not empty talk."
70. Cf. Chiang Kai-shek, *A Philosophy of Action, or What I Mean by Action* (Chungking, 1940), p. 21, n. 1.
71. *Ts'un Hsüeh*, chap. 1, p. 1*a*.
72. Quoted by Hou Wai-lu, *Chin-tai Chung-kuo Ssu-hsiang Hsüeh-shuo Shih* ("History of Modern Chinese Thought and Learning") (Shanghai, 1947), p. 423.
73. *I-shu*, chap. 10, p. 14*a–b*.
74. *I-shu*, chap. 2, pp. 5*b*–7*a*.
75. *I-shu*, chap. 10, p. 3*a–b*.
76. Fung, p. 1011.
77. *Jen Hsüeh*, p. 36.
78. *Ibid.*, p. 91.
79. Fung, p. 1029.
80. *Jen Hsüeh*, pp. 91–92.
81. Fung, pp. 1034–37.
82. Fung, p. 1036. I am indebted to Professor Derk Bodde for calling Liao P'ing's views of the Classics to my attention.
83. Hu Shih and Lin Yu-tang, *China's Own Critics* (Tientsin, 1931), pp. 44–46.
84. *Ibid.*, p. 47.
85. Chiang Kai-shek, *China's Destiny*, with Notes and Commentary by Philip Jaffe (New York, 1947), p. 186.
86. Hu Shih and Lin Yu-tang, *op. cit.*, pp. 46–47; Chiang Kai-shek, *China's Destiny*, p. 185.
87. Hu Shih and Lin Yu-tang, *op. cit.*, p. 49.
88. *Ibid.*, p. 55.
89. *Ibid.*, p. 52.
90. Instruction of the Nanking party to the State Council, *Shanghai Evening Post*, September 30, 1929; quoted in the Editor's Preface of *China's Own Critics*, p. vii. This incident was called to my attention by Mr. Conrad M. Schirokauer, Stanford University.

91. *A Philosophy of Action*, p. 7.
92. *Ibid.*, p. 20.
93. *Ibid.*, p. 9.
94. *China's Destiny*, p. 19.
95. *Ibid.*, pp. 158–60; for Chiang's interpretation of Sun see also pp. 183–90.
96. Mao Tsê-tung, *On Practice* (Peking, 1951), Editor's Note.
97. *Ibid.*, pp. 4 ff.
98. *Ibid.*, pp. 19 ff.
99. *Ibid.*, p. 16.
100. Liu Shao-ch'i, *Lun Kung-ch'an Tang Yüan Ti Hsiu-yang* (2d ed.; Hong Kong, 1949), pp. 32–33; cf. the English translation, *How To Be a Good Communist* (Peking: Foreign Language Press, 1951), pp. 51–57.

"HISTORY" AND "VALUE": THE TENSIONS OF INTELLECTUAL CHOICE IN MODERN CHINA

J. R. LEVENSON

A traveller, who has lost his way, should not ask, Where am I? What he really wants to know is, Where are the other places? He has got his own body, but he has lost them.

ALFRED NORTH WHITEHEAD, *Process and Realty*

1. Premises

WITH THE passing of time, ideas change. This statement is ambiguous. It refers to thinkers in a given society, and it refers to thought. With the former shade of meaning, it seems almost a truism: men may change their minds or, at the very least, make a change from the mind of their fathers. Ideas at last lose currency, and new ideas achieve it. If we see an iconoclastic Chinese rejection, in the nineteenth and twentieth centuries, of traditional Chinese beliefs, we say that we see ideas changing.

But an idea changes not only when some thinkers believe it to be outworn but when other thinkers continue to hold it. An idea changes in its persistence as well as in its rejection, changes "in itself" and not merely in its appeal to the mind. While iconoclasts relegate traditional ideas to the past, traditionalists, at the same time, transform traditional ideas in the present.

This apparently paradoxical transformation-with-preservation of a traditional idea arises from a change in its world, a change in the thinker's alternatives. For (in a Taoist manner of speaking) a thought includes what its thinker eliminates; an idea derives its particular quality from the fact that other ideas, expressed in other quarters, are demonstrably alternatives. An idea is always apprehended in relative association, never in absolute isolation, and no idea, in history, keeps a changeless self-identity. An audience which appreciates that Mozart is not Wagner will never hear the eighteenth-century *Don Giovanni*. The mind of a nostalgic European medievalist, though it may follow its model in the most intimate and accurate detail, is scarcely the mirror of a medieval mind; there is sophisticated protest where simple affirmation is meant to be. And a harried Chinese Confucianist among modern Chinese iconoclasts, however scrupulously he respects the past and conforms to the letter of tradition, has left his complacent Confucian ancestors hopelessly far behind him.[1]

Vocabulary and syntax, then, may remain the same, late and soon, but the statement changes in meaning as its world changes. Is there another postulate, besides the postulate of the changing world, which confirms this change in meaning, as time passes, in the statement whose sensible content remains unchanged?

There is such a postulate, the logical principle which states that "a body of knowledge consists not of 'propositions,' 'statements,' or 'judgments' . . . but of these together with the questions they are meant to answer."[2] By this token, a proposition's meaning is relative to the question it answers.[3] A change, then, in the question behind an idea, like a change in the alternatives beside it, imposes change on the persisting positive content of the idea itself.

Let us consider, for example, European acknowledgment of the worth of Asian civilizations. In both the eighteenth and the nineteenth centuries there were Europeans who denied the doctrine of European superiority to China. But this denial, this European antiparochialism, was quite a different idea in the eighteenth century than in the next one; for in the first instance it was primarily an expression of a rationalistic bias, while in the second instance it was antirationalistic.

Voltaire's admiration of China was an aspect of his deistic appeal to a universal as against a particular revelation. His denial of European pretensions was a negative answer to the question, "Is Christianity the criterion of cultural excellence?" But nineteenth-century opponents of Europocentrism derived not from Voltaire but from Herder, with his principle that every age and every people has its own particular genius. Rationalism, with Turgot and Condorcet, had developed a theory of stages of progress of civilization and had turned from uncritical admiration of the non-European world to uncritical condemnation; Condorcet lowered China in the scale of nations to the level of the primitive agricultural state of society. "Civilization," to the rationalists, now mean exclusively European civilization. The romantics, therefore, in their denial of European pretensions, meant to answer the question, "Is 'secular progress' the criterion of cultural excellence?" Thus, successive "same" ideas, European expressions of extra-European sympathies, change as the questions behind them change.[4]

An idea, then, is a denial of alternative possibilities and an answer to a question.[5] What a man means cannot be inferred solely from what he asserts; what he inquires and what other men assert invest his ideas with meaning. In no idea does meaning simply inhere, governed solely by its degree of correspondence with some unchanging objective reality, without regard to the subjective motivations of its thinker.

In nineteenth-century China claims of "history" (predisposition toward the offerings of one's own particular culture) began to intrude on judgments of "value" (quest for universal truth), and ideas which were losing their philosophical command continued to be espoused by thinkers compelled by history, emotionally, as their intellectual convictions faltered, to attribute value to these ideas. As the thinker and his thought are inseparable, his motivations participate in his idea. When value is ascribed to ideas out of considerations of history, the very value ascribed is thereby prejudiced. When Confucian traditionalism comes to be accepted not from a confidence in its universal validity but from a *traditionalistic* compulsion to profess that confidence, Confucianism is transformed from a primary, philosophical commitment to a secondary, romantic one, and traditionalism from a philosophical principle to a psychological device.

And then this inner change in a persisting idea, this change which works through the thinker's loyalty, furthers the trend to the other type of intellectual change in time—alienation.

In this essay the terms "history" and "value" stand for two incompatible systems for classifying human activities. The conflict between them can be defined philosophically and identified psychologically; for men have commitments to both these systems, and implicit in the process of thought is the thinker's effort to smother the conflict. The impact of the modern West has intensely stimulated this conflict in China. And modern Chinese intellectual history, which is the decay of traditional Chinese civilization (i.e., two reciprocal processes—progressive abandonment of tradition by iconoclasts and petrifaction of tradition by traditionalists), can be analyzed as a sequence of intellectual expedients to make these commitments seem to coincide.

The conflict in philosophy is over this issue: Is precedent properly a special determinant in intellectual choice, precluding man's free exercise of reason according to general principles?

The defenders of general principles maintain that the value of anything is independent of its history.[6] All people make value judgments, and, when they do, their touchstones are truth and beauty—absolutes, universals, ideally uncolored by relativities of time and place. Historical particularism, a philosophically contemptible social excrescence, may blur the fact, but standards of value have universal application because men share a common humanity. According to this point of view, history cannot govern choice, because history has no life; it is only a dead receptacle for value judgments exercised in the past.

The spokesmen for historicism claim quite another character for history. History, to them, is by no means simply a dead scheme of classification of individual choices made from considerations of value. History is organic, history is living tradition, not to be modified at will according to unhistorical value criteria. History does not just receive intellectual choices; it intrudes on them. A man makes choices not as a member of a bloodless, universal humanity but as a member of his proudly particular, vibrant people, with its own national spirit. For a people (Hegel, for one, especially stresses this point) is an organization which pre-exists its members.[7]

If intellectual choice which contravenes the "spirit of the people" is impious or impossible (and, depending on its thoroughness, historicism makes it one or both), then the individual thinker, his scope determined for him in a world he never made, can have no standards of value which make him free to judge what his people's history offers him. Yet, in fact, history is made of his judgments, for a completely binding traditionalism would keep a people forever at the post, never moving into history. Some tempering of traditionalism by value judgment must occur, or history is frozen by the law that nothing can be added to a way of life, no matter what value claims can be made for it, if it seems a departure from what has gone before. Absolute traditionalism is a completely hypothetical, self-destructive concept; a sense of the past can never develop if an original unmitigated reverence for "what is" precludes its ever becoming past.

Traditionalism, then, the exaltation of the claims of history, in its fullest philosophical implications denies absolutely the right of value to enter a counterclaim. But the existence of traditionalism belies its ultimate doctrine. For traditionalism can take its subjective tone only in a world in which alternatives to the worship of the "eternal yesterday" have been sharply presented. A traditionalist may insist that "Mine or thine?" is the only relevant question which a man may ask before making a choice among cultural elements. But the conscious will to narrow the vision (and this will, not the blind plodding in the footsteps of the past, is the essence of traditionalism) can never exist apart from the realization that another question is always being asked: "True or false?"

As a prelude to choice, the second question logically supersedes the first. A man's decision that something is true and something false constitutes, in logic, his intellectual choice between them. But, psychologically, the question, "Mine or thine?" is never superseded; it, too, stubbornly particularistic, beyond all the plausible insistence on the primacy of universal value, is always being asked.

For values depend, in the last analysis, on their natural sources in particular places and times.[8] A man may not feel predestined to accept the institutions, science, morality, or aesthetics which his history offers him, but he knows that whatever he does accept has its place in someone's history. And no one is so ethereal, so cleanly delivered from native soil and the limited culture which formed him, that he can see its relative disqualifications with perfect equanimity. Freedom from the determinism of history, which forbids a man to think, brings little release if the only alternative is the dictation of value, which forbids him to feel. History and value are worlds apart, but men are drawn to both, with an emotional commitment to the first and an intellectual commitment to the second; they need to ask the two incompatible questions, and they yearn to be able to answer "Mine" and "True."

Intellectual alienation from a tradition and emotional tie to it reciprocally intensify each other. As the former proceeds, the continued attribution of value to historical inheritances stems more and more from the thinker's emotional need to harmonize history and value, less and less from a genuine intellectual conviction that he has the best of both possible worlds. And finally the tie is snapped. No idea commended solely by the historical imperative that it must be true, and not at all by an unclouded confidence that it *is* true, can persist.

The reverse of this situation, however, is equally impossible. Whatever succeeds that moribund idea from which intellectual alienation has become complete must be congenial to the claims of history. Man is not a neutral machine, calmly recording right answers; if a foreign answer is to be intellectually accepted as right, the emotional claims of history must somehow be squared.

I believe that an understanding of this principle makes the chronological sequence in modern Chinese history logically comprehensible. As traditional ideas change in losing their intellectual respectability, and traditionalists fail thereby to maintain the harmony of history and value, iconoclasm thrives. But iconoclasts, of the mildest or the deepest hue, face the danger of the same failure, and their own ideas change—in a series of acceptance, rejection, and acceptance of something new—as they seek a formula which will keep the psychological peace. The quest for this formula has been the common ground of all the new currents of Chinese thought since the Opium War (1839–42). How can the thinker scrap Chinese ideas which the Western impact has made to seem inadequate, while he preserves his confidence of Chinese equivalence with the West? How shall he satisfy the claims of value and the claims of history together?

2. *Eclecticism in the Area of Native Chinese Choices*

A. CONSIDERATIONS OF TIME BECOME CONSIDERATIONS OF SPACE

In intellectual controversies within the Confucian tradition, each school tried to score a point by claiming for itself a sort of apostolic succession from the sages. Opponents would almost invariably be accused of deviation from a path laid down in antiquity. The old was prized over the new, and seventeenth- and eighteenth-century critics of Sung and Ming thought charged primarily not that it failed to meet the needs of the present but that it strayed from the truths of the past.[9] Ch'ing critics of the Neo-Confucian "Sung learning" were known as the school of the "Han learning," not as the school of the "Ch'ing learning."

The pedigree, then, of an intellectual position was one of the main criteria of its value, its truth. This was true for traditional thought before the Western intrusion, and it was true after it. But, with antiquity still a criterion of value, the West forced revision of Chinese judgments on the older contending philosophies. Petty distinctions and conflicts between Chinese schools paled into insignificance before the glaring contrast of Western culture to everything Chinese. Grounds for discrimination between Chinese schools were blurred when a new Western alternative existed for them all, a more genuine alternative than they afforded one another. Chinese thought was shocked into a semblance of unity; when the West was a serious rival, Chinese rivals closed their ranks. The question "New or old?" as a test of value continued to be asked, but the question was removed from a Chinese world to the larger world of the West and China. As a first effect of their comprehending that Western culture had to be taken seriously, the Chinese schools ceased contending about which of them was old. They all were old (having existed before the West came), and the West was new.

Why did the nineteenth-century West and not the seventeenth-century West, which had been interpreted to China by the Jesuits, present a sufficiently strong alternative to press the Chinese schools together? For one thing, of course, the Jesuits were immeasurably fewer than their Western successors on the Chinese scene, and their voices reached fewer ears. The difference in the intellectual implications of these two Western incursions, however, can probably be explained only slightly as a difference simply in the weight of numbers. It is noteworthy that the Jesuits largely fulfilled traditional Chinese expectations as to the likely course of intelligent barbarians in Chinese society. They gave their actions a Chinese cast and accommodated their ideas as closely as possible to Chinese civilization. But the Europeans who established themselves in the nineteenth-century treaty ports were independent spirits, unconcerned with Chinese susceptibilities; where the Jesuits had tendered the Chinese a graceful invitation to embellish and enrich their universally respected Chinese civilization, the later Europeans exposed to China an uncompromisingly foreign alternative.

The Jesuits were culturally conciliatory because Chinese society, in their day, was stable, and they would receive a hearing more or less as candidates for membership or not at all. But the Chinese who heard them were only casually interested in such frankly Western knowledge as the Jesuits offered. For, since seventeenth-century Europe was unable to jeopardize the stability of Chinese society, Western knowledge was superfluous to the Chinese literati; it had no relevance to power or success. A mastery of traditional Chinese learning was not only necessary but sufficient—at least, to the extent that intellectual factors counted—to enable a Chinese to get the most out of Chinese life and the Chinese state.

But after the Opium War, when European industrialism and commercial enterprise began to act as a catalyst in traditional Chinese society, new roads to power, roads smoothed by Western knowledge, came to be dimly seen. A challenge was offered to the usefulness of Chinese thought, and, when the question of its usefulness could be raised, the question of its truth became alive. Chinese thought, all schools of it, had a genuine, serious Western rival.

B. THE ECLECTICISM OF TSENG KUO-FAN

The tendency to lose interest in purely Chinese intellectual disputes was characteristic of those who recognized the fact of the Western intrusion. But facts, of course, may run well ahead of awareness of them, and in the nineteenth century, particularly in its earlier decades, there were many parochial minds who persisted in treating China as the world and in analyzing Chinese thought according to its traditional refinements. T'ang Ching-hai (1778–1861), for example, in his *Ch'ing Ju Hsüeh-an Hsiao-shih* ("Short History of the Intellectual Situation in Ch'ing Confucianism"), published in 1845, made a systematic and thoroughly partisan classification of Ch'ing philosophers. He exalted the *li-hsüeh* of the Sung Neo-Confucianists Ch'eng I and Chu Hsi and disparaged the *hsin-hsüeh* of Lu Hsiang-shan and Wang Yang-ming, of the Sung and Ming dynasties, respectively.[10]

Tseng Kuo-fan (1811–72), however, the most powerful governor-general during the T'ai-p'ing Rebellion and the T'ung-chih reign, was implicated in dealings with the West and exposed to Western ideas as few of his contemporaries among the Chinese literati could be. He remained certain of the universality of Chinese spiritual values; nevertheless, his Chinese ethnocentrism was not that of a man whose complacency has never been challenged but that of one who has known a rival claim and disposed of it. And though Tseng flatly rejected the rival Western claim (and condemned the anti-Confucian, pseudo-Christian T'ai-p'ing rebels of mid-century for seeming to have accepted it), Tseng's very facing it affected his view of the Chinese heritage which he defended.

He came to admire the practical techniques of the West and to feel, correspondingly, that the peculiar Chinese excellence (which he always affirmed) need not be held to characterize traditional Chinese practice in that sphere of practical techniques. And in the sphere of the ultimate values of civilization—the sphere which was left to Tseng for the indulgence of his pride as a Chinese—he became more of a composite Chinese, an antithesis to Westerners, and less of a partisan sectarian, an adherent of one pre-Western Chinese school against another. As a loyal Chinese, but a Chinese among Westerners, he lost the will to dwell on intramural distinctions. An eclectic in the larger sense, ready to infuse something of Western civilization into Chinese civilization, he was catholic, too, in the field of native Chinese choices and sought to impose a peace on traditional Chinese enemies.

He would synthesize the best points of all systems of thought, he asserted. The various philosophers of the late Chou period were not so great as Confucius, because they were biased or one-sided. But if the biases could be rectified and the deficits made up, if these philosophers could lend themselves to a composite—with Lao-tzŭ's and Chuang-tzŭ's doctrine of emptiness and tranquillity for relaxing the mind, and Mo-tzŭ's doctrine of industry and frugality for regulating the self, and Kuan-tzŭ's and Shang Yang's doctrine of severity and orderliness for unifying the people—then all of them would be worth following and indispensable.[11]

> To combine the industry and frugality of Emperor Yü and Mo-tzŭ with the tranquillity and emptiness of Lao-tzŭ and Chuang-tzŭ—is not this the art of simultaneously accomplishing self-cultivation and group-regulation?[12]

> By gratifying oneself with the way of Chuang-tzŭ and restricting oneself with the way of Hsün-tzŭ, may not one be a princely man attaining the Way?[13]

Coming to classical Chinese conflicts in this conciliatory spirit, Tseng had similar views about more recent intellectual controversies.

He intimated that modern writers liked to dwell on comparisons between Chu Hsi and Lu Hsiang-shan just for the joy of sectarianism; and he had a low opinion of most of the criticism of the Lu-Wang (Yang-ming) idealistic school which had become so widespread.[14] Tseng wrote approvingly, too, of both the "Sung learning" and of the later "Han learning" which attacked it, "discarding the tradition of the five Sung philosophers." The scholars of the "Han learning" had been attacked in turn, accused of "splitting the classical tradition into fragments and causing the true path such harm as would never come to an end." Yet according to Tseng, the peacemaker, there was little distinction between them, and he urged their adherents not to be inflexible. Their differences could be easily adjusted, and the schools could fit together. Why should the two denounce each other?[15]

C. THE ENCROACHMENT OF HISTORY ON JUDGMENTS OF VALUE

Why, with Tseng and others like him, was there a waning of discrimination between Chinese alternatives, while to their predecessors and their less worldly wise contemporaries such discrimination was both natural and important? The positive content of the "Sung learning" and the "Han learning," for example, had not changed. But some change had occurred—a redefinition of the Chinese ideas in terms of new alternatives, and a consequent reordering of the psychology of the Chinese thinker. When Tseng, unlike some others, declared such Chinese controversy intellectually insignificant, perhaps he did so, in part, because for him, at least, it was emotionally undesirable.

For all his consistently serene Chinese self-confidence, he knew the West as a rival—a rival so formidable that he felt compelled to recommend an infusion of Western culture into Chinese civilization. This recommendation, this implied deference to the West as a center of value, was wrapped in a saving rationalization, which preserved the pretensions of China to superiority to the West. If, then, in this broader eclecticism (which we shall shortly examine), we find Tseng unable to accept the Western value simply, as a matter of intellectual persuasion, but find him concerned instead, from considerations extraneous to value, to make it seem legitimate for a *Chinese* to accept, may not this same commitment to history have a place in his narrower preliminary, Chinese eclecticism? It is easy to see how this eclecticism indulges the will of Chinese traditionalists, of whatever stamp, to hold their own against Western rivals who have raised the specter of doubt among them all. For agreement might seem to shore up the defenses of the Chinese intellectual world. Literati who could recognize, even dimly, the Western onslaught for what it was could have no stomach for civil war. It was more than unjustifiable—it was unwelcome. However freely they had indulged themselves in the luxury of dissension in the safe old days, now, when the West had challenged Confucius himself, all the bickering contenders for the mantle of Confucius were in a dangerous situation, and they all were in it together.

When Chinese history had not been threatened, the quest for value had been undertaken freely, and the several Chinese philosophies had been hammered out as distinctive serious efforts to describe the way of the world. But when Chinese philosophers, defensively ranged against the West, came to see truth in all these philosophies and to sip at all the flowers, their eclecticism was an intellectually sterile thing; for the flowers would have never existed, had not serious thinkers formerly cultivated their own individual gardens and developed their ideas by marking them off from the others.

Therefore, as considerations of history oust considerations of value in the Chinese approach to Chinese ideas, Western ideas, to some extent, are forced on reluctant Chinese minds. And Sino-Western syncretisms, inspired by that force and that reluctance, pre-empt the field of Chinese intellectual history.

3. Cultural Syncretism No. 1: T'i *and* Yung
"Substance" and "Function"

A. THE RATIONALIZATION

Soon after the Opium War a few farsighted literati proclaimed the need for change in Chinese culture. Paradoxically, they insisted on change because they had a traditionalistic bias against it. They parted company with unshakable traditionalists not over the question of ends—the ascription of value to Chinese civilization—but over the question of the means to preserve it. To admit innovation in certain areas of life, declared the bolder spirits, was the only means.

Uncompromising anti-Westernizers had an attitude of radical simplicity: the way to stay Chinese was to stay Chinese in all the aspects of culture. But the cautious eclectics, protesting their perfect loyalty to the basic Chinese values, believed that immobility would be a self-defeating tactic and an impossible ideal. The only alternative to outright destruction of Chinese civilization by foreign conquerors was selective innovation by dedicated Chinese traditionalists. To justify their proposal historically, to satisfy their will to believe that Chinese superiority was still unchallenged, they emphasized that these areas of innovation were areas of only *practical* value, not of essential value. Western knowledge would be used only to defend the core of Chinese civilization, and it would not impinge upon it.

If there should be argument on this point, if some traditionalists should doubt that Western ideas could be sterilized just by Chinese rhetoric, or be turned into passive instruments simply by decree, any one of this school of Westernizers would respond, in effect, like Li Hung-chang, cutting off discussion with the blank, apodictic apologia: "If one knows one's self and knows one's opposite number, in a hundred battles one will have a hundred victories."[16]

This rationalization, whereby something of Western culture could have a place in China and yet be kept in its place, was an article of faith for a whole school of Confucian-official Westernizers, the "self-strengtheners," from Lin Tse-hsü (1785–1850) to Chang Chih-tung (1837–1909). It was Chang who made the most explicit philosophical statement of what they all assumed—that, since elements of Western culture would be introduced only for use, condescension could be heaped on "practicality," and China could seem, not beggarly, but even queenly in borrowing Western methods. Taking his terminology from Chu Hsi, he advocated Chinese learning for *t'i* ("substance," "essence") and Western learning for *yung* ("function," "utility"). In value, China could still seem more than equivalent to the West. The tie to history need not be strained.[17]

B. THE FALLACY

Why should this rationalization not serve its purpose? Why should the Chinese not be able to rest on this middle ground? The *t'i-yung* dichotomy might well appear to be adequate to the claims of history, a psychologically suitable camouflage for the infiltration of foreign value —at least in the field of science. In that field, considered apart from other areas of civilization, the modern Chinese have had the least hope of harmonizing history and value and making an emotional Chinese particularism respectable intellectually. Valid conclusions of science, the sphere of the empirically demonstrable, finally enforce their claims to acceptance, regardless of their cultural origins. But scientific values are distinguished from moral and aesthetic values not only by being empirically demonstrable but by being widely and obviously useful. Now, since the Chinese are forced to accept Western science, what could be more plausible than that they should accept it in the spirit of Chang Chih-tung, emphasizing not that Western science is more valuable than Chinese science but that Western science is less valuable than Chinese morals and aesthetics, less valuable because of its usefulness? As something useful, it is a means, and a means is less than an end.

Yet, this rationalization, which was meant to compromise the differences between the *avant-garde* and the obscurantists, was attacked in both these quarters, and with considerable cogency. Both stubborn traditionalists and impatient Westernizers came to feel that history and value were not really welded together by the *t'i-yung* formula. Since that formula seemed to fail to justify innovation, traditionalists rejected innovation, and Westernizers sought a new formula.

The failure of the *t'i-yung* rationalization to consolidate Chinese devotion to Chinese culture in the modern world of Western techniques can be explained in its own terms: Chinese learning, which was to be the *t'i* in the new syncretic culture, was the learning of a society which had always used it for *yung*. Western learning, when sought as *yung*, did not supplement Chinese learning—as the neat formula would have it do—but ousted it. For, in reality, Chinese learning had come to be prized as substance because of its function, and, when its function was usurped, the learning withered. The more Western learning came to be accepted as the practical instrument of life and power, the more Confucianism ceased to be *t'i* ("essence"), the naturally believed-in value of a civilization without a rival, and became instead a historical inheritance, preserved, if at all, as a romantic token of no surrender to a foreign rival which had changed the essence of Chinese life.

Positivistic historians have been criticized for imagining a vain thing—that they can "appease a new discovery by fitting it into an old world, not allowing it to transform the whole of that world."[18] It was the illusion of the *t'i-yung* dichotomists that they could succeed in just such an effort. If a man read Mencius and an engineering manual, they felt, Mencius would speak to him just as he had to his father, who read Mencius and Tu Fu. But they were wrong, for the meaning of Mencius changed in his new context, the questions changed which Mencius was taken to answer, and the Western ideas accepted as *yung* were not tame, or dead, but dynamic. For,

> whatever we know, we know as a whole and in its place in our whole world of experience. . . . The process of knowledge is not a process of mere accretion. To speak of "adding to knowledge" is misleading. For a gain in knowledge is always the transformation and the recreation of an entire world of ideas. It is the creation of a new world by transforming a given world. If knowledge consisted in a mere series of ideas, an addition to it could touch only the raw end. . . . But, since it is a system, each advance affects retrospectively the entire whole, and it is the creation of a new world.[19]

C. REJECTION OF "T'I-YUNG" AND REJECTION OF INNOVATION: WO-JEN

The traditionalists who failed to be persuaded by the official Westernizers recognized the *t'i-yung* dichotomy for what it was, a formula for self-deception about the implications of innovation. If the Western learning were let loose in China, the Chinese learning would not stay safely screened off and unsullied. And if the Western learning came in because the Chinese deluded themselves that there could be two separate components to a culture, the Western learning would speedily end the separation and expose the delusion—the new *yung* would become also the new *t'i*.

Wo-jen (d. 1871), one of the most inflexible anti-Westernizers in a position of influence in nineteenth-century China, would not defend Chinese culture by accepting Western culture as a complement, a *yung* to a *t'i;* he defended it by rejecting Western culture as a rival, an alternative *t'i* to the traditional one. That is why we see Wo-jen tracing the origin of Western values (which others wish to admit as *yung*) to Chinese history, and saying, in effect, that they had had their chance to become Chinese *t'i* and had been rejected.

In other words, he denied the conflict between history and value by alleging that all possible value choices had already been posed and settled in Chinese history; he maintained that the Chinese history which was his nineteenth-century inheritance was good and that it should be sustained not only because of the ties of history but also because of the ties of value. His ideas were consistent, in accord with his comprehension that, if elements of Western culture were admitted, eventually the only grounds for clinging to Chinese culture would be historical ones, and the *t'i-yung* rationalization, which was supposed to smother conflict between history and value, would only make conflict certain.

Thus, while Chang Chih-tung assumed a radical separation in the conditions of origin of the Western and Chinese learning, Wo-jen assumed their identity. For Chang, Western learning was a foreign development, a promising candidate for Chinese acceptance as *yung;* for Wo-jen, "Western" learning was a domestic development, a discredited candidate for Chinese acceptance as *t'i.* While Chang thought Western learning could be accepted as means, Wo-jen feared it would usurp Chinese learning's prerogatives as end, and he condemned the Western learning, therefore, as an end already judged and rejected in the course of Chinese history. The Western scientist, in Wo-jen's view, cannot be an aide to Confucius—he is a fallen angel cast out by Confucius, and the relation between them is not collaboration but struggle.

So Wo-jen emphasized the distinction, the incompatibility, between the Chinese ideal of the "human heart" and the Western ideal of "techniques." He explicitly disavowed any effort to bring them together as complementary partners, for the Chinese had had the techniques and had let them go. He and like-minded literati delighted to maintain that ancient China had known the prototypes of that scientific learning which the Westernizers so uncritically admired. Astronomy and mathematics, it was alleged, derived from the *Chou-pi Suan-ching* (a book which was thought to be of Chou dynasty authorship) and the *Ch'un-ch'iu*. Chemistry derived from the *Shu-ching*, especially the *Hung-fan* ("The Great Plan") section, and from the Taoist Huai Nan-tzŭ. The part of physics which covers problems of solids, liquids, and gases was outlined in the *K'ang-ts'ang-tzŭ* (a book by an eighth-century Taoist, Wang Shih-yüan, though it purported to be Chou). Mineralogy was expounded in the *Shu-ching*, optics and mechanics by Mo-tzŭ, and electricity was explained by Kuan-yin-tzŭ, a Taoist supposed to have been a disciple of Lao-tzŭ.[20]

Wo-jen's intellectual position, of course, was shaped by social considerations. When he declines to exempt Western science from the ban of the conservative Chinese, one hears, not Wo-jen the abstract logician speaking, but Wo-jen the head of the *Han-lin Yüan*, the spokesman for the most honored masters of the ancient learning, men whose prestige and careers depended on the discrediting of the Western learning, a potential rival. It was just this social sensitivity to the cold blast at the back, perhaps, which accounts for Wo-jen's apprehension of the weakness of the *t'i-yung* rationalization. The social position of the Confucian gentry-literati-officialdom was tightly linked with the intellectual pre-eminence of Confucianism; no formula, embroidered with whatever Confucian pieties, which threatened to break the Confucian intellectual monopoly could expect general support from the old bureaucracy.

All question of vested interest aside, Western "matter" could not, in fact, be tamed to the service of Chinese Confucian "spirit." And the intellectual inadequacy of the *t'i-yung* formula as a principle for a viable syncretism is no better illustrated than by its general rejection among the pillars of the old society. For to say that Wo-jen saw the logical fallacy in the *t'i-yung* rationalization is only to say that he saw its social perils; if the literati, whose pre-eminence was as traditionally *Chinese* as the classics they guarded, were really imperiled by innovation according to a *t'i-yung* formula, a formula which ostensibly protected tradition, then the formula was illogical indeed.

D. REJECTION OF "T'I-YUNG" AND SEARCH FOR A NEW RATIONALIZATION: THE CLASSICAL SANCTION

Wo-jen, refusing to settle for a syncretism of Chinese ends and Western means, tried to save Chinese tradition by staking everything on it. Anything, he felt, which Westerners were presumptuous enough to offer and Westernizers blind enough to accept as a complement to Chinese civilization had already been found wanting by that civilization; and, indeed, the latter could hardly expect to be unaffected in admitting scientific techniques, when it had taken its present spiritual form by frankly demeaning them.

Now, Wo-jen's devising of a Chinese precedent for modern Western science is more familiar to us as a tactic of the opposite camp, the syncretists. No theme is more hackneyed in modern Chinese intellectual history than that of proud discovery of modern Western values in pre-modern Chinese history. Modern Chinese thinkers, once they have allowed themselves to unleash their imaginations, have found this by all odds the easiest manner to acknowledge the prestige of certain Western values, when they feel they must, without thereby casting reflections on Chinese history. Sun I-jang (1848–1908), for example, a traditionalist who nevertheless bowed to the persuasiveness of Western science, believed as Wo-jen did, that Mo-tzŭ's ideas were very close to modern conceptions of physics.[21]

When *t'i-yung* innovators resorted to this sorry searching for precedent, they were less consistent in their reasoning than the Wo-jen school of obscurantists in two ways. First, in trying to buttress their case for innovation by maintaining that Western science was really Chinese anyway, they tripped themselves up; for their basic argument, of course, was that science, non-Chinese but manageable by Chinese, could be accepted by Chinese without embarrassment because it was basely utilitarian. And, second, the paucity of specimens which the precedent-seekers could dredge up rather favored the reactionaries than the progressives. If Chinese examples were rare, this would be consistent with Wo-jen's contention that they lacked value and were found out early. But when Westernizers, on their side, were forced to scour Chinese history to find a few poor scraps of Chinese priority in the creation of modern values, they had to explain away the difficulty of their search, while their opponents could rest their case on it. Why, one might ask (and nineteenth-century Chinese did so), if Western ideas are commended to Chinese minds by their allegedly Chinese lineage, should this lineage be so hard to trace? If science was valuable, as the Westernizers admitted, and if ancient China had known this value, as the Westernizers tried to establish, then it was embarrassingly obvious that the Chinese critical faculty had become terribly dulled somewhere along the way. Why else would China in the nineteenth century have to make such a new beginning?

The *t'i-yung* rationalizers, if they diluted their reasoning with appeals to precedent, could never answer that question. And on their own proper ground they had less feeling than the reactionaries for the ominous potentialities of Western methods imported solely "for use." Nevertheless, although the reactionaries might well plume themselves for sensing the logical inadequacies of that particular rationalization for innovation, their conclusion—that the innovation must be stopped rather than the rationalization changed—was unsound. For they were obscurantist in failing to realize that innovation was inevitable and that some rationalization, logical or not, was a psychological necessity. This may not have been crystal-clear in the 1860's, when stand-patters like Wo-jen were harrying "self-strengtheners" like Tseng Kuo-fan, whose premises Chang Chih-tung was later to systematize; but by the 1890's, after further years of bitter lessons, it was hard to deny that drastic changes, whether made under Chinese or foreign auspices, were on the way for China.

Among those who saw this clearly were the late-nineteenth-century reformers of the *chin-wen* ("modern text") school of K'ang Yu-wei (1858–1927), who undertook to attain the goal of the *t'i-yung* school—Westernization with honor—while avoiding the basic fallacy in the *t'i-yung* formula. The *chin-wen* school made no attempt to separate *t'i* from *yung* (and thereby doom China to the drain of Chinese *t'i* into Western *yung*) but tried, rather, to link *t'i* and *yung* in the Chinese learning. The reformers would not leave the Chinese learning alone as *t'i*, with nothing of *yung* about it, and thereby condemn it; they would rather reinvigorate it, making the values of the modern West not a complement to the Chinese tradition but an integral part of it. In short, K'ang Yu-wei would keep Western values (which Wo-jen would not do) but would find them *inside* Confucianism (which Chang Chih-tung would not do).

Instead of saying, like the obscurantists, that Chinese tradition should dispense with Western values or saying, like the *t'i-yung* school, that Chinese tradition should be supplemented with Western values, the *chin-wen* school said that Chinese tradition should possess Western values. And it does possess them, said the *chin-wen* reformers, as the Chinese would realize if they only went back to their *authentic* Confucianism, which had long and sadly been under eclipse.

4. *Cultural Syncretism No. 2: The* Chin-wen *School and the Classical Sanction*[22]

A. NEW VALUES INJECTED INTO CHINESE HISTORY: K'ANG YU-WEI

Although Kang's reformers believed as little as the obscurantists that a Sino-Western civilization would be cleanly partitioned between Chinese essence and Western utility, they shared with the official Westernizers of the *t'i-yung* school a willingness to proceed toward some such civilization. Indeed, they improved on that willingness. On the spectrum of attitudes toward Westernization in nineteenth-century China, *chin-wen* stood as a mean, not between implacable anti-Westernizers and *t'i-yung* Confucian officialdom, but between the latter and the Protestant missions.[23]

The officials saw themselves as padding their civilization, a pearl of great price, with useful Western ideas. China was still alone, they felt, in possessing intrinsic value. The missionaries, however, while perfectly ready to spread useful ideas, were far from ready to accept these Chinese strictures on the culture of the West as a whole. Religious missionaries, after all, could hardly agree that the West was simply materialistic, that practical techniques were the only respectable products of Western history. If Confucian officials disparaged Western values in the nonmaterial sphere, Christian educators returned the compliment. Not only science, they insisted, but Western political and ethical values must come into China and displace their Chinese counterparts.

Between these two groups there stood the reformers. Before their brief moment of political influence in the summer of 1898, they conducted schools and study projects neither official nor Christian, though some aid came to them from both those quarters.[24] The reformers disparaged neither the Western spirit nor the Chinese spirit but prized them both and tried to believe them identical. Intellectually alienated from much of what passed for Chinese ideals, yet invincibly Chinese themselves, they strained to establish that history and value, in spite of appearances, had not been severed for China in the meeting of East and West.

The reformers, it must be apparent, had more disaffection to explain away than had the liberal, *t'i-yung* officials. The latter, in their confidence of the value and staying power of the "essentials" of Chinese civilization, were only a shade less complacent than the outright reactionaries. Old-school modernizers felt simply that China was weak; and the weakness was only relative to an evil Western strength. But once they had taken "self-strengthening" to be a Chinese ideal, properly

Chinese because supposedly harmless to the Chinese essence, the essence itself became subject to criticism if it seemed to inhibit the program designed to protect it. And so a younger generation, no more anxious than their elders to break the tie of history, but even more sorely troubled by the gathering wave of disasters, diplomatic and military, which China suffered in the later nineteenth century, came to a paradoxical conclusion: to preserve the Chinese spirit, they must change the spirit as well as the tools of their Chinese civilization.

The only way in which they could reconcile their traditionalism with their condemnation of the Chinese way of life was to strip from the latter its cloak of tradition. China was not only somehow weak, they felt, but somehow wrong. To escape the consequences of this admission, they tried to show that it was not the genuine principles of Chinese culture which were wrong. These had been perverted, distorted, or suppressed. And if these true principles were asserted again, China could have what the West had and still be true to herself. The values which the missionaries saw as the issue of European progress and Christian faith, K'ang would make Chinese.

All Chinese traditionalists, whatever their opinions on Westernization, had to agree that Confucius was the sage of Chinese culture, and Confucianism its very essence. But if the tables could be turned on the self-deceptive, ostensibly Confucian, despisers of the West, and contemporary Chinese culture be described as un-Confucian, then innovations in a wholesale measure, by no means simply in the material sphere, might not discredit the Chinese essence but make for its rediscovery. Accordingly, when K'ang recommended sweeping changes in Chinese society, he presented his views in three great works of Confucian exegesis. In the *Hsin-hsüeh Wei-ching K'ao* ("On the False Classics of the Hsin Learning"), he challenged the authenticity of certain texts of the Confucian canon, texts which he wished to see superseded by others more "exploitable." In the *K'ung-tzŭ Kai-chih K'ao* ("On Confucius as a Reformer"), he drew on his revised Confucian canon to interpret Confucius as a progressive, not a conservative, in his own day. And in the *Ta-t'ung Shu* ("Book of the Great Harmony"), he made Confucius the prophet of progress to a utopian Confucian future, toward which the West, with its modern values, was also on its way. K'ang set a course for Chinese history in the stream of Western optimism, and he called it a Chinese stream. When K'ang, building on the foundation of the "Han learning" of the seventeenth and eighteenth centuries, seemed to discredit the *ku-wen* ("ancient text") Classics of the orthodox Confucian canon, and when he heavily over-interpreted the early Han *chin-wen* ("modern text") Classics which he believed he had rehabilitated, all the impressive Western values fell into their Chinese places.[25]

B. PASSING OF THE "CHIN-WEN" SANCTION

Another eclectic utopia, inspired by the visions of K'ang Yu-wei, was the *Treatise on Benevolence* (*Jen Hsüeh*) of T'an Ssu-t'ung, one of the "six martyrs" to the reform movement who died in September, 1898, after the Hundred Days of reform. In this work, T'an set up a striking parallel between Western and Chinese histories. The papacy killed Christianity in the West, he said, and Luther revived it. Confucianism, done to death in China by the false scholarship of authoritarians, needed a Luther, too.[26] This suggestion that the Chinese reformers had had their Western counterparts recurred frequently in reformist writings, and Liang Ch'i-ch'ao, in his biographical tribute to K'ang written in 1901, expressed it with simple clarity: "My teacher is the Martin Luther of Confucianism."[27]

But the invocation of K'ang as the Chinese Luther was an ambiguous argument, which the *chin-wen* Confucian reformers pointed first at their conservative opponents and then turned inward on themselves. On the one hand, it supported metaphorically the essential position of the *chin-wen* school; for, as Luther claimed to be only restoring the pure Christianity of the Gospels and the Fathers, which had long been distorted by its self-styled representatives, so K'ang could maintain that he, also, had cut through the fog of centuries and restored the doctrine of the real Confucius of the earliest days. And if K'ang's Confucius, the prophet of progress, was the genuine article, then the fruits of progress, which had seemed to be solely Western fruits, could spring from the roots of Chinese tradition.

But, on the other hand, the K'ang-Luther analogy could suggest the equivalence of China to Europe in quite a different manner. Instead of forcing the Chinese to contemplate Western success and to find its principle, through tortuous reasoning, in an "authentic" Chinese past, it could lead him to dwell on Western failure, the age of darkness before Luther came, and to feel that China, not unrespectably, develops in parallel fashion. In other words, there need be less emphasis on Chinese deviation from the right way and more on the Chinese advance toward it, an advance which Europeans, with their own dark ages, had been forced to make painfully, too. And K'ang could be a Chinese Luther, not as a rediscoverer of an ancient truth, but as a hero of freedom of thought who breaks the grip of a smothering, mindless orthodoxy.[28]

This analogy of stages of progress remained, when the classical sanction lost its force, to cover a Chinese sacrifice of traditional Chinese values. If the West had once been benighted like China, and "Reformation" and "Renaissance" were all that was asked of China, then there was an implication of parallel histories and of China redeemed from a naked conflict of history and value. Neither intellectually stubborn, out of concern for Chinese history, nor flatly submissive to Europe, China could grow into modern times with self-respect.

T'an died before the doctrine of social progress—with Confucian orders to that effect no longer being relevant—was clearly extracted from the *chin-wen* reasoning. And K'ang, as long as he lived, never lost his *chin-wen* convictions: that the stages of progress were Confucian stages and that the values of progress, modern values, were really values because the Sage had once conceived them. But with Liang we see Confucianism trailing off to its twentieth-century ruin; for he comes to accept the second meaning of the K'ang-and-Luther analogy and insists that what China needs, and can have with no indignity, is *not* a commitment to a pure Confucianism but a break with it.[29]

Historical evolution, in the basic principle of the *chin-wen* Confucianists, was a universal progress from the "age of chaos" (as Confucius called it) to the "great peace" or the "great harmony." Confucius, it seemed, had licensed China to listen to new ideas. But the new ideas were so many, and so clearly subversive of the stable Confucian society, that it soon was merely fanciful for moderns to claim the Confucian imprimatur.

And so the classical sanction seemed only for a moment to deny the conflict between history and value in modern China. But it gave a new direction to the Chinese search for a formula which might succeed. Since Confucianism could neither exclude nor absorb Western ideas, since neither *t'i-yung* nor *chin-wen* could really save the Chinese *t'i*, then Chinese thinkers must cease to feel that equivalence with the West was staked on it. And a new possible defense for China, a new sanction for innovation, could be salvaged from the *chin-wen* doctrine. For if evolution is the way of the world, as the *chin-wen* school had taught, an ancient *t'i* is properly superseded. Men may turn, if they lose the heart to compare the values of Europe and China, to comparing their histories and see a morphological analogy between the life of China and the life of the West. These may seem to evolve with similar sequences, as the dismal stages of their pasts are succeeded by stages to a brighter future, as their bondage to intellectual orthodoxies gives way to intellectual freedom.

5. *The Modern* Ku-wen *Opposition, Reactionary and Revolutionary, to* Chin-wen *Reformism*

A. THE REACTIONARY "KU-WEN" ATTACK

The *chin-wen* school, as its name indicates, was not eclectic in the field of Chinese choices. Though even more aware of Western incursions than Tseng Kuo-fan had been, the reformers failed to respond as he did, and to ancient domestic intellectual conflicts they brought not peace but a sword. Han dynasty scholarship had finally accepted the so-called *ku-wen* Classics as the really authentic texts, and the rival *chin-wen*, in the third century A.D., went into eclipse. The "Han learning" of the early Ch'ing, to a large extent, reversed this judgment, and K'ang Yu-wei, for his generation, kindled the conflict anew.

Yet, K'ang's truculence was not inconsistent with the peaceable eclecticism of Tseng Kuo-fan. For Tseng saw the West as a common rival of all the Chinese schools and meant to distinguish the West from China as *yung* is distinguished from *t'i*. But K'ang had no hopes of separation and preferred to see peace between civilizations, with the West and China sharing common values. With peace abroad, a battle at home was possible. And, for a semblance of peace abroad, a battle at home was necessary. Orthodox Confucianism of the *ku-wen* school could never appear to shelter Western values.

It was the need to accommodate Western values, then, which impelled the reformers to revive the *chin-wen* scholarship. Since that was the case, since the reformers' scholarship was hardly "pure," it was impervious to attack by the pure scholarship of *ku-wen* conservatives. When the classical sanction faded, when Chinese rebels ceased protesting that Confucius was their master, it was not the conservative *ku-wen* scholars who effected that development. For the issues now were not the same as in the *ku-wen—chin-wen* conflicts of earlier centuries. Social facts, not textual critics, were the damaging antagonists of the modern *chin-wen* school.

The serious question for these latter day *chin-wen* scholars was whether their doctrine was really compatible with Western experience. They had seized on the *chin-wen* scholarship not as simple Confucians, who wanted only to know the truth about what their Sage had said; they had acted rather as Westernizers, for whom the *chin-wen* doctrine *had* to be true if they were to be Confucians at all. Western values possessed the younger minds, and, the harder they found it to cram their new knowledge into K'ang's Confucianism, the less they cared about any Confucius, either the one who spoke through the *ku-wen* texts or the one who spoke through the *chin-wen*.

Thus, when the reactionary *ku-wen* traditionalists attacked the reformers on textual grounds, they were engaging in an irrelevant battle. "Irrevelant" does not mean unsound. On textual issues, for assertions such as these—that Confucius composed the Six Classics, that Liu Hsin (d. 23 B.C.) forged the *Tso-chuan*—the *chin-wen* scholarship was certainly open to grave indictment.[30] But K'ang's mistakes were more important than other men's corrections, and the indictment had no significance for future Chinese history. For the *ku-wen* critics never answered the real question which the *chin-wen* school was asking: not, "What does Confucius say?" but, "How can we make ourselves believe that Confucius said what we accept *on other authority?*"

Therefore, although the lines were drawn as at earlier times, there was an air of unreality about the textual conflict. For *chin-wen* Confucianism was a different idea before and after the Western invasion of China. And a hostile *ku-wen* argument, which might have been telling against an eighteenth-century *chin-wen* scholar of the "Han learning," was an answer later to a dead question. The Confucian canon was simply not the issue. Liang Ch'i-ch'ao attested to this in 1902, when he abruptly ceased, in his reformist writings, to exhort his readers to care about the Classics.[31] And the keener members of the *ku-wen* camp realized this as well. Yeh Te-hui (1864–1927), brushing past the question of what Confucius said, seized quite certainly on what K'ang meant, though K'ang himself was always in the dark: "K'ang Yu-wei, secretly proposing to be a 'reforming Luther' in his own life, desired to clear away the Six Classics, and composed first the *Wei-ching K'ao;* and he desired to stir up the imperial regime, and went on to compose the *Kai-chih K'ao*."[32]

B. THE REVOLUTIONARY "KU-WEN" ATTACK

The *chin-wen* school was reformist in political action, never anti-dynastic, and it blamed Chinese for distortion of the genuine Chinese tradition. But other dissidents in the last years of the empire were revolutionaries. For them the Manchu usurpers of Chinese power were fair game, in cultural attacks as well as political. If it had to be acknowledged that the contemporary West, intellectually and politically, was far in advance of China, the blame could be heaped on the Manchus, and the Chinese spared.[33]

Therefore, anti-Manchu revolutionary nationalists had no need to arraign Confucian "heretics" for Chinese ills and every reason to consider that K'ang's diagnosis was counterrevolutionary. In his *Po K'ung-chiao I* ("Refutation of the Confucian Religion"), Chang Ping-lin, a virulently anti-Manchu revolutionary, skilfully defended the *ku-wen* Classics against the *chin-wen* textual criticism.[34]

Yet, though *ku-wen* scholarship may seem proper in revolutionary circles, as a symbol of the denial of reformism, the great majority of *ku-wen* scholars were consistent conservatives, whose loyalty to the orthodox *ku-wen* canon was an affirmation of the status quo; and there was a peculiar complexity about Chang Ping-lin's position. For he came by his *ku-wen* opinions honestly, as a cultural conservative himself, defending the old literary style and the traditional materials of the old imperial examinations.[35] He was an important contributor to the Shanghai monthly *Kuo-sui Hsüeh-pao* (1904–11), which defended the Chinese cultural heritage against the "European wind and American rain," the storm of Western ideas.[36] He did not derive his conservative views in classical scholarship from his revolutionary political views. He seems, rather, to have derived the latter from his concern to save the "Chinese essence." And, in this, he parted company with most of his fellow-traditionalists.

He saw more clearly than they that change must come to the Chinese scene; and if traditionalism was not to be sentimentality alone, and intellectually indefensible, he must hold, he knew, a rational theory which would keep the Chinese past from being discredited by the change. But he was wrong to think that Manchu-baiting was a serviceable theory in the twentieth century. It could seem to protect the reputation of traditional Chinese culture, but it would help to end its existence.

For the institution of the monarchy, the ultimate target of the anti-Manchu revolutionary movement, was as traditionally Chinese as Confucianism itself. The *chin-wen* school, it is true, in attacking the accepted Confucian canon, was culturally subversive, opening the way for cultural drift; when the Classics could be doubted, anything could be doubted. But it was hardly striking a blow for tradition to reject the *chin-wen* heresy and to spare the Classics by condemning the throne. When the imperial system could be doubted, anything could be doubted. Who could be sure of any rule, when almost the oldest rule of all was broken? "My older uncle was drunk, and angry about the revolution most of the time. . . . He would stare at the relatives, and say ironically: 'But, excuse me, we have the revolution. What difference does it make who is the oldest in the family? What can I have to do with the marriage of my brother, Tan Tsi-pu?' "[37]

6. Cultural Syncretism No. 3: The Role of Nationalism in the Disowning of the Past

A. THE ATTACK ON THE MANCHUS

When nationalism swept the Chinese student world, in the first years of the twentieth century, inevitably the Manchus felt the blast of hatred. They were such obvious targets, and on two counts—as usurpers of the Chinese power and as rulers of China in a bleak age of national degradation. But anti-Manchu feeling was only an effect of nationalism, only a manifestation, not its cause or its core.

The cause of Chinese nationalism, and the core of its content, was intellectual alienation from traditional Chinese culture. Nationalism, as a meaningful concept on the Chinese scene, had not only a positive but a negative significance; in accepting the nation as the proper object of Chinese loyalty, the nationalist rejected the historic alternative, the "culturalistic" reverence for the "Chinese way of life," above and beyond all other loyalties. Theoretically, nationalists were free to make any intellectual choice, however unorthodox in terms of Chinese culture, if only it were nationally useful.

By the twentieth century the Manchus were almost impervious to attack on a culturalistic basis, for they had become the champions of the Chinese way of life. In the seventeenth century they may have seemed to pose a cultural threat to China. But, as time passed, Western culture became the only dangerous alternative, and, as long as the Manchus were anti-Western, Chinese culturalists could rally around the Ch'ing. And where their predecessors had flaunted the slogan, "Fu Ming, Mieh Ch'ing" ("Uphold the Ming, Destroy the Ch'ing"), the "Boxers" of 1900, xenophobic and culturalistic, rose to the cry, "Fu Ch'ing, Mieh Yang" ("Uphold the Ch'ing, Destroy the Foreigner").[38]

Thus, the Manchu cause and the traditional cause had become the same. But there was a brand of Chinese traditionalists, not sublimely confident, like the Boxers, but defeatist, like Chang Ping-lin, who chose to believe that the Ch'ing had thwarted the Chinese genius. It was a straw to clutch at, something to keep them from sweeping along to either cold iconoclasm or arid traditionalism. And so, as a gesture of respect for Chinese culture, they called themselves nationalists, and they reissued, as supposedly nationalistic fare, seventeenth-century, long-outmoded culturalistic invectives against the Manchus.[39]

Rigorous nationalists like Liang Ch'i-ch'ao, who since 1902 had been proclaiming the need for a "new people," opposed the specious nationalism of the easy anti-Manchus, for the latter seemed to proclaim that the old people was good enough, if only the Manchu incubus could be taken off its neck. Therefore, although the ruin of the Manchus was certain if nationalism spread, as Liang intended it should, he refused to accept his own anti-Manchu conclusions, because the "official," republican anti-Manchus appeared to reject his premises. Nevertheless, the new state, the republic, belongs in the history of the new people. Chang Ping-lin was iconoclastic and Liang was revolutionary, each in spite of himself.

B. CULTURALISM AND NATIONALISM AS COMPETITORS FOR LOYALTY

When nationalism began to flourish in Chinese intellectual circles in the earliest years of the twentieth century, it represented a bold attempt to sweep away the cant which had become all too obvious in the usual apologia for Chinese tradition. The dilemma posed by intellectual alienation from tradition and emotional tie to it still existed. History and value were still apart. But the nationalist dispensed with the effort to bridge the gap by somehow justifying Chinese tradition. He still hoped to establish the cultural equivalence of China with the West; but his ingenious way of accomplishing this was to deny that culture was the proper unit of comparison.

That unit was the nation. When the Confucian efforts of the *chin-wen* school subsided, and yielded the figure of "parallel histories" for the syncretist to work with, the Chinese nation became his first concern. The ideas of progress and freedom of thought were his new possessions, but these, by themselves, were useless to guide him in intellectual choice. "Progress to what, thought about what?" he must ask, before tampering with the Chinese tradition. To what end should change take place?

The end of change, he must answer, is the strengthening of the nation. For if the nation, not the culture, has the highest claim on the individual, then the abandonment of traditional values, if they seem to be indefensible, is a cheerful duty, not a painful wrench. And the laws of evolution, not Confucian now but social-Darwinist, exalt the nation as the highest unit in the struggle for existence and proclaim that the past must die and should never be lamented.[40]

When nationalism developed in China as the denial of culturalism, the latter changed in itself; for culturalism, now, in its turn, had Chinese nationalism as something new to deny. Chinese culturalism had defined itself formerly as the alternative to foreign barbarism. But now, with the rise of nationalism, when Chinese "barbarism" was the real alternative, a calculated intemperance seemed to replace the old complacency of spokesmen for tradition. "Better to see the nation die than its way of life change," said Hsü T'ung, and Ku Hung-ming protested that foot-binding should be sacrosanct, as an important element in the Chinese spirit.[41] One can sense a note of defiance here, a willingness to shock, and a grim decision to stand on principle, though the principle be out of fashion.

C. THE REINTEGRATION OF TRADITION INTO NATIONALISM

Such men as these were quite correct in believing that nationalism and culturalism were irreconcilable and that the rise of nationalism was somehow linked with the disintegration of Chinese civilization. But there is a complication in the picture.

We have ascribed to nationalism the freedom to dispense with the cultural loyalties which are the sum and substance of culturalism. Nationalism thus becomes, it appears, the basis of a cool iconoclasm; without feeling tied by the cord of history, a restive Chinese generation can follow the dictates of value, which lead it to Western examples. For the traditional culture need not be protected. Its claims have been explained away. When nationalism follows culturalism, necessity, not precedent, has the right to govern choice.

Yet, if we examine the actual content of nationalistic expression in China, we see that this definition is too abstract.[42] An absolute breach between the *chiao* and the *min*, doctrine and people, "essence" and nation, is not ruthlessly enforced. On the contrary, there are nationalists who insist on loyalty to the old. They prescribe fidelity to what history has established as Chinese. They will never admit that a Chinese careless of Chinese tradition can be a Chinese nationalist.

Traditionalism, then, retains a place in nationalism. But, in that case, where is the nice distinction between Chinese nationalism and Chinese culturalism? When loyalty to the past is so clearly one of its features, can nationalism really contribute to a deliverance from the past? How do the following sentiments, from a Chinese Nationalist (Kuomintang) handbook of 1934, clash with the culturalism of Chang Chih-tung?

> A nation must always remain faithful to its own history and its own culture in order to maintain an independent existence on earth. For a people to keep faith with itself and progress courageously, it ought not to renounce its own old civilization lest it become like a river without a source or a tree without roots. While wishing to assimilate the new knowledge of western civilization, we ought to give it for a base the principles of Confucius. The whole people must learn the doctrines and conform to the thoughts of Confucius.[43]

That statement, with its apparent reaffirmation of the culturalistic *t'i-yung* philosophy, actually shows the difference between the nationalism which celebrates a traditional way of life and the culturalism which does the same. For Chang Chih-tung's convictions about Confucius as a base for Western knowledge were absolutistic, not relativistic. He saw value, absolute value, in the Chinese *t'i*. In his inherited way of life (or in that part of it which he cordoned off, yielding to the West the world of "practical utility"), he found not only the appeal of history but the appeal of value. It was not just *his*—it was right. And it was its rightness which justified the allegiance he was moved to assert. Chang, like all true culturalists, did not see the *t'i-yung* formula as universally applicable, *mutatis mutandis;* not just *any* nation's national essence, its *t'i*, was entitled to preservation, with a foreign *yung*, perhaps, to shield it. The Chinese learning, for Chang, was commended by both value and history. He believed, at least overtly, that there was more than mere traditionalism to enjoin its preservation.

Thus, Chang retained a philosophical attachment to Confucianism, the heart of the Chinese *t'i*. But nationalists had a romantic attachment, not a primary belief in Confucianism, but a belief in the need to profess belief. The nationalistic passage quoted above, so near on the surface to culturalism, which attributes absolute value to the culture to which it refers, is really a statement of cultural relativism; and the latter is a tenet of romanticism, which denies the contention of rationalists that abstract value should be the sole criterion in intellectual choice.

One must note the anonymity in that Kuomintang pronouncement. Who should remain faithful to its own history and its own culture? "A nation"—that is, every nation. China must be loyal only as other nations must, each to its own culture.

This note of relativism, so unfamiliar to Chinese minds in the halcyon days of the empire, was sounded clearly by Liang Ch'i-ch'ao, writing as a nationalist in 1915. It was disastrous, he said, for a nation to break with its past. It must act in keeping with its national character, which is manifested in language, literature, religion, customs, ceremonies, and laws. For a nation dies when its national character is obliterated. That happened, said Liang, to Korea and Annam. So many Chinese elements entered their cultures that their national characters could never be more than half-developed. Hence, they fell into subjection.[44]

It is easy to see the distinction between such an appeal for traditionalism and the earlier, culturalistic one. It had been the assumption of Chinese civilization, in the old days, that if Annam and Korea adopted a certain amount of it, to that degree were they civilized. Traditionalism had not been a blind charge on the Chinese, not an imperative ("We must"), but an axiom ("How could a reasonable man think otherwise?"). For modern nationalists, however, traditionalism was no longer necessary in the primary sense of the word, as axiomatic, but in the hortatory sense: it must exist if an end is to be achieved. Traditionalism was no longer an end in itself, self-justified.

Its end is nationalism. It must exist in nationalism, shorn of its claim to value as it is, in order that nationalism may exist. The sense of community which is essential to nationalism depends on people's acknowledgment of a common past. And the common past must be prized if a man is to let it forge a bond between himself and his fellow-nationals. Otherwise, why should it matter?

Yet, the fact that traditionalism had to be "worked at" in Chinese nationalism, instead of exerting a natural charm, reminds us why nationalism swept into favor. The reason was that the tradition had lost its natural charm; Chinese thinkers, however reluctantly, had lost their faith in its value. And nationalism justified emotionally the departure from tradition, which was already justified, only too well, by intellectual conviction.

Chinese nationalism, therefore, began as a paradox, a doctrine with increasingly obvious internal tensions. The nationalist protected tradition so that he might *be* a nationalist and be able to attack it. And a tradition requiring protection instead of compelling belief became increasingly open to attack. In the search for a credo in modern China to appease the conflict of history and value, nationalism failed to provide the final resting place; for nationalism was not at rest itself.

7. *The Ostensible Attribution of Significance Exclusively to Value As a Defense of Tradition*

A. "SELECT THE BEST IN EAST AND WEST"

Chinse nationalism came into being with two prescriptions for the Chinese thinker which were hard to reconcile. He was to have a special sympathy for the Chinese past, and he was to review the Chinese past with a disinterested critical honesty. A decision to combine the best which the West and China offered seemed the most suitable way to meet the requirements of this complex point of view. The willingness to pool the resources of the two civilizations was to be a genuine willingness, without the reservation of the culturalistic *t'i-yung* Westernizers, who always grudgingly added that the Western best was a poor one.

This formula seems to call into play the iconoclastic potentialities of nationalism. Ostensibly, value alone shall be the concern of the thinker. This is clear from the fact that "best," a culturally neutral value term, describes the object of the thinker's search. The importance of tradition as an influence on judgment seems completely denied, for whatever part of the Chinese heritage which a Western "best" displaces is just as commendable on traditional grounds as what remains.

Nevertheless, just as the past retains a significance in Chinese nationalism, though the latter was designed to deny it, so it intrudes in this formula, making the "best" equivocal. In the apparent need to specify the origins of values, a continuing conflict between history and value is tacitly admitted though outwardly denied. Men are to choose, of course, solely according to the dictates of universal reason; but the suggestion is insistently offered that our objective thinker will doubtless find the East as well as the West a repository of values from which he may draw.

Now, if value judgment were being rigorously applied in an honest, impartial search for the best, such insistence that the West *and* China shall inspire the brave new culture would be irrelevant. For the traditional Chinese values which a modern could reaffirm would be those which conformed to his own standards (i.e., those to which he would subscribe even if he knew nothing of tradition). Therefore, the only motive which a Chinese could have in toasting the beauty of blended values would be a desire—entirely foreign to the world of value—to see China and the West as equal partners. The supposed commitment to value alone is made as a gesture to history.

B. EXAMPLE: TS'AI YÜAN-P'EI

For the first two decades of the twentieth century, an important educator, Ts'ai Yüan-p'ei (1867–1940), was an influential advocate of values-across-the-sea. His fundamental conviction was that truth has no national boundaries. Truth, that is, belongs to the man who knows it, who may be and should be Chinese, even though a particular article of truth has perhaps been discovered in Europe. Ts'ai's position can be characterized as a tautological statement that value is universal and, therefore, a fortiori, Chinese. If the Chinese only "select the best," they are true to themselves.

Ts'ai, then, asking only for an appreciation of truth, was ready to settle for a composite culture based, ostensibly, on a commitment exclusively to value. Yen Fu (1853–1921), the conservative translator of many philosophical Western works, went only so far as to say that, if the ancient sages could have survived to modern times, they would have dismissed neither Western learning and culture nor the Chinese ideals of "investigation of things" and "extension of knowledge."[45] But in Ts'ai's appeal for syncretism he meant truth to be absolutely its own sponsor. It was unnecessary for the "sages" to grant it the freedom of China; truth had its freedom naturally.

Therefore, when he stressed the importance of "right knowledge of Liberty, Equality, and Fraternity," it is particularly significant that he related liberty to the classical principle of righteousness (*i*), equality to the principle of forbearance or reciprocity (*shu*), and fraternity to benevolence (*jen*).[46] For, unlike the *chin-wen* doctrine, his philosophy did not demand of him that he legitimize cultural borrowing by a reference to the Classics. He sought only the best from East and West—but with an unspoken wish to see the East as a genuine partner.

One can see that desire, too, behind his advocacy of "world education," something broad enough, he urged, to allow expression to the best in man.[47] Living in a particular culture, he implied, was too severely limiting. Implying this, he simultaneously attacked both Chinese ethnocentrism and Chinese self-abasement. For, if China ought to throw her values into a common pool, so ought the West, whose culture was just as limited. And in this spirit he envisioned the "world citizen," a man with rights and duties, tempering Nietzsche's egoism with Mencius' and Mo-tzŭ's altruism.[48]

Ts'ai's zeal for universality, his eagerness to see both the West and China sacrifice their individualities, was a balm for cultural defeatism. For, if value was all, then no one's history was at stake in intellectual choices, no culture won or lost. China could choose selectively from the storehouse of its past or from the storehouse of the West, without lapsing into either a petrifying imitation of its own old manners or a soul-destroying imitation of Western manners.

But there was a flaw in the premises of Ts'ai's appeal for the reign of sweet reason. He was magnanimously willing to sacrifice what the West had already killed—the power of traditional Chinese culture to contain the Chinese mind. The Westernization of China was becoming a fact; the "Sinification" of Europe was out of the question. Ts'ai had proclaimed that the cultures should meet, but he meant "halfway." The West had to sacrifice, too. Westerners were supposed to acknowlege the value of Chinese things and acknowledge value not just with their critical faculties, as the Western collectors of Sung landscapes did, but with their creative faculties, as the Chinese did who went to Paris to learn to paint like Matisse. Yet, the West would be obliged to sacrifice only if a significant amount of the Chinese heritage was universally commendable to modern minds. If the attribution of significance exclusively to value was to aid the defense of Chinese tradition, value *had to be* found in the

Chinese past. The lack of concern with anything but quality—the emancipation from history—was an illusion.

Ts'ai's theory, then, which some nationalists used to stave off suspicion that traditional Chinese civilization was bankrupt and in no condition to set the terms of its modification, hastened the day when its ruin could no longer be concealed. For compulsion *a tergo* to admire a heritage, even the compulsion of one's own nostalgia, instils a doubt that the heritage attracts on its own merits. As their reassertion of old values became thoroughly deliberate and smacked of artifice, Chinese were driven to make other adjustments to the modern world or were confirmed in them.

C. "MATTER" AND "SPIRIT": THE "T'I-YUNG" RATIONALIZATION "IN EXTREMIS"

For many Chinese recognition of the hollowness of such defensive eclecticism was deferred by the first World War. The West seemed open then as never before to a plausible charge of evil materialism, and Chinese traditionalists were immensely cheered by the Western debacle. A mass of Chinese apologetics is summed up in Yen Fu's gloating statement, in his stubbornly classical style, that three hundred years of European progress had brought only "profit self and kill others, diminish incorruptibility and banish shame."[49]

In the nationalists' dedication to an impartial search for the best in East and West, it was refreshing to seem able to be impartial on the Chinese side. Before the war, many of the nationalists who most firmly insisted that China and the West had equal title to whatever was best for modern man had disowned their past more in sorrow than in anger. After the war, they were more than pleased to rediscover it and, instead of defensively pleading "no contest," to proclaim again their triumph over the West. The West was matter—China, spirit.

Matter could be used, spirit was essential, and *t'i-yung* analysts were abroad again in the land. Their finest flowers appeared in the writings of Ch'en Li-fu and in the *China's Destiny* of Chiang Kai-shek, where the West was assigned the task of revealing the secrets of sordid material power, while China won the halo for her spiritual achievement in traditionally neglecting the search.

We have already suggested, however, that nationalistic eulogies of the Chinese essence were only a counterfeit of culturalistic confidence in it; and the *t'i-yung* formula of Ch'en and Chiang differed in meaning from the *t'i-yung* formula of Chang Chih-tung. The latter, in urging that Western learning be introduced as *yung*, addressed himself to traditionalists, who seriously doubted that Western learning would really protect the Chinese *t'i*. And they were right to be skeptical. For, when nationalists revived the *t'i-yung* rationalization, they were forced to confront iconoclasts, who doubted that the *t'i* deserved protection.

8. The Ostensible Attribution of Significance Exclusively to Value As an Attack on Tradition

A. THE CHARGE OF STERILITY AGAINST CREATIVE EFFORTS IN THE TRADITIONAL SPIRIT

When science, though disparaged, was admitted under the *t'i-yung* or matter-spirit sanctions, care had to be taken that China should, in fact, preserve her traditions in the realm of spirit. In the field of painting, for example, the Chung-kuo Hua-hsüeh Yen-chiu Hui ("Society for the Study of Chinese Painting") was founded in Peking in 1919, under the sponsorship of Hsü Shih-ch'ang, a political figure of scholarly and traditionalistic bent.[50]

What happens to a traditional aesthetic when it is perpetuated as a symbol of something outside its field? The painter Wu Hu-fan (b. 1894), a devotee of the art of Sung, Ming, and early Ch'ing, has left us some useful testimony. He has taken no interest, he says, in new or Western techniques of painting because he feels that new things can grow only out of old. They must have roots.[51]

This statement is unexceptionable. It is clearly true, as Sapir has remarked, that an individual is helpless without a cultural heritage to work on: "He cannot, out of his unaided spiritual powers, weave a strong cultural fabric instinct with the flush of his own personality. Creation is a bending of form to one's will, not a manufacture of form *ex nihilo* . . . the creator from out of a cultural waste gives us hardly more than a gesture or a yawp."[52]

In undertaking to work within a tradition, then, Wu made a legitimate decision, and one, moreover, with more promise of value than the undisciplined eclecticisms which other modern artists have embarked upon. We are all familiar with that species of sociological coloration of aesthetic purposes which has led so many Chinese painters to do their bit to select the best from East and West, thus to redeem China from either sterile imitation of its own past or servile imitation of the West.[53]

But Wu Hu-fan himself, it becomes clear, was far from free from sociological motivations, which led him to see in his traditional forms something quite different from what his traditional masters had seen in them; he emerges as a spokesman for just that course of sterile imitation which has driven some other contemporary painters to their hopeless symbolic syntheses, and still others to outright rebellion. For, although his concern with "roots" implies an interest in development and in the relation between past and present, Wu's interest is in the past itself, a past which he sees as sharply distinct from the present.

One of his paintings is a landscape, with a girl dressed in ancient Chinese costume in the foreground. When asked why the girl could not have been dressed as Chinese women dress today, he replied: "If I did that, the style would change and in a few years the picture would look old-fashioned and ridiculous. My pictures are not painted for people of today only, but for those who will look at them during a thousand years."[54]

A credo such as this reveals the ravages which the West has wrought in traditional Chinese art and, by implication, in traditional Chinese thought in general. Creativity presupposes a state of tension between a fresh imagination and the weight of tradition, a tension which leads to development within a tradition. But how was there to be development within the Chinese artistic tradition when the West stood across its path? The West, it seemed, had anticipated the possible new departures, and Chinese painters who might have been tempted to apply their fresh imaginations to Chinese tradition, and to create their own ideals of value within the stream of Chinese history, were caught up short when they recognized that such an action would be historically indefensible. Back in their groove, where once they had valued tradition as the spur to creativity, now they valued tradition because only there could they find the shelter of history, and history and value had to seem united.

The search for roots, then, really meant the search for the old flowers. Development, and with it the hope of creativity, were sacrificed to an idealization of the past, and one undertaken for reasons not solely aesthetic. Wu Hu-fan's statement on costume seems totally illogical unless one sees that the past is idealized and far removed from the plane of the present. For if a change in the fashion tomorrow would be sufficient to render ridiculous the painting of a woman in the costume of today, what principle, except the idealization of the past, could authorize the painting of the costume of yesterday? The present must be ephemeral, and the past, the ancient past of the authentic China, eternal.

When traditionalists lost the will to develop tradition and sought instead to repeat it, they changed its content. They no longer saw it, with a spontaneous aesthetic vision, as a world of beauty which could pique them to new discoveries. They saw it rather as an antithesis to the West, and development could only weaken it in that capacity. The strength which tradition should have brought them was lost, for they put themselves under the ban: "An automatic perpetuation of standardized values, not subject to the constant remodeling of individuals willing to put some part of themselves into the forms they receive from their predecessors, leads to the dominance of impersonal formulas. The individual is left out in the cold; the culture becomes a manner rather than a way of life, it ceases to be genuine."[55]

Therefore, when Western pioneers appeared to be astride all avenues of development, Chinese traditional thought went stale. Traditionalists, seeking to avoid a conflict between history and value, drained the value from what they perpetuated. The conflict grew sharper, and it became inevitable that some Chinese should try a course of outright iconoclasm and see where it took them. It took them, in large numbers, from nationalism to communism.

B. THE PRESSURE OF ICONOCLASM AGAINST NATIONALISM

We have seen that there were nationalists who were willing to innovate but whose earnest desire was to let the tradition down gently. Nationalism also sheltered a group which felt it possible, under nationalism's auspices, to spare the tradition nothing. If a man would see things honestly, they felt, in the clear, cold light of value, his release from tradition was unconditional.

Ch'en Tu-hsiu, a leader and mentor of the young intellectuals who gathered under such significant banners as *Hsin Ch'ing-nien* ("The New Youth") and *Hsin Ch'ao* ("The New Tide, or 'Renaissance' "), was one iconoclast who refused to accept his release from tradition at the hands of nationalism. He was wary about nationalism as a foe of tradition, for he feared that nationalism would let tradition in by the back door.[56] Many of his students and disciples, however, did combine political nationalism and cultural iconoclasm in the "May Fourth movement" of 1919, and, in later periods of political crisis, student-patriots continued to link these strains of thought. In the decade of the 1930's, in the anti-Japanese student world, the old education was stigmatized as "poison left over from feudalism."[57]

This brand of patriotism was unpopular with official nationalists, who suspected a student affinity with communism. The suspicion was well founded, for the desertion to communism of the younger generation of Chinese intellectuals was apparent during the war against Japan, and signs of it had been noticeable in the 1920's.

In so far as nationalists really thought as Ch'en did about Chinese tradition, they overloaded their nationalism with iconoclastic content and became quasi- or actual Communists. For communism, as we shall see, appeared to be able to absorb a higher degree of antitraditionalism than simple nationalism was able to do and yet justify a Chinese, emotionally or historically, in breaking intellectually with his Chinese past. And there, in communism, they met Ch'en Tu-hsiu, one of the founders of the Communist party of China. He had refused the sanction of nationalism for his antitraditionalism, but he could not, as a Chinese, do without any sanction at all.

C. THE SOCIAL COMPULSION ON NATIONALISM TO DEEPEN AND DENY THE STERILITY OF TRADITION

As long as an iconoclast could believe that nationalism sanctioned iconoclasm unreservedly, as a prerequisite to the strengthening of the nation, he could remain a nationalist. But when he observed that nationalism seemed to encourage the preservation of tradition as a dead museum piece, he was forced to rethink his position. One thing was clear—nationalists killed tradition in one way or another, whether they cast it out or congealed it. Why, then, the iconoclasts must ask, should men as modern as they themselves pay lip service to a tradition in which all nationalists must really have lost their confidence?

Actually, in their diagnosis of sterility in the traditional thought and art which persisted in a nationalistic China, the iconoclasts implied a decision about its causes. The charge of sterility suggested that the new traditionalists had no primary intellectual or aesthetic commitment to what they were doing but only a social commitment: this was the reason why what they produced lacked value, and equally the reason why they continued to praise and produce it, its aesthetic or intellectual worthlessness notwithstanding.

Incisive iconoclasts, then, like Lu Hsün (1881–1936) used social analysis in directing the battle in the 1920's between a morally motivated naturalism in the arts and what they condemned as "art for art's sake," traditional Chinese art in particular. Elaborate concern for style was interpreted as a denial of the importance of content and a refusal to say what had to be said about the desperate problems of society. Traditional expression in the modern context, it was charged, was socially significant as an effort to establish form as a rival of content, not aesthetically significant as an effort to maintain that traditional form was the best vessel for content. Thinkers and artists must speak out, said the naturalists, and, when thinkers and artists with a traditionalistic bias gently remonstrated that speaking out was vulgar, they were speaking out themselves. In their aesthetic purity they took a stand on the social issues which they disclaimed as proper subjects of their concern.[58]

In believing that cultural traditionalism in modern China had a social purpose, the iconoclasts were surely right. But the fostering of tradition was hardly just a cynical maneuver in social policy. Traditionalism was, indeed, socially useful to nationalists as anti-Communists. It was also, however, psychologically necessary to nationalists as non-Communists, barred by their social requirements from the Communist means of renouncing a moribund system.

Socially, nationalism was a formula for denying that class warfare should exist. Chinese must all have solidarity as Chinese, the nationalist could say, and an affirmation that Chinese culture had a universal claim on Chinese loyalty would be a sign of solidarity. Since iconoclasm was linked with social protest (and who knew it better than the nationalists, emerging as critics of the gentry-literati from treaty-port positions of power, outside the control of the traditional society?), traditionalism, successfully nurtured, would be a palliative.

Their range of intellectual choices having been circumscribed by the social conflict between Chinese and Chinese, non-Communist nationalists had to make the most of traditionalism in the cultural conflict between China and the West. Nationalistic enough to feel alienation from their traditional culture, they had nowhere to go for compensation but socially impossible communism. Therefore, their only way to treat the malaise which alienation engendered was to deny the alienation. They had to try to believe in the value of Chinese tradition, and believe sincerely, not as a tactic. Modern Chinese traditionalists have been, not political manipulators in a smoke-filled room, but self-deluded heirs of a dying culture.

9. Cultural Syncretism No. 4: Communism

A. COMMUNISM'S APPEAL TO THE WRACKED CHINESE INTELLECTUAL

When Chinese nationalists felt the social compulsion to use their traditional legacy for all it was worth, they weakened its claim to value and made Western intellectual alternatives more compelling than ever. But raw intellectual conviction had never been enough to sustain a Western-oriented Chinese iconoclasm, and, if nationalism was unable to cover a ruthless rejection of traditional Chinese values, the step to communism would be taken by those who were socially free to do so. The very Western origin of the Communist call to revolt, instead of putting a psychological hurdle in the way of Chinese acceptance, smoothed the path, for it guaranteed that the pre-Communist West, the West which had impinged on China, was as firmly rejected by its own critics as by the most hidebound Chinese traditionalist. A Chinese who wished to be confident, then, of the equivalence of China and the West need not fall back on a desperate traditionalism, since anti-traditionalism, under Communist aegis, would serve his purpose. Instead of being the laggard, following in Western footsteps, a Communist China, with Russia, could seem at the head of the queue.

B. RESIDUAL TRADITIONALISM

But the Communists found that a complete disavowal of old China was psychologically impossible even for them. Occasional statements attest to this. The poet Ai Ch'ing remarks that the May Fourth movement went too far in destroying the images of the past.[59] The philosopher Ai Ssu-ch'i calls for a search for evidence of dialectical materialism in traditional Chinese philosophy.[60] And the important party statesman Liu Shao-ch'i, writing that the thought of Mao Tsê-tung is the best expression of Marxism applied to a given nation, adds, "It is as Chinese as it is thoroughly Marxist."[61]

Liu seems to say this under an emotional compulsion to assert the tie to history, for the statement does not issue logically from the Communist assumption, affirmed by Liu himself, according to which the "Chinese-ness" of Chinese Communist doctrine, its particularity, is irrelevant as long as its Marxism, its universal truth, is established.

The assumption which Liu states and which makes Mao's "Chinese-ness" irrelevant is the frequent assumption, familiar to us, of those who try to protect a jeopardized history: only value matters. For Liu says: "As regards historical heritages, whether Chinese or foreign, we neither accept nor reject them without discrimination, but accept critically what is valuable and useful and discard what is valueless and inapplicable, basing ourselves on Marxist dialectical materialism and historical materialism."[62] Similarly, a contributor to a symposium at the First All-China Conference of Writers and Artists, in July, 1949, says that Communists respect and humbly welcome the fine, useful legacy of all native and foreign traditions.[63] But here, too, although the specification "useful" supersedes history's commendation of tradition, he goes on wilfully to reintroduce particularism; for any foreign forms, he says, once they have been used to depict Chinese struggles and been accepted by the masses, will have inevitably changed into a Chinese national and people's form of art.[64]

C. CONCESSION TO TRADITIONALISM: RATIONAL TACTIC OR EMOTIONAL COMMITMENT?

Should such concern for the "Chinese spirit" be explained not as a kind of emotional manifestation but simply as a tactic to lure the people, the less-advanced thinkers?

We must note at the outset that concern with what is viable does indeed enter into the Communists' analysis of problems of innovation. Chou Yang, the contributor to the symposium whose words we have already quoted, observes that the old-form drama ("the main pillar of feudal literature") still commands a huge audience. This drama is an important legacy of Chinese national art, he remarks. It is closely linked with the masses, who know it and love it, and yet the old ruling class has used it as a tool to deceive and drug the masses. It is the Communist duty, therefore, both to preserve and to revise it. As the political consciousness of the masses increases, their liking for the old-form drama will diminish, but the watchword in revision must be practicality.[65]

Here, then, is a seemingly clear statement that old forms have *ipso facto* no claim on Chinese, but, for tactical reasons, the Communists should preserve them and sweeten their content. The old-form drama, it is suggested, can be used to give the masses, not the interpretation of history generally contained in it, one "saturated with the ideology of a feudal ruling class," but a new and scientific interpretation.[66]

Elsewhere, the same writer reports that the Liberated Area literature most popular with the masses is that which preserves close ties with national and popular-traditional literature.[67] And Chou En-lai is another who holds that traditional forms have their Communist uses. If any form of the old literature or art has taken root among the masses, it has a claim to survive and deserves Communist reform. Any attempt to eliminate and replace the old forms of expression, he believes, would surely fail.

Chou is not of the opinion that everything in the old literature and art is good and should therefore be preserved. He is far from suggesting that all Chinese should be conservative admirers of the past. But neither does he think that everything in the old literature and art is bad and should therefore be discarded. Such an attitude, he says, is one which totally disregards the Chinese national traditions and the sentiment of the Chinese people and which is therefore wrong. It is wrong in the sense that it would keep the Communists from their primary objective of popularizing literature and art.

Thus, Chou seems to indicate that the Communist concession to traditionalism is after all no more than a conscious stratagem. But he goes on to dispel that illusion. For he holds that unsparing denunciation of the old is wrong also in a second sense: it does not fit in with the Chinese Communists' historical point of view.[68]

Chinese Communist theory, then, is not something to which, intrinsically, the claims of tradition are extraneous. We cannot interpret the Communists' tenderness to the particular claims of the Chinese past simply as an artful manipulation of traditionalistic sentiments, to the end of eventually drawing the people past them to a coldly utilitarian iconoclasm. On the contrary, on Chou En-lai's testimony, Communist theory demands concessions to the Chinese past not in the interests of its success but as a condition of its existence. The theory is concerned with tradition in its own right, not as a sop to the feelings of the backward.

D. CLASS ANALYSIS

Communism in China, like nationalism, permits iconoclasm while sheltering an impulse to reconstitute a tie with the past. But it is the strength of Chinese communism that this impulse is not an embarrassment to it, something either to be smothered or uneasily tolerated, with a nagging sense of inconsistency. As Chou En-lai has indicated, Communist theory does not merely suffer the reconstitution of such a tie; it demands it.

In the Communist explanation of history in terms of class struggle, ideas are represented as ideologies, not compelling acceptance for their abstract value but themselves compelled into existence as expressions of class interest. Chinese communism, then, can authorize the rejection of the content of a historical heritage while it preserves the urge to inherit. *The* Chinese tradition can be scrapped; but a Chinese tradition exists which can be prized.

The antigentry and anti-Confucian T'ai-p'ing rebels (active 1850–64), whom the Communists regard with critical affection as precocious children, but immature, tentatively came to class analysis of Chinese society and introduced the idea, or the feeling, that Confucian tradition was not Chinese tradition but gentry tradition.[69] Now, when Confucian tradition (and so much else which is associated with it) is consigned to a class, then China, a nation, not a class, has no necessary historical commitment to it. China's natural historical commitment is to its own history.

Who is China? The gentry is not China, say the Communists; it is a class, and the gentry culture is a class culture. China is the nongentry, comprising all those whom the Communists loosely designate as "the people," who, by their numerical predominance, can identify China with themselves. The tradition which is China's, which is to be appreciated and not disowned and which iconoclasm cannot touch, is the tradition of the nongentry, one which has always existed but has always been submerged and scorned as long as the social and cultural domination of the gentry persisted. The people's tradition is the Chinese past which can be reclaimed, while what had been represented as the Chinese past (when it was only gentry) is freely disowned. The T'ai-p'ings themselves become for the Communists an element in a living Chinese tradition which supplants the spurious Chinese tradition of the official spokesmen for gentry China.

E. "ICONOCLAST-NATIVIST" SYNTHESIS

Such is the formula which the Communists use to keep history and value together. An alternative Chinese tradition intervenes between the classical Chinese tradition, which they excoriate, and the Western tradition; for the latter would rush in to fill the vacuum left by the removal of traditional (gentry) China, if this "people's China" were not unearthed to fill it. The class analysis which disposes of traditional Chinese values as "gentry" or "feudal" disposes of a prospective successor, Western values, as "bourgeois."

The Communists seek, in effect, to find a synthesis to displace the Western antithesis to the rejected Confucian thesis. China should embrace neither the traditionally celebrated Chinese values nor the modern Western ones in whose name the former were first attacked. Thus, the well-known literary figure Kuo Mo-jo speaks critically both of Chinese feudal scorn for the novel as a literary medium and of bourgeois appreciation of the novel when capitalist civilization entered into it, after the May Fourth movement.[70] And Chou Yang states the Communist theory clearly. Formerly, he says, Chinese considered the forms of the feudal literature as old. This is correct, but to consider those of the bourgeois literature as new is an error. The latter concept originated from an inclination to worship the West blindly, and this inclination, to put it bluntly, was a reflection of semicolonial ideas.[71]

In the fine arts, similarly, there is condemnation of complete traditionalists and complete Westernizers. Traditional Chinese painting is called "*shih-ta-fu*" (i.e., "gentry-literati," the term deriving from the title of certain clerical aides to the aristocracy in antiquity), and associated with the *pa-ku*, or "eight-legged essay," the symbol of all that was stylized and stereotyped in the old imperial China.[72] And the modern movement in Western art is called the product of a capitalist-class ideology, whose basic tenet is that no such thing exists, that fine arts, literature, philosophy, and science are "spiritual" manifestations, having no relation to the material conditions of society.[73]

Mao Tsê-tung has told us (and he was not the first) what Communists think of such a contention. In 1942, in an address which has been accepted as approximately an official directive in aesthetic matters, he declared: "All culture or all present-day literature and art belong to a certain class, to a certain party or to a certain political line. There is no such thing as art for art's sake, or literature and art that lie above class-distinctions or above partisan interests."[74]

It is this approach which enables the Communists to "see through," as they would put it, or be liberated from, as an observer may conclude, both traditional China and the modern West. For it is precisely in the name of the purity of art, says the Communist critic, that Chinese perpetuate traditional Chinese art ("Imitate Sung, Resemble Yuan," he quotes the slogan of this school) or chase after the European moderns.[75]

After the May Fourth movement, "capitalist painters" either displayed an extreme "revive-the-old" spirit, in order to quash the revolutionary movement, or surrendered to the art of capitalist countries (running-dogs of the impressionists?). The reactionary spirit was especially strong in the two decades after the Kuomintang coup of 1927. *Sung Yuan Chia Fa* ("The Rules of the Sung and Yuan Masters") were widely advocated; in Communist opinion, the great monument to this tendency was the Burlington Art Exhibition of 1936, sponsored in London by the Chinese government. As for the surrender to the West, the founding of the T'ien-ma Hui, a society to advocate impressionism, in Shanghai in 1921 is cited. In 1931 a passion for post-impressionists, *fauves*, and surrealists swept the art circles in the big Chinese cities, but this phase petered out when the patriotic fervors of the anti-Japanese resistance movement began to take hold.[76]

As it steers between these two shoals, then, which class analysis helps it to mark out and avoid, what does the Chinese Communist aesthetics value? It has only contempt for the eclectics who use traditional Chinese brush technique for realistic pictures or who try to paint "atmospheric life-movement" pictures in oils. These painters, who imagine that they produce a new art, neither Chinese nor Western, are simply mired down, it is charged, in the futile *t'i-yung* reformism.[77] This is not the compromise which the Communists seek.

What they value in painting is realism.[78] Realism has the virtue, for modern Chinese, of seeming to be a mediant between the idealistic values of classical Chinese painting and the nonrepresentational, architectural values (among others) of the modern movement in the West. Among art forms less ambitious than painting, woodcuts of homely scenes have been given tremendous encouragement, as have simpler peasant arts, techniques called "scissors-cuts" and "knife-cuts," silhouette designs of flowers, birds, insects, people, or scenes from well-known stories. And the judgment passed on them by one Communist critic is this: "The decadence of China's old-style literati or of the so-called 'modernists' has not touched them."[79]

F. CONCLUSION: HISTORY AND VALUE REVISITED

This compulsion to find a middle ground in art between old Cathay and new Paris symbolizes a general compulsion in modern China. The need to find a new tradition at home and a new principle of critical selectivity abroad shows that it costs something for a Chinese to scrap the old tradition at home and invite in the West, costs something to the Chinese Communist as well as to any other. The need for compensation implies an attachment to the old tradition, an attachment on the part of the Communists which is not belied but evinced in their repudiation of that tradition.

The Communists' denial, by class analysis, of the right of the classical tradition to claim their loyalty is perhaps as pious an act toward their ancestors as resolute traditionalism. For, in rejecting the historical claims of a tradition which has lost its value, they release it from death-in-life and release themselves from the pain of contemplating that melancholy condition. The Communist introduces class analysis, not joyously to kill the traditional Chinese culture, but, in the latest of a series of efforts, all of which have previously failed, to exorcise the specter of decay.

Communism in China can hardly be defined as a rarefied intellectual refuge from an introspective despondency; earthy social protest is behind it. But the breakdown of traditional Chinese society is the result of the Western impact, the same Western incursion that ruffled and finally ruined Chinese confidence in China's intellectual self-sufficiency. The question of cultural loyalty comes alive only with the question of social upheaval.

To suggest, therefore, that Chinese communism has a role to play as a device for an intelligentsia in its effort to escape an intellectual dilemma is not to deny but to confirm the fact that Chinese communism has come to the fore because of awesome social pressures. Alienation from Chinese tradition is inseparable from restlessness in Chinese society; and a revolutionary effort to cure the malaise which alienation engenders is the inescapable counterpart, in intellectual history, of the effort, by revolution, to pass through social restlessness to a social equilibrium.

NOTES

1. Cf. the discussions of "prehensions" (whereby everything somehow absorbs what is outside itself into its own being) and of the "fallacy of simple location" (i.e., "the belief that it is adequate, in expressing the spatio-temporal relations of a bit of matter, to state that it is where it is, in a definite finite region of space, and throughout a definite finite duration of time, apart from any essential reference of the relations of that bit of matter to other regions of space and to other durations of time"), in Alfred North Whitehead, *Science and the Modern World* (New York, 1925); *Process and Reality* (New York, 1929); and *Adventures of Ideas* (New York, 1933), *passim.*

2. R. G. Collingwood, *An Autobiography* (Harmondsworth, 1944), p. 25.

3. *Ibid.*, p. 27. Cf. Susanne K. Langer, *Philosophy in a New Key* (New York, 1948), pp. 1–2: "A question is really an ambiguous proposition; the answer is its determination. . . . Therefore a philosophy is characterized more by the *formulation* of its problems than by its solution of them. Its answers establish an edifice of facts; but its questions make the frame in which its picture of facts is plotted. . . . In our questions lie our *principles of analysis* and our answers may express whatever those principles are able to yield."

4. For this distinction between Voltaire and Condorcet as rationalists see Duncan Forbes, "James Mill and India," *Cambridge Journal*, V (October, 1951), 20–21. For Herder see Ernst Cassirer, *The Problem of Knowledge* (New Haven, 1950), pp. 203–4.

5. Collingwood, who defends the concept of the question-answer synthesis as the substance of ideas, also states the complementary concept, the definition of ideas in terms of alternatives. See *An Essay in Philosophical Method* (Oxford, 1933), pp. 106–9, where he states that every philosophical statement is intended to express rejection of some definite proposition which the person making the statement regards as erroneous. A philosophical assertion, whenever it affirms something definite, also denies something definite. "If we cannot understand what the doctrines were which a Plato or a Parmenides meant to deny, it is certain that to just that extent we are unable to grasp what it was that he meant to affirm."

6. Morris Raphael Cohen, *Reason and Nature* (New York, 1931), p. 369.

7. Jean Hippolyte, *Introduction a l'étude de la philosophie de l'histoire de Hegel* (Paris, 1948), p. 20. Cf. Oswald Spengler, *The Decline of the West* (New York, 1934), p. 105: "History [is] not the mere sum of past things without intrinsic order or inner necessity but . . . an organism of rigorous structure and significant articulation, an organism that does not suddenly dissolve into a formless and ambiguous future when it reaches the accidental present of the observer. Cultures are organisms, and world-history their collective biography."

Cf. also Cassirer, *The Myth of the State* (New Haven, 1946), p. 73, where he compares Hegel as a spokesman for traditionalistic historicism and Plato as the founder of the opposing philosophical school in Western thought. Hegel maintains that "the striving for a morality of one's own is futile and by its very nature impossible of attainment. In regard to morality the saying of the wisest men of antiquity is the only true one—to be moral is to live in accordance with the moral traditions of one's own country." Plato's view is that tradition follows rules that it can neither understand nor justify; implicit faith in tradition can never be the standard of a true moral life.

8. Richard McKeon, "Conflicts of Values in a Community of Cultures," *Journal of Philosophy*, XLVII (April 13, 1950), 203.

9. E.g., Ku Yen-wu (1613–82), criticizing the Ming-Ch'ing school of Wang Yang-ming, charges that this school is really a revival of the ill-famed fourth-century *ch'ing-t'an* ("pure-talk") school, but, whereas the original *ch'ing-t'an* was frankly Taoist, their modern descendants masquerade as Confucians. In truth, they far diverge from the thought of Confucius and Mencius. They "dwell upon the surface (lit. 'coarseness') without reaching the essence (lit. 'fineness') [of the sages]." They "never ask about the great principles of the master's sayings on learning and government." See Ku Yen-wu, *Jih-chih Lu* ("Record of Knowledge Day by Day") (Huang Ju-sheng ed., 1834), chap. 7, p. 6*b*.

Cf. Lu Shih-i (1611–72), who also states, in his *Ssŭ-pien Lu* ("Record of Speculation"), that many of his contemporaries in the intellectual world are really like the *ch'ing-t'an* school which had been so injurious in the Chin period. As empty speculators, they were guilty of straying from the path of Confucius, in whose *Lun-yü* Lu discerns a call to practical activity. See *Ssŭ-pien Lu Chi-yao* ("Summary of the *Ssŭ-pien Lu*"), in Chang Pai-hsing (ed.) and Tso Tsung-t'ang (suppl. ed.), *Cheng I T'ang Ch'üan-shu* (1866–87), ts'e 109, chap. 1, pp. 10*b*–11.

10. Hsü Shih-ch'ang, *Ch'ing Ju Hsüeh-an* ("Ch'ing Confucian Scholarship") (Tientsin, 1938), chap. 140, pp. 9*b*–11.

11. Tseng Kuo-fan, *Jih-chi* ("Diary"), in *Tseng Wen-chang Kung Ch'üan-chi* ("Collected Works of Tseng Kuo-fan") (Shanghai, 1917), ts'e 44, chap. 1, p. 6*b*.

12. *Ibid.*

13. *Ibid.*, p. 6.

14. Tseng, *Tseng Hou Jih-chi* ("Marquis Tseng's Diary") (Shanghai, 1881), p. 6*b*.

15. Tseng, *Sheng-chih Hua-hsiang Chi* ("Portrait Record of Philosophical Masters"), in *Tseng Wen-chang Kung Ch'üan-chi*, ts'e 27, chap. 2, p. 3. As examples of works executed in the same eclectic spirit by disciples of Tseng Kuo-fan, see Chu Tz'u-ch'i (1808–82), *Ch'ing-ch'ao Ju Tsung* ("Confucianism during the Ch'ing Dynasty"), discussed in Hsü, *op. cit.*, chap. 171, p. 1*b*, and Ch'en Li (1810–82), *Tung-shu Tu-shu Chi* ("Record of My Reading") (Shanghai, 1898). The latter is particularly close to Tseng's eclecticism, attempting to harmonize the "Sung learning" and the "Han learning" on the grounds that some members of the "Han school" had made metaphysical researches like those of the "Sung school" (though the "Han learning" generally emphasized textual criticism), while Chu Hsi, the leader of the highly metaphysical "Sung school," was the fountainhead of the "Han school's" textual criticism. See chap. 15.

16. This phrase, from the ancient *Mou-kung* ("Art of War") by Sun Tzŭ, was used by Li Hung-chang in a memorial (1863) urging provision for instruction in foreign languages, and used again by Ma Chien-chung in a memorial (1894) recommending the establishment of a translation bureau. See Jen Shih-hsien (Yamazaki Tatsuo, trans.), *Shina Kyoiku Shi* (Tokyo, 1940), XII, 95–96. Hellmut Wilhelm has pointed out in "The Problem of Within and Without, a Confucian Attempt in Syncretism," *Journal of the History of Ideas*, XII (January, 1951), 50, that everyone in this group of innovators conceived of Westernization as a matter of national defense.

For a translation of statements by representative Confucian Westernizers—Lin Tse-hsü, Hsü Chi-yü, Tseng Kuo-fan, Hsüeh Fu-ch'eng, *et al.*—see Fairbank, Têng, and Sun, *China's Response to the West* (in press).

17. Chang Chih-tung, *Ch'üan-hsüeh P'ien*, translated (rather, paraphrased) by Samuel I. Woodbridge under the title, *China's Only Hope* (New York, 1900), p. 63: "In order to render China powerful, and at the same time preserve our own institutions, it is absolutely necessary that we should utilize western knowledge. But unless Chinese learning is made the basis of education, and a Chinese direction given to thought, the strong will become anarchists, and the weak, slaves."

Ibid., pp. 137–38: "To sum up: Chinese learning is moral, Western learning is practical. Chinese learning concerns itself with moral conduct, Western learning, with the affairs of the world. . . . If the Chinese heart throbs in unison with the heart of the sages, expressing the truth in irreprovable conduct, in filial piety, brotherly love, honesty, integrity, virtue; if government is loyalty and protection, then let government make use of foreign machinery and the railway from morning to night, and nothing untowards will befall the disciples of Confucius."

18. Michael Oakeshott, *Experience and Its Modes* (Cambridge, 1933), p. 98.

19. *Ibid.*, p. 41.

20. Jen, *op. cit.*, p. 107.

21. Ch'en Teng-yüan, "Hsi-hsüeh Lai Hua Shih Kuo-jen Che Wu-tuan T'ai-tu" ("Arbitrary Chinese Attitudes at the Time of the Coming of Western Knowledge to China"), *Tung-fang Tsa-chih*, XXVII, No. 8 (April, 1930), 61.

22. I have given a general account of the sources, content, and implications of the *chin-wen* reformist doctrine in an article, "The Breakdown of Confucianism: Liang Ch'i-ch'ao before Exile—1873–1898," *Journal of the History of Ideas*, XI (October, 1950), 448–85; and in a book *Liang Ch'i-ch'ao and the Mind of Modern China* (Cambridge, 1953).

23. In the nineteenth century, Protestant missionaries were much more active than Catholic missionaries in the field of secular Western education. See Kenneth Scott Latourette, *A History of Christian Missions in China* (New York, 1929), p. 478.

24. The collaboration of missionaries with reformers is well known—e.g., the Welsh missionary Timothy Richard, after reading one of K'ang Yu-wei's memorials on the subject of modernization, wrote him a letter which expressed his surprise that K'ang had arrived at Richard's conclusions, remarked that their aims seemed to be the same, and suggested consultations. A meeting of K'ang and Richard took place in Peking, and K'ang's disciple, Liang Ch'i-ch'ao, became Richard's Chinese secretary soon after. See Ch'en Kung-lu, *Chung-kuo Chin-tai Shih* ("History of Modern China") (Shanghai, 1935), pp. 439–40.

Reformers and official Westernizers met on the common ground of *tzu-ch'iang* ("self-strengthening"). This phrase, which appears in texts of official recommendations for Westernization at least as early as 1863, in Li Hung-chang's memorial recommending the study of foreign languages, was a favorite phrase of the reformers, whose principal organizations, active in Peking and Shanghai in 1895–96 were called the Ch'iang-hsüeh Hui ("Society for the Study of Strengthening"). For this aspect of Li's memorial see Shu Hsin-ch'eng, *Chin-tai Chung-kuo Chiao-yü Ssu-hsiang Shih* ("History of Modern Chinese Educational Thought") (Shanghai, 1929), pp. 25–26.

25. For a summary of the *Ta-t'ung Shu*, K'ang's most explicit effort to outline his program for action and to make Confucius its patron, see Sakano Nagahachi, "K'ang

Yu-wei No Taido Shisō" ("K'ang Yu-wei's Idea of the 'Great Harmony' ") in Niida Noboru (ed.), *Kindai Chūgoku no Jukyō Hihan* ("A Criticism of Modern Chinese Confucianism") (Tokyo, 1948), pp. 47–59.

26. Kuo Chan-po, *Chin Wu-shih Nien Chung-kuo Ssu-hsiang Shih* ("History of Chinese Thought in the Last Fifty Years") (Shanghai, 1926), p. 35.

27. Liang Ch'i-ch'ao, "Nan-hai K'ang Hsien-sheng Chuan" ("Biography of Mr. Kang Yu-wei"), *Yin-ping Shih Wen-chi* ("Collected Essays of the Ice-Drinkers' Studio") (Shanghai, 1925), chap. 39, p. 64*b*.

28. For this identification of Luther with freedom of thought see Liang, "Lun Hsüeh-shu Chih Shih-li Tso-yu Shih-chieh" ("On the Power of Learning To Control the World"), *Yin-ping Shih Wen-chi*, chap. 6, pp. 38–39*b*, and elsewhere. Liang wrote of Luther in this fashion after he abandoned the *chin-wen* school's practice of invoking the Classics to justify innovation.

29. An extended description and analysis of the iconoclasm which succeeded *chin-wen* Confucianism in Liang's writings during the first decade of the twentieth century appears in my *Liang Ch'i-ch'ao and the Mind of Modern China.*

30. See Ch'i Ssu-ho, "Professor Hung on the Ch'un-ch'iu," *Yenching Journal of Social Studies*, I, No. 1 (June, 1938), 49–71, esp. pp. 55–66.

31. See Liang, "Ch'ing-tai Hsüeh-shu Kai-lun" ("A Summary of Ch'ing Scholarship"), *Yin-ping Shih Ho-chi—Ch'üan-chi* (Shanghai, 1936), chap. 9, pp. 34, 63, where he says that in his thirtieth year he ceased discussion of the "false classics."

32. Wei Ying-ch'i, *Chung-kuo Shih-hsüeh Shih* ("History of Chinese Historiography") (Shanghai, 1941), p. 243.

33. E.g., Sun Yat-sen's manifesto at Nanking on January 5, 1912, after he had been named by revolutionaries the first president of the Chinese Republic: "Hitherto irremediable suppression of the individual qualities and the natural aspirations of the people having arrested the intellectual, moral, and material development of China, the aid of revolution was invoked to extirpate the primary cause. . . . Dominated by ignorance and selfishness, the Manchus closed the land to the outer world and plunged the Chinese into a state of benighted mentality calculated to operate inversely to their natural talents." See Benoy Kumar Sarkar, *The Sociology of Races, Cultures, and Human Progress* (Calcutta, 1939), pp. 177–78.

34. Kuo, *op. cit.*, pp. 64–65.

35. Henri Van Boven, *Histoire de la littérature chinoise moderne* (Peiping, 1946), p. 11.

36. Roswell S. Britton, *The Chinese Periodical Press, 1800–1912* (Shanghai, 1933), p. 122.

37. S. M. Tretiakov (ed.), *A Chinese Testament, the Autobiography of Tan Shih-hua* (New York, 1934), p. 83.

38. Ichifuku Chuzō, "Giwaken No Seikaku" ("The Characteristics of the *I-ho T'uan*"), *Kindai Chūkoku Kenkyū*, p. 252.

39. Chang Ping-lin, for example, edited a compilation of works by the anti-Manchu scholar Wang Fu-chih (1619–92). Wang did, indeed, denounce the Manchus fiercely, but his diatribes were directed against the threat of barbarism to Chinese culture, not the threat of invaders to the state. Note the tone of these extracts from his *Ch'un-ch'iu Chia-shuo* (1646), wherein it is implied (allegorically) that the Manchus are so thoroughly uncivilized that the Chinese need not abide by civilized rules in their dealings with them:

"Any strife with the barbarians the Middle Kingdom should not call a war. . . . For to annihilate them is not cruel, to deceive them is not unfaithful, to occupy their territory and confiscate their property is not unjust. . . .

"To annihilate them and thereby safeguard our people is called benevolent, to deceive them and thereby do to them what they must dislike is called faithful, to occupy their territory and thereby transform their customs by virtue of our letters and morals as well as to confiscate their property and thereby increase the provisions of our own people is called righteous." See *Ch'uan-shan I-shu* ("Remaining Works of Wang Fu-chih") (Shanghai, 1933), ts'e 29, chap. 3, pp. 16*b*–17.

In the text Wang specifically distinguishes between strife among the various states of the empire (hence, civilized states) and strife between a Chinese state and barbarians. Thus, there is a cultural, not a political, test as to whether strife is pursued under rules of honor or ruthlessly.

40. For a documented account of social-Darwinism in early Chinese nationalism see my *Liang Ch'i-ch'ao and the Mind of Modern China.*

41. Ts'ai Shang-ssŭ, *Chung-kuo Ch'uan-t'ung Ssu-hsiang Tsung P'i-p'an* ("General Criticism of Traditional Chinese Thought") (Shanghai, 1949), pp. 13–14.

42. But not meaningless just because it does not apply in actual individual instances. Cf. Ernst Cassirer, "Einstein's Theory of Relativity Considered from the Epistemological Standpoint," supplement to *Substance and Function* (Chicago, 1923), p. 419: "The philosopher . . . is ever again brought to the fact that there are ultimate ideal determinations without which the concrete cannot be considered and made intelligible."

43. Henri Bernard-Maitre, *Sagesse chinoise et philosophie chrétienne* (Paris, 1935), p. 260.

44. Liang, "Ta Chung-hua Fa-k'an-tz'ŭ" ("Foreword to *Ta Chung-hua*"), *Yin-ping Shih Ho-chi—Wen-chi*, chap. 12, pp. 33, 83–84.

45. Hsiao Kung-ch'uan, *Chung-kuo Cheng-shih Ssu-hsiang Shih* ("History of Chinese Political Thought") (Shanghai, 1946), II, 424.

46. Robert K. Sakai, "Ts'ai Yüan-p'ei as a Synthesizer of Western and Chinese Thought," *Papers on China* (Harvard University), III (May, 1949), 180.

47. *Ibid.*

48. *Ibid.*, pp. 182–83.

49. Kuo, *op. cit.*, p. 61. Ya-tung T'u-shu-kuan (publ.), *K'o-hsüeh Yü Jen-sheng-kuan* ("Science and the Philosophy of Life—a Symposium") (2 vols.; Shanghai, 1923), and Yang Ming-chai, *P'ing Chung-Hsi Wen-hua Kuan* ("A Critique of Views on Chinese and Western Civilizations") (Peking, 1924), probably provide the best introduction to the vast literature in this vein.

50. Ch'in Chung-wen, *Chung-kuo Hui-hua-hsüeh Shih* ("History of Chinese Painting") (Peiping, 1934), p. 188.

51. Judith Burling and Arthur Hart, "Contemporary Chinese Painting," *Magazine of Art*, XLIII, No. 6 (October, 1949), 218.

52. Edward Sapir, "Culture, Genuine and Spurious," in David G. Mandelbaum (ed.), *Selected Writings of Edward Sapir in Language, Culture, and Personality* (Berkeley and Los Angeles, 1949), p. 321.

53. The definition of eclecticism in Theodore Meyer Greene, *The Arts and the Art of Criticism* (Princeton, 1947), p. 383, applies: "Eclecticism in the bad sense may be defined as the arbitrary juxtaposition of antipathetic stylistic factors or, alternatively, as the use in a single work of art of unassimilated aspects of sharply divergent styles."

54. Burling and Hart, *op. cit.*, p. 218.
55. Sapir, *op. cit.*, p. 321.
56. Benjamin I. Schwartz, *Chinese Communism and the Rise of Mao* (Cambridge, 1951), pp. 17–18. *Hsin Ch'ing-nien* and *Hsin Ch'ao* were periodicals first appearing in 1915 and 1919, respectively. The Hsin Ch'ao Society, which sponsored the periodical of that name, was founded in December, 1918.
57. Fukuda Masazo, "Shakai Bunka Hen (Kyoiku)" ("Section on Society and Culture—Education"), in Hideshima Tatsuo (ed.), *Gendai Shina Kōza* ("Lectures on Modern China") (Shanghai, 1939), VI, 4.
58. Cf. Lu Hsun, "The Diary of a Madman," in Wang Chi-chen (trans.), *Ah Q and Others* (New York, 1941), pp. 205–19, a condemnation, in the form of tragic irony, of the classical tradition as a scourge of society. The tradition's claims to a rarefied philosophical value are denounced as pretense, as a camouflage for vicious social control. "Twenty years ago I trampled the daily account book [Wang: i.e., the Classics, characterized by critics as of no more value and no more edifying than the account book kept by shopkeepers] of Mr. Hoary Tradition under my feet, a deed which he greatly resented. . . . I thought I had read somewhere that man-eating was a common practice in ancient times, but I was not sure. I decided to look it up in my history. This history contained no dates, but over every page was scrawled the words, 'Benevolence and Righteousness.' It was not until I had read half through the night (I could not sleep anyway) that I began to make out the words hidden between the lines and to discover that the book was nothing but a record of man-eating!" (pp. 207–9).
59. Robert Payne, *China Awake* (New York, 1947), p. 378.
60. Benjamin Schwartz, "Marx and Lenin in China," *Far Eastern Survey*, XVIII, No. 15 (July 27, 1949), 178.
61. Liu Shao-chi, *On the Party* (Peking, 1950), p. 31.
62. *Ibid.*, p. 29.
63. Chou Yang, "The People's New Literature," in *The People's New Literature* (Peking, 1950), p. 105.
64. *Ibid.*, pp. 105–6.
65. *Ibid.*, pp. 115–16.
66. *Ibid.*, pp. 116–17.
67. *Ibid.*, p. 103.
68. Chou En-lai, "The People's Liberation War and Problems in Literature and Art," in *The People's New Literature*, pp. 32–34.
69. Communist interest in the T'ai-p'ing Rebellion has been enormous. There has been a great output of Communist literature on the subject, particularly in 1950, the centenary year. A cursory study of modern Chinese intellectual history, but one which gives the quintessence of Communist opinion, describes the T'ai-p'ing Rebellion as *k'ung-hsiang* ("fantasy") socialism. See Fei Min, *Chung-kuo Chin-tai Ssu-hsiang Fa-chan Chien-shih* ("Brief History of the Development of Modern Chinese Thought") (Shanghai, 1949), p. 12.
70. Kuo Mo-jo, "Culture chinoise et occident," *Démocratie nouvelle*, V, No. 2 (February, 1951), 69.
71. Chou Yang, *op. cit.*, pp. 104–5.
72. Li Ch'ang-chih, *Chung-kuo Hua-lun T'i-hsi Chi Ch'i P'i-p'ing* ("Chinese Systems of Aesthetics and a Criticism of Them") (Chungking, 1944), pp. 9–13.

73. Wen Chao-t'ung, *Hsin Chung-kuo Ti Hsin Mei-shu* ("The New Fine Arts of the New China) (Shanghai, 1950), pp. 1–3.

74. Mao Tsê-tung, *Problems of Art and Literature* (New York, 1950), p. 32.

75. Wen, *op. cit.*, p. 1.

76. *Ibid.*, pp. 11–12.

77. *Ibid.*, p. 2.

78. Cf. the description of an exhibition of proletarian paintings in Peking in 1949 in Derk Bodde, *Peking Diary* (New York, 1950), p. 182.

79. "Scissors-Cuts and Knife-Cuts," *People's China*, III, No. 6 (March 16, 1951), 26.

PLATE II

Courtesy of the Metropolitan Museum of Art

CHINA'S EARLIEST DISTINCT SYMBOLISM

Bronze sacrificial vessel of the early Chou (type *p'ou*) showing "*T'ao-t'ieh*" (on lower half) formed by two confronted masks to make a single one.

PLATE III

HAN COSMIC SYMBOLISM

A "TLV" mirror of the first century A.D. showing the characteristic angular markings, the twelve zodiac symbols around the inner square, and the Four Spirits, which were originally silvered to make them stand out.

PLATE IV

THE FOUR SPIRITS

The Black Warrior (tortoise and snake) of the north, the Azure Dragon of the east, the Red Bird of the south, and the White Tiger of the west, on a silver-backed mirror of the late T'ang.

PLATE V

Courtesy of the University Museum, Philadelphia

An Imperial Flying Dragon

An aggressive *ying lung* on a medallion from the robe of a Ming emperor

PLATE VI

Courtesy of the Seattle Art Museum

T'ANG MARRIAGE SYMBOLS

A T'ang mirror showing a small cosmic diagram in the center, ancient auspicious symbols in the inner ring, and the Twelve Animals of the Zodiac in pairs.

PLATE VII

More T'ang Marriage Symbols

A T'ang mirror with paired magpies carrying symbolic cords, balanced by the moo disk to represent *yin* opposed to a *yang* dragon.

PLATE VIII

ourtesy of the University Museum, Philadelphia

A MING FESTIVAL BADGE

A Ming princess' phoenix badge, with tigers, artemisia leaves, and the Five Poisons, added as symbols for the Dragon Boat Festival.

PLATE IX

Some Late Ch'ing Pun Symbols

A nineteenth-century mandarin square for a first-rank official, showing the five red bats in the clouds, the halberds in a vase, and flower rebuses, as well as the crane—an old symbol of longevity.

TYPES OF SYMBOLS IN CHINESE ART

SCHUYLER CAMMANN

1. *Introduction*

THE WORD "symbol" as used here refers primarily to pictorial forms that were designed to express ideas. Taken in groups, these representations tended to form a kind of language, much as the Chinese characters—which in themselves were symbols of a slightly different type—made up the written language of China and her neighbors. By using the appropriate pictures or images, even the illiterate could express their hopes and beliefs or convey good wishes to each other. Another correspondence between the language of symbols and China's written language is that many symbols became obsolete in time, or at least underwent changes in meaning at later periods, just as the characters did. Therefore, a great many that were easily understood in their own day are extremely difficult to translate now.

A few of the early symbols expressed their ideas so simply and clearly, such as the many-seeded pomegranate as an emblem of fertility, that their meanings could be obvious to anyone even in another civilization. However, it is risky to accept what may seem to be the obvious meaning as the traditional one. Like the Chinese characters again, the symbols seldom had single, constant meanings, and they were sometimes borrowed to convey entirely different thoughts.

Not only can one symbol refer to different things in different localities or at different periods, but it may convey various ideas to a number of people seeing it at the same time. This is because a symbol evokes a thought, and the basis for that thought has to be in the mind first. Thus, depending on their backgrounds, environments, or degrees of sophistication, several people might read into a single symbol a number of ideas of more or less complexity. The open pomegranate, for example, might connote "many children" to most viewers, but to some Chinese it suggests just an abundance—of joy, of money, or even of wisdom, depending on the viewer's temperament. For this reason we have tried to choose fairly simple examples to illustrate the types of symbols discussed below, ones that would not be susceptible of too many interpretations at one time.

Even in the case of symbols that had only one clear intention, while occasionally the intended idea may still be easily grasped by a modern person with some knowledge of Asiatic culture, the situation is seldom so simple. Usually the symbol pictures were very topical or were based on allusions long since forgotten, in which case, even though they might have been understood by practically anyone at the time of depiction, they could no longer be recognized without special knowledge of the cultural background of the times when they were used. Even a Chinese could not interpret such symbols correctly today unless he was particularly steeped in the ancient culture, just as modern Chinese cannot read archaic characters without long training.

For these reasons it is necessary to be as wary of modern Chinese explanations for symbols as of the attempts to explain them made by most Western writers on Chinese art. In both cases the interpretations tend to be merely late rationalizations; but the former are especially misleading because most Occidentals uncritically assume that "any Chinese would know his own culture." It is too frequently forgotten that only extreme specialists in European art can possibly know the meanings of certain pun symbols or allegories found in European paintings of as recent a period as the seventeenth century and that there were styles and fads in Chinese art and thought which caused various symbols to fall out of favor just as there were in our Western tradition.

The rationalizing of Chinese symbols began a long time ago. Some of the ancient Chinese symbols were "explained" in medieval Chinese books, particularly in the works of the all-too-imaginative Sung and early Ming antiquarians. Since the original meanings had long since been lost, the later writers generally felt compelled to read into the old symbols what they personally thought they must have meant, with the result that the symbols were inevitably interpreted in terms of later concepts.

Such "explanations" may be of some help for determining what certain symbols meant to the people of a later period, when they reappeared in decoration due to an antiquarian revival; but it would be foolish to accept them uncritically as being valid for an earlier time. However, later Chinese scholars have almost invariably passed on, without question, the false rationalizations of their predecessors, out of reverence for the opinions of past writers, no matter how irresponsible such writers might have been. From the later Chinese scholars, then, these misconceptions have passed into the Western literature on Chinese art and folklore. That is why it is necessary to attempt a new and more thorough study of Chinese symbols.

The only truly reliable way to find out what one of the more difficult symbols originally meant is to locate some reference to it in the writings of the time when it was current. This is often impossible, as the symbols and their meanings were usually taken for granted in their own time. But, when a specific remark cannot be found, some chance allusion to a contemporary belief or a popular folk tale of the period may supply a clue which can ultimately lead to the solution; or the mention of an associated symbol may suggest a tentative interpretation by analogy which can later be checked.

The meanings of certain symbols may conveniently turn up even in such formal works as the dynastic histories—those of the Former Han and the Liu Sung dynasties being especially rewarding. They may be found there under such disparate headings as "Astronomy," "Clothing," or "Music." Equally profitable for the symbol-seeker are popular works on philosophy or religion which expressed ideas in current terms, or the local gazeteers and travel memoirs written by scholars or officials who frequently referred, in passing, to customs and beliefs which they had personally observed. From such sources certain key symbols can be traced from period to period. In following their development, it can often be seen that a given Chinese symbol may have begun with deep religious or philosophical connotations, then passed over into the realm of magic and superstition to serve as a lucky charm, finally degenerating into a mere ornament for meaningless decoration.[1]

The sections that follow will present nine groups of symbols which can be considered characteristic of the major periods of Chinese culture. In discussing as far as possible how they were used, what they seem to have meant, and why they were probably chosen, we may find that they often present valuable clues to the currents of thought in their time. For this reason alone, the development of graphic symbols cannot be neglected in any consideration of the history of Chinese thought.

A. THE "T'AO-T'IEH" MASK AND OTHER EARLY CHINESE SYMBOLS

The "earliest Chinese symbols," if they were symbols at all, are found in the decoration on the Neolithic painted pottery discovered by Anderson and others in northwestern China.[2] The handsome decorative forms on these pots are so highly stylized that one can do little more than guess at possible hidden figures and abstract meanings. But such guesswork can seldom be more than an exercise in imagination.[3]

Even in the case of the early historic period, there seems to be little chance of our ever discovering beyond question the meanings of the principal motifs that were displayed on the ritual bronzes and other relics of the Shang and Chou dynasties, such as can be seen in many of our American museums. The inscriptions on the famous oracle bones seem to have been primarily concerned with fairly practical matters such as questions concerning war and the hunt; and, with the Burning of the Books in 213 B.C., most of the records that might have shed some light on the subject of religion and rites were completely destroyed.

One motif occurs again and again, especially on the bronze sacrificial vessels, and by its very repetition has tantalized every student who has ventured into the field of ancient Chinese art. This is a monster mask, shown full face, composed of prominent features from several large animals, such as the teeth of a tiger, the ears of an ox, and the horns of a ram. The combinations often differed from one example to another, although the general effect was about the same. Sometimes it has short bandy legs with claws extending down on either side of the mouth. Frequently the mask is formed of two faces in profile, joining at the nose to form a single one.[4]

People of later ages called this figure the "*T'ao-t'ieh*" 饕餮 or "Glutton," because the conventional absence of a lower jaw gave the effect of a wide-open mouth with infinite capacity for swallowing. The Sung antiquarians went even further, explaining that the monster was figured on vessels for food and wine as a warning against overindulgence. The latter is a fine example of a later rationalization. Even if overindulgence was considered a vice in the earliest period of Chinese history—which is by no means certain—it would have been most impolite to convey a pointed warning against it to the gods or spirits who were being propitiated by the sacrifices contained in the vessels decorated with this monster. Furthermore, there is much indirect evidence to suggest that the monster was intended to symbolize much more than that.

The way in which the monster was displayed might help to tell how it was regarded in its time. The fierce mask, with its teeth and claws prominently displayed, is usually shown looming, half-formed, through scroll patterns which a continuing Chinese tradition has interpreted as representing thunderclouds. In later, less rigidly conventionalized renderings, the monster is depicted as either giving forth or devouring birds, animals, plants, or men, which suggests a great power capable of creating or destroying living things.

In view of its frightening aspect, its location among the clouds, and its terrific powers, one might think that the monster might have been conceived to symbolize a supreme sky deity. As possible supports to this supposition, the men of Shang called their principal god, or deified ancestor, "the Ruler Above" (*Shang Ti*), while the Chou people who succeeded them, sometime around 1027 B.C., referred to theirs simply as "the Sky" (*T'ien*); and the somewhat modernized form of the ancient

"*T'ao-t'ieh*" mask which still survives in the highly conservative religious art of Tibet is explained as representing a supreme sky-god.[5]

However, tradition says that the Chinese were not accustomed to representing their gods until the coming of Buddhism introduced the use of images, sometime after the beginning of the Christian Era. Therefore, it does not seem likely that the monster itself was considered as an idealized portrait of one of their early deities. More likely it was simply an attempt to represent the awesome power of their god or their deified ancestor or of the mysterious sky.

If the "*T'ao-t'ieh*" actually was such a symbol of divine power, then the form in which two faces combine to make a single one might have represented the idea of two great forces in nature combining to make one, that concept of Unity in Duality which so pervades later Chinese religion and thought. In later times this idea was more simply represented by a sacred diagram called the *T'ai-chi t'u*, formed by two interlocking comma-shaped figures, one red and one black, symbolizing the *yang* and the *yin* principles inherent in all of life and nature.

Further clues to early Chinese attitudes might be revealed by investigating some other commonly used motives in the arts of the Shang and early Chou, notably the snake and the cicada. The Chinese of that time had doubtless noticed that a dusty and bedraggled snake could shed its skin to become a sleek and brightly colored, new-looking creature, suggesting a renewal of youth, while the cicada was probably already associated with immortality—as it was in later times—because of its strange life-cycle, in the course of which it emerges from underground life as a grub and then finally breaks out from an earthbound shell to fly away into the air. It would seem likely that the Chinese of the Shang and early periods probably regarded actual snakes and cicidas as potent spirits because they possessed much-desired powers which man would crave to have for himself and that they depicted them as such. However, the men of that time might also have represented them on their sacrificial bronzes as symbols of the renewed life and immortality which were also associated with their deified ancestor and their god.[6] In the absence of more concrete evidence we can only speculate.

B. COSMIC SYMBOLS

Although the exact meanings originally ascribed to the early Chinese symbols are still a matter of speculation, arriving at the next period we begin to walk on firmer ground, since we have literary evidence to help shed light on contemporary symbolism.

The earliest of the Chinese cosmic symbols that can be easily deciphered is a group known as the *Pa kua*, or "Eight Trigrams." This consisted of a set of eight rectangular figures, each composed of three lines, whole or split in two, to make eight separate combinations. They symbolized the basic elements in nature—earth and sky, swamps and mountains, wind and thunder, water and fire—as well as the Eight Directions: the four cardinal points with the intermediate ones. Their origin is ascribed to remote antiquity, and they were evidently known in Chou times. At that period an elaborate system of divination was developed out of these symbols. By using six lines instead of three, the ancient Chinese devised a system of sixty-four hexagrams. Fortunes were then told, and prophecies made, by casting down sets of sticks and observing the patterns into which they fell, to see which of the hexagrams the resulting combinations most resembled.

After the T'ang dynasty the Eight Trigrams were usually displayed in a circle around the interlocked symbols of the *yin* and *yang* (the *T'ai-chi t'u*), in order to suggest the origin of all matter from the interaction of the two fundamental principles, which together made up the Unity in Duality, or the Great Absolute. In this later period sometimes only four of them were used to symbolize the Four Directions of space.

Beginning with this set of eight simple figures—few symbols could be any simpler than the trigrams—there gradually arose a whole series of cosmic symbols portraying in far more graphic form the principal elements in nature and the directions of space.

This type of symbolism reached its height in the long period which began about the fourth century B.C., toward the end of the Chou, and continued on through the Han dynasty. This seems to have been an age of magic, to judge from the accounts of the efforts made by the first emperor of the Ch'in to learn the secrets of immortality and from the story of Wang Mang's unsuccessful attempt to avert assassination, as his empire crumbled around him, by relying on an instrument of divination. At this time we begin to find clearly recognizable cosmograms or representations of the universe and its phenomena. The problem is: Were these indeed symbols in the sense of pictures of ideas, or were they considered as actual little universes, through which could be performed magic and wonder-working that might affect the greater universe? From what we know of the temper of the times, the latter would seem to have been the case.

Before going on to discuss some of these symbols in detail, we should pause to consider one more problem: Was this type of symbolism, and the beliefs that went with it, entirely indigenous, or was it, at least in part, the result of foreign influences? The magic arts had been highly developed in the Near East in connection with astronomy, particularly in Chaldea, for centuries before this time, and—as Maspero and other writers have pointed out—foreign elements including "Iranian" notions of astronomy were coming into Chinese civilization about the end of the Chou dynasty.[7] There seems to be plenty of evidence that the state of Ch'in, whose ruler established the first empire in 221 B.C., had been borrowing important cultural traits from western Asia considerably before that date.[8]

One of the indigenous elements seems to have been the concept of a cosmic house, the *Ming T'ang*. This building had a square plan "to resemble the earth" and was covered by a circular roof "to resemble the sky." Meanwhile, other features reflected calendrical beliefs—such as twelve rooms for the twelve months of the year—so that the whole structure was apparently a vast space-and-time diagram, reflecting contemporary beliefs.[9] In late Chou times, at least, this must have been unquestionably more than a symbol. To the people of that time it was still "like the universe," partaking of the same qualities; and, even though it was seen as distinct, it was undoubtedly thought to be intimately related to the greater universe. Only in late revivals of the *Ming T'ang*, such as occurred in the late seventh century under the T'ang, would it have been seen by the sophisticated courtiers that it was a *symbol* of the universe, having no real connection, but set up to designate the greater entity. Only then could we speak of it as a pure symbol.

Regardless of the precise attitude toward them, the representations of the universe in microcosm that were made at this period are important because of what they can tell us about the conceptions of the world at that time. Perhaps the most detailed examples available to us are the diagrams on the backs of the Han bronze mirrors of the so-called "TLV" type, which reached their highest development during the reign of Wang Mang in the first quarter of the first century A.D.[10]

The patterns on these mirrors show that the earth was conceived as a large square form, with the center set off within a smaller square, the latter representing China, "the Middle Kingdom" at the center of the world. The four corners of the large square were further cut off by right angles (the *V*'s of the pattern), so as to leave four rectangular fields extending out in the four directions. Lest there be any doubt of this, each of these fields was labeled by the presence of one of the Four Spirits: south, which was always shown uppermost on the old Chinese maps and plans, was represented by the Scarlet Bird, west by the White

Tiger, east by the Azure Dragon, and north by the Black Tortoise coupled with a snake. To the old Chinese these had the same significance as the letters *N*, *S*, *E*, and *W* on our Western maps. The four rectangular arms which stretched out from the central square, separated from it by a figurative wall with gates (the boundary of the inner square with its projection *T*'s), were apparently intended to represent the "Four Seas" surrounding China. This term did not refer to bodies of water but was a figurative expression referring to the lands of the barbarians beyond the gates of the civilized Middle Kingdom. This concept is further emphasized on some mirrors by placing small figures of spirit-men or "barbarians," along with strange birds and animals, in the four outer fields. The sky was symbolized by a circular rim which fitted down over the great square of the earth, cutting off its outer corners, and the sun and moon were indicated by disks containing, respectively, the three-legged sunbird and the four-legged toad of the moon. These very numbers were important because the sun was a prime exponent of the *yang* principle, and three was a *yang* number, while the moon was the chief representative of the *yin* principle, and four was a *yin* number.

The *yin* and *yang* concept also was intimately related to the Four Directions as symbolized by the Four Spirits. South was considered as the region of pure *yang*, represented by the resplendent Firebird, while north was thought to harbor pure *yin*, in the realm of the neutral and moisture-loving tortoise; east was considered as having more *yang* than *yin*, and west more *yin* than *yang;* while the center—emphasized on these mirrors by a high, prominent boss—marked the axis of balance between the two vital forces.

The axis of the universe, located at the center of the world, was also considered as the source of the divine energy which came down from Heaven through the gate in the middle of the sky.[11] Countless mirror inscriptions, and references in contemporary metaphysical writings such as *Chuang Tzŭ* and the *Tao-tê-ching*, allude in rather mysterious terms to "attaining the center," which was apparently one of the aims in early Taoist practices.[12] Thus, it is not surprising to find the bosses on these cosmic mirrors so prominently displayed as to dominate the rest of the pattern. Furthermore, a popular game of the time, *liu-po* 六博, which was played on a board laid out with a square on a cross on a larger square, like the diagram of the earth on the mirror pattern, apparently had as its goal the placing of a player's "man" in the center of the board —that is to say, at the center of the universe. Even the games expressed the deep feeling of the times regarding the possibility of acquiring harmony, integration, and even occult powers by somehow establishing one's self at the center of one's individual universe, where one would be equally responsive to both *yin* and *yang* and under the direct influence of Heaven.[13]

Lastly, the element of time was expressed on these mirrors, and on other cosmic symbols of that period, by a set of twelve archaic characters, later known as the "Twelve Branches," which were used to refer to the twelve two-hour periods in each day as well as to designate successive years in the sixty-year cycle. These characters were often arranged around the central square of the mirror, which was intended to represent China, as though symbolizing the science and order to be found within the cultured precincts of the "Middle Kingdom," as opposed to the lands of the wild men and strange beasts beyond the four gates.

The basic elements of the Han cosmic mirror pattern reappeared on a group of mirrors from the Sui and early T'ang periods (*ca.* 590–650). These had the small central square in the middle of a cross, set off by the *V*'s, and the four projecting arms were generally figured with somewhat larger pictures of the Four Spirits.[14] The Twelve Branches, which had been represented on the Han mirrors by archaic characters around the inner square, were now frequently replaced by their alternates, the Twelve Animals of the Asiatic Zodiac, arranged in an outer ring of the design.

These twelve animals are found—with minor variations—all across Asia, from China to Turkey. Chavannes, who wrote about them at some length, thought that they had been borrowed by the Chinese from some Turkic people farther to the west.[15] However, Léopold de Saussure presented ample evidence to show that they could have sprung from indigenous Chinese animal symbolism.[16] The case of the Four Spirits is by no means so clear cut, and there is still some question about a possible foreign origin. The latter are also associated with the Four Elements: Fire, Water, Wood, and Metal, and this type of symbolism is very characteristic of the ancient Near East.

One especially interesting cosmic mirror pattern of the middle T'ang has the Four Directions symbolized by the Four Elements, instead of the Four Spirits.[17] North is indicated by a pool of water, east by a tree (for wood), south by flames of fire, and west by a tripod vessel of metal. The change from animals to element symbols was probably caused by the current interest in alchemy.

Other middle T'ang mirrors had cosmic patterns of great complexity, drawing from the entire repertoire of Chinese symbolism since before the Han. Some of the most elaborate examples had concentric zones or bands of symbols, with the Four Spirits at the center, followed by the Eight Trigrams, the Twelve Animals of the Zodiac, and the Twenty-eight Constellations—shown in the form of dotted star figures.

It would seem that the strong revival of ordered, cosmic patterns on the Sui and early-to-middle T'ang mirrors, following a series of badly composed and disordered patterns made during the previous Six Dynasties period, may have been an expression of a basic current in contemporary thought. We know from other sources that the people of that time felt a deep sense of relief and renewed assurance, with the knowledge that China was once again reunited and stable after the centuries of civil strife and foreign invasions that had succeeded the fall of the Han.

C. IMPERIAL SYMBOLS

Foremost among the emblems associated with the emperors of China was a group known simply as the "Twelve Symbols" (*Shih-erh Chang*). Traditionally these went back beyond the Chou, although there is only doubtful evidence to indicate that they were used much before the period we were just discussing, which began with the late Chou. They would certainly have been characteristic expressions of the temper of those times, for as a group they represented the universe in microcosm just as effectively as any cosmic diagram. However, their use was by no means limited to that special period which lasted from the late Chou through the Han, with occasional later survivals into the T'ang. In fact, they have a special significance for the study of Chinese symbolism because of the way in which they survived into the twentieth century, having long since lost their original cosmic symbolism, changing in meaning as attitudes toward them altered with the passage of time.

Intended primarily to be worn on the emperor's sacrificial robes, they consisted of the sun disk, the moon disk, stars and mountains, dragons and pheasants, an ax and an odd symbol known as the *fu* 黻, bronze libation cups, water weeds, flames, and seeds of grain. The first four represented primarily the heavens and the earth. The next two represented animate nature as expressed in bird and animal life. The ax and the *fu* (the latter possibly once a seal of authority) probably represented the power to reward and punish. Finally, the last four represented four of the Five Elements: metal, water, fire, and grain (instead of the more usual wood); while earth, the fifth, was already represented by extension in the mountain symbol. Thus, originally at least, the imperial robe figured with these must have comprised a kind of *mandala*, or symbolic representation of the greater universe and its component elements.

That this was evidently the original meaning of the Twelve Symbols is indicated in a passage in the *Book of Rites*, which was compiled during the Han from Chou sources. This says: "On the day of sacrifice, the sovereign wears the robe with the Twelve Symbols to represent Heaven (i.e., the Ruler of the Universe)."[18] The same passage goes on to explain, somewhat indirectly, why there were precisely twelve of these symbols. In telling why the sovereign had twelve strings of jewels on his ceremonial crown, it says, "Twelve is the number of Heaven."[19]

The fact that grain was represented as one of the Five Elements instead of wood shows the relative antiquity of these symbols,[20] as does

THE TWELVE SYMBOLS

the use of the pheasant, rather than the Chinese phoenix, to depict the chief among birds. Moreover, the *fu* symbol—which roughly resembles two capital *E*'s placed back to back—was so old that its original significance was apparently forgotten even before the T'ang. Whether or not their use began before the late Chou period, the Twelve Symbols were in use for a very long time.

During the T'ang dynasty the meaning of these symbols was reinterpreted. Instead of being considered as representations of elements in nature, collectively forming a kind of cosmic plan, they were now explained as being purely symbols of the emperor's superior qualities. This complete shift of emphasis occurred at about the time when the reign dates were being changed from traditional auspicious expressions to others with more secular connotations, both developments being symptoms of a growing trend toward materialism.[21]

The T'ang attitude was first expressed in a memorial to the throne by Yang Ch'iung, in the seventh century. He said that the sun, the moon, and the constellation symbolized the light of the good and wise king shining upon the world; that the mountain which distributes clouds and rain thus symbolized the beneficence of the good and wise king to his people; while the dragon, ever infinite in its changes, symbolized the adaptability of the good and wise king, who publishes his laws and instructions according to the needs of the time; etc.[22]

This new type of rationalization was much more succinctly expressed by a later Sung writer who said: "The sun, moon, and stars represent enlightenment; the mountain represents protection; the dragon, adaptability; the pheasant, literary refinement; the libation cups, filial piety; the water weed, purity; the grain, ability to feed (the people); the flames, brilliance; the axe, the power to behead (or punish); and the *fu* symbol, discrimination (between right and wrong)."[23]

Thus it can be seen that there was no longer any standard explanation of these symbols, and anyone could rationalize about them, provided that he represented them as reflecting the wisdom and glory of the ruler in an approved Confucian manner.

By Sung times, therefore, they had become so much associated with the emperor—even though his highest officials were still wearing them (in descending numbers) at the times when he wore them—that the rulers of the alien dynasties also took them over. The Khitan Tartars of the Liao adopted the Twelve Symbols in A.D. 946, the Ju-chên Tartars of the Chin in 1140, and the Mongols of the Yüan in 1274.[24]

The Ming emperors created an innovation by adding these symbols to their less formal robes as well as to their ceremonial ones, and in the portraits of the Ming emperors it is interesting to see that, sometime before (probably in the T'ang or Sung periods), the representation of the sun had changed, so that its disk now carried a three-legged cock, instead of a three-legged crow, while the moon animal had changed from a toad to a rabbit (through the influence of Buddhism).

The Manchu emperors of the Ch'ing at first indignantly resisted such a "Chinese trait" in the struggle to maintain Manchu cultural identity, but the Ch'ien-lung emperor was a confirmed traditionalist, and sometime about 1760 he added the Twelve Symbols to his robes, both formal and informal. He kept them small and unobtrusive so that they did not detract from the main pattern of his robes, which in itself represented the universe in microcosm: rocky land masses, wave-tossed seas, and cloud-filled sky. To him they were simply a mark of emperorhood, which linked him with the great sovereigns of the past.[25]

In later times, however, beginning about the Sung period, the dragon began to be a paramount symbol of the emperor, and the Chinese phoenix, or *fêng-huang* 鳳凰, became the symbol of the empress. The Yüan dynasty regulated this by prescribing that the imperial dragon should have five claws, while that used by lesser nobles and officials should have four, and they were thence designated by separate names, being called *lung* 龍 and *mang* 蟒, respectively. Until the Sung period dragons had only had three claws, and this usage survived in Japan. However, almost the only three-clawed dragons found in China after the Yüan were those used by the early Ch'ing emperors, for a brief period, as an alternative to the five-clawed ones.[26]

Dragons in China were generally—but not always—considered as benevolent, rain-bearing creatures associated with clouds and were usually represented as soaring through the clouds with their sacred flaming pearls. As chief among the animals, the *lung* dragon was made up of superior or outstanding elements from other creatures, just as the "*T'ao-t'ieh*" had been many centuries before. The traditional description of the Chinese dragon, ascribed to a writer of the Han period, says that it has horns like a stag, a (fore-) head like a camel, eyes like a demon, a neck like a snake, a belly like a sea monster (the *shên*), scales like a carp, claws like an eagle, pads like a tiger, and ears like an ox.[27] It was also supposed to have exactly eighty-one scales, since nine times nine was the most auspicious *yang* number, and the dragon, who as one of the Four Spirits had been considered only half *yang*, was now considered as the outstanding symbol of the *yang* principle. (This association with the *yang* caused some confusion, incidentally, in regard to the various *Lung Wang*, or Dragon-kings of certain springs and pools, especially in South and Southwest China. For in those regions the Indian legends of the *Nāga-rāja*, or Serpent-king, had been transferred to the dragons, so that the latter accumulated a number of *yin* associations connected with darkness and dampness.)

The *mang* dragon resembled the *lung* in every particular except for the number of claws, but there were lesser types of dragons that looked quite different. One was the *tou-niu* 斗牛, which had down-curling horns, usually only three claws, and no pearl. Another was the *ch'ih* 螭, traditionally described as a "baby dragon." The latter had no scales and only a single rudimentary horn, but its outstanding characteristic was a long split tail, of which the two ends curled outward in opposite directions. The *ch'ih* dragon was the emblem for grandsons of the emperor in the later Ch'ing dynasty.

The resplendent Chinese phoenix, or *fêng-huang*, traditionally the emblem of the empress of China, was regarded in old Chinese folklore as being the ruler of birds, corresponding to the dragon as king of animals. Therefore, just as the dragon was made up of various outstanding features from several animals, the Chinese phoenix was endowed with spectacular elements from different birds. For example, it is shown with a cock's comb, and sometimes its wattles as well, the throat of a mandarin duck with delicate golden feathers, the back of a peacock with scalelike feathers in blue or green, two to five long tail plumes ultimately derived from the peacock or the Argus pheasant, and the long legs of a crane, usually colored red. Just as the *lung* dragon had a lesser representative in the *mang*, there was a less spectacular type of phoenix, known as the *luan* 鸞, which was the emblem of princesses.

Even though the phoenix sounds highly fanciful, this does not mean that it was considered as purely imaginary. On the contrary it was thought to be occasionally seen, and, when it appeared, this was such an auspicious occurrence that it was reported in the official records. Its appearance, either actual or in the form of an auspicious apparition (*jui t'u* 瑞圖), was thought to be an omen of good government. To take one of the many quotations on the subject: "When the state is peaceful, and its ruler enjoys literary pursuits, then the *fêng-huang* makes its home there; when the state is in turmoil, and its ruler enjoys warlike pursuits, then it leaves."[28]

Both the dragon and the Chinese phoenix were taken down into the folk arts, especially in later times. The dragon was usually portrayed as a rain-bearing deity, and, in order to avoid all official censure, its feet were frequently hidden behind clouds so that no one could count the number of its claws. The phoenix, on the other hand, was an emblem of brides and as such was often painted or embroidered on wedding gifts and trousseaux, because in China, as in other parts of the world, the bride was considered an "empress for a day."

D. AUSPICIOUS SYMBOLS

Very characteristic of the Han period and of the lesser dynasties immediately following was a collection of strange animals or birds, either rare or imaginary (by our modern standards), grouped together with various unusual plants to form a category which we might call "auspicious symbols" because of the way in which they were regarded. For example, we have seen that it was imagined at that time that, if a sovereign ruled well, phoenixes would appear. Similarly, many other kinds of animals, birds, or plants were believed to present themselves at special times in order to signalize the pleasure of Heaven regarding the activities of men.

In contrast to these were some even more awesome manifestations of nature, such as unusual appearances among the stars and planets, loathsome freaks in the animal world, or even large-scale disasters such as floods and earthquakes. This second group might be classed as "portents," since they were considered as symbols of Heaven's displeasure, warning of still worse things to come. Although even in Han times there were scoffers, such as Wang Ch'ung, the author of the *Lun Heng*, most people took all these manifestations very seriously. They were even recorded in the various dynastic and local histories down to the present century.

Some especially fine illustrations of symbolic portents can be found in the entries in the Yünnan histories describing the events preceding the Manchu army's attack on Wu San-kuei, the local king, in 1673. There was an earthquake on New Year's Day, but in the third month things really began to happen. The ornamental fish at the east end of the roof on the North Gate tower gave forth a white vapor, five feet high and four feet broad, which on examination turned out to consist of mosquitoes. Then the bronze phoenix atop the pagoda in the Western (City) Temple screeched without stopping, until it was decapitated. Finally, an enormous bird appeared, which baffled even the experts on strange matters.[29] One can imagine the consternation in the city.

Ridiculous as this may sound to us, our European ancestors held similar beliefs as late as the Elizabethan period. Shakespeare was merely expressing a concept of his own times when he made Richard II exclaim, "Down court, down king. For night-owls shriek where mounting larks should sing."[30]

Although the portent symbols occupy no less a place in Chinese symbolism in general, especially from the literary and historic points of view, these were rarely depicted in art. In terms of sympathetic magic, in which most Chinese implicitly believed, the act of portraying something could be quite sufficient to cause it to happen. Thus to draw or carve a portent symbol might have actual danger. By the same token, symbols of good augury were quite capable of producing good fortune, so they were very popular in the vocabulary of the Chinese artist.

The first large-scale depiction of these auspicious symbols known to us from ancient China was in the carving on the roof slabs of the tomb shrine of the Han scholar, Wu Liang, who died in A.D. 151.[31] Among the oddities portrayed were a pair of "birds with mutual wings" (*pi-i niao* 比翼鳥), each having but one eye and one wing, so that they could fly only when joined together, and a pair of "fish with mutual eyes" (*pi-mu yu* 比目魚) that similarly had to work together to make their way about. The picture of the paired birds is inscribed, "When the virtue of the ruler extends high and far, they will appear," while that for the paired fish says, "When the virtue of the ruler is wide and bright, and there is no place where it does not penetrate (i.e., even into the deep sea), then they will be seen."[32]

Because of the damage to the stones in the course of centuries, many of the inscriptions on the Wu Liang shrine are now indecipherable, and representations of these symbols in other places were seldom so conveniently labeled, so we would be hard pressed to work out the meanings of these Han auspicious symbols were it not that the *History of the Liu Sung Dynasty* (*Sung Shu*) devotes three chapters to a discussion of them, in addition to having the usual *wu hsing* section reporting their occurrence, such as can be found in most dynastic histories.[33]

Not only does the *Sung Shu* mention the "birds with mutual wings," but also nine-tailed foxes, red bears, six-legged animals, and others with three horns. Among other rare beasts it mentions the white elephant, telling under what circumstances it would appear.[34] In view of the overwhelming importance of the sacred white elephant in the Buddhist kingdoms of Southeast Asia in much later times, it is especially interesting to note that the white elephant was considered as an auspicious animal in the pre-Buddhist traditions of China. Later, it reappears quite frequently in Chinese Buddhist art as a purely Buddhist symbol, particularly associated with bodhisattva P'u-hsien (Samantabhadra).

A second chapter in the *Sung Shu* has a number of additional bird omens and some auspicious trees and plants, of which two typical examples are a pair of millet stalks growing together to produce a single ear of grain, or two lotuses joining to bring forth a single flower. It also speaks of "auspicious clouds" in five colors (*ch'ing yün* 慶雲). The latter was an especially valued omen for centuries after, and occurrences of it were duly recorded in the dynastic and local annals as late as the last century. In fact, "five-colored clouds" formed an integral part of the ornamentation on the robes of the Ch'ing emperors because they were considered so lucky.[35] This was the fate of a great many symbols by Ch'ing times: they had lost all significance except as emblems of good fortune.

With the exception of the auspicious clouds and a few of the more outstanding birds and animals, most of these omen symbols had dropped out of favor before the end of the Six Dynasties period. A few of them were briefly revived under the T'ang by someone called upon to produce a design for a bronze mirror. He took twelve of these symbol combinations including the paired birds and fish who were helpless alone, and the plants which joined together to bear fruit, etc., as logical symbols of matrimony to decorate a marriage mirror.[36] Otherwise they were forgotten except for occasional use as ornaments on some antiquarian's ink slabs.[37] The designers of ink slabs, often scholars themselves, were always searching for obscure literary allusions to illustrate in order to achieve novelty, and probably that is how these happened to be revived for that purpose.

As to the mythical creatures who survived when these other Han symbols were forgotten, chief among them were the dragon, the Chinese phoenix, and the *ch'i-lin* 麒麟. Western writers often describe the *ch'i-lin* as "the Chinese unicorn," which seems singularly inappropriate, as it has two horns. Furthermore, it differs in every other respect from the unicorn of medieval European bestiaries, having the body of an antelope, covered with scales, a dragon-like head, cloven hoofs, and a bushy tail. Since the time of Confucius this creature was mentioned as a creature of vast wisdom and especially good omen. The *Sung Shu* gives a typical quotation about it: "If the King moves with decorum and has a dignified mien, then it will appear."[38] After the belief in such symbols had passed, it was still retained as a symbol of fertility, capable of obtaining an illustrious progeny because of an ancient allusion to it in the *Shih Ching* as a bringer of children.[39]

E. BUDDHIST SYMBOLS

Leaving aside some of the portent symbols which were drawn from Confucian pronouncements regarding wise or evil rulers, most of the religious symbols in Chinese art come from Buddhism and Taoism. During the troubled times in the Six Dynasties period, Buddhism became not only a popular religion but a powerful one as well, especially under the patronage of the Wei emperors; and Buddhist iconography found roots in China. Even periods of persecution under the T'ang did not check the development of this religion and its art to any marked degree.

In the course of development the stark, spiritual icons of the Wei dynasty gave way to images of greater realism, as China's "gothic" phase succumbed to the baroque with the more material attitudes of T'ang times, losing dignity and spirituality as well as their simplicity in the process. The change in the form of the images seems to have led to altered attitudes toward them—at least among the thinkers. To the masses a Buddha figure was still an idol, if not an actual god, but it seems probable that before the end of the T'ang period deep-thinking Chinese must have thought of the images as personifications of ideas.

The Buddha figures, for example, were intended to depict former beings who had found release from rebirth, and hence the average Chinese Buddha expressed a relaxed calm and compassion toward those still on the path, personifying a spirit of peaceful yet kindly detachment. To the spiritual-minded Chinese a Buddha image suggested primarily release from cares, after which might be added various associations drawn from a knowledge of Buddhist teachings.

More obviously, an image of Kuan Yin, goddess of Mercy, suggested compassion and divine assistance. When she held a child in her outstretched arms, in later times, it required no imagination or esoteric knowledge to see that she symbolized hope for the barren. Similarly, Wên-shu (Manjusri) not only was the bodhisattva of Wisdom but, with his serious face and his book or scroll, personified wisdom; while P'u-hsien, the lord of Happiness, holding his wish-granting *ju-i* scepter, grinned down from atop his equally grinning elephant as the actual personification of happiness. Even the figures of the Lohans, as disciples of Buddha, were in a sense personifications of the ability to conquer sin and the world, for they represented rather worldly looking people who had found rewards in the spirit. And the fact that they looked rather mundane could encourage the average believer that there was hope for him too.

An essential part of any Buddhist image was always the attribute, that extra object in the hand or on the crown, perhaps, which identified that particular figure from others of the same category in the hierarchy, and, in the more familiar cases, could stand for the figure alone. These attributes, or "identification symbols," as one might call them, have been somewhat loosely used by the Chinese Buddhists of recent centuries, who were not so serious about their iconography as their Mongol and Tibetan neighbors of the Lama faith. In fact, almost the only places in Peking where one could find precise iconography were in the Yung-ho Kung and other Lamaist shrines, although the spiritual quality in such places was obviously far below the standard of exactitude in image-making.

Chief among the Buddhist symbols of ultimate Indian origin was the lotus. Usually it was represented as opened out, with eight petals to recall the Eight Noble Truths taught by Sakyamuni Buddha. Moreover, as Buddhist deities were commonly shown as supported above the earth on lotus thrones, and since the plant grows up from muddy waters to flower in the clear air, the lotus flower also came to be considered as an emblem of purity and detachment from earthly cares. Because of this, and because it was a familiar attribute of the ever popular Kuan-yin, it became a constant symbol in Chinese art from the T'ang dynasty onward. It must be admitted, however, that in the later Ming and throughout the Ch'ing it was largely used for its pun values. Combined with emblems of good fortune, it carried meaning of continuing felicity because of a pun on its name *lien* 連, or it meant "harmonious" because of a pun on its other name, *ho* 荷. But we shall have more to say about puns in another section.

Equally significant as a Buddhist symbol was the Wheel of the Law. Its eight spokes also recalled the Eightfold Path of the Buddha's teachings, and the flames which usually surrounded it were a reminder of solar connotations, since the wheel was an ancient sun symbol in India and Central Asia. Both the wheel and the lotus are included in the group of emblems commonly known as the Eight Buddhist Symbols. The other six are the vase and conch shell, the endless knot and the twin fish, the royal canopy and the state umbrella. All these were Indian symbols of remote antiquity, revered long before Buddhism, and around them had clustered a long tradition. In Ming China they were so frequently used for mere ornamentation that they rapidly degenerated into mere lucky symbols, of which only the wheel and the lotus retained any especial significance.

A number of other attribute symbols came to China from India with Buddhism, such as the sacred pearl, the alms bowl, and the *vajra* or ritual thunderbolt. The original flaming pearl came to be associated with the dragon—no one quite understands why—and lesser versions of it appear among the group known as the Eight Jewels (*Pa pao*). This sacred pearl was originally identified with the *Cintamani*, the "Wish-granting Jewel" of Indian folklore, but somehow that concept came to be represented by another related symbol. It would seem that the latter was represented in the Middle Ages by a pearl set in a trilobed gold plaque, the whole being called the "Wish-granting Jewel" (*ju-i chu* 如意珠). Although this continued on as a symbol into the present century in that form, it is perhaps more commonly known in the form of the "*ju-i* scepter," which in its purest representation is simply the "Wish-granting Jewel" with a handle. It is this that is the special attribute of P'u-hsien. The begging bowl is seldom represented except as an attribute in the hand of an image, but large stone bowls of marble or jade in certain old Chinese temples were often described as holy begging bowls. The *vajra* is chiefly seen as an attribute in the hands of certain Lamaist deities in North China temples; for, in Chinese Buddhism, when the sacred texts call for such an object, it is usually simply represented by a Chinese mace. However, it sometimes appears in its common Indo-Tibetan form as a decoration around the base of throne daises or cast on bells. A particularly fine example of the latter usage appears on the Great Bell of Kunming, in Yünnan, cast in 1424, near the beginning of the Ming.[40]

Lastly, there is a whole series of "jewel symbols" which are used in groups of eight and then referred to as the *Pa pao*, as mentioned above. These apparently originated as depictions of Buddhist offerings, and sometime about the end of the Yüan dynasty they began to be used in the decoration of porcelain, and other secular purposes, until they finally degenerated into mere luck symbols. The series as a whole comprises pearls (single large ones or groups of smaller ones), gold circular ornaments and gold rectangular ornaments, *ju-i* jewels and *ju-i* scepters, rhinoceros horns, ivory tusks, sticks of coral and rolls of tribute silk, ingots of silver and gold, holy books (sutras), sacred pictures, swastika emblems, leaves of the *patra* palm, and a number of other things which Buddhists would consider rare or valuable. It did not seem to matter which of these were chosen to make up a given group, but the total number should ordinarily not exceed eight. This peculiarity will be noted in a number of other groupings to be mentioned. It would seem that, in the Far East, the idea of a symbolic number of things was considered more important than the specific objects chosen, and the number eight was evidently an especially propitious one. It occurs frequently in Buddhist writings and in native Chinese literature, art, and folklore.

F. TAOIST SYMBOLS

Taoism began some centuries before the birth of Christ as a great metaphysical philosophy embodying some of the best of early Chinese abstract thought. By the later Han dynasty, however, the mystical strain began to be replaced by another with a great emphasis on magic. The latter soon evolved into a popular faith much concerned with the pursuit of long life, to be attained by such devices as breathing exercises or "pills of immortality," and with means for procuring release from evil influences that were thought to be generated by the *yin* principle. For these magical-minded Taoists the *yang* and the *yin*, instead of representing the active and passive forces of nature in harmonious relationship, had come to be considered as the very essence of good and evil, respectively.

The second form of Taoism even gained imperial favor under some of the T'ang emperors, to the extent that for certain periods it replaced Buddhism as the state religion of China. Even though the Buddhists and Taoists were rivals, and often enemies, the Taoists drew a lot from the Buddhists, especially in literature, iconography, and sculpture. Before the coming of Buddhism, the Taoists are supposed to have had no imagery, but under the influence of the foreign faith they rapidly developed an elaborate system of images. By the end of the T'ang dynasty, therefore, Taoism had a sizable pantheon.

The Taoists did not slavishly copy the Buddhist figures but devised their own. Two of their personifications, in fact, were so dramatic that they impressed even the Buddhists, who ultimately adopted them. These were the Thunder-god and the Lightning-goddess. The former is half-man and half-bird. He has a savage semihuman face ending in a huge beak, a powerful human torso with vast wings, and sometimes bird's feet, while in his hands he brandishes the hammer and spike which are the source of the thunder's sound. The Lightning-goddess, by contrast, is a slender, graceful damsel deftly balancing two polished mirrors which are supposed to create the lightning flashes as she dances in the sky. The contrast between brute strength and agility shown in this pair is especially striking, even to a foreigner unfamiliar with the tradition.

Most of the other Taoist deities are legendary sages in ancient Chinese dress who were believed to have achieved immortality by esoteric practices. Since popular Taoism devoted so much attention to magical methods for prolonging life, it was only natural that great reverence should have been placed on such worthies. Eight of these, in particular, had gained a firm hold on popular imagination by the Ming period. Each of these was identified by one or two constant attributes: a gourd and crutch, a flower basket, a bamboo rattle, lotus, fan, flute, sword, and castanets. In time, these identification symbols came to be depicted in place of the personages they represented, as being wonder-working in themselves. By the later Ch'ing the symbols of the Eight Taoist Immortals were being used so much for incidental decoration that, like the Eight Buddhist Symbols, they quickly degenerated into mere emblems of good fortune.

The second preoccupation of the Taoists, which lay in finding and exploiting methods of exorcising evil forces generated by the *yin* principle, was also linked with the search for longevity, since diseases and the evil spirits who strove to shorten the span of life were also believed to be embodiments of the *yin*. Thus, anything associated with the opposing *yang* principle was believed to have great power as a counteracting force and demon-repellent. For this reason, anything colored red (the *yang* color) was considered as especially auspicious.[41] Certain flowers, usually red ones like the scarlet peony and medicinal plants with real or fancied curative properties, such as the artemisia, were thought to be especially effective for repelling demons, as were most of the spike-leafed plants such as the iris.

The evil forces of *yin* were collectively expressed in the early Taoist iconography by small demons, or *kuei*, and an even more demoniac figure, by the name of Chung K'uei 鍾馗, was devised to keep the latter in check. Until recent years his picture alone was considered as a powerful symbol for exorcising evil. By Ming times the powers of the *yin* were more usually expressed in art under the form of five loathsome creatures (usually the spider, lizard, centipede, snake, and toad), collectively known as the Five Poisons. Paradoxically, it was believed that, if figures of these animals were displayed, they could ward off the evils that they represented, especially if they were depicted being trodden underfoot by a spirit tiger or by Chang T'ien-shih (otherwise known as Chang Tao-ling), the first "Taoist Pope."[42] In this group of five any one of the animals may be exchanged for another equally detestable one, but the total number must always remain the same. This is another case where the symbolic number of things seems more important than the specific objects.

G. SYMBOLS MORE DIRECTLY FROM NATURE

In discussing previous Chinese symbols from nature, we were dealing with earlier periods when, from our point of view, the line between natural history and unnatural history was frequently crossed, although the old Chinese never recognized that there was any such line, any more than our medieval forefathers did. The dragons, phoenixes, and other mythical animals were probably just as "alive" to the men of the Han as were horses and cats, though of course considered as far more rare. It was only quite late that they were thought of as imaginary and purely symbolic.

The change in the attitude toward nature symbols seems to have begun in the T'ang, when pairs of animals or birds, particularly the latter, were figured in pairs as the principal design on marriage mirrors to symbolize constancy and affection. Among the chief birds used for this purpose were phoenixes, mandarin ducks, orioles, geese, and magpies, but parrots and peacocks were also represented. There was no question about their being considered as symbols representing human devotion. The tendency to represent animals and birds realistically, which began in the relatively materialistic period of the T'ang, received further impetus in the Sung. That was a time when great painters, both academicians and impressionists, were striving to learn more about nature from actual observation in order to depict it better, and they frequently chose subjects which could be given a symbolic interpretation.

Such mythical monsters as the dragon and the Chinese lion were still favorite subjects, especially in paintings of a semireligious character, but the tendency of the times ran more to birds and animals such as the crane and the deer, which because of their reputed great age were symbols of longevity. Until the Mongol Dynasty, the turtle was also considered one of this group of long-lived creatures. But, because of the shape of its head, it came to have lewd associations and has been assiduously avoided in Chinese art ever since. Therefore, it was very seldom seen in modern China except in children's drawings on some wall or gate. The dragon-tortoise, supporting the imperial edicts and other important documents carved on stone tablets, as a symbol of stability, did not come under this general ban, as its dragon-like head was above reproach, and besides it was considered as an accredited member of the dragon family and no ordinary turtle. Even though it was abandoned in China, the turtle of longevity is one of the many Chinese symbols that was passed on to the derivative cultures in Japan, Korea, and Annam, and in those regions it retained its original meaning into recent times.

In the Sung, mandarin ducks and other auspicious birds were painted in pairs to symbolize happy marriage, because of their reputed devotion to their mates, but it seems probable that, like other subjects painted by the artists of that time, they were chosen more to show the artist's versatility at painting feathers and a realistic habitat than as meaningful symbols. The pairs of ducks on dishes and plates of the time may have been more truly symbolic. Later the quail acquired the same reputation for devotion to its mate that the mandarin ducks had long enjoyed, and thus quails are sometimes portrayed in pairs on porcelains and small jades of the Ming and Ch'ing to symbolize domestic felicity.

The carp, though known to the Occident as a sluggish fish, somehow acquired in China a more aggressive reputation. Accordingly, it became a symbol of vaulting ambition, and a carp leaping through the Dragon Gate, a favorite subject in all media of Chinese art, represented a successful candidate in the triennial imperial examinations. This was a particularly important symbol in a land where the highly organized civil service system made success in such examinations the prerequisite for any official position. Probably it meant more under the Sung and the Ming than in other periods, because in both those dynasties the number of imperial nobles was limited, and their power negligible, so the power and prestige of the officials was especially strong, and this symbol of their rise to power had correspondingly more significance.

Various trees and plants, such as the pine, the cypress, and the tree fungus (*ling chih* 靈芝), have been considered as symbols of longevity for many centuries, and with the new vogue for decorating porcelain in blue on white, which began in the Yüan period, they were much in demand. They continued popular through the Ming and the Ch'ing, from time to time being joined by other plants which for various reasons seemed equally appropriate as symbols of long life, notably the marigold, which was called the "Everlasting Flower" (*wan shou hua* 萬壽菊) and the evergreen *Nandina*. The pine tree also figures in other symbolic groups, such as that of the pine, the bamboo, and the prunus. Collectively known as "the three friends in winter," these three serve as a symbol of constancy in adversity. This particular symbol has always had an especial appeal for the Japanese, who borrowed it from China.

Some flowers seem to have become symbols because their fancy literary names were taken literally. A notable example of this was the peony, known as "the flower of riches and honor" (*fu-kuei hua* 富貴花)[43] and hence used as a symbol of advancement. Others became popular as symbols because of puns on their names, like the lotus, as a symbol of harmony, as previously mentioned.

The Chinese, always fond of flowers, seem to have begun their special cult of the "Flowers of the Four Seasons" back in the Sung dynasty, at the time when so many of these other symbols taken directly from nature were entering the repertory of the Chinese artist. Special flowers were assigned not only to each season but to each month of the year; however, the former grouping is certainly the best known. The Flowers of the Four Seasons are generally considered as the following: the prunus or bamboo (or pine) for the winter, peony or grass orchid for the spring, lotus or tree peony for the summer, and various types of chrysanthemum for the autumn. These tend to vary from artist to artist, and the same applies to other details in paintings of the Four Seasons, such as the types of bird chosen or the details of the background landscape. Combinations of flowers and birds have always been favorite subjects, and appropriate sets have often been chosen to represent the passing seasons of the year. A typical selection might show, for example, sparrows on snow-laden bamboo leaves, magpies perched among plum blossoms, an egret in a lotus pool, and a phoenix posed among chrysanthemums. Just as in previous examples of groups of symbols, there do not seem to have been any rules or conventions to determine which birds or flowers were chosen for the combinations, as long as they came in four sets and were not too inconsistent with the time of year to be depicted.

In addition, there were various fruit symbols, such as the peach, the pomegranate, and the Buddha's-hand citron, collectively known as the "Three Abundances." Peaches were a symbol of long life, because of their association with the immortal queen, Hsi Wang-mu, while the Buddha's-hand (*Fo shou*) was a symbol of happiness from an old pun on its name, when the first syllable was pronounced like the word for happiness, as it still is in many parts of China. By contrast, the meaning of the pomegranate, cut open to show its many seeds, was much more obvious. Like the melon and the gourd, it was a natural symbol of fertility or "abundant children"—or, by extension, abundance in general.

The gourd, in addition to symbolizing fertility, also was an emblem of medicine, referring especially to the elixirs of the Taoist immortals, which according to tradition were carried on the backs of the sages in gourd canteens. Hence, the gourd bottle not only was used as the sign of a druggist's shop but also became a symbol of longevity. It seems extraordinary to think how many of the Chinese plant symbols directly or indirectly symbolized long life. But, then, that was one of the great preoccupations of Chinese folklore and symbolism throughout history.

H. FESTIVAL SYMBOLS

Festival symbols, that is to say, special emblems for the great occasions of the year in the old Chinese calendar, were especially highly developed in the later Ming dynasty. We are fortunate in having fairly detailed information on this development from the writings of two Ming courtiers of the later sixteenth and early seventeenth centuries, both of whom left rather full accounts of late Ming court customs as they had personally known them, thus preserving data of the type seldom found in the conventional histories.[44]

There were several good reasons why the Ming court should have placed much emphasis on the great annual festivals. In the first place, these had not been celebrated according to the traditional Chinese customs by the alien Mongol rulers during the previous dynasty of the Yüan, and during that period of foreign occupation the native Chinese had observed these days according to their old observances in the privacy of their homes, fervently clinging to them as a mark of their cultural identity in the face of "barbarian" rule. Then, when they had finally expelled the Mongols, together with most of the foreigners whom the latter had had in their employ, these festivals took on a special patriotic significance; in celebrating them, the Ming Chinese felt that they were reinforcing their national culture.[45]

There were other reasons for emphasizing these occasions in the later Ming dynasty, the time from which we know most about them. That period was a time of trouble and great stress, with constant pressure on the northern frontiers from both the Mongol chieftains and the newly constituted "Manchu nation," accompanied by serious internal uprisings, which by 1644 were eventually to accomplish the overthrow of the dynasty. In view of all this, regular periods of gaiety and relaxation throughout the year were especially welcome to the rulers who were so burdened with anxiety about the present and the future. Also, the Ming dynasty was one of those unfortunate periods when the palace eunuchs had special control over the court. They had to keep the semicaptive members of the imperial family sufficiently interested so that they would not become restless and look for means to alter the situation, and at the same time they were no doubt frequently bored themselves by the endless routine of court life and thus inclined to welcome anything that would temporarily alter its tempo. Thus the palace went to extraordinary lengths to celebrate these festivals, with symbolic decorations, symbolic foods, and even symbols of the occasion on their clothing.

The first of the great annual festivals of the old Chinese calendar was New Year's, which fell in January or February of our Western calendar and marked the beginning of spring.[45] The special symbol for this occasion was a gourd. We have seen that the gourd had long been an emblem of abundance and fertility because of its numerous seeds, but this was a particular one, "the gourd of Great Good Fortune" (*Ta chi hu-lu* 大吉葫蘆), and its name was emphasized by decorating the surface of the gourd with a large poleax or halberd (*ta chi* 大戟). Other punning symbols were used as well, to make rebuses within rebuses. In fact, this was a great period for the development in pictorial puns, as we will see further in the next section. Not only was this gourd pictured on paper streamers and cutouts hung up for the occasion, but its image was impressed on New Year's cakes, and it also appeared on the robes of the eunuchs and courtiers, either as an all-over pattern or figured in the background of the dragon insignia on breast and back, as is illustrated by Ming textile fragments in some of our American museums.

The next festival was the Feast of Lanterns on the fifteenth of the first month. This was marked not only by setting out lanterns in every conceivable form and color, to welcome the increasing light and warmth of the sun after the winter's cold, but also by impressing the lantern symbol on the little cakes which were baked for that occasion and by embroidering it on the robes and dragon insignia of the courtiers. Rather sensibly, some of the courtiers apparently felt that it was needlessly expensive to have special robes for two festivals so near together, so we find surviving textile fragments on which the gourds have been furnished with a lantern canopy, so that they could double as gourd-shaped lanterns and thus be appropriate on both occasions.

The next of the special festivals with its own particular symbols was the Dragon Boat Festival, at the summer solstice, on the fifth day of the fifth month. As this was a season when the *yang* forces were considered to be at their lowest ebb, the symbols used were intended to placate or ward off any evil influences inspired by the ascendant *yin* elements. Thus the paper signs and placards depicted Chang T'ien-shih, the semi-legendary, magic-working founder of later Taoism on his tiger, or a sword-brandishing goddess on her tiger, or simply a very large tiger standing alone, opposing the Five Poisons, consisting of a toad, a centipede, a lizard, a scorpion, and a snake, which were considered as representing all the forces of evil. The artemisia plant was considered equally effective for counteracting the Five Poisons, and whole plants or portions of them were hung in gates and doorways. As in the previous cases, the clothing of the courtiers had these symbols on them for the occasion. The accounts speak of an all-over pattern of little tigers, or of additions to the dragon insignia in the form of the tiger, artemisia leaves, and the Five Poisons.

On the seventh of the seventh month occurred a minor festival which had a romantic rather than a ritualistic appeal. This was to celebrate the legendary meeting of the Oxherd and the Spinning Maiden, who had been doomed to live in the sky as certain constellations (Aquila and Lyra, respectively), but who were permitted to meet on this one night each year. The means by which they crossed the Heavenly River (the Milky Way), to accomplish this, was said to be a bridge formed by magpies, which, as we have seen, were included among the traditional symbols of happiness and marriage. Thus, on that occasion the palace eunuchs and courtiers wore the symbol of the Magpie Bridge, formed by a cluster of these handsome birds.

The Midautumn Festival, on the eighth of the eighth month, had special significance in the Ming, as we have seen, but its chief importance was as a Moon Festival. This day called for special sacrifices to the moon, and to the rabbit in the moon, as well as moon-viewing parties in the evening and the eating of moon-cakes. The special symbols for this occasion were thus the moon disk, which appeared on the eunuchs' hats, and representations of the greenish-white Moon Rabbit on the robes of the ladies of the palace.

On the ninth of the ninth month, the Chrysanthemum Festival was especially celebrated by a great display of these flowers before the Ming emperor, and, to signalize this, the palace eunuchs and courtiers wore robes with chrysanthemum patterns, or chrysanthemums with their dragon insignia, and figures of the same flower on an embroidered patch on their hats.

On the first of the tenth month there was an important court ceremony for the proclamation of the calendar for the coming year, which the courtiers all attended in order to felicitate the emperor and wish him many more years to come. For this the appropriate symbol was *wan nien*, "ten thousand years (to come)," symbolized on the courtiers' hats by a swastika (*wan*) and a catfish (*nien* 鮎), another of those Ming puns!

Lastly, the winter solstice in the eleventh month was a special occasion at the Ming court, to herald the change in the length of days and the coming return of the sun, with the attendant rising of the *yang* principle. The records say that on this occasion the robes of the courtiers displayed badges for the (re-)birth of the *yang*, but they do not explain these, so we cannot be sure exactly what the symbols were. However, we can gain some clue from the hat ornaments of the courtiers and palace eunuchs, which were described as having plum blossoms (as emblems of the winter season) and sheep (*yang*) with a crown prince (*T'ai tzŭ*), making an outrageous pun on *T'ai Yang*, meaning, "The Great Yang Principle," or "the Sun."

When the Manchus came into China after the fall of the Ming to a usurper in 1644 and founded a new dynasty, they did not continue the custom of festival emblems. One late Ch'ing Manchu antiquarian explained this by saying that his dynasty with its august frugality considered it too frivolous.[46] However, the native Chinese in Peking and elsewhere continued their customs as they had before under previous foreign domination. So the gourd and the lanterns and the tiger with the Five Poisons and the Moon Rabbit continued to appear on the cakes and on the cut-paper ornaments and the folk embroideries of the common people well into the twentieth century.

The important thing to note about these Ming festival symbols is that, with the possible exception of the puns, they were all essentially folk symbols taken over by the court and were no doubt still being used by the common people at the same time, although we have no specific record of it. Therefore, when the Chinese court abandoned them with the change of dynasties, these symbols were merely reverting to their former, original status. This, then, is an example of how folk symbols were sometimes taken up by the court to find their way into palace art, by contrast to the way in which symbols of palace art, such as the dragon and the phoenix, found their way down into the folk arts, through a reverse process.

1. PUN SYMBOLS OR REBUSES

We have noted in passing that one of the chief manifestations of the later Ming and the Ch'ing dynasties, as far as the history of symbols is concerned, was the gradual breakdown of meaning in what were once religious symbols, so that they became merely lucky emblems. In fact, by constant repetition they tended to lose even that significance and became mere ornaments. Equally characteristic was the development of new sets of decorative motifs that, at first glance, would seem difficult to account for, such as bats carrying swastikas, and poleaxes standing upright in a vase.

On investigation, most of these apparently arbitrary motifs turn out to be rebus symbols, like those which were so characteristic of the Ming court in the early seventeenth century. In other words, when the names of the things pictured were pronounced, they were supposed to recall other words that had the same sound but different meanings; combined in groups, they made up phrases which usually expressed hopes for much-desired things, such as happiness, fortune, and long life.

It might seem that these plays on words were purely literary symbols, but it was not necessary to write down the characters for each object depicted in order to detect the puns. By simply pronouncing the names of the objects, even an illiterate person could recall the similar-sounding words which would make up a familiar auspicious phrase. In fact, the basic ideas which were expressed in these rebus symbols—hopes for long life, great wealth, marital happiness, numerous children, eventual official rank, and tranquillity—were not confined to the literati. Their frequent occurrence in the folk arts would indicate that they represented the actual values of Chinese life in recent centuries, regardless of class.

The earliest clear-cut rebuses of any complexity are those which appeared on the festival robes and hats of the late Ming courtiers. However, such symbols did not begin to appear in Chinese art in general until the early eighteenth century, about the time of the reign of Yung-chêng (1723–35). Then they are found more and more in designs on embroidery and in porcelain decoration. It is interesting to find that they seem to have been used in cycles. A given rebus would enjoy considerable popularity for a while, until it lost its novelty and was no longer thought to be amusing. Then it would drop out, perhaps for good, or possibly to be resumed in somewhat altered form at a later time. It is not too difficult to determine the periods of popularity for the commoner ones.

The fact that such rebuses existed in later Ch'ing art was pointed out by Bushell, Chavannes, and Hobson, in their pioneer reviews of Chinese symbolism.[47] Fortunately, they preserved for us the meanings of quite a number of them that were being used at the end of the Ch'ing dynasty. But there are a great many others, few of which have ever been properly interpreted. Nothing seems to have been written about them in China since the Ming, when they were probably still a novelty, except by two Japanese antiquarians living in China during recent years.[48] During the Ch'ing dynasty the Chinese apparently considered them as part of an accepted tradition known to all, which it was unnecessary to reduce to writing. This is the old story with any branch of Chinese symbolism.

The simplest and one of the commonest of the rebus symbols is the bat, because its name, *fu*, is a pun on the word for happiness 蝠 福. Frequently five bats were shown, to recall the five chief forms of happiness (*wu fu*). And, when colors were used, the five bats were depicted in red, flying among cloud wisps, because the descriptive phrase "red bats attaining the sky" (*hung fu chih t'ien*), by a substitution of homophones for the first two words, becomes, "vast happiness reaching unto heaven" 紅蝠至天 紅福致天. Often the bats are shown dangling swastikas on ribbons from their jaws, as mentioned above, because the swastika is used as an alternative character for *wan* meaning "ten thousand," and the picture then means, "May you have happiness in a myriad forms."

Quite commonly shown with the bat as an element in pun symbols is a jade musical stone (*ch'ing*), used as a pun on *ch'ing* meaning good fortune 磬 慶. With them is often placed a *ju-i* scepter, or a *ju-i* jewel (as described above). Either of these recalls the second meaning of *ju i*, "as you wish." Thus, the bat and the musical stone with the jewel or scepter, together mean, "May you have (as much) happiness and good fortune as you desire." Alternatively, two carp may be shown with the bat and the musical stone, to give the phrase *fu ch'ing yu yü*, "May you have happiness and good fortune in abundance" 蝠磬有魚 福慶有餘. Or another kind of fish, the spotted catfish (*nien*), may be used with them to make the phrase *nien nien fu ch'ing*, "May you have happiness and good fortune from year to year" 鮎鮎蝠磬 年年福慶.

The above are all illustrations of the common or garden variety of rebus. The situation becomes far more complex when, as often happens, a single rebus picture offers the possibility of more than one interpretation. This can occur in at least two ways. A given picture may stand for a single word with more than one meaning, like the lotus (*lien*), which suggests a word of the same pronunciation meaning "lasting" 蓮 連, "continuous," or "in succession," or a picture can stand for two separate words with the same sound but entirely different meanings, like the bamboo mouth organ (*shêng*), which can stand for either the *shêng*, meaning "to rise in rank," or *shêng*, "to give birth" 笙 昇 生. Thus, in a familiar symbol used on wedding gifts, a noble child is shown riding on a *ch'i-lin*, holding in his hands a lotus flower and a bamboo organ, to make the phrase *lien shêng kuei tzŭ*, "May you successively give birth to noble sons" 蓮 笙 桂[花] 子 連 生 貴 子 (a sentiment which was already implicit in the figure of the *ch'i-lin*, as we have seen, and hence doubly reinforced). However, when the same musical instrument is shown in the sky along with two lotuses on certain Ch'ing mandarin squares, the combination suggests the phrase, *lien lien shêng kao*, "May you continually mount to higher rank" 蓮蓮笙高 連連昇高. In such cases the precise meaning can only be determined by the associated symbols which establish the context.

Another common pun symbol with two meanings is the halberd or poleax (*chi*) such as was used on the Ming New Year's badges. This can either be used as a pun on the word for "good luck," its common use in Ming puns, or as a pun on the word for "official rank." In the first case it is often used with the musical stone and the *ju-i* scepter, to make the phrase *chi ch'ing ju i*, "May you have as much good luck and good fortune as you desire" 戟磬如意 吉慶如意. In the second case, a vase is shown with three halberds jutting from its mouth, to form the descriptive phrase *p'ing shêng san chi;* but by replacing the first and fourth characters with homophones, and using a variant one for the second, this gives the phrase, "May you rise without opposition three degrees in official rank" 瓶升三戟 平昇三級. Popular variations may show the halberds rising from a lotus or from an ingot of silver instead, in which cases the resulting phrases are *lien shêng san chi*, "May you gradually rise three degrees in rank" 蓮升三戟 連昇三級, or *i ting shêng san chi*, "May you certainly rise three degrees" 一錠升三戟 一定昇三級. Both of these appear on middle Ch'ing mandarin squares.

We now come to a compound type of pun picture which can convey two or more complete auspicious phrases. The best example, perhaps, is a variation of the three halberds rising from the vase, in which the jade musical stone is superimposed against the shafts of the weapons. In considering one of these double puns, it is necessary to disregard one or more of the elements shown, to find the first meaning; then one must take up the object (or objects) neglected the first time, and ignore one or more of the elements first considered, to find a second meaning. In this particular case, for example, we first disregard the musical stone and get the usual hope for an easy ascent of three ranks, *p'ing shêng san chi*. Then, by taking up the musical stone but overlooking the specific number of halberds, we get the descriptive phrase "Halberds and musical stone together with a vase" (*chi ch'ing ho p'ing*), and after replacing the first, second, and fourth characters by homophones, and taking another meaning for the third, we get the hope, "May you have good luck, good fortune, and tranquillity" 戟磬合瓶 吉慶和平.

Another, less familiar series of compound rebuses is based upon the humble spotted catfish (*nien*) as a pun for year, as in the case mentioned above. Thus we find on a nineteenth-century official's dragon robe an elaborate design consisting of a bat with a ribbon hanging from its mouth, to which are fastened a lotus (*lien*) and a cintamani jewel (*ju-i*), and from these in turn hang two catfish, each with a swastika. Taking one catfish with its swastika, and the lotus and a bat, we get the pun phrase *wan nien lien fu*, "May (the wearer) have ten thousand years of continuous happiness" 卐·鮎蓮蝠 萬年連福. Then if we disregard the bat, the lotus, and the swastikas, and take simply the two fish and the jewel, we have the wish *nien nien ju i*, "Year after year may everything be as (the wearer) desires" 鮎鮎如意 年年如意. Third, by taking the lotus and the bat with both fish, considering the latter as fish in general rather than as a specific variety, we have the phrase *lien fu yu yü*, "May the wearer have lasting happiness in abundance" 蓮蝠有魚 連福有餘.

Of course there are countless more examples, but these are enough to illustrate the underlying principles behind the rebus symbols.[49] We have seen that some individual symbols, like the *shêng* mouth organ or the halberd, can have more than one pun meaning based on the same sound; others, like the lotus or the catfish, can have more than one pun meaning based on different words; while sometimes two or more symbols may be used to express the same word. But one rule is almost constant, and that is that the pun equivalents should generally have both the same sound and the same tone as the originals, a fact which was ignored by the Japanese scholar Nozaki in his attempts to decipher some.

It is not enough to guess at the meaning of a given rebus combination, unless it is composed entirely of familiar stock elements, in which case one already has the vocabulary. It is also unadvisable to accept without question the explanation of Chinese laymen, for, since the symbols are no longer current, these people are usually guessing, too. The only safe way to handle an undeciphered rebus is to look for a case in which the symbol group in question is somewhere shown accompanied by the phrase in characters—and such cases are quite rare—or else to search for popular auspicious phrases which were current at the time when the symbol in question was made. Such phrases may be found in lists of proverbs,[50] in conventional remarks on New Year's Day gate-papers,[51] on embroidered mottoes, or in inscriptions on wood carvings. In short, one must apply the methods which have to be used to a greater or less degree for the proper elucidation of any Chinese symbol. But, as these were among the most sophisticated symbols of all, they are correspondingly harder to work out.

2. *Final Remarks*

The nine groups of symbols which we have been considering were assembled primarily to illustrate some of the principal types of Chinese symbols and to present a general view of the mechanism underlying Chinese symbolism in general. At the same time, however, they have demonstrated how certain categories of symbols came into favor at different periods apparently as expressions of contemporary currents of thought.

We have seen that the earliest symbols of the Neolithic period were impossible to decipher with any certainty because of their extreme vagueness and the total absence of any records; and, although the symbols in the early historic period of the Shang and early Chou became more distinct, the lack of proper records makes it difficult to decipher them as anything more than expressions of the powers of force and transformation in nature. From the late Chou through the Han there was a great interest in magic, and cosmic symbols abounded. In the time of political chaos during the later Han and through the Six Dynasties, auspicious symbols had their day, probably as talismans to compensate for the distress and uncertainty of the times. The early T'ang dynasty saw a revival of earlier cosmic symbols, together with a great development of new religious symbols under the inspiration of Buddhism and Taoism, but a gradually increasing spirit of materialism led to a secularization of older symbols, including the ancient imperial emblems. The Sung interest in observation of nature because of developments in painting gave rise to symbols drawn directly from nature. Ming nationalism and antiquarianism led to emphasis on festival symbols. Finally, since most of the older symbols had lapsed into lucky emblems or mere decoration by Ch'ing times, the men of that dynasty developed a new type to satisfy their jaded appetites, carrying to extreme lengths the late Ming pun symbols. We have also seen that, although many symbols from each group passed out of fashion at the end of their respective periods, others lingered on into later times, often changing their meanings to conform to new moods and new philosophies.

The nine groups might have been arranged differently. For example, the longevity symbols which reappeared in various forms throughout Chinese history might have been sorted out from the other groups and put into a class of their own. Other categories might have been listed, such as "symbols based on literary allusions," and a whole section could have been devoted to the question of the symbolic nature of Chinese characters—apart from the few which were regularly used as decorative symbols in themselves. Also, numerous other examples could have been added to each of the existing groups. However, it has seemed best to confine our attention to the essential principles which are required for an appreciation of the symbols in Chinese art, with just enough examples to bring out each point clearly and to illustrate the problems that are involved in seeking out the symbols and in trying to track down their meanings.

It should be emphasized that this is still a pioneer field, needing a great deal of further research. Moreover, this study must be undertaken as speedily as possible, because even the recent symbols of the Ch'ing period are now quite dead, and few people now living remember their meanings correctly. The farther we get from that period when some of the symbols were still in use, the more difficult it will be to reconstruct them accurately. Though the Ch'ing symbols are relatively trivial compared with earlier types, these later symbols are no less important for study because they serve as bridges to the earlier ones. It is always easier to begin with things from the recent past and then work back into the less well-known periods.

Eventually, it should be possible to demonstrate even more clearly how the old Chinese symbols often preserve relics of the thought currents of various periods to supplement what has survived in literature, philosophy, and legend. And it might even be found that evidence from symbols will be able to fill actual gaps in the existing knowledge of Chinese thought, thus providing new insights into the great periods of China's past civilization.

NOTES

1. For an example of how a symbol may change its meaning see S. Cammann, "The Symbolism of the Cloud Collar Motif," *Art Bulletin*, XXXIII, No. 1 (March, 1951), 1–9.

2. See Dagny Carter, *China Magnificent* (New York, 1936), plate facing p. 4, for several examples.

3. The latest attempt to explain the symbols on the Neolithic painted pottery from

Kansu has been made by Anneliese Bulling, *The Meaning of China's Most Ancient Art* (Leyden, 1951).

4. For some typical "*T'ao-t'ieh*" examples see the Metropolitan Museum catalogue, *Chinese Bronzes* (New York, 1939), Figs. 1, 10, 53, 89, 96, etc.

5. See S. Cammann, "Tibetan Monster Masks," *Journal of the West China Border Research Society*, XII, Ser. A (1940), 9–19. (This article is full of misprints, as the war prevented the writer from receiving any proofs.)

6. These animals were depicted on jades as well as on the bronzes. For some representative Chou jade cicadas see Carter, *op. cit.*, plate facing p. 14.

7. See Henri Maspero, *La Chine antique* (Paris, 1927), chap. ix, pp. 507 ff., and Léopold de Saussure, "Le Système cosmologique sino-iranien," *Journal asiatique*, I, Ser. 12 (January–June, 1923), 235–97.

8. See L. Carrington Goodrich, *A Short History of the Chinese People* (New York, 1943), pp. 26–28.

9. See Huan T'an, *Hsin Lun* 桓譚，新論 (*Ssŭ-pu Pei-yao* ed.), p. 9.

10. The writer first demonstrated the meaning of this pattern some years ago (see S. Cammann, "The 'TLV' Pattern on Cosmic Mirrors of the Han Dynasty," *Journal of the American Oriental Society*, LXVIII, No. 4 [1948], 159–67).

11. For further details about the Sky Gate concept see Cammann, "The Symbolism of the Cloud Collar Motif," *op. cit.*, pp. 2 ff.

12. See Cammann, "The 'TLV' Pattern," *op. cit.*, pp. 166–67.

13. For an example of cosmic symbolism (of a slightly different sort) surviving in modern Asiatic games see S. Cammann, "Chess with Mongolian Lamas," *Natural History*, LV (1948), 407–11.

14. For an example of a late survival of the Han cosmic mirror pattern see Liang Shang-ch'un, *Yen-ku Tsang Ching* 梁上椿，巖窟藏鏡, III (1941), 11.

15. E. Chavannes, "Le Cycle turc des douze animaux," *T'oung Pao* (*Leiden*), VII, Ser. 2 (1906), 50–122, esp. pp. 69 and 85. He points out that this animal cycle was also used by the Annamites, Cambodians, Chams, Siamese, Japanese, Mongols, Manchus, Tibetans, Persians, and Turks, as well as by the Chinese. He might also have cited the Koreans.

16. L. de Saussure, "Le Cycle des douze animaux," *Journal asiatique*, XV, Ser. 11 (1920), 55–88, esp. the last two pages.

17. For an example see the *Yen-ku Tsang Ching*, p. 38. In his accompanying inscription, the author shows that he failed to understand the symbols.

18. *Li Chi*, *Chiao-t'ê-shêng* 禮記，郊特牲 (2), *Shih-san Ching* (Commercial Press ed.), I, 924. See further comments on this by the writer, in *China's Dragon Robes* (New York, 1952), p. 92, n. 42.

19. *Li Chi*, *Chiao–t'ê–shêng*, I, 924.

20. This feature also shows a Near Eastern connection, if not a derivation (see De Saussure, "Le Système cosmologique sino-iranien," *op. cit.*, pp. 279–80).

21. Arthur Wright first called the writer's attention to this parallel development (see Wright and Fagan, "Era Names and *Zeitgeist*," *Études asiatiques* [Bern], V, Nos. 3 and 4 [1951], 113–21).

22. For the original memorial see the *Chiu T'ang-shu*, chap. 45, p. 17. Translations appear in various museum exhibition catalogues, such as "Costumes from the Forbidden City" (Metropolitan Museum, 1945), p. 7.

23. Ts'ai Shên, *Shu-ching Chi-ch'uan* 蔡沈，書經集傳, chap. 1, pp. 38*b*–39.

24. See the *Liao Shih*, chap. 56, p. 1*b;* the *Chin Shih*, chap. 43, p. 7; and the *Yüan Shih*, chap. 78, p. 3.

25. See S. Cammann, "A Robe of the Ch'ien-lung Emperor," *Journal of the Walters Gallery*, IX (1947), 16–18; and "Imperial Dragon Robes of the Later Ch'ing Dynasty," *Oriental Art*, III, No. 1 (1950), 8–10.

26. See *China's Dragon Robes*, pp. 25–26, 78–79. Aside from its presence on the Ch'ing imperial robes, cited in this reference, the only post-Sung occurrences of the three-clawed *lung* dragon known to the writer are on a few blue-and-white porcelains with Hsüan-tê date marks and one or two later Ch'ing pillar rugs for lama temples, one of which is in the Newark Museum.

27. This description is quoted from a Sung work, the *Erh-ya I* 爾雅翼, chap. 28, p. 1*b*, but it is originally ascribed to Wang Fu, a writer of the later Han.

28. *Sung Shu*, chap. 27, p. 2*b*.

29. *K'un-ming Hsien-chih* (1901 ed.), chap. 6, pp. 13*b*–14.

30. *Richard II*, Act III, scene 3. A longer, very vivid example is found in Act II, scene 3, of the same play, in the remarks of the Welsh captain; and of course there are countless more passages of a similar nature among others of Shakespeare's plays.

31. See the reproductions in Chavannes, *La Sculpture sur pierre en Chine aux temps des deux dynasties Han* (Paris, 1893).

32. Chavannes completely failed to understand these symbols (see S. Cammann, "A Rare T'ang Mirror," *Art Quarterly*, IX, No. 2 [spring], 1946, 112, n. 50).

33. *Sung Shu*, chaps. 27–29.

34. *Ibid*., chap. 28, p. 11.

35. See *China's Dragon Robes*, pp. 84–85.

36. This mirror has been fully discussed by the writer in "A Rare T'ang Mirror," *op. cit*.

37. See, e.g., Fang Yü-lu, *Fang-shih Mo-p'u* 方于魯，方氏墨譜, a Ming work of 1588.

38. *Sung Shu*, chap. 28, p. 1.

39. See Legge, *Chinese Classics*, Vol. IV, Part I, *She King*, p. 19.

40. See S. Cammann, "The Bell That Lost Its Voice," *Folklore*, LVII (December, 1946), 187.

41. This explains the frequent occurrence of fine Chinese embroideries in silk and gold on imported red flannel or baize, which often shocked foreign visitors to China. The flannel was chosen for its auspicious color as well as its contrasting texture.

42. See C. B. Day, *Chinese Peasant Cults* (Shanghai, 1940), pp. 51–52, etc.

43. The peony was apparently first given this title, and hence this association, by the Sung scholar Chou Tun-i, in his famous essay on flowers, *Ai-lien Shuo* 愛蓮說, which is quoted at length in the *Kuang-ch'ün Fang-p'u* 廣群芳譜, chap. 29, p. 13.

44. Liu Jo-yü, *Cho-chung Chih* 劉若愚，酌中志 (reprinted in the late Ch'ing as the *Ming-kung Chih* 明宮志), and Chiang Chih-ch'iao, *T'ien-ch'i-kung Tz'ŭ-chu* 蔣之翹，天啟宮詞注. Most of the festival badges cited are described in the former; but additional information has been obtained by examination of actual specimens from the Metropolitan Museum, the Nelson Gallery, Kansas City, and the University Museum, Philadelphia.

45. For some well-written and detailed descriptions of how these festivals were celebrated later, in the Ch'ing dynasty, see Derk Bodde, *Annual Customs and Festivals in Peking* (Peiping, 1936). This is a translation of Tun Li-ch'ên's *Yen-ching Sui-shih-chi* 敦禮臣, 燕京歲時記.

46. Tun Li-ch'ên, quoted by Bodde, *op. cit.*, p. 58.

47. See R. L. Hobson, *Chinese Pottery and Porcelain* (New York and London, 1915), II, 299–301; Chavannes, "L'Expression des voeux dans l'art populaire chinoise," *Journal asiatique*, XVIII, Ser. 9 (September–October, 1901), reprinted as an individual pamphlet (Paris, 1922); and S.W. Bushell, *Oriental Ceramic Art* (New York, 1897).

48. Nozaki Seikin, *Kisshō Zuan Kaidai* 野崎誠近, 吉祥圖案解題 (Tientsin, 1928), and Nagao Ryōzō, *Shina Minzoku-shi* 永尾龍造, 支那民俗志 (Tokyo, 1940–41).

49. A number of other examples, together with some of these, appear in *China's Dragon Robes*, pp. 100–107, etc.

50. A very useful book for this sort of research is C. A. S. Williams, *Manual of Chinese Metaphor* (Shanghai, 1920).

51. A number of posters of this type are illustrated, and more described, in Day, *op. cit.*

SOME PROBLEMS OF INTERPRETATION

ARNOLD ISENBERG

1. Introduction

THE STUDY of human thought embraces at least these three kinds of work: (*a*) interpretation, (*b*) explanation, and (*c*) criticism or evaluation.

a) Always we have before us a speech, a book, a monument, a record of thought or action. This text must be understood. Sometimes, as when we read a newspaper article in our own language or as when specialists discourse in a technical terminology, the understanding presents no difficulty. But sometimes it is necessary to expound, translate, paraphrase, decipher, condense, or summarize, in short, "explain the true meaning"; and those who do this, though they may bear such other titles as editor, translator, or textual critic, are one and all interpreters.

b) Every text has a background in personal psychology, literary or scientific tradition, social history, the national or class membership of its author; and there are those who interest themselves in investigating relationships between this text and elements in this background. This kind of study is termed "genetic" and sometimes also "contextual"; and it is here mainly, of course, that the various doctrines about the causation of ideas—psychoanalysis, historical materialism, sociology of knowledge, history of ideas—endeavor to apply themselves.

We may describe it as the ideal of genetic study to explain ideas through their causes. But, for any purpose I hope to accomplish in this paper, it will be unnecessary to insist upon a very strict conception of causal explanation. Any example of loose and general relevance between a work of the mind and various items in its background (such as might be found almost anywhere in Parrington or in Van Wyck Brooks) will serve us well enough.

c) Clearly it is part of the study of ideas to determine not just their contents and their antecedents but their truth or falsity, aesthetic merits, general significance for human life, special values and disvalues. This is criticism; and those considerations which have, for a critic, some bearing on the value of an idea may be called its "domain of verification."

This threefold division, not of labors but of kinds of labor, is the tritest but still the most useful framework for the study of ideas that one could propose.

Among these three processes interpretation certainly does not hold the final or sovereign position; on the contrary, we interpret a text for the sake of the criticism or the explanation which, we assume, is to follow. But interpretation is, by all odds, the central part of the study of ideas and the one on which everything else depends; for it would seem that we can neither criticize nor explain without first understanding what it is we are speaking about.

The lines between interpretation and explanation, between interpretation and evaluation, are thus speciously clear: interpretation comes first; explanation comes later and goes backward to causes; evaluation comes later and goes forward to reasons. But in truth the case is not so simple. The earliest phase may be in certain ways dependent on the later ones; the fields merge, or overlap, or variously partake in each other. In contemporary thought (e.g., Mannheim's) it is suggested that even genesis and validity are not such distinct dimensions as had been previously assumed. This paper will, in fact, consider only such problems of interpretation as have been created by the mutual entrenchment of these processes on each other, the indistinctness of the lines of division between them. We may expect to discover a situation of which the following analogy provides a sketch. Psychologists divide the response system into three parts: a receptive process, a connective process, and an effective process—we look, then we think, then we act. But on closer examination it appears that each phase has all three phases within itself. In "looking," for example, the position of the eyeballs produces sensory signals which determine perpetual readjustments of the eyeballs. So with "thinking," which incorporates subtle sensory and motor processes. So with "walking," which incorporates sensory and associative processes. It is convenient to retain the rough division of phases for the description of human response on the gross scale; the finer analysis does not conflict with this scheme. So, I would suggest, the rough demarcation of the idea from its causes on the one hand, its validating reasons on the other, will sustain itself on one level, notwithstanding the minute interconnections which may reveal themselves on others.

A problem *in* interpretation is one which reflects some doubt as to the meaning of a text: it is the sort of problem with which interpreters are faced. "What is it the poet means just here?" "How shall this Chinese phrase be rendered in English?" "Of these two strains of thought, which is predominant in this author?" "Does he mean this seriously, or is he being sarcastic?" These are examples of the ways in which problems in interpretation tend to couch themselves.

A problem *of* interpretation is (or will be so understood here: I do not recommend the general observance of this distinction between "in" and "of") the sort of problem which confronts the semanticist, logician, or student of general linguistics who wishes to understand the interpretative process. Interpretation, as we have noted, is not always problematical; and, even if it were never so, people would still raise questions about the nature of interpretation. But it will be convenient for us to assume that a problem of interpretation has some special connection with the *doubts* of the interpreter; it is, in other words, a question about the proper method of solving some class of problems in interpretation. Such questions belong, therefore, to the methodology of the interpretative disciplines; and, in contrast to the examples listed above, we may cite such questions as these: "What degree of equivalence, as between a translation and its original, is it reasonable to demand or to hope for? How do we judge such equivalence? What, in other words, is a relatively 'faithful' translation?" "Does a text have a single meaning, fixed by the author, which it is necessary to ascertain? How shall we know when we have reached this meaning?" "How, if at all, can a knowledge of the tradition to which a work belongs clarify the contents of that work?"

Problems of interpretation are not foisted upon honest scholars by a set of scheming methodologists. Practicing interpreters seem to be impelled, by the material in their hands, to the development of some theory or principle of method; one could examine a roster of eminent interpreters without finding one name that was not identified with some conception of interpretative procedure.

But though the interpreter is inevitably led over into questions of method, it is another question whether he can ever find his way out of them and still another whether it will have profited him to have been for a time so beguiled. And we have to ask: What value would the solution of some problem of interpretation have for the practice of any craft? Could we "apply" it, with increased prospect of success, to the interpreter's problems as they come along? Or would it leave him where he was, dependent for his achievement not on any conception of method but on his intuition, experience, and skill?

It would be easier to frame an answer to such questions if we could point to some outstanding problem of interpretation the solution to which was known. We could then see whether this solution had some lesson or implication for the practice of interpreters. But the truth is that the art of interpretation has by far outstripped the theory of interpretation. We have, for instance, accurate translations; we do not have any clear conception of the meaning of accuracy in translation. It is therefore hard to say whether such a conception, if we did have one, could or should make life simpler for the translator. In default of such an ability to demonstrate the pertinence of methodology, I can only give voice to the *opinion*, which does however seem to me to be plausible, that no method, and no theory of interpretation, will ever relieve the interpreter of the need to settle his problems by the use of nice judgment in the individual case. At the present time, certainly, methodology can do no more for him than to make him aware of the kinds of decision he has to make and the sorts of factor which enter into his decisions. I attempt no more in this paper than to mention some of these sorts and these kinds.

In presenting some issues in the theory of interpretation to the reader of this volume, I have to make one further assumption: that the differences between one language and another, one intellectual tradition and another, are not such as to prevent some of the same problems from arising for the interpreter of each. Distance is always a matter of degree. Chinese thought and language are no doubt different from English; but Joyce's thought and language are different from those of Pound and of Yeats, who are also different from each other. There must be some works of ancient Chinese art which are clearer, or more accessible, to American students of that subject than are the most recondite contemporary poets to their best students. If one insisted that every difficulty in interpreting Chinese were uniquely characteristic of that field, one would not know where to stop short of saying that there were no general problems of interpretation, recurring in two or more places; and that would seem to be absurd. It is more reasonable to postulate a certain continuity among differences in thought and language, assuming that, while indeed there are problems peculiar to each subject, there are also some which repeat themselves everywhere.

2. *Interpretation and Explanation*

Let us then suppose it may prove to have some slight relevance to oriental studies to consider closely the situation in which we find ourselves when we read a passage from a work relatively near to us in time and space. I am thinking of a single sentence from Thoreau's essay on *Resistance to Civil Government:* "That government is best which governs least," together with some of the remarks which follow: "This government never of itself furthered any enterprise, but by the alacrity with which it got out of its way. *It* does not keep the country free. *It* does not settle the West. *It* does not educate . . . ," and so on. A doctrine is stated here. This doctrine belongs to the field of abstract political theory. It was taken up, as we know, by persons called philosophical anarchists, as being similar to their own tenets. Philosophical anarchism is a theory with a universal reference; that is, it is meant to apply to human society as such, regardless of special conditions. If Thoreau's views are an example of such a theory, they will naturally provoke a *criticism* of a very general type. Abstract considerations of human nature and social organization will be in order; so will particular questions about any society we may care to think of. We shall feel it entirely proper to ask, for instance, what would happen to the life of modern cities if they were to have no government at all or only a very weak one. And if Thoreau's views, so interpreted, are to be *explained*, we must ask ourselves how a doctrine of anarchism could have sprung from the soil of mid-nineteenth-century New England.

How did Thoreau come to think as he did? It is sometimes pointed out that his mentality was a product of the primitive American Republic, with its expanding frontier, its pioneer spirit, its predominantly agrarian society, its Jeffersonian politics reflecting the interests of that society, its laissez faire capitalism operative in some degree both in practice and in theory. I do not propose to consider the adequacy of such explanations, that is, the ability of the specified conditions to account for the individual thought of Thoreau. But there is no paradox whatever in the fact that conditions as limited and specialized as these should give rise to a political doctrine bearing the stamp of those conditions, yet universal in its intended scope and reference—any more than in the fact that certain cosmological theories in Greece should have reflected the structure of the city-state yet should have been theories about the world and not about the city-state.

Yet, in Thoreau's case, an investigation of his background will surely make us begin to wonder whether our original interpretation of his ideas was correct—whether they are indeed quite such an abstract and general version of anarchist philosophy as we thought. As it happens, the purely literary context is sufficient to modify our opinion, for Thoreau says: "To speak practically and as a citizen, unlike those who call themselves no-government men, I ask for, not at once no government, but *at once* a better government." But the external context also has a bearing, for the conditions of nineteenth-century America not only influenced Thoreau to think as he did but were also borne in mind by him as he wrote; he counted on his readers to bear the same conditions in mind and insert his thoughts, as it were, into that setting. Some of the conditions of his thought were, in short, also objects of reference in his thinking. In that case his meaning becomes more particularized than the meaning of the words as they stand on the page. His libertarian principles were asserted, in view of some of the experienced benefits of individualism, against a government which supported slavery and imperialism; and whether they were also intended as general principles of political theory is a question that cannot be judged apart from that special reference. The Mexican War—one of the two great immediate evils in the eyes of Thoreau—was one in which the role of government was secondary to that of the sturdy individualist. The slaveholder also professed himself an advocate of weak central government. Phrases about "strong government" and "weak government" do not discriminate between such positions and that of Thoreau—who would, perhaps, have hailed any strong federal government which had undertaken to abolish slavery. It is, of course, possible for a writer to be inconsistent, confused, and careless about the implications of his words, or (in any of a dozen senses) "not really mean what he says." But we wonder whether Thoreau can have been oblivious of such discordances as those I have just noted; and we come, perhaps, to propose to ourselves an interpretation which trims the meaning of some of his words. "That government is best, at least in some times and places, which interferes as little as possible with some activities, which I could specify, of some kinds of men, whom I could name."

There is, at any rate, an option here for the interpreter of Thoreau. The circumstances of his time may set a man thinking and instigate him to the promulgation of a universal doctrine. On the other hand, those same circumstances, taken as a setting for that doctrine, may curtail its intended significance and application. The point is that this option has been created, and indeed enforced upon the interpreter, by contextual knowledge; so that background factors which seem at first to have a purely genetic significance turn out to be engrossed in the very text whose "origins" we thought we were exploring. It is not difficult to show, in general terms, how this comes about. When two people who are engaged in communication have common objects in their environment—as a husband and wife may have their dog and as Thoreau and his readers had the basic issues and institutions of their time and country—they can rely on the awareness of these objects to supply a larger or smaller part of the ideas which they are exchanging and do not need to have the exact meaning embodied in their speech. One can say, "The animal is sick," meaning specifically this dog; and Thoreau can say, "That government is best which governs least," meaning just that certain functions of the American government should be restricted in certain ways. When one can really count on the presence of these surrounding circumstances to fill out or specify one's meaning, one's speech is not so vague or ambiguous as it might seem to a person who had only the speech before him. But later times are apt to be in just that position and, in order to understand what was said, must try to reconstruct the situation of the writer. The need for this effort, and its usefulness to the interpreter, will vary according to the document or the passage. Scientific treatises tend to disclose themselves pretty fully to one who understands merely the language in which they are written; and the context of a scientific doctrine is something superadded to its content. But anyone who, though not at all puzzled by the language of political writings in the seventeenth century, has felt himself to be in the dark as to their import until he could know just what persons and parties they were written against, what those persons and parties stood for, with what or whom the authors in turn affiliated themselves, etc., will not question the merits of contextualism as a philosophy of interpretation.

But these merits can be exaggerated and can become a source of confusion. When the historian Taine said that "to comprehend a work of art, an artist, a group of artists, we must represent to ourselves with exactitude the general state of the spirit and customs of the time to which they belong," he was taking the verb "to comprehend" in two ways: first, in the way in which we speak of comprehending the Northern Lights or the growth of population, that is, to explain through its causes; second, in the way we speak of understanding Stravinsky's music or a poem by Rimbaud, that is, to know what it says or contains. The program called for the causal explanation of literature, in keeping with the deterministic assumption of Taine that works of the mind were "products, like sugar or vitriol"; and it is, indeed, for his failure to provide sufficient explanations that Taine is usually criticized. But the program sought for itself the extra credit of being the means of clarifying literature and of providing canons of interpretation. Now we have conceded, or even insisted, that historical knowledge can illuminate literature. But this—an incident or a by-product of the historian's mission—should not obscure the difference between the nature of a thing and its causes, the meaning of a text and its background. A writer can refer to things which do not form part of his own background at all: historical research may be largely wasted if we are trying to clarify this part of his meaning. And, conversely, circumstances which have had a material influence on the formation of his personality may be unknown to him or, if known, not even remotely alluded to in his writing.[1] The historian is interested primarily in things which do not enter into the sense of a passage; the interpreter, primarily in things which are not found among its antecedents. Many texts (e.g., treatises on the stars) show no overlapping whatever between meaning and background; and our attention is called to entirely different things when we investigate one and the other. When we do touch upon background factors which are significant also for interpretation, we are taking them two ways over: first, as related existentially to a person's thought and, second, as part of what he is thinking about. The same *fact* belongs to two classes, but this does not mean that the classes are not distinct.[2]

Any given portion of historical context will have unequal values as applied to the purposes of interpretation and explanation. Thus I should think that the general history of Thoreau's time is rather more useful to us in clarifying his position than in showing why he took it, while psychogenetic factors, if they were known, might have a different kind of utility.

A slack historicity in interpretative criticism, contenting itself with some formula about the "need to see every work in its place in the tradition," ignores its own controlling motives. When the over-all purpose is interpretative, history will function as a moment within that broad intention. The interpreter will make short excursions into the historical background, selecting items for notice through an implicit sense of their relevance to the meaning of his text. When the aim is basically historical, quite a different emphasis is shown; and certain questions in interpretation will be raised as minor incidents in the prosecution of that aim.

Establishing the general principle of contextual relevance does nothing to simplify the problems of the interpreter; it simply exposes areas in which there are decisions for him to make. Contextual relevance has its limits, beyond which the genetic method becomes either useless or baneful to the interpreter. And let us say, first of all, that there are limits to the plasticity of the text.

What sort of context could compel us to interpret Thoreau as advocating absolute government? What kind or amount of external evidence would force us to read "that government is best which governs least" as meaning "that government is best which governs most"? Suppose we found Thoreau, elsewhere in his life or in his writing, admiring contemporaneous absolute monarchies or dictatorships. We would say that he had changed his mind, that he contradicted himself, or that he was ambivalent in his political attitudes. We would say that there were "conflicting strains of thought" in his work. We would say that he was speaking of different things (as Marxists speak of a *provisional* dictatorship and an *eventual* anarchy). We would say any of these things before conceding that the right interpretation of the passage in the text was the reverse of the apparent one. There is something fixed and rigid about the words and their public usage, though there is something else that is not rigid but variable with the complementary context. The purely linguistic content has a gist which contextual study can modify but which cannot be twisted at liberty into any shape proposed.

A Japanese colleague with whom I once shared an office would sometimes enter when I was there and say, "Please don't make trouble." I could easily interpret this: "Please do not trouble yourself on my account." One could hardly—apart from codes in which, by secret agreement, familiar words are given wholly arbitrary meanings—encounter a greater reversal of the apparent meaning by the true meaning, a greater difference between what a man "says" and what he "means." And, since I was able to effect the reversal by knowledge of the speaker's character and probable intention, it becomes tempting to say that the true sense is what the author intends. But one then forgets that the words as uttered, in their common public American connotation, did after all lend themselves to the "correct" interpretation; the probable intention did fit in, however awkwardly, with the words as spoken. Scholars working on literary texts which have for the most part public conventional meanings find special choices posed for them among possible alternatives (i.e., readings which fit the text); and in these circumstances they may declare, for good reasons or bad, that the author's sense is the true or decisive one. But lifting this out of situation and framing it as a naked rule of interpretation, which might apply automatically to any case, they convey the preposterous suggestion that an author who had written "Cats eat mice" could by his own say-so make it mean "Three two's are six." This is to overlook the need for the dovetailing of internal and external evidence, the weighing of kinds of evidence one against another. The recognition of this need will reduce any overweening claim for the "uses of history" and provide in its degree the justification for those who say that, life being short, they wish to get what they can from art and philosophy, directly confronted.

There is a principle of diminishing returns in the application of knowledge. Appreciative understanding does not grow in exact correspondence to the growth of contextual information; and the interpreter must know when and where to stop—he must separate the extrinsic facts which help to reveal the sense from those which encrust and conceal it. Let us consider an extreme example. One of Balzac's heroes, prowling through an antiquary's shop, scans object after object with reflections similar to these: "A salt-cellar from Cellini's workshop carried him back to the Renaissance at its height, to the time when there was no restraint on art or morals, when torture was the sport of sovereigns; and from their councils, churchmen with courtesans' arms about them issued decrees of chastity for simple priests."

This manner of engrossing the context of a work in its meaning is a perpetual temptation to the historically minded; but—apart from Balzac's particular errors of fact and of taste—it is really *un*historical, since it assigns a meaning which could not have been shared by the artist and his contemporaries, who, being at no distance from themselves, had no way of enjoying the pathos of distance.

Like a stone or a flower, in which the naturalist sees whole volumes of natural history written out, a work of art can "speak" to the historian of anything which, however remotely, has entered into its composition. It is not improper to speak of the "meaning" an object possesses in virtue of its relations to other things; but this is certainly not the same as the thought contained in and conveyed by works of the human mind. In the example from Balzac the mistake is obvious, since a work by Cellini makes no statement about the "Renaissance luxury" of which it was a product. If one could always draw as sharp a line, the discipline of interpretation would be less taxing than it is. But when, for example, we think we see a whole system of Christian theology in the *Disputà* of Raphael, we may be thinking of historical elements in the painter's background which lead up to and more or less explain the presence of certain visual forms on the wall; or we may be apprehending farther and higher ranges of significance, of which the visual forms have been set down as vehicles. In all probability, we are doing something of each. The artist has rendered a conception of theology, to which the history of that subject is the only clue but which is nonetheless present in the painting. But he has not put into the painting everything which pedantry can spell out of it, down to the last letter of every work by St. Augustine or St. Jerome. It is surely very difficult to decide what "belongs" and what does not; but such decisions must be ventured, lest, on the one hand, such a work seem poorer to us than it is or, on the other, we confuse our appreciation of our own historical knowledge with an appreciation of the work we are interpreting.

3. Interpretation and Evaluation

It would seem that interpretation should be complete before criticism can so much as get started. Yet it is easy to show that criticism can function as a moment within the interpretative process. We need only consider a remark as common, among interpreters, as this: "If he meant what he seems to be saying here, he would not only be wrong but inexcusably so. But we know from the rest of his work that he is an intelligent man. He could not have committed an error like this. He must mean something else." The argument here is complicated, employing different sorts of premise; but one of the reasons for rejecting a certain hypothesis as to the author's view is the interpreter's own opinion of the absurdity of that view. Such a rebound from criticism to interpretation could be illustrated in divers ways. A first guess as to the sense of the text starts us thinking about the truth of that text, so interpreted; and the result of that appraisal sends us back to the text for a surer understanding. Criticism is then resumed from this new interpretation. Following the suggestion of the last section, we could, then, reach a view of the functions of interpreter and critic which might be epitomized in the phrase, "Broad difference in principle; minute interrelations in practice."

The ravings and maunderings of mental patients have, it is said, a "meaning" for the student of psychology, as do other worthless products of the human mind—advertisements, convention speeches, and the like. And so also the poorest or most ordinary products of the Chinese mind may attract the interest of the Sinologist, for whom they have a "value," symptomatic or documentary. One understands very well, for instance, why a historian should feel impelled to study astrology, a subject in which he personally cannot take any stock. The sterner devotees of an objective scholarship, who say it is not their business to say what they think about other people's ideas but only to say what those are and how they came to be what they are, have a good deal of reason on their side. Anyone who countenances a general distinction between interpretation and criticism must admit that the latter can, ideally, be dispensed with. No criterion of value is assumed merely in selecting a thing for study. The Four Gospels, the dialogues of Plato, and the Confucian writings, which must seem to any impartial reader to be documents of great intrinsic interest and merit, have also been thought to be such by thousands or millions of Europeans and Chinese; and this historical importance, which they share with poor stuff like the works of Hitler and of Alfred Rosenberg, is enough to recommend them to the historian.

Yet one supposes, after all, that one motive for studying China is the appreciation, perhaps the appropriation, of its positive achievements, in science, art, philosophy, and government. But this presupposes a principle of selection, an ability to tell the difference between what is valid and what is spurious or indifferent. In the end it is difficult, and not particularly desirable, for men to refrain from criticism.

The assertion of the right to criticize is, however, hedged about with epistemological problems of such depth and intricacy as to have defied solution from the time of Protagoras to the present day. Some of these can be couched in a perfectly general form. They show up, without noticeable variation, in the philosophy of science as well as in ethics and aesthetics or in comparative religion as well as in political theory; and they are exemplified just as well by a difference of opinion arising between two colleagues working side by side in the same laboratory as by the difference in outlook between a dervish and a mathematical statistician. But others seem to present themselves with peculiar force in the criticism, say, of art or of moral philosophy; or they appear as obstacles to the criticism, in particular, of distant cultures. A scholar who would not, on account of the difference in sex or station, hesitate to criticize the opinions of his wife or his congressman would consider it madness in himself to presume to evaluate the beliefs of the Hopi or the ethics of an ancient Chinese thinker. And this not merely for contingent reasons—the relative lack of information and concrete insight into a foreign body of thought, the need for exceptional caution in procedure—but for fundamental ones, such as a sense of the unfairness in the act of judging a body of thought by norms of cognition which it does not itself recognize, a fear of the distortion which would seem to be inherent in the imposition of one's own categories of truth and value upon one who had never dreamed of such categories.

The student is caught between the need, and the very nearly irresistible impulse, to determine the validity of the ideas he is examining and the objections which tell so powerfully against any attempt on his part to do so. I could not hope, in the space of this article or in a dozen like it, to resolve such an impasse. But our subject is interpretation; and I would like to point out that there is a mutual exacerbation of the critic's troubles and the interpreter's when we shift their responsibilities one onto the other. The result is a vaguely desperate feeling about the inaccessibility of foreign modes of thought, a feeling which prevents the truly troublesome questions of epistemology from ever being clearly posed.

I. A. Richards, in *Mencius on the Mind*,[3] asks:

> Can we in attempting to understand and translate a work which belongs to a very different tradition from our own do more than read our own conceptions into it? . . . Can we maintain two systems of thinking in our minds without reciprocal infection and yet in some way mediate between them? And does not such mediation require yet a third system of thought general enough and comprehensive enough to include them both? And how are we to prevent this third system from being only our own familiar, established tradition of thinking rigged out in some fresh terminology or other disguise?

It will be noted that the question has to do solely with the understanding of the foreign work. Yet, particularly in the third sentence, it is stated in a way which reminds us of those who feel that, to avoid lapsing into a complete relativism, it is necessary to find a neutral and impersonal set of standards for *deciding* between our own views and those of people who disagree with us. In other words, the question is modeled upon a problem of epistemology.

Let us suppose we had two human minds that were, to begin with, as different as possible in all their manifold expressions. How could one of these undertake first to understand and then to evaluate by its own lights the contributions of the other while still doing them complete justice?

For convenience we might confine the question to ideas about nature. There is a point often made about the basic concepts of the natural sciences which I think also holds for those ordinary concepts which are represented by the vocabulary of a language. It is a commonplace of logic textbooks that basic concepts in a science are to be rated by their heuristic value—as productive and useful, or sterile and obstructive, rather than as true or false. Thus the concept "mammal," which groups the whale and the bat together with cats, rodents, etc., and separates them from the fishes and the birds is not in any way truer than the ideas of sea, air, and land animals but is better, in ways that I need not explain, as a foundation for zoölogy. But the propositions in which such concepts, good ones or poor ones, occur will be true or false. Thus, if you have perversely chosen to call the whale a fish, then to say that all fish lay eggs will be false.[4]

Now the concepts represented by the average man's vocabulary—dog, cat, sit, stand, walk, red, green, blue, etc.—constitute, like the concepts of natural science, a grouping and selection of the phenomena of nature. The formation of those concepts is not, as in the case of the sciences, dictated by or responsible to explicit goals of predictability, system, and order. Yet there is a general resemblance in the fact that our ordinary concepts were influenced in their growth by practical needs, by emotional and aesthetic factors, by motives of convenience, simplicity, utility, and by accidents of all kinds; that no one set of them has any kind of exclusive legitimacy; on the contrary, that many different sets may exist side by side without logical conflict. Thus, to make up an example at random, we might well imagine that some group of people should have no concept corresponding to the English "shadow." It is hard to believe that any people living under the sun should not sometimes have noticed shadows; but recalling the fact that in some painting no shadows are found at all while in the works of the painter Braque the side of the pitcher which is turned from the light, instead of modeling into the third dimension, becomes a flat area of dark color contrasting with the lighter side, we can well understand that shadows might to some people seem not interesting or important enough to deserve a separate name as a class. Perhaps they are comprehended together with other things under the word for "dark spot." Now imagine further that someone should attempt a translation into such a language of an English text containing the word "shadow." Such a person, to be competent, would have to be a bilinguist; and this means that he knows the meaning of a word like "shadow," as well as the words in his own language, through seeing its use in dozens of literary contexts, its application to hundreds of experiences in daily life, its definition in the English dictionary by means of other English terms the meaning of which he already knows. In other words, he knows the range of objects which this word denotes; and he knows it is not the same as that of his word for "dark spot"; so he is able to say, "We have no exact equivalent for the English 'shadow.' " His ability to say this presumes an understanding of the English word. The ability to speak about the difficulties of translation, about the perils of crossing the gap between an ancient author and ourselves, presumes an achieved identification of the interpreter with the mental process of the subject, a vantage point from which he can belabor distorted readings. No "third system" of concepts is either possible or necessary. He will perhaps in a roundabout fashion and using many words attempt a construction of the concept "shadow" out of the concepts his language already possesses. If instead of "shadow" you will think of psychological or religious concepts or think of the translation of metaphors and puns from a language as close to ours as German, you will readily admit that the position just described is one in which translators really do find themselves. Now it seems to me that the real difficulty of communication, and the real danger of distortion, exists at this level of exchange of concepts. To say that two people "live in different worlds" is to say, very largely, that the world is carved up and organized differently by their respective systems of concepts; and to say that one "imposes" his own categories on the other is to say that he assumes for the other's concepts meanings which are readiest at hand and most familiar to him in his own thought and language. There then often follows a glib "appraisal" in terms of truth or falsity. But it does not follow from this that, if one *had* achieved precise understanding of the other mentality in its own terms, one would *still* be in no position to evaluate its ideas. One thing is to understand the word "shadow," to learn the extent and the limits of the idea, to overcome the strangeness of having to pick out a class of phenomena never before noticed as a class. But to be able then to judge the truth of propositions concerning shadows, their causes and effects, their increase or diminution with various kinds of lighting, is a matter of plain experimental verification, of which in principle any human being is capable.

I have been trying to meet an objection to intercultural criticism which stems from a confusion between communication and judgment. No doubt there exist more sophisticated and formidable objections. It may, for instance, be urged against the foregoing paragraphs that "concepts" and "propositions" are not so easy to keep separate, since a given concept, say, of human nature may reflect or incorporate a whole battery of previous convictions. But even if the foregoing analysis were wholly acceptable, it still is restricted to ideas of natural science, both the understanding and the appraisal of which are—by comparison with art, politics, religion, and metaphysics—exceptionally plain and simple. Since the meaning and validity of ethical judgments are as such in dispute among professional moralists, there is a double risk and temerity involved in the evaluation of alien systems of ethics. Such difficulties I must leave undiscussed, but with the suggestion that to clear up problems of interpretation first and take up problems of judgment later would probably be a useful procedure everywhere.

NOTES

1. Of course there are many moot cases. A famous one is the question whether we can say there is an "unconscious" allusion to an Oedipus complex in *Hamlet*—granted that we have any reason to attribute an Oedipus complex to the author and to suppose that it was a genetic factor in the creation of the play. But, to bring out the difference between meaning and background, we should look to the clear-cut case: an Oedipus complex might have played a part in turning a man away from his father's occupation to the study, say, of geology; it has, therefore, causal or genetic significance; but it will probably not show up, even in the faintest way, as an object of reference in the work on geology.

2. A short and pointed example may be useful here. When, in Victor Hugo, a Spanish grandee, who with some of his fellows is about to be executed in the presence of the king, refuses to take his hat off and remarks—

> "Oui, nos têtes, O roi,
> Ont le droit de tomber couvertes devant toi!"—

and a footnote tells us, "A Spanish nobleman had the traditional right of standing with his head covered before the king," we admit that the historical fact is helpful; without it the play on words, on which the whole effect of the lines depends, would be lost. But does it have to have been a *fact?* Might it not as well have been a legend, or an invention of Hugo's, so long as the *idea* of such a traditional right somehow gets framed for consideration by the audience along with the explicit sense of the lines?

3. (London, 1932), p. 86.

4. See M. R. Cohen and Ernest Nagel, *An Introduction to Logic and Scientific Method* (London: Routledge, 1940), pp. 223–24.

TOWARD A THEORY OF TRANSLATING

I. A. RICHARDS

That dolphin-torn, that gong-tormented sea.

W. B. YEATS, "Byzantium"

LOOKING BACK, across more than a score of years, on the considerations with which *Mencius on the Mind* was concerned, it seems to me now that the togethernesses, the mutualities, of those considerations were omitted. There were distinctions made and differences stressed between sorts of meaning, but why they should be so made and so stressed hardly became apparent. The last chapter, "Towards a Technique for Comparative Studies," was suitably tentative in title and in treatment. It stammered away persistently, but what it was trying to say never, *as a whole*, got said. I have some doubts whether any whole was in any steady way in the mind of the sayer. The book was written hurriedly, in a whirl of lecturing on *Ulysses* and on *The Possessed*, during a first teaching visit to Harvard. It was worked up from notes made between Tsing Hua and Yenching, under the guidance of divers advisers, and written out with much of the feeling one has in trying to scribble down a dream before it fades away. The intellectual currencies of the Harvard scene, not to mention Leopold Bloom and Stavrogin, were driving out those Chinese *aperçus* all the while. Then the only manuscript was lost, stolen by Li An-che's cook by mistake. It lay on a house roof for some months, tossed there by the thief the instant he perceived how worthless it was. Then odd pages began blowing up and down the *hutung*; rumor spread and a search was made; it was found and returned to me—just in time to be compared with the proofs of a second version I had been recollecting back home again in Cambridge, where yet another local logical game had been offering yet other guide lines to be avoided. All useful experience, no doubt, in guessing about *what* makes *what* seem to mean *what*—*when*, *where*, and to *whom*—but not then and there conducive to a single comprehensive view of comprehending.

This, I now suppose, is what one should attempt to form. I suppose too that a first condition of the endeavor is a recognition of its inherent wilfulness. It is purposive; it seeks. If asked *what* it seeks, its only just answer should be: "Itself." It seeks to comprehend what comprehending may be. What is sought is the search.

Yet it advances. When it looks back upon its earlier phases, what it most notes are the things it took for granted *without* having put its requests into any but most indefinite form. It can bring the request and the grant nearer to terms forever without any fear of arriving. The process of refining its assumptions must be just as endless as the endeavor itself.

Through these assumptions it divides and combines[1]—dividing in order to combine, combining in order to divide—and simultaneously. Whatever it compares is compared in a respect or in respects. These respects are the instruments of the exploration. And it is with them as with the instruments of investigation in physics but more so: the properties of the instruments enter into the account of the investigation. There is thus at the heart of any theory of meanings a principle of the instrument. The exploration of comprehension is the task of devising a system of instruments for comparing meanings. But this system, these instruments, are themselves comparable. They belong with what they compare and are subject in the end to one another. Indeed, this mutual subjection or control seems to be the ἀρχή for a doctrine of comprehension—that upon which all else depends.[2]

There is a seeming opposition to be reconciled here. We may suppose there to be a hierarchy of instruments, each caring for those below and cared for by those above. Or we may suppose the system to be circular. I have leaned here toward a position somewhat like that of the constitutional monarchist who supports an authority which is itself under control (see Aspect VI below). The same question seems to me to appear again as: "How should we structure the most embracing purpose?" and this I take to be an invitation to an inquiry into Justice on Platonic lines.

This mutual control shows itself in any segment of activity (any stretch of discourse, for example) as accordance and discordance of means with ends. Ends endeavor to choose means which will choose them. The entirety of activity, if, obeying Aristotle, we may venture to attempt to conceive it, seems to consist of *choices*. Initial choices would be free; but, when choice has been made, the sequent choices are bound thereby while the choice is held. An interpretation knows only a part, often a very small part, of the entailments of its choices. These entailments may later seem to it to be "brute fact"—something in no way and in no measure due to its choices, something upon which their success or failure depends. This is the defectiveness of the choices—made too soon or not made when choice was needed.

Enough of these preliminaries. They seemed necessary to the introduction here of the word LET as the first and all-important move in this undertaking. Let *let* rule every meaning for every word in every sentence which follows. These sentences will seem for the most part to be in the indicative, but that is for brevity and for custom's sake. Everything which seems to be said in the indicative floats on a raft of optative invitations to mean in such wise. Any theory of meanings which can serve as authority, as more embracing purpose, to a theory of translation is concerned with the mutual tension of whatever can be put together to serve as that raft.

Such are among the reflections which translation between diverse cultures can occasion. How may we compare what a sentence in English may mean with what a sentence in Chinese may mean? The only sound traditional answer is in terms of two scholarships—one in English, the other in Chinese. But a skepticism which can be liberating rather than paralyzing may make us doubtful of the sufficiency of our techniques for comparing meanings even within one tradition. How can one compare a sentence in English poetry with one (however like it) in English prose? Or indeed any two sentences, or the same sentence, in different settings? What is synonymy?[3] A proliferous literature of critical and interpretative theory witnesses to the difficulty. It seems to have been felt more and more in recent decades. Is there any reason to doubt that analogous difficulties await analogous efforts for Chinese? They may well have been attending the conduct of that language all along.

These troubles come, perhaps, in part from insufficient attention to the comparing activity itself. How do we compare other things? Let us see whether what we do in comparing boxes or rooms can be helpful in suggesting what we might do in comparing meanings. What would a sort of geometry of comprehendings be like? With rooms, we need, in the simplest cases, three dimensions. With length, breadth, and height ascertained, we have gone some way toward discovering how far one room is like another. Would it be useful to ask in how many "dimensions" meanings may agree or differ? It might be wise to drop the geometric word and generalize at once. Let us say, then, "in how many respects"—remembering that meanings may, if we so wish, be compared in an indefinitely great number of respects or in as few as will serve some purpose. The purpose decides which respects are relevant. This is true of rooms, too. So our problem is one of choice. What is the simplest system of respects which would enable us to compare meanings in a way serviceable to the translator's purposes? (As three dimensions serve us in comparing sizes and shapes.)

I have just called this a *problem*. If a problem is something which has a solution, I should not have done so. In my opening sentence I called such things *considerations*, hoping thereby to suggest that they are fields of unlimited speculation—held within only the most unlimited framework that even sidereal space could symbolize—and not, as problems in a branch of mathematics may be, formed and given their solutions by the assumptions which set them up. What this theory of meaning should be or do is not in this narrow sense a problem.

It is, on the other hand, the most searching of all considerations, for it is concerned with arranging our techniques for arranging. Since the system of respects is set up to serve our comparings, the respects in it must not be too many or too few, and they will probably vary with the comparing. But this cannot itself be described except by means of the respects which serve it, being the comparing which these respects implement and enable. (Similarly, the comparing of sizes and shapes cannot be

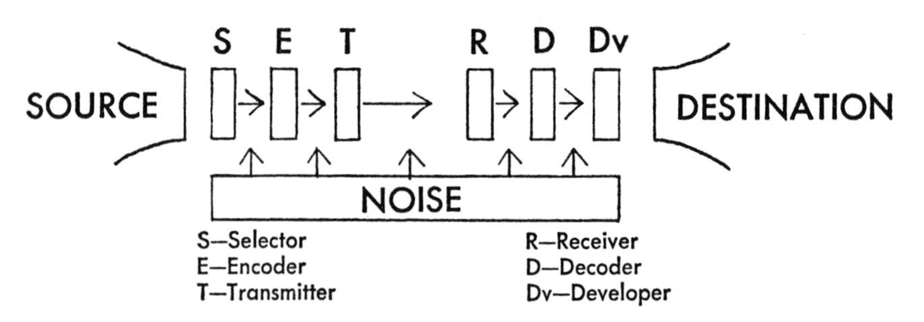

described except by reference to the spatial dimensions.) In brief, we make an instrument and try it out. Only by trying it out can we discover what it can do for us. Likewise, only such trial can develop our comprehending of what it is with which we seek to explore comprehending. Thus what ensues will be a depiction of the whereby and the wherefore as well as the what.

We may begin by adapting the conventional diagram of the communication engineer to our wider purposes.[4] In translation we have two such diagrams to consider as a minimum. There will be (say) a Chinese communication for which we find ourselves in the role of Destination; and we assume thereupon the role of Source for a communication in English. But since other communications in Chinese and other communications in English, having *something in common* with the present communication, come in to guide the encodings and decodings, the process becomes very complex. We have here indeed what may very probably be the most complex type of event yet produced in the evolution of the cosmos.

Between two utterances[5] the operative *something in common* whereby the one influences the other may be any feature or character or respect whatever and can be itself highly complex. It may be some conjunction of respects. The comprehending of any utterance is guided by any number of partially similar situations in which partially similar utterances have occurred. More exactly, the comprehending is a function of the comparison fields from which it derives. Let the units of which these comparison fields consist be *utterances-within-situations*—the utterance and its situation being partners in the network of transactions with other utterances in other situations which lends significance to the utterance. Partially similar utterances made within very different situations are

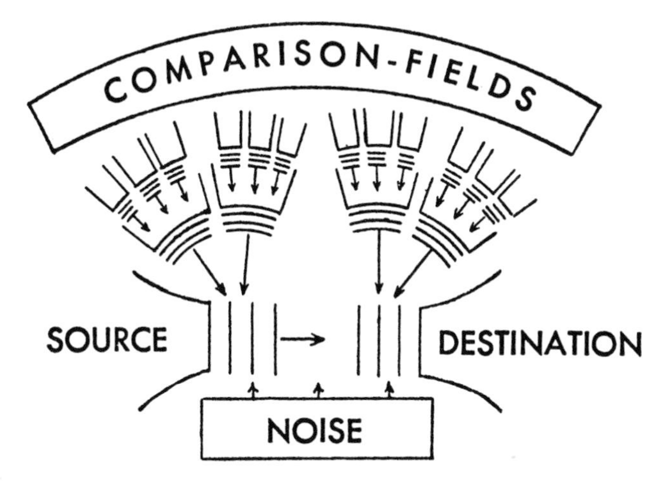

UTTERANCES-in-SITUATIONS

likely to require different comprehendings, though language is, of course, our collective attempt to minimize these divergences of meaning.

A comprehending, accordingly, is an instance of a nexus[6] established through past occurrences of partially similar utterances in partially similar situations—utterances and situations partially co-varying. The past utterances-within-situations need not have been consciously remarked or wittingly analyzed; still less need they be explicitly remembered when the comprehending occurs. Thus the word *comparison* in the technical term "comparison-field" may mislead. It is not necessary that the members of a comparison-field—widely diverse utterances-within-situations as they may be—should ever have been taken together in explicit analytic scrutiny and examined as to their likenesses and differences. The discriminations and connections (dividings and combinings) which arise in the development of meaning are, in some respects, *as though* this had been done. Sometimes they are so produced; but, for the most part, they need no such elaborate reflective procedure. Let me generalize "comparison" here to make it cover whatever putting together and setting apart (however unremarked) has been operative in the formation of the nexus. The routine of concept formation and of discriminative behavior even down to what we might call merely perceptual levels has an interesting resemblance to the highest activities of systematic conceptual classification. It is as though the nervous system had been taught Mill's Joint Method of Agreement and Difference.

What I have been sketching applies, for the translator, in the first place to the Decoding and Developing of the Chinese utterance. In the second place it applies to the Selecting and Encoding which (it is hoped) will produce an utterance in English acceptable as a translation from the Chinese. But, plainly enough, the co-varyings of utterances-within-situations for English are other than they are for Chinese. Any translator has acquired his Chinese and his English through "comparison-fields" which are different and systematically different in structure: different not only with respect to the ways in which utterances change with situations, but also with respect to those changes that are significant in utterances (e.g., phonemics) and with respect to those changes that are significant in situations (e.g., status recognition). The comparative linguist could, if he wished, illustrate this for the rest of his natural days. And it is one of the pedagogue's reasons for preferring a "direct" method to a "translation" method in beginning language learning. He finds that by keeping to one language only he can provide comparison-fields (through sequences of sentences-in-situations) which are more effective, that is, more propitious to full and deep comprehending later on. This structuring of experience will of course differ with our aim. The linguist—for his purposes—will set up one schema of respects in which comparisons will be made; the pedagogue—for his purposes—will set up another. What schema will a translator set up to serve as a theory of the sorts and interrelations of meanings to guide him in his own tasks?

Limitless in their variety, these tasks present themselves, the words, phrases, sentence forms and the situations, and the meanings, to be compared being as varied as the ways in which they may be compared. How are we to choose the respects (or dimensions) which will serve us best as headings under which to arrange those similarities and those differences of meanings which the translator must try to discern in one language and to achieve in another? In the concrete, in the minute particulars of practice, these comparison-fields are familiar enough; though we tend to forget, as scholars, what we must always, as pedagogues, recall:

that these comparison-fields go back into infancy. All we have to do is to arrange, in a schema as parsimonious as adequacy will allow, a body of experience so common that if the purposing of our arrangement could be agreed on, there might be little we would then differ about.

Let us turn our communications diagram through 90 degrees now and look down it. Here is a cross-section of the activities to be found there, made at the points where what is prepared for transmission and what has been decoded and developed may be supposed—in a successful communication—to resemble one another most nearly. I have marked and numbered for labeling the seven[7] divisions in my proposed schema.

I. Points to, selects. . . .
II. Says something about, sorts. . . .
III. Comes alive to, wakes up to, presents. . . .
IV. Cares about. . . .
V. Would change or keep as it is. . . .
VI. Manages, directs, runs, administers itself. . . .
VII. Seeks, pursues, tries, endeavors to be or to do. . . .

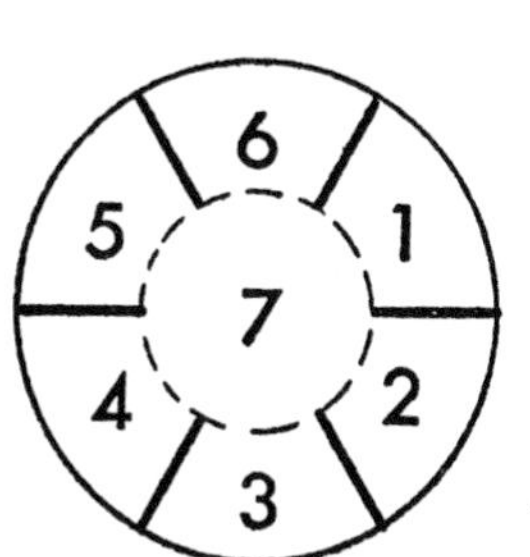

I. Indicating
II. Characterizing
III. Realizing
IV. Valuing
V. Influencing
VI. Controlling
VII. Purposing

Let us label these *sorts of work* which an utterance may be doing with two or more sets of names, academic and colloquial—on the assumption that communication will be made more probable if we use here a multiplicity of largely equivalent indications. I am numbering them for convenience of reference; but I do not want to suggest that there is any fixed temporal order, that first we Select, then we Characterize, then Realize, then Value, then would Influence, then Organize and then Purpose. Nor is there any constant logical order. Let us keep these jobs as independent one of another as we can. In individual cases we will find many sorts of detailed dependence, but let us put none in by definition.

In applying this schema to translating, we can ask of two utterances in two languages:

I. How far do they pick out the same (or at least analogous) things to talk about?

II. How far do they say the same (or at least analogous) things about them?

III. How far do they present with equal vividness and/or actuality, weak or strong?

IV. How far do they value in the same ways?

V. How far would they keep or change in the same ways?

VI. How far are the dependencies and interplay between I, II, III, IV, V, and VI itself, the same in them both?

VII. How widely would they serve the same purposes, playing the same parts, within the varying activities they might occur in?

Let me label this seven-fold event which my diagram depicts COMPREHENDING, as comprehensive a name as I can find. Any full utterance does all these things at once, and invites all of them in the comprehender. In some instances, however, one or more of these dimensions, aspects, powers, functions, jobs, variables, parameters, components, ingredients, tasks, duties (all these words are in need of the comparative study my diagram should be an instrument for), will shrink toward the null, the vanishing point. There is swearing and there is mathematics. In swearing there *may* be nothing but IV, V, and VII; in mathematics only I, VI, and VII may matter. It would appear that VII never lapses; without purposing, without the feed-forward[8] which structures all activity, no utterance and no comprehending. A full comparison between two utterances (between an original and a translation of it, for example) would require us to discern what all their dimensions, aspects, functions, may be and compare them as to each and as to their relations within the entire comprehending. In comparing boxes or rooms, we need three dimensions; in comparing comprehendings, we need, I suggest, at least these seven.

Even of a single comprehending we can ask our seven sorts of questions: Under I, we ask WHICH things are being talked (thought) of? Under II, WHAT is being said of them? Under III, EVEN so? Under IV, SHOULD this be so? Under V, WON'T YOU (WON'T I)? Under VI, HOW? Under VII, WHEREIN, WHEREBY, and WHEREFORE, TO WHAT END?

Of these, I and II may be felt to be more narrowly, more clearly, *questions* than the others; and III especially may seem to be rather a wondering than a questioning. Under III, what is in question is the nearness and fulness with which something is to be present to us. *Doubting* ("is this so or not, possibly, probably, certainly?") belongs (in this schema) rather to V or VI ("to be accepted or not, and how?").

Let us consider these functions in turn.

Indicating and *Characterizing* will need less comment than the others. They have been more discussed, for they correspond to the distinction logicians make under the labels "Extension-Intension" and "Denotation-Connotation." In the logicians' use, the denotation of a term is whatever may be covered by the term and the connotation is the set of properties (characters) anything must have if it is to be so covered. But there is also a well-established literary use of "connotation" in which the connotation is III, IV, and V in my diagram rather than II (which is likely then to be called the "bare, or mere meaning"). These two uses of "connotation" parallel what may be the chief difference between scientific and poetic use of language. There is some parallel, too, with what I have discussed (*Interpretation in Teaching*, p. 311) as the rigid and the fluid uses of language. If we make Characterizing be "*saying something about* what is being pointed to," we have obviously to narrow down the meaning of "saying." It can open out to take in anything that an utterance can do, anything in any way said, suggested, evoked, hinted, required, and implied (the literary connotation), or it can be kept down to the logician's connotation—the "definition" (as it is sometimes put) of a term.

The last paragraph illustrates—as must any attempt to write about the language we use or should use about language—the heavy duties we have to put on quotation marks. I have suggested (*How To Read a Page*, pp. 68–70) that we should develop sets of specialized quotes, as a technical notation by which we could better keep track of the uses we are making of our words, and I have tried out the use of a few such quotation marks in that book and elsewhere. I am now more than ever persuaded of the usefulness of this device. It can serve us to distinguish many different uses we make of quotes. For example:

^{w} . . . ^{w} to show that it is a word—that word in general, Peirce's ^{r}type^{r}—which is being talked of.[9] For example, ^{w}use^{w} is a highly ambiguous word.

^{oc} . . . ^{oc} to show that occurrences of a word—Peirce's ^{r}token^{r}—are being talked of. For example, I have been using ^{oc}uses^{oc} above in various ways.

^{r} . . . ^{r} to show that some special use of the word or phrase is being *referred* to. The marks may be read as *refer to* and the implication may be that only by having that particular use of the word in that passage present to us in lively attention (Realizing) can we distinguish it from other uses and avoid confusion.

^{t} . . . ^{t} to show that the word or phrase is being used as a *technical term* anchored by a definition to some state of affairs or procedure—to an operational technique perhaps or to a set of performances.

^{q} . . . ^{q} to show that how the word or phrase is to be comprehended is the question. It may be read as *query;* and we can develop this notation further by adding I–VII after the *q* to show where the focus of the question lies in my diagram. These *q*'s should carry no derogatory suggestion; their work is to locate and orientate inquiry; they are servants of VI. Thus we might write ^{qII} connotation ^{qII} or $^{qIII, IV, V}$ connotation $^{qIII, IV, V}$ to direct attention either to the logical or to the literary questions.

^{sw} . . . ^{sw} to show that we are considering what may be *said with* a certain word or phrase without decision as yet to what that is. This enables one to bring together meanings of words and phrases, for examination, without settling anything prematurely as to how they may be related. We need to bring these meanings together *before* we pick out those we may profitably compare. I have written elsewhere at length (*Interpretation in Teaching*, chaps. xv and xix; *How To Read a Page*, chap. x) on the troubles which the lack of such a warning mark may lead us into.

$^{!}$ . . . $^{!}$ to show astonishment that people can write or talk so. Some will want to put this whole paper within such marks.

Once we recognize to what an extent thinking is a taking care of and a keeping account of the conduct of our words, the need for a notation with which to study and control their resourcefulness becomes obvious.

^{sw}Indicating^{sw} or ^{sw}Selecting^{sw}—especially if we picture it to ourselves with the image of a pointer (an arrow as of a wind vane)—may seem instable. It can be so; but some of our selectings are the most constant things we do. Angus Sinclair puts a further point well: "What is thus loosely describable as the selecting and grouping which each of us carries out is not an act done once and thereby completed, but is a continuing process which must be sustained if our experience is to continue as it is. If for any reason it is not sustained, i.e. if for any reason a man follows a different way of grouping in his attention, then the experience he has will be different also. Further, this requires some effort. . . . Knowing is not a passive contemplation, but a continuously effort-consuming activity."[10]

Sinclair's ^{sw}grouping^{sw} seems to be my ^{sw}Characterizing, Sorting^{sw}. We have, in English, what may seem an excess of analytic machineries to help us in distinguishing $^{!}$its$^{!}$ from $^{!}$whats$^{!}$, that is, Indicating, I, from Characterizing, II. Such are (in most uses): for I, ^{w}subject, substance, entity, particular, thing, being, group, class^{w}; for II, ^{w}predicate, attribute, property, quality, relation, character, essence, universal^{w}. A large methodological question which can seem to fall near the very heart of any endeavor to translate philosophy is this: does use of different ^{q}analytic machineries^{q} entail difference of ^{q}view^{q}? I put my *q*'s in here to remind us that both ^{sw}analytic machineries^{sw} and ^{sw}view^{sw} have to do with little-explored territories though they are surrounded by the most debatable land in ^{q}the Western philosophic tradition^{q}. Current use of most of this machinery is erratic: at a popular level it cares little which of the above words are employed; more sophisticated use varies from one philosophic school to the next.[11] There is little likelihood of increased clarity unless some new factor enters. The exercise of choice required when thinking which is remote from ^{q}the Western philosophic tradition^{q}—thinking which uses, perhaps, no such machinery—has to be thoroughly explored in English, might be just such a new factor. The distinction between Indicating and Characterizing, and their queer interplay, might, through translation studies, become again the central growing point for thought.

Realizing, III, needs more discussion here, though what the discussion should bring out is something familiar to everyone. The two meanings we separate most easily in this cluster are exemplified by: (*a*) "She realized how he would take it" and (*b*) "He thus realized his ambition." It is with (*a*) that we are concerned, though the background influence of (*b*), [sw]realizing[sw] as [sw]the becoming actual of the possible[sw], is frequently apparent. This duality may be as relevant to Chinese modes of [q]knowledge[q] as it is to some Aristotelian doctrines of becoming.

Within (*a*), two lines of interpretation offer themselves: (i) it may be taken as equivalent to [sw]She imagined vividly and livingly how he would feel[sw]; or (ii) [sw]She foresaw how he would act[sw]. (The vagueness of [oc]take it[oc] reinforces the ambiguity of [oc]realized[oc].) This exemplifies a frequent shift in [sw]realize[sw]: the shift between a lively, concrete, actualized presence and a cognizance of implications and consequences which may be (and commonly is) highly schematic. A statesman may realize what the outcome will be all the better for not realizing too vividly how *X* may feel. It thus appears that while the use of [w]realize[w] in (i) does entail a high degree of Realizing, III, in my schema, [w]realize[w] in (ii) does not. The entirety of apprehension which is ascribed by remarks such as "He fully realized," and the contrast with "He didn't at all realize," can be handled in terms of I, II, V, and VI.

What is highly realized may be distinct, explicitly structured, detailed, [q]definite[q] in most of the senses of this strategic word.[12] But it may equally well be very indefinite. That unlocatable, indescribable, almost unidentifiable qualm which is the first emergence of nausea is something which can be Realized to the full without as yet being Characterized in any but the sketchiest fashion. Conversely, Characterizing may be most complete and minute without much Realizing having developed. In fact, fulness and detail in Characterizing frequently prevent our Realizing, though the details may be offered expressly to increase it. On the other hand, many devices—from headlines to the routines of the dispatch editor and the commentator—reduce the reality of what is presented. Much that is called [q]sensationalism[q] has this effect. We may suspect that this is sometimes its justification. We need to be protected from the wear and tear of actuality. It would not be surprising if this wrapping-up professed to be unwrapping.

> Human kind
> Cannot bear very much reality.

Nonetheless, increase in Realizing is in general accompanied by increased particularity in Characterizing, and by increased choosiness and discrimination in the Selecting of what shall be Characterized.

Realizing is very frequently brought about through metaphor, as may be illustrated by the following vivid account of a moment of Realization from Virginia Woolf: "Suddenly, as if the movement of his hand had released it, the *load* of her accumulated impressions of him *tilted up*, and *down poured in a ponderous avalanch* all she felt about him. That was one sensation. Then *up rose in a fume* the essence of his being. That was another. She felt herself *transfixed* by the intensity of her perception; it was his severity; it was his goodness."[13] (My italics.)

Metaphor, however, can serve under all my headings. It is worth remarking with regard to Chinese-English translation that the great traditional metaphors of Western thought play so large a part in shaping our conceptions that a study of any metaphors which have played a comparable part in Chinese thought suggests itself as possibly a key move. Examples in the Western tradition would be: the metaphor of conception used in the previous sentence (see *Phaedrus* 276E); the analogy of the Self and the State from the *Republic*, and the tripartite structure of both; that other Platonic metaphor of intellectual vision, the eye of the mind; the comparison of the idea of the good with the sun; the metaphor of light as truth generally; the metaphor of inspiration; and, from Hosea, the metaphor of a marriage contract between the Lord and Israel, and indeed the use of the ideas of love (not sex) and fidelity in theology. These great originative structurings have acted in the West in innumerable minds which have had no notion of how important such metaphors can be. It would be hard to say, indeed, of the Self-State analogy whether thought about personality or about government has been the more influenced by it, for the traffic has been two-way. Where such a metaphor is absent in Chinese or where Chinese has a traditional metaphor which English lacks, the loss in translation is likely to be grave. The remedy is, perhaps, through a deeper, more systematic study of metaphor.[14] Assistance in such studies is, of course, one of the aims of the schema of comparisons offered in my diagram.

Valuing, IV, is a modern philosophic battleground, the dispute being in part whether the language of valuation, obligation, and justification is to be comprehended in some peculiar fashion or fashions (as !qemotiveq!) or in the ordinary way of description. For the purposes of comparative study of meanings, this warfare, on which so much time and talent is being spent, may not be important. It is not clear that any decision would help us to compare meanings better. It may be wise to hold that: rEvaluations are a form of empirical knowledge,r[15] which might put considerable strain on our concepts of qempirical knowledgeq; or it may be wiser still to hold that will and desire may enter into valuations in more ways than those in which they enter our type specimens of empirical knowledge. To decide which view would be wiser, we would have to be able to make comparisons between meanings beyond our present scope. What does seem certain is that, *as an instrument for the comparison of meanings*, our diagram should avoid prejudging this issue. It should be able to represent the opposed positions more justly; they look as if they were almost equally in need of restatement. But notice here how ^{oc}should^{oc} and ^{oc}justly^{oc} and ^{oc}in need of^{oc} appear in this very remark. Any formulation of these problems will itself be valuative as well as factual; the conflict it hopes to adjudicate is alive in the bosom of the judge. The difficulties ensuing from this I shall discuss under Aspect VI, the Management, Control, or Administration of Comprehending. Meanwhile, my diagram assumes that ^{sw}Valuing^{sw} is different from Realizing, Characterizing, and Indicating; and that it ^{q}should^{q} be defined in such a way as to avoid implying any fixed relations to them—though, of course, the interplay between all three will be varied, incessant, and all-important. All study of language and thought *in action* is both an exemplification and a study of this kind of interplay.

As another precaution, we may leave the full variety of Valuing unconfined. We are concerned here not only with all the attitudes which may be uttered by the aid of ^{w}good^{w} and ^{w}bad^{w}, ^{w}right^{w} and ^{w}wrong^{w}, ^{w}beautiful^{w} and ^{w}ugly^{w}, ^{w}pleasant^{w} and ^{w}unpleasant^{w}, ^{w}important^{w} and ^{w}trivial^{w}, but with the ranges of love and hate, desire and fear, hope and despair, belief and disbelief. These fields are all polar, and there is a middle zone where it may be doubtful whether any valuing is going on and whether it is positive or negative. So Valuing may often seem to lapse.

Similarly, and perhaps as a consequence, Influencing, V—that part of a Comprehending which endeavors either to change or to preserve unchanged, to be changed or to remain unchanged—may be too slight to be remarked. If we ask what it is here which would change or be preserved, it may be best to reply ^{sw}the onflowing situation^{sw} and to remind ourselves that this ^{sw}onflowing situation^{sw} is at least twofold. It is (*a*) that motion of affairs within which the Comprehending is proceeding; it is also (*b*) the Selecting, Characterizing, Realizing, and Valuing, and the rest, through which the Comprehending is taking account of and dealing with (*a*). It is what is happening *and* what we take to be happening. We are lucky when these sufficiently accord. Influencing—the keeping of the stream of events so or the changing of it—concerns (*a*) as offered to us in (*b*) and, within (*a*), it includes our adjustment to the not-us as well as the adjustment of the not-us to ourselves. In general, a

Comprehending is concerned to change part of the onflowing situation and keep the rest unchanged. Something has to remain unchanged; there has to be some continuant, if change is to be possible: so at least we may be wise to suppose.

Controlling or Administering, VI, has to do with these decisions as to what it will be wise to suppose, and with what arises through these supposals. Wisdom, we may remember, "lies in the masterful administration of the unforeseen."[16] We may be highly surprised to discover what we are supposing. The supposals may be conscious, and arrived at through explicit reflection and deliberation and choices wittingly made, or they may be unwitting, picked up from the tradition or from the accidents of habit formation. And they may concern every aspect of meaning—from Selecting round to Controlling, this would-be executive, itself. Many of our most important supposals concern the nature of meaning and the connections of the sorts of meaning with one another, in brief, the very topic our diagram should help us to explore.

It is here, in this aspect of the mind as a self-ordering endeavor, as a government hoping to maintain itself,[17] that compromise appears most clearly as the practical art of the translator. To ask: Where in general will compromise be most needed? is to try to divide the fields of possible discourse. There are areas of settled routine—much of trade, for example—where the fixed and comparatively simple structuring of the things and events to be dealt with allows of a fine practical equivalence between the languages used. Wherever there is a clear operational check upon Comprehendings this happy condition is likely to prevail. Mathematics, physics, the strict sciences can be translated without loss—by the introduction of the technical term and the use of the type-specimen, the model and the operational definition. Here functions I, II, and VI are serving a Purposing so general that it can hide behind the ordering, VI, of what is said, II, about what, I. But as discourse grows less abstract and hypothetical, more entire and actual, the probability of loss and therefore the need for choice and compromise become greater. With narrative and philosophy and poetry in so far as the growth and history of the language and of other social and cultural institutions enter in, a self-denying statute is required. If we take Ethics to be "the bringing to bear of self-control for the purpose of realizing our desires,"[18] we have to decide which of our desires must give way to which. The translator has first to reconcile himself to conceiving his art in terms of minimal loss and then to balance and adjudicate, as best he can, the claims of the rival functions. His question is: Which sorts of loss will we take in order not to lose what? And answering that is in practice a series of decisions, VI, on behalf of a policy, VII, which may very well have to declare itself openly, in a preface or in footnotes. The mind-state analogy is at work all through, it will be perceived. The translator is called upon to become a statesman and serve a limitless oncoming state. His chief advantage over his analogue is that he can, sometimes, go back and undo his mistakes. He can cancel and choose again. But for the rest his practical sagacity must accept the hard general truths: if we try for too much, we will get less than we might, and what we can go on to do will depend on what we have done and are doing now.

Translation theory—over and above the aid it may afford the translator—has thus a peculiar duty toward man's self-completion, to use a concept which seems to be suggestively common to the Chinese and the Western traditions. We are not weather vanes, I; we are not filing systems, II; we are not even agonies or delights only, III; we are not litmus paper, IV, or servo-mechanisms, V. We are guardians, VI, and subject therefore to the paradox of government: that we must derive our powers, in one way or another, from the very forces which we have to do our best to control. Translation theory has not only to work for better mutual comprehension between users of diverse tongues; more central still in its purposing is a more complete viewing of itself and of the Comprehending which it should serve.

NOTES

1. *Phaedrus* 265D–266B. I have written further on "these processes of division and bringing together" in *How To Read a Page* (New York: W. W. Norton & Co., 1942), pp. 217–22.
2. *Republic* 511C. See *How To Read a Page*, Index: "Dependence."
3. See, e.g., Willard V. O. Quine, "Two Dogmas of Empiricism," *Philosophical Review*, Vol. LX (1951).
4. Adapted with considerable changes from Claude E. Shannon and Warren Weaver, *The Mathematical Theory of Communication* (Urbana: University of Illinois Press, 1949), p. 5.
5. I need a highly general term here, not limited to any mode of utterance, such as *overt* speech or writing. An act of comprehending may itself be regarded as an utterance, being a rebirth, after passage through the lifeless signal, of something more or less the same as the original which was transmitted.
6. See C. K. Ogden and I. A. Richards, *The Meaning of Meaning* (New York: Harcourt, Brace & Co., 1941), pp. 52–59 and Appendix B. The word "context" there used seems to have been misleading. See my *Interpretation in Teaching* (New York: Harcourt, Brace & Co., 1938), p. viii.
7. A possible eighth division might be Venting (that one of the multifarious meanings of the word *expression* which seems least well covered by my seven). Utterances from a simple "Ouch!" or "Ooh!" up to *The Divine Comedy* can be regarded as drive-reducing—in terms, that is, of the psychology of the utterer. But, since the purposes of a

psychological investigator are not those of a translator, I would expect different schemas to be suitable. And to me, at present, this respect seems well enough taken care of—for the translator's purposes—through my seven which may *all* in their varying ways be drive-reducing. I am indebted to Dr. Irving Singer for making me see the need for this note, and to Charles Morris' *Signs, Language, and Behavior* (New York: Prentice-Hall, Inc., 1946) for suggestions contributing to my schema.

8. See *Cybernetics: Transactions of the Eighth Conference* (Josiah Macy, Jr., Foundation, 1951); I. A. Richards, "Communication between Men," pp. 54–60; and *How To Read a Page*, Index: "Purpose."

9. *Collected Papers of Charles Saunders Peirce* (Cambridge: Harvard University Press, 1933), IV, 423.

10. Angus Sinclair, *The Conditions of Knowing* (London: Routledge, 1951), p. 35.

11. See my *Interpretation in Teaching*, chap. xxi, "Logical Machinery and Empty Words."

12. See *Interpretation in Teaching*, chap. ix, " 'Definite.' "

13. *To the Lighthouse*, p. 41.

14. See my *Philosophy of Rhetoric*, Lectures 5 and 6.

15. C. I. Lewis, *An Analysis of Knowledge and Valuation* (La Salle, Ill.: Open Court Publishing Co., 1946), p. 365.

16. Robert Bridges, *The Testament of Beauty* (Oxford, 1939).

17. *Republic* 591.

18. *Collected Papers of Charles Saunders Peirce*, I, 334.

SOME REFLECTIONS ON THE DIFFICULTY OF TRANSLATION

ACHILLES FANG

All a man ever thought would go onto a half sheet of notepaper. The rest is application and elaboration.

THE PROBLEM of translation may be treated from three angles: adequate comprehension of the translated text, adequate manipulation of the language translated into, and what happens in between. The last question properly belongs to linguistic psychology, of which I know little. The second question has been treated eloquently by Matthew Arnold in the last century (*On Translating Homer*) and by Ezra Pound in the present (*Notes on Elizabethan Classicists* and *Translators of Greek*); I do not see any way of adding to their excellent studies on the subject of the style of translation.[1]

All studies on the problem of translation take it for granted that the translator has comprehended the language and thought of his text. But comprehension is not an easy thing, as we all know through bitter experiences. Especially so in Chinese, a language reputedly invented by the devil to prevent the spread of the Gospel in the Middle Kingdom. Besides, as D. G. Rossetti once wrote, "a translation remains perhaps the most direct form of commentary." Hence it may not be irrelevant to treat the first problem of translation in this paper.

1. *Test and Protest*

J'estime les Danois et leurs dents de fer.

When a professional phonologist reads 六書音均表 as *Liu shu yin kün piao* in place of *Liu shu yin yün piao* or when the greatest of all Sinologists entitles his *magnum opus Les Mémoires historiques* instead of *Les Mémoires du* (or *d'un*) [*grand*] *historien*, we should remind ourselves that Benjamin Jowett occasionally "mistranslated" δέ. We should not put them in the same class with Rapaud of the Institut F. Brossard who amuses us with his original rendition of *timeo Danaos, et dona ferentes* (see George du Maurier, *The Martian*). The phonologist ("the world's authority on Ancient Far Eastern Art" according to a New York book-dealer) was perhaps intentionally practicing the art of deception beloved of Chinese art-dealers; and the Sinologist probably was following the inaccurate but tradition-hallowed interpretation of the title. It is reasonable to believe that these two eminent scholars sinned with their eyes open; at least they have earned the benefit of a doubt.

On the other hand, when so eminent a Japanese student of Sinology as Professor Shionoya, an *ordinarius* and himself a practicing poet *à la chinois* or at least a versatile versifier, misleads and continues to mislead (in edition after edition) his readers with a totally impossible interpretation of the second line in an almost pellucid poem of Yüan Ch'en's

元稹 遣悲懷,[2]

昔日戲言身後事 今朝都到眼前来
衣裳已施行看盡 針線猶存未忍開
尚想舊情憐婢僕 也曾因夢送錢財
誠知此恨人人有 貧賤夫婦百事哀,

we cannot but raise our eyebrows. The line in question simply means that after his wife's death the poet gave away her dresses one after another (to her friends and relatives) until almost all of them disappeared and that he could not bear to open her sewing basket with its needles and thread simply because he found the reminder painful. MM. Bynner and Kiang render the line thus:

> Almost all your clothes have been given away;
> Your needle work is sealed, I dare not look at it.

The sentiment can be understood by anyone who has, *inter alia*, read the two really sentimental stories of Elizabeth Villiers and Elinor Forester in *Mrs. Leicester's School*. But Professor Shionoya, who seems to be characteristically "deficient in love,"[2] cannot understand such a human sentiment. Instead he paraphrases the line

身ニ衣裳ヲ着ケテ,ツブツグト眺メ,
針線ガ尚ホ存シテイテモ,取去ルニ忍ビナイ.

In a recent English translation of *Tao-te-ching* the well-known translator Edward Erkes seems to have surpassed all his past originalities: instead of taking Ho-shang-kung's glosses as glosses, he reads them as homiletics. For example, the simple sentence 知者不博,博者不知 (chap. 81) should not puzzle even a tyro provided that he knows how to locate the four characters in his dictionary. Nor should a sophisticated tyro worry himself to death over this couplet, for our translator's oracle is quite explicit:

知者謂知道之士,不博者守一元也,
博者多見聞,不知者失要真也.

Furthermore, Ho-shang-kung's commentary quoted in *I-lin* seems to make the point still more explicit:

知道守一，則不必博，多見聞失要真，故不知.

All that the couplet purports to say is that a true philosopher need not be a walking encyclopedia and that a man of encyclopedic learning is not necessarily a true philosopher. After giving the couplet a Chestertonian twist, "The knowing one is no scholar. The scholar is ignorant," our translator turns to his oracle: "The knowing one is the knowing Taoist. The unlearned one comprehends unity at the origin. The scholar sees and hears much, but as he is ignorant, he loses what is important and true." His translation of the *I-lin* quotation is no less original: "Who knows Tao and preserves unity is surely no scholar. As he sees and hears much, he loses what is more important. Therefore he is ignorant." It looks as though the translator could not see the gloss for paraphrase, or the pedant for the preacher.

A Chin dynasty poet wrote a touching poem on "The Desecration of the Han Tombs," in which occurs the line: 毀壞過一抔. A remarkably competent translator renders it as "Of earth they have carried away more than one handful" (second edition: "crumbled" for "carried away") and informs his readers in a footnote, "In the early days of the dynasty a man stole a handful of earth from the imperial tombs, and was executed by the police. The emperor was furious at the lightness of the punishment." (Second edition: "In the early days of the Han dynasty a man who stole one handful of earth from the Imperial Tombs was put to death.") The story refers to *Shih-chi* 102 (or *Han-shu* 50), where it is told that when the chief justice of the empire, Chang Shih-chih, sentenced to death a man who stole a jade ring from the temple of the founder of the Han dynasty, the emperor Wen-ti was furious at the lightness of the sentence and wanted to exterminate the man's entire family, but that Chang Shih-chih stood firm on the text of the criminal code and tried to make the emperor reasonable by asking him what severer sentence remained to mete out to the man who should (Heaven forbid, 萬一) carry away a handful of earth from the tomb of the later emperor, upon which the emperor had to satisfy himself with confirming the original sentence. As commentators agree, the phrase "to carry away a handful of earth" is a euphemism for "to desecrate the imperial tomb." There is no question of anybody's desecrating the tomb "in the early days" of the Han dynasty.

How, then, do absurdities like these come about? *Lapsus calami?* Deficiency in love? Or (as St. John of the Cross would have said) *un no sé qué?* It is easy to say that there is such a thing as sheer incompetence in comprehending a foreign language and a system of alien and often "subversive" thoughts enmeshed in that language, and to prescribe a strict and sensible regimen in the Sinological techniques to cure such a malady. But the matter goes a bit deeper than that. For the so-called Chinese language is a really froward child, a most recalcitrant thing in the hand of the logical-minded.

The Literary Revolution may be viewed as in part an attempt to eliminate some of its recalcitrance. The original program for that revolution was something far more comprehensive in scope than a mere restoration of the spoken language as the literary medium, for it demanded that all allusions, clichés, parallelism, stock-in-trade emotions, and ancient tradition be thrown overboard; it insisted on grammar, content, and colloquialisms. But the revolution started a bit too late for the students of Chinese literature. Practically every important piece of writing dating before 1916 (and even some subsequent to that date) abounds in allusions, clichés, parallelism, stock-in-trade emotions, and ancient tradition with little grammar and sometimes with less content to speak of. (It is in a way a blessing in disguise that colloquialisms were not the order of the day; which of us do not groan when we try to read Yüan drama, written in the dead colloquial speech of the time?) In fact, "obscurity, erudition, allusiveness, . . ." as a critic in *Partisan Review* describes the modernist poetry of Europe and America, have always characterized Chinese literary style.

T. E. Hulme, the ancestor of Imagism and Amygism, once wrote: "Personally I am of course in favor of the complete destruction of all verse more than twenty years old." If there had been a dozen or more Ch'in-shih-huang-ti (First Emperor of all China, burner of the books), the state of Chinese literature could have been more accessible to Sinological comprehension. But there was only one Ch'in-shih-huang-ti. And, by the nature of things, it is doubtful if more than one could have been tolerated. As Hulme continues, "But that happy event will not, I am afraid, take place until Plato's desire has been realized and a minor poet has become dictator." (Perhaps Ch'in-shih-huang-ti was a minor poet.)

2. *Text and Context*

Pensiamo perche non sappiamo.

A translator must comprehend the text he is translating in the light of its own context as well as of that of other texts. He cannot be too subtle about this matter; it would be nothing short of folly to translate a passage before he is perfectly satisfied with the text and can explain every word in it. He must, furthermore, look into variant editions and compare the basic text with the fragments and excerpts as quoted elsewhere, such as *T'ai-p'ing Yü-lan*, etc. It is very fortunate that a large number of Chinese texts are duplicated: a huge segment of *Han-shu* is almost, but not quite, identical with *Shih-chi*, which in its turn overlaps with many pre-Ch'in texts; there are also two *T'ang-shu*, two *Wu-tai-shih*, and two *Yüan-shih*. A translator has to compare his text with a parallel passage in other books before he is entitled to feel satisfied with his comprehension.

He must furthermore make a thorough study of all available scholia. True, most of them are rather silly and stuffy; yet a translator will profit much if he assesses them for what they are worth. In short, a translator must comprehend not only his text but also its numerous glosses, actual and possible. If he cannot understand the language of the scholiasts, he would be well advised to postpone his translation until he is competent in this respect.

Take, for example, the sentence:

雖說擇術不正，可知時會使然.

It is translated: "You may say that they didn't go the right way about their business, but you must know that it is really the fault of the times." What the passage means is that the two men who applied their ingenuity to the invention of bagatelles like the opium lamp and the smoking pipe were misguided, hence they deserved to remain in obscurity, and yet it is to be conceded that, had they been citizens of Europe or America, they could have made themselves famous by their inventions. It definitely does not mean that they were ignorant of the value of publicity. The phrase 擇術不正, of course, alludes to *Hsün-tzu* (非相篇):

故相形不如論心，論心不如擇術，
形不勝心，心不勝術，術正而心順，則形相
雖惡，而心術善，無害為君子也.

The meaning of the original text may come out more accurately in: "You may blame them for their misguided intelligence, yet you will have to agree with me that their obscurity was due to a lack of opportunity." This sounds a little *non sequitur*, but this is what was intended.

Another instructive example is the passage

士為知己者死，女為悅己者容，

translated as follows: "A man will die for the one who appreciates him; a woman will beautify herself for the one who pleases her." The text, found in *Shih-chi* 86, is derived from *Chan-kuo Ts'e* (Chao-ts'e). Ssu-ma Ch'ien himself uses this sentence in his letter to Jen An, where he alters 死 to 用 (see *Wen-hsüan* 41; the letter is also in *Han-shu* 62, where the two 者 are omitted). Whether 悅 means "to please me" or "to be pleased in me" is a minor point, but the translator could have been a bit more painstaking and accurate. Lü Hsiang's paraphrase 女為愛己貌者而飾其容 (in *Wen-hsüan*) definitely shows that the translation may be revised: ". . . A woman will beautify herself for the man who is pleased in her." Why not even "for her lover"?

Of course it is not an easy matter to evaluate glosses and commentaries. Some of the Ch'ing scholars have thrown much light on ancient texts; hence a student of, say, the *Shih*, must acquaint himself with Ch'en Huan's contributions. But it is quite likely that the writer of the text the translator is interested in, and who is quoting the *Shih*, may not have followed or anticipated Ch'en Huan's interpretations; he may have been a follower of Chu Hsi. In other words, the translator must decide which interpretation the writer had in mind when he adopted the particular *Shih* passage.

Another serious task for the translator is to be critical of his text. The sentence 嘗從觀畫虞舜見娥皇女英 is nonsensical; it cannot be translated. But a translator has interpreted the passage as: "On one occasion they were looking at a picture of the emperor Shun gazing at [his wives] E-huang and Nü-ying." As the text does not make sense, the translator ought to have emended it before translating. The emendation should be made on the basis of the original Ts'ao Chih text: either as 嘗從觀畫,過虞舜之像,見娥皇女英 ("On one occasion she was looking at pictures in his company: they were inspecting the portraits of the Emperor Shun [and his entourage], when they saw the portrait of E-huang and Nü-ying") as in *T'ai-p'ing Yü-lan;* or as

嘗從觀畫,過虞舜之廟,見娥皇女英

("On one occasion, etc., when they visited the temple of Shun, they saw the portraits of E-huang and Nü-ying") as in *I-wen Lei-chü*. (The second reading seems to be inferior.) At any rate, there is no question of the good emperor's leering at his wives in public.

The sentence

後漢光武明德馬皇后.美於色,厚於德,帝用嘉之

is translated: "Under the later Han, 'the Empress Ma, [termed] "Illustrious Virtue," consort of Kuang Wu Ti, was as beautiful in face as she was great in virtue, so that the Emperor took much delight in her.' "

Now the empress Ma was not the consort of Kuang Wu Ti but of his son Ming Ti, hence the character 明 here. The text seems to be derived from an essay of Ts'ao Chih (now existing in excerpts in *T'ai-p'ing Yü-lan* 137 and 750 and *I-wen Lei-chü* 74), where the telltale 光武 does not occur. (The translator could have looked into Giles's *Biographical Dictionary*, which he seems to be familiar with, under No. 1471, "Ma Hou" 馬后, where the information is correctly given.) 明德, then, means "Consort of Ming-ti and canonized 'Virtuous.'" Furthermore, 明 in the canonization is supposed to mean 照臨四方 (i.e., it means "omnilucent," not "illustrious"). Incidentally, "illustrious" seems to be a favorite word with Sinologists: a newcomer thinks he is improving on MM. Bynner and Kiang by translating 不才明主棄 as "Because I lack talent, the *illustrious* ruler has rejected me." Of course, 明主 means "a wise ruler," as Bynner and Kiang have it. The phrase always refers to the intelligence of a ruler as in 明王 in *Shu* ("intelligent kings," Legge's translation, p. 526), and in 明主好同而暗主好獨 in *Hsün-tzŭ.*

The problem of context can be best illustrated by an actual example. When James Legge makes Mencius say (*The Works of Mencius*, pp. 321–22), "The great man does not think beforehand of his words that they may be sincere, nor of his actions that they may be resolute;—he simply speaks and does what is right," it is not fair to father on Mencius the intention to absolve the great man from sincerity of words and resoluteness of action. Yet one of the acutest minds in the West can comment: "The opportunism which has been regarded as the chief merit and the chief defect of Confucianism shows clearly here." Does it? What was it that Mencius had in mind when he made "this rather sinister seeming pronouncement"? Opportunist as he may now and then have been in actual life, Mencius was not preaching anything very sinister, for he was merely trying to make more precise what Confucius had said. Once asked by Tzŭ-kung to describe an "officer" (*shih*), Confucius described three types, in the following anticlimactic scale—a man with the sense of shame in him, never failing in his mission for the sovereign; a man praised for filial piety and fraternal love; and "a man who makes point of sincerity in his words and resoluteness in his actions, a truly obstinate little man," 言必信，行必果，硜硜然小人哉. Now, Mencius probably was asked to describe a great man (*ta-jen*); and he chose to state the opposite of what Confucius described as "a little man," by inserting the negative *pu* into the two Confucian sentences and adding something positive after them:

大人者言不必信，行不必果，惟義所在. As Ezra Pound once wrote, "Mencius nowhere turns against K'UNG, all of Mencius is implicit in K'ung's doctrine" (see *The Criterion*, July, 1938). The poet himself translates the passage in question as follows:

> not words whereto to be faithful
> nor deeds that they be resolute
> only that bird-hearted equity make timber
> and lay hold of the earth.

There is no compromise in this version (except the compromise with popular etymology in the last two lines). In spite of the fact that Mencius' mind has been analyzed and his book is used in classrooms, it does not seem always to be easy to understand Mencius' text in the light of context.

3. *Rhetoric and Sentiment*

> Tain't what a man sez, but wot he means that the traducer has got to bring over.

Bernard Berenson, in his *Sketch for a Self-portrait*, has recently thrown down the gauntlet to translators from the Chinese:

> When one comes to German and attempts to translate its abstract and qualitative terms the task is fraught with almost insurmountable difficulties, as the English or French or Italian versions of German poets and philosophers prove amply. Yet, though many of us have a living language group to help us out, who can offer a contemporary satisfactory rendering of *Gemüt?* When it is a question of Greek—Plato, for instance—how convey in any speech of today the exact meaning of *σωφροσύνη*? Then dare to translate the ancient Chinese and Indian thinkers.

Surely, most of us wince at this challenge, for it is a very serious one. And the reason why such a challenge is so difficult to meet is that we know very little of what might be called the rhetoric and sentiment of the ancient Chinese thinkers. If it is true, as T. S. Eliot says in *The Sacred Wood*, that "an understanding of Elizabethan rhetoric is as essential to the appreciation of Elizabethan literature as an understanding of Victorian sentiment is essential to the appreciation of Victorian literature and George Wyndham," affairs are still more complicated in the case of Chinese writers and thinkers. Where nothing is obsolete or even obsolescent and all writers of reputation are conscious of and groan under the dead weight of the past, it is no easy matter to disentangle true sentiment from false rhetoric, to distinguish between tradition and individuality, to discriminate a sentiment of the heart from mere lip service to respectable rhetorical devices—in short, to place every word in the proper perspective of space and time.

There is a good example illustrating the rhetorical aspect: in the "Canon of Shun" we read

詩言志　謌永言　聲依永　律和聲.

There has been some earnest controversy over the precise meaning of this passage. In spite of the fact that the first two sentences have been bandied about by almost every literary historian or critic, it is a moot point whether to take the words at their face values (if there are such things). Moreover, the matter becomes complicated when each writer appropriates the sentences in his own fashion and makes them put on some new coloring, without being aware (I have the temerity to assert) of their rhetorical nature.

If "psychosinology" (we must thank the author of *Finnegans Wake* for inventing this handy word) is a necessary discipline (how else do we hope to get at each writer's sentiment?), "etymosinology," otherwise known as "the ideogrammatic method," is usually frowned upon. But we will have to apply the methodology of that discredited discipline to evaluate the first two sentences of Shun's definition. We all know that 詩 ˳si < *siag and 志 tsi° < *t̂iag were to all intents and purposes homophonous in ancient phonology; furthermore, the 寺 element of 詩 and the character 志 have an identical component, 之 (degenerated in conventionalized writings to 士); finally, 言, the other component of 詩, is the same as the second character in the first sentence. In other words, the sentence is a very clever but essentially etymological or etymosinological trick. In fact, the *Shih-ming* 釋名, whose characteristic feature is its definition by homophones, defines 詩 as 之也, 志之所之也.[3] In the second sentence, 謌永言, none of the three characters is homophonous; but we must note that one component of the first character in the phrase stands independently as the third character. To that extent the second sentence is also an etymological definition.

How seriously, then, do we have to take those two statements? Etymology by itself lends neither credit nor discredit to any definition; only when it excludes all other things does it become suspect. A translator faced with a passage like the above must see it in its true light before he attempts to comprehend its import or sentiment. Furthermore, he ought to interpret all subsequent adoptions of such a passage (e.g., in Liu Hsieh's *Wen-hsin Tiao-lung*) in the light of the adopters' inferred understanding of the original passage. A veritable Chinese box indeed.

Years ago G. L. Dickinson wrote, naïvely I am sure, of Chinese poetry: "It is of all poetry I know the most human and the least symbolic or romantic. It contemplates life just as it presents itself, without any veil of ideas, any rhetoric or sentiment." Many of us would agree with most of this statement; it is not for nothing that Dickinson claimed to have been a Chinaman in one of his former incarnations. But "without rhetoric or sentiment"? Of course, Dickinson is here using the two words in slightly different senses from Eliot; perhaps he meant that Chinese poetry is entirely sincere and without cant. And yet there is enough of rhetoric and sentiment—even in Dickinsonian senses—in Chinese poetry and prose to confuse innocent translators.

The second aspect, that of sentiment, may be better treated in connection with a word that has played a paramount role in the history of China and seems to have lost not a particle of its efficacy today. I mean 民 or 人民.

We hear often of the so-called oriental contempt for human life. China may be a part of Orient or, as Dickinson and Harold Acton would insist, may not be one, but the salient feature of Chinese political philosophy has always been its attention to the idea of the people. In fact, 民 has always been identified with *Homo sapiens* and never with *Homo pekinensis* alone. It is a word which never has sunk as low as "vulgar," "plebeian," "popular," "le bas peuple" (下民 never meant anything of this sort), "peuple" (used as an adjective), "populace" (as in Matthew Arnold's renowned tripartite classification of English society into Barbarians, Philistines, and Populace).

It would be the height of folly to believe that the Chinese have always realized their political ideal. Nor is it relevant to discuss the gap between ideal and action here, for our immediate concern is with the simple words *min* and *jen-min*. The problem for the translator, then, boils down to this: Has he done justice to the full connotation of those words by rendering them as "the people"? Is there any other way of rendering them?

More or less allied with the problem of rhetoric and sentiment is the annoying nature of Chinese literary style in general. In most of the civilized languages the two categories of prose and verse are usually distinguished more or less sharply. Speaking of prose rhythm, George Saintsbury wrote: "The great principle of foot arrangement in prose and of Prose Rhythm, is Variety." With regard to diction and other technical devices, T. E. Hulme thought that "prose [is] a museum where all the old weapons of poetry [are] kept." It is, on the other hand, pretty much of an impossibility to demarcate between the two categories in the Chinese literature of the past. If they have developed as more or less separate entities in the West, they coalesce and merge in

Chinese; in fact, it would not be incorrect to say that the genius of Chinese prose is verse. Take the case of *p'ien-t'i-wen*, "parallel prose." Is it prose or verse? (That some of the things written in this genre are anything but *poetry* is beyond question, but it is not so simple to decide whether parallel prose is *verse* or prose.) And parallelism or symmetry are ingrained in Chinese thinking.

In the West a prosateur who writes blank verse is the butt of critics; Charles Dickens with his "As we struggle on, / nearer and nearer to the sea, from which / this mighty wind was blowing dead on shore, / its force became more and more / terrific, etc.," has served as an object lesson. But a Chinese prosateur is all the more appreciated for the blank verse he might scatter through his prose writing.

The matter becomes still more complicated when we consider the appalling amount of evocation in Chinese prose. It is not only in regard to rhythm and diction that Chinese prose approaches verse but also in the quality known specifically as poetic. When a well-known student of Chinese art translates a verse inscription on a painting as a piece of prose, chopping the lines into bars of two, three, or even eight, nine characters, we cannot simply deplore his incompetence; it must be quite difficult to recognize verse as verse. The same applies to the Japanese musicologist who punctuated a *lü-shih* ("regular verse") as if it were a *tz'u;* probably he also thought it was a piece of prose.

4. *Parataxis versus Syntaxis*

> For purposes of translation one has to cut various knots, and make arbitrary decisions.

Most Chinese texts can be readily punctuated; moreover, a large number of important texts have been printed with punctuation marks, especially those reprinted in recent years. If a translator cannot correctly put dots and circles in the body of his text, obviously he is not ready for translation; he will have to wait some more years.

A serious problem, however, remains; it is not to be disposed of so lightly. Unless the translator is really competent, he will be at a loss to obtain syntaxis out of the predominantly paratactical structure of Chinese texts. For the so-called punctuation marks in Chinese texts, which any school child of ten can put down, represent nothing much beyond breathing pauses. They are neither grammatical nor logical.

There are, of course, two kinds of parataxis; one in the strict sense of the word, and the other in a loose sense. When Louis MacNeice (*Modern Poetry* [1938]) speaks of Arthur Waley's translation of Ode No. 26:

Tossed is that cypress boat,
Wave-tossed it floats;
My heart is in turmoil, I cannot sleep.

汎彼柏舟，亦汎其流
耿耿不寐，如有隱憂

as paratactical, he is using the word in the strict sense. The problem that concerns us here is not poetic devices like this but how to group a series of breath-units (called *chü*) into logically coalescent units. Take the passage: "My humble opinion is this concerning Master Ch'ang, who undertook the practice of art while dwelling amid the shadows of the North, and was truly competent without ever having received the cultural influence of the Middle Kingdom; who could not be moved by force nor beguiled by profit: this was indeed a MAN! How could it have been easy to get hold of him?" It is hard to understand what these sentences mean. Quite possibly the translator did not have access to a syntactically punctuated text, which would read:

愚以為：常生者擅藝，居幽朔之間，不被中國之聲教，果能不可以勢動，復不可以利誘；則，斯人也，豈易得哉。

The translator must have punctuated the text something like the following:

愚以為常生者擅藝，居幽朔之間；不被中國之聲教果能；不可以勢動，不可以利誘；則斯人也；豈易得哉。

If the correct syntactical punctuation is followed, the text may be translated: "I would like to observe:—Master Ch'ang, a devotee of art, cannot be moved by force nor beguiled by profit, in spite of the fact that he lives in the Northern Land where Chinese civilization has not penetrated. In other words, this man is a rare phenomenon." (Here the two characters 果能 are only emphatic; they do not mean that the painter was a competent artist. The last four characters 豈易得哉 merely mean "How is it possible that such a man exists?")

A rather instructive example is furnished by a recent translation from the biography of the poet Meng Hao-jan in *Hsin T'ang-shu:* "[Already] in his youth, he loved steadfastness and righteousness, and liked to help people in distress." This should sound strange to anyone who has done any translation: what connection is there between the poet's love of steadfastness and of righteousness and his willingness to help others?

Now, the text has:

少好節義，喜振人患難.

It is possible that the translator was aware of Legge's translation of the Confucian sentence 夫達也者質直而好義, "Now the man of distinction is solid and straightforward, and loves righteousness" (*Analects*, XII, 20). But how does one love steadfastness? Did the poet love that quality in other people? or in himself, or is it that the poet was steadfast himself? If so, steadfastness in what? "Steadfastness and righteousness" for *chieh-i* is, to be sure, far better here than Giles's "chaste and good,—as a widow who does not remarry." Nor do the examples given in *P'ei-wen Yün-fu* (widows who remained steadfast to their late husbands' memory, a girl who took revenge on her father's killer by killing him, men who held fast to the course of life their conscience had dictated to them) fit with the context in question. But Meng Hao-jan (remarkable a personality as he was) was not particularly distinguished for *chieh-i* in the usual sense; the translation strikes a false note.

As the translator himself knows, the passage is derived or rewritten from Wang Shih-yüan's preface to the collected poems of Meng Hao-jan:

救患釋紛，以立義表.

Which sounds very much like Ssu-ma Ch'ien's prefatory remark on his chapter on knight-errants:

救人于戹，振人不贍 — 仁者有乎；
人既信，不倍言 — 義者有取焉；

except that Ssu-ma Ch'ien uses 仁 in place of Wang Shih-yüan's 義.

The writer who penned the *Hsin T'ang-shu* passage must have intended it to be a syntactical, not a paratactical, sentence; that is, he was not enumerating three qualities that distinguished Meng Hao-jan's youth (love of steadfastness, love of righteousness, and readiness to come to men in distress); he rather expected his readers to punctuate the sentence as follows:

少好節義：喜振人患難.

Moreover, he must have used 節 either as a synonym of 義 or as its qualifier or even intensifier; at any rate, he must have thought 少好義 was not rhythmic enough. In other words, all he intended was that Meng Hao-jan was fond of playing the role of a knight-errant, *for* he was ready to come to the help of anyone in distress. The phrase 好節義, then, must mean the same thing as 好義 or 樂義 in the following sentences from *P'ei-wen Yün-fu:*

其輕財好義如此(漢書,楊惲傳)杜季良豪俠
好義：憂人之憂,樂人之樂(馬援,誡兄子書)
輕財樂義：急人之急,憂人之憂(宋史,孝義傳).

The phrase 好義 occurs also in the colloquial saying 急公好義. If 義 is translated as "righteousness," the translator must warn the reader that he is using the word in the sense of Hebrew *zedokah*, "justice, righteousness," which stands for "charity," for 義 in the *Hsin T'ang-shu* does not connote the same thing as when the word is joined with 執 or 守, etc.

As a syntactical sentence, the passage should then mean: "As a youth he was generous to other people, always ready to help them when they were in distress."

5. *Particles and Principles*

> You crush all particles down into close conformity, and walk back and forth on them.

It is fortunate that few Sinologists, except those who are still struggling with their characters, have been victimized by particle specialists. Quite justifiably, they leave their particles to take care of themselves. Particle books are necessary evils: a standard treatise (P'ei Hsüeh-hai), very valuable for the number of illustrative examples, is a delectably concocted *olla podrida* of grammatical and lexicographical equations. And what equations indeed! The final 夫 is first equated with 乎, under which heading instances of its interrogative and interjective usages are marshalled; then it is equated with 也, 矣, and 焉, the illustrative passages put under each of these equations being all indicative sentences. That is, the particle *fu* seems to spice almost any kind of sentence. The truth of the matter is that it is not the particle which makes a sentence indicative, etc., for the sentence itself is already indicative enough, with or without the additional seasoning.

A parallel instance is furnished by a textbook meant for classroom use, in which 罷, which is more or less a colloquial counterpart of the final 夫, is handled in the same fashion; only that the author, who incidentally does not go into any equation, invents a special category called "idiomatic" into which he puts a phrase like 就是罷, "bien entendu."

Our quarrel with the analytic particlist is that his work, legitimate and often necessary as it is, stops with analysis. We are justified in demanding that such an expert, who does not mind spending his time and energy on such rarefied things, give us some over-all and synthesizing outlook, an outlook that would tell us why a particle behaves as it does and not otherwise. He should call quits with his in-gathering of particles and samples, which has become as *recherché* as Eric Partridge's study of Shakespeare's bawdy, and with his penetrating analysis, as *raffiniert* as in the *Kama Sutra*. He should instead think boldly on the larger plane of his problem.

A tentative suggestion may be offered to such a student. All particles are divided, like Caesar's Gallia, into three tribes: functional particles (e.g., pronominal 其), which should be dealt with as a regular part of speech; decorative particles (like 之 in certain context), ubiquitous in parallel prose and allied genres; and attitudinizing particles, which convey the writer's mood toward the statement to which they are attached. (There is another category of particles, which grammarians call 辭 or 助辭 or 助字, "expletives," out of sheer despair, because they are ignorant of their real functions. But this class may turn out to belong to one of the three categories mentioned above.)

Take the Confucian saying 辭達而已矣. The last *i* is generally accepted as expressing the speaker's modesty (or mock-modesty) because it expresses the conclusion drawn from a supposition, whether expressed or not. In the present case, the protasis is a gentleman (à la Confucius) and his activities; Confucius is here making the statement *tz'u-ta* with his idealized gentleman as the frame of reference or even as the point of departure. The compound *erh-i* (而已) is translated, in the classroom cant, with "and that's all." But from what point of view? The heretical translation, "Problem of style? Get the meaning across and then STOP," seems to prove that the translator took *erh-i* as referring to or continuing the act expressed in the verb *ta*. What Confucius intended to say was probably something like this: "As for your question about the problem of style, there is nothing more for me to say in answer than that you should be able to get your meaning across." Which should have reminded the interrogator of the poor estimate Confucius had of a mere "literary" man, who may be eloquent with the three hundred odes but performs miserably as an ambassador. In short, it is a mistake to read such particles into the words of the statement itself. Attitudinizing particles, then, have to be given a psychological and even a psychoanalytical treatment.

When it comes to decorative particles, a totally different approach is needed: an aesthetic treatment. A convenient parallel is to be found in the practice of calligraphy. As is well known, no calligrapher starts a stroke abruptly; he rather deploys and maneuvers for a while the forces of his brush back and forth, up and down. Then he carries his brush resolutely forward until he reaches a point where the direction is to change; here he does the same thing as in the beginning. Nor does he lift the brush without warning, for he tarries a while before he completes the stroke. Just as there are many ways of executing the initial, medial, and final stages in executing a stroke (see the *Eight Techniques of Yung*, 永字八訣), there are any number of particles for the initial, medial, and final positions in a sentence. Take for example the beginning of Ou-yang Hsiu's essay,

相州畫錦堂記：仕宦而至將相，富貴而歸故鄉，此人情之所榮，而今昔之所同也.

The three 而 can hardly be called functional. In fact, according to Chu Hsi, Ou-yang Hsiu did not insert the first two *erh* in the original draft; it was probably for rhetorical or decorative reasons that Ou-yang Hsiu inserted them later, for they would make the first sentences less abrupt. The reader has to take a pause when he comes to *erh*, looking backward to the two conventional and hence challenging words and looking forward, with certain anticipation, to what is coming; in a way, Ou-yang Hsiu is playing a cat-and-mouse game with his reader. Thus considered, the two initial *erh* are merely stylistic. It is baffling, therefore, to understand what Dr. Walter Simon means when he asserts that the particle *erh* placed before "the verb of which it is the object" contributes to "greater precision of thought" (cf. *Asia Major*, New Series, II, 1). The two *chih* here are also quite superfluous medial particles. The final 也, of course, belongs to the third category, but it has also a rhetorical use here: by its assertative force it challenges the reader to think, and (if he is so minded) to disagree even; but, if he wants to read on, he has to grant the truth of the statement *pro tem* at least.

Frankly, all these particles could have been excised without damaging an iota of the writer's meaning and attitude; even the functional 此, which subsumes the two preceding sentences, could have been omitted. 仕宦至將相，富貴歸故鄉，人情所榮，今昔所同(也) could have conveyed everything meant and implied in the original passage; the reader could take recourse to, what John Addington Symonds in his book on blank verse terms, "sense and pauses" in his own fashion. Indeed, the characteristic feature of particles, as far as they are of the second and/or third category, is their dispensability.

This being so, it is wisdom not to translate particles at all rather than to translate wrongly; rather *suppressio veri* than *suggestio falsi*. As long as particlists do not come forth with some synthetic suggestions, the principle of particles can be stated thus: Particles are like pornography; one may study them if one has a taste for them and one ought to know them (just as Tseng-tzŭ maintained the necessity of knowing the art of burglary in order to protect his property), but it is not wise to talk about them publicly.

The *Hsin T'ang-shu* sentence 年四十乃遊京師 is faultlessly rendered in: "At the age of forty, he finally traveled to the capital." But the translator must give himself away in a footnote: "Possibly the particle *nai* 乃 here merely serves to connect the preceding adverbial phrase with the predicate. But I believe it fits the context better to take it in the sense of 'finally,' 'at last.' Literati interested in an official career usually went to the capital when they were about thirty years old." The original *Chiu T'ang-shu*, however, has: 年四十來遊京師, which shows that the *Hsin T'ang-shu* writer altered 來 to 乃. He could equally well have altered it to 而 or 始, or even omitted it altogether. When the translator wrote "finally" he was not translating 乃 but was merely interpolating a felicitous word. One wonders how he would have translated all the 迺 (乃) occurring in the spirited story of Hsiang Yü in *Shih-chi*. (Chavannes didn't.) Would he also translate the twenty 也 in Ou-yang Hsiu's piece 醉翁亭記? (Giles didn't.)

It seems that the Anglican archbishop of Quebec was right when he said, "Logical-minded unimaginative people make great mistakes by studying the texts too intensively. . . . You need to relax—to open your heart—to listen."

6. *Quotation and Allusion*

> I have heard that the finest flower of Chinese education is that which, steeped in the Chinese classics, can convey in three pages of allusive writing, to the right readers, what would otherwise take thirty.
>
> E. E. Kellett

Allusive style, of course, is not the monopoly of Chinese literature; it is a truly universal aspect of all literatures, past and present. The modernist poetry in the West seems to vie with ancient Chinese literature in this respect. We know that in spite of vociferous denunciation *The Waste Land* has been translated into several languages by men without serious claims to comprehending all the *bêtes noires* of the *Saturday Review of Literature;* and yet they seem to have produced tolerably accurate versions.

Whether because of the supposedly abysmal gulf between the Chinese mind and occidental mentality or for other reasons, Sinological translators seem to stumble very frequently over quotations and allusions. Yet, one cannot but admire the tolerably accurate versions they have produced in spite of the odds. The fact is, it is almost always rewarding to track down the immediate and ultimate sources of allusions and quotations, for more often than not they are glossed or commented on in those sources; hence, a translator works against odds, by despising those sources.

The sentence

記曰，將貽父母令名，必果，將貽父母羞辱，必不果

is rendered: "In the scriptures there is the saying: whoever adds to the honor and renown of his parents will be successful, whoever disgraces his parents will be unsuccessful." What scriptures? Certainly not Exod. 20:12 ("Honor thy father and thy mother . . .")? Had the translator looked into *Li-chi*, "Nei-tse," he would have found that in

父母雖沒，將為善，思貽父母令名，必果；
將為不善，思貽父母羞辱，必不果

where the key word *kuo* means, as Cheng Hsüan says, 決 ("resolute, unwavering"). "Certe perficiet . . . certe non perficiet" (Couvreur).

It is not difficult to discover the *locus classicus*, but it is, on the other hand, not so easy to be able to recognize a quotation or allusion as such; a second sight or a sixth sense is perhaps needed for this. The most difficult and most important thing for the translator, however, is to be able to evaluate the quoted passage in the context of the text he is translating. It is not enough to refer the reader to the *locus classicus* or quote someone else's translation of the passage. For it often happens that the writer of the text may not have interpreted the passage in question in the same way as the translator thinks, on the best authority, it should be interpreted. Furthermore, it is quite possible that the writer was not a conscientious scholar; he may have quoted the passage indirectly from a secondhand source. A parallel instance is furnished by the later French Symbolists who thought they were true disciples of Edgar Allan Poe, all the while they were misinterpreting him on the basis of a secondhand authority.

> Literary history has neglected this process of misinterpretation and misunderstanding. We need to investigate, not the dreary chains of influence where we can show that one writer copied another in literal detail, but the more fascinating chains which link one poet to another he has never read but only read about or heard about, whose ideas vaguely apprehended or even misapprehended serve as catalytic agents for his own development [Jacob Isaacs, *The Background of Modern Poetry*].

To give a concrete example, Lu Chi's *Wen-fu* has the following two lines:

雖區分之在茲，亦禁邪而制放，要辭達而理
舉，故無取乎冗長。

What does Lu Chi mean by 辭達, which is here made parallel to 理舉? In my version in the *Harvard Journal of Asiatic Studies* I rendered the last line with "Essentially, words must communicate, and reason must dominate; prolixity and long-windedness are not commendable," and referred the reader to Legge's *Analects*, page 305. This bare reference to an existing translation is highly irresponsible, not much more creditable than the total silence maintained by the three previous translators. From the very fact that the two lines containing the phrase conclude a discussion of the ten genres, it seems beyond doubt that Lu Chi did not take the Confucian saying 辭達而已矣 in the usual acceptation. The traditional interpretation of this enigmatic saying seems to have gone into Legge's translation: "In language it is simply required that it convey the meaning." That is, a gentleman as idealized by Confucius was essentially a *Homo politicus*, whose interest in life should be much more comprehensive than mere stylistic accomplishment; hence, he has no time to waste on polishing his literary ability, for all he has to do is to be able to make others understand him—a sentiment which is so poignantly echoed by Hsiang Yü when he said that all he wanted in the art of letters was the ability to write down his name (書足以記姓名而已). And this interpretation seems to have been in Yen Fu's mind when he set up as desiderata of translation 信達雅, "Accuracy, Intelligibility, Elegance."

It is, however, doubtful if Lu Chi accepted this interpretation in his context, especially when he rounds out the paragraph (or strophe) with an injunction against prolixity and long-windedness. It is quite possible that he intended what Ezra Pound meant when he interpreted the Confucian saying with

> in discourse what matters is
> to get it across *e poi basta.*

If he did, there is no question of Lu Chi's "vaguely apprehending" the Confucian meaning; a scholar of no mean accomplishment, he must have wilfully distorted the import of the Sage.

> And I like Augustine Birrel. I happened to correct him when he said that the Apocrypha was not read in the Church services; and again when he said that Elihu the Jebusite was one of Job's comforters. He tried to override me in both points, but I called for a Bible and proved them. He said, glowering very kindly at me: "I will say to you what Thomas Carlyle once said to a young man who caught him out in a misquotation, 'Young man, you are heading straight for the pit of Hell!' "

Like Robert Graves, the Sinological student has to cite Scripture for his purpose, unmindful of the consequence.

7. *Grammar and Dictionary*

Lisez, lisez; jetez la grammaire.

GUSTAVE SCHLEGEL

Un dictionnaire peut toujours être amélioré.

CHAVANNES

In recent years a number of vernacular grammarians, some of them determined to live down the allegedly idiosyncratic analogic or anagogic or even bifocal reasoning of the Chinese, have been producing grammatical treatises. And there have been also no small number of Sinologists who, laudably following the dictum *docendo discimus*, do not seem to mind washing their dirty linen in public. When in 1916 Mr. Hu Shih wrote to the editor of the *Hsin Ch'ing-nien* advocating Literary Revolution, he managed to put "Insist on Grammar" as one of the eight points in his program. This is a bit surprising because such a schoolmasterly *Gebot* was not to be found in the Imagist credos which must have inspired that program. But it is not so surprising to see Ch'en Tu-hsiu (the editor of the journal) and Ch'ien Hsüan-t'ung reacting violently against that injunction.

Ch'en Tu-hsiu thought (and Ch'ien Hsüan-t'ung confirmed it) that, as grammar in the usual senses of the word does not exist in Chinese, what Dr. Hu Shih considered to be grammar should be, as had always been, relegated to *Stilistik* (or rhetoric). Probably the writer had in mind Yü Yüeh's *Ku-shu I-i Chü-li* and its continuations. At any rate, it cannot be seriously disputed that books like that have more use for Sinological students than Gabelentz or even Stanislas Julien. Gustave Schlegel was not the best of Sinologists; yet he had a modicum of sound sense when he advised his students to forget their grammar. Indeed, no one has ever learned to read ancient Chinese texts from analytical grammar; a warning example is that of Angelo Zottoli, S.J., who is known for his imposing tomes of *Cursus*. In his Latin grammar written in Chinese the phrases (*chü*) are mostly perfect, but the juxtaposition is nightmarish. It would take a genius to string together those phrases (some in the *Shih-chi* style, some in the *fu* style, some sheer colloquialisms) into coherent sentences. The sooner we forget grammar, the speedier will we recover our sanity.

Another fetish of a group of Sinologists who still think Chinese (classical Chinese) is a "language" in the conventional sense is their firm conviction that a perfect dictionary will smooth their way. Alas, they are whoring after false gods. First, such a dictionary is impossible to make; next, what earthly use is a two-hundred-volume dictionary to anyone? After all is said and done, the meaning is determined from the context; *ergo*, a translator must get a firm grasp of his context in the largest sense of the word, and there no dictionary will avail him. Moreover, a dictionary is no help if the wrong entry is chosen.

It is generally known that Chinese scholars themselves seldom use any dictionary except the *Shuo-wen* and the *Ching-chi Tsuan-ku* (Juan Yüan); certainly, Sinologists can profit from the monumental *Shuo-wen Chieh-tzŭ Ku-lin* and *Shuo-wen T'ung-hsün Ting-sheng* (which incorporates most of the *Ching-chi Tsuan-ku* entries), plus *P'ei-wen Yün-fu*. No self-respecting translator should use Mathews, Giles, Couvreur, etc., after he has studied a year, unless it be to find English synonyms.

As an illustration, take the sentence 作長夜之樂 of *Han-shu* 100 A/3*b* (ed. Wang Hsien-ch'ien) or 為長夜之樂 as in *Lieh-nü Chuan*. What does 樂 mean here? Which of the three dictionary meanings should be accepted? "Music" (**nglŏk* / *ngåk*$_{\circ}$ / *yüeh*^{4})? "Joy, dissipation" (**glåk* / *lâk*$_{\circ}$ / *lê*^{4})? "To like" (**nglŏg* / *ngau*$^{\circ}$ / *yao*^{4})? A recent translator seems to have accepted the first meaning, for his version makes the sentence "to make the night long with music." He probably did not look into the corresponding passage in *Shih-chi* 3: 為長夜之飲, "il donna des orgies qui duraient toute la nuit" (Chavannes). Of course there is no reason why Pan Ku should not have meant *music* when he altered 飲 to 樂. But Pan Ku was no puritan, nor had he to reckon with Mrs. Grundy. Hence it is more likely that he used 樂 in the second sense, which comes nearest to 飲. In fact, it must have been used in the sense of 淫樂 in the phrase 好酒淫樂 occurring a few lines ahead in Pan Ku's own text. What boots a dictionary then? Probably the translator was trying to give a sophisticated translation; witness "to make night long" for 為長夜 ("in order to prolong the night"?). If it comes of sophistication it is quite unfortunate, for the sense of the entire sentence is totally altered.

The couplet

微雲淡河漢，疏雨滴梧桐

is rendered by a recent scholar as:

> Delicate clouds dim the Milky Way,
> Drizzling rain drops from the wu-t'ung trees.

The translator seems to have labored on this; witness the alliteration, more or less corresponding to the original scheme. But "drizzling rain drops *from* the wu-t'ung trees" is totally false, for it drops onto the wu-t'ung leaves; the poet could hear the tatoo of raindrops. Of course, no dictionary or grammar can ever hope to take notice of such individual examples.

Needless to say, amateur Sinologists whose obsession with their pet theories is as great as their veneration of dictionaries tend to lose sight of context. Take a translation of the passage which summarizes the gist of dialectical metaphysics of the "Book of Changes":

> When the sun goes, the moon comes;
> When the moon goes, the sun comes.
> Sun and moon alternate; thus light comes
> into being.
>
> When cold goes, heat comes;
> When heat goes, cold comes.
> Cold and heat alternate, and thus the year
> completes itself.
>
> The past contracts.
> The future expands.
> Contraction and expansion act upon each other;
> hereby arises that which furthers.

It is almost unbelievable that the translator took 往者 and 來者 as "the past" and "the future." The third strophe means that the sun, the moon, heat, and cold go because they have to stoop (lit. "bend") before the cyclic law, and come because they are allowed to have their due (lit. "unbend") in the cyclic system. That *che* here serves the function of quotation marks can be seen by anyone who has examined the context. (It is also possible that *che* is a personifier; i.e., *wang-che* may mean "the goer.")

A similar example of the oversophistication is: "When anger, sorrow, joy, pleasure are in being but are not manifested, the mind may be said to be in a state of Equilibrium; when the feelings are stirred and co-operate in due degree the mind may be said to be in a state of Harmony." Which is meant to be a translation of

喜怒哀樂之未發謂之中，發而皆中節謂之和.

As the translation is made to support the synaesthesis theory, there is no doubt that the word "co-operate" is to be understood in a normal sense: the four feelings, after they are stirred one and all, *work together* in an ideally harmonious manner. This is a unique interpretation of the passage. Of course, the original text is vague; and there is nothing to forbid our translator from taking the four feelings as working and acting simultaneously, but anyone who has studied all the competent commentaries on the text will have no doubt whatsoever that the writer of the passage probably intended to leave the matter to the reader's sense of proportion as to whether he should consider one feeling or more than one stirred. He will at any rate have no hesitation in thinking that the stirred feeling or feelings work in harmony with the personality of the man whose feeling or feelings are stirred and, *ipso facto*, with the cosmic scheme itself. The translator is likely to defend his position by referring to the dictionary meaning of 皆 as "all."

8. Traduttore, Traditore

And the end of all our exploring
Will be to arrive where we started
And know the place for the first time.

All the difficulties mentioned in the above can and should be surmounted, sooner or later, by honest and earnest students. But there is a big roadblock still looming large before them: our ignorance of Chinese psychology. What do we know about terms like 性, 情, etc.? And what does 義 really mean? And when shall we come to know more precisely about all these terms?

illa cantat, nos tacemus: quando ver venit meum?
quando fiam uti chelidon ut tacere desinam?

As long as we are ignorant of their meanings, we will have to be cautious about what we do with them; we should certainly abstain from reading our favorite theories into the innocent texts.

Meanwhile I see no reason why we should desist from translating Chinese texts; we cannot expect to enjoy "another lifetime," nor would our translations be perfect if we enjoyed several. But translations made with all conscientiousness are the *sine qua non* of all Chinese scholarship, and the effort to translate heightens one's awareness of his own heritage even as he seeks to understand another.

NOTES

1. The last word on the art of translation was said in 1950 by Marianne Moore, the gifted translator of La Fontaine's *Fables:* "The first requisite of a translation, it seems to me, is that it should not sound like a translation. That similacrum of spontaneity can be a fascinating thing indeed. A master axiom for all writing, I feel, is that of Confucius: 'When you have done justice to the meaning, stop.' That implies restraint, that discipline is essential."

2. Which is what Goethe charged Heine with but is also a term used by Lu Chi (寡愛).

3. Cf. 詩者志之所之也，在心為言，發言為詩 in the "Great Preface" to the *Shih*. Does this mean the same thing as Ezra Pound's definition: "Poetry is a verbal statement of emotional values. A poem is an emotional value verbally stated"?

THE CHINESE LANGUAGE AND FOREIGN IDEAS

ARTHUR F. WRIGHT

For more than nineteen hundred years the proponents of various foreign ideas have been at work in China. Each and every one of them, whether he was a Buddhist or Christian missionary, a teacher of modern science, or a Communist organizer, has had to find the means of expressing his ideas in Chinese. For most of this long period foreign ideas had to be expressed within the framework of a vigorous Chinese literary tradition and in a language whose fundamental principles remained unchanging. Again, for most of this period, foreign ideas could only make their way by challenging or compromising with an indigenous body of thought remarkable for its perennial vitality and for its intimate relation with every Chinese value and institution. These two contexts, the linguistic and the cultural, are in a broad sense the constants in the histories of the introduction and naturalization of foreign ideas in China. But a number of variables are also important. Some of these are the relative vitality of indigenous thought and institutions in different periods, the changing degrees of consent or acceptance elicited by Chinese ideas and values, the varying pressures—internal and external—affecting the acceptance or rejection of alien ideas.[1]

This paper is a preliminary effort to discuss the histories of certain foreign ideas in relation to the first of the constants noted above: the linguistic medium in which those ideas had to be expressed. It is neither possible nor desirable to attempt such an inquiry entirely apart from considerations of the cultural constants or of the historic variables. Nevertheless, it may be useful here to concentrate attention on the linguistic problem and make only minimal reference to other factors. Wherever possible I shall attempt, in the interests of simplicity, to illustrate aspects of the problem by reference to single words. At the end I have ventured to suggest a few instances of the influence of cultural factors on the communication of foreign ideas.

The proponents of foreign ideas—whether they were Chinese or foreigners—have recognized that the Chinese language was a singularly intractable medium for the expression of their ideas. Many felt that the language, by its nature and structure, inevitably distorted or deformed the foreign ideas expressed in it. It should be noted that all foreign proponents of alien ideas had, as the original medium for those ideas, some Indo-European language. Thus the monks from medieval India, the Jesuits from Renaissance Europe, emissaries of modern scientific thought such as Bertrand Russell, and representatives of the Comintern all spoke inflected polysyllabic languages. They faced, each in their turn, the bewildering strangeness of an uninflected isolating language utterly different from anything in their background. Structurally Chinese was a most unsuitable medium for the expression of their ideas, for it was deficient in the notations of number, tense, gender, and relationships, which notations were often necessary for the communication of a foreign idea.

Moreover, Chinese characters as individual symbols had a wide range of meanings accumulated in the long history of the language plus a still wider range of allusive meanings derived from their use in a richly developed literary tradition. A more elusive but equally important characteristic of the individual symbol was what one can only call its "weight." It was a far more esteemed and significant symbol than any syllable of Indo-European languages. Granet has described this phenomenon: "Solidaire d'un signe vocal dans lequel on tient a voir une valeur d'emblème, le signe graphique est lui-même considéré comme une figuration adéquate, ou plutôt, si je puis dire, comme une appellation efficace."[2]

Further, the Chinese was relatively poor in resources for expressing abstractions and general classes or qualities. Such a notion as "Truth" tended to devolve into "something that is true." "Man" tended to be understood as "the people"—general but not abstract. "Hope" was difficult to abstract from a series of expectations directed toward specific objects.

These characteristics of the Chinese language reduced many proponents of foreign ideas to despair, the depth of their despair being the greater as their knowledge of Chinese increased. Kumārajīva (344–413), devoted Buddhist and stouthearted missionary, after long experience in translation, was moved to sigh: "But when one translates the Indian [originals] into Chinese, they lose their literary elegance. Though one may understand the general idea, he entirely misses the style. It is as if one chewed rice and gave it to another; not only would it be tasteless, but it might also make him spit it out."[3] More than fourteen centuries later a leading Protestant cleric complained: "The Chinese language is so defective and clumsy an instrument for being made the medium of spiritual truth. . . ."[4] Still later a student of the problems of Western education in China was moved to propose that "for the purposes of teaching Western ideas, especially Western scientific ideas, the best course would be to adopt a Western language as a medium."[5]

These are all statements by foreigners, expressing a common feeling of frustration at the difficulty of expressing their ideas in Chinese. The feeling was also shared by Chinese interested in foreign ideas. Tao-an (A.D. 312–85) and other great exegetes continually chafed at the difficulty of communicating Buddhist ideas in the Chinese language. It is probable that the great translator of Western scientific and sociological works, Yen Fu (1854–1921), was influenced by his difficulties to join the movement for a simplified Romanized Mandarin.[6]

The difficulties which brought forth these varying expressions of frustration can best be grasped by a consideration of the two principal devices for signifying a foreign idea in Chinese: translation (the rendering of the meaning into Chinese) and transliteration (the rendering of the sound). An examination of instances of the use of these devices may perhaps also isolate for our consideration some of the ways in which they acted to modify the foreign ideas they were used to express.

1. Translation

The most common means of signifying a foreign concept in Chinese is to choose an existing Chinese word which seems to have an equivalent meaning. This device, rather than transliteration, is one which appeals immediately to anyone who seeks to express a foreign idea. This is because it introduces the unknown in terms of the known and mitigates the strangeness and the outlandishness of the foreign idea by expressing it in words that are familiar and respected symbols. For example, in the earliest period of Chinese Buddhism it was customary to render the Indian word *dharma* by the Chinese word *tao*. We do not know how far this choice was influenced by (*a*) missionary strategy—making use of a prestige-full native term—or (*b*) an honest, if fumbling, search for the most appropriate term. The early Buddhist apologetic *Li-huo Lun* contains a multitude of examples of early efforts to "translate" both in the narrow sense of rendering Indian words into Chinese and in the broader sense of explaining groups of Indian concepts through Chinese argumentation. The second of these varieties of translation was first systematically developed in the system known as *ko-i*, "equation of concepts," which flourished in the first three quarters of the fourth century.[7] *Ko-i* sought to pair the concepts and the categories of Indian thought with those which existed in China. It seems to have especially sought equivalences between those Buddhist notions which were traditionally stated in enumerated groups and such Chinese notions as had, from the Han dynasty onward, been similarly grouped. For example, it "equated" the Indian notion of the four elements (*Mahabhutas*) with the Chinese five elements (*wu-hsing*).

Both the use of simple equivalents, such as *tao* for *dharma*, and the elaborated system of *ko-i* were soon seen as having marked disadvantages. These methods of translating the unfamiliar into the familiar were useful in breaking down initial resistance to alien ideas. But the Buddhists—foreign and Chinese alike—early became aware that a key Buddhist term tended to lose its specific Indian meaning and to take on the accumulated meanings of the Chinese term which had been used to translate it. While it was strategically advantageous to equate an Indian term of this sort with such a venerable and revered Chinese word as *tao*, the very power and authority of the indigenous term and concept tended to make it simply absorb the Indian notion into its already ramifying galaxy of meanings.[8] This tendency was strengthened by the age-long propensity of Chinese thinking for syncretism—a tendency which, I believe, is to be explained as the transmutation into intellectual processes of the social ideal of harmony. The dilemma for Buddhists and for later advocates of foreign ideas was this: Select, as equivalents for key terms, native terms which already enjoyed great prestige, and in so doing risk the obliteration of the distinctive meaning of the original concept; or select as equivalents terms which, when used in an explained technical sense, more adequately translate the meaning of the original, but at the cost of familiarity and prestige and at the risk of uncouthness.

The "term" question which exercised both Catholic and Protestant missionaries for three centuries was essentially a prolonged attempt to get off the horns of this dilemma. The early Jesuits came to China with useful Japanese experience behind them. Xavier's uninformed selection of Japanese terminology for his catechism had, in the eyes of the order, jeopardized Catholicism in Japan. The danger to Catholic doctrine in his selection, for example, of Dainichi (Vairocana-Buddha) as the equivalent for God soon became obvious. By 1576, after a short sharp struggle between "Europeanizers" and "Japanizers," the former prevailed, translation was abandoned, and Catholic terms were expressed by transliterations from Portuguese and Latin.[9]

Thus the early Jesuits in China were aware of the confusion likely to result from the translation of Catholic terminology into existing indigenous terms. Nevertheless, the strategy of Ricci and his immediate successors was to relate and ally Catholicism with "classical" Confucianism so that they would win the confidence and support of the Chinese educated elite. To do this meant to explain and rationalize the relation between the two groups of ideas. Ricci's most famous apologetic *T'ien-chu Shih-i* quoted from six Chinese Classics, showing how their teachings harmonized with the doctrines of Christianity. The ultimate effort of Confucian-Christian synthesis was *Confucius Sinarum philosophus* published in Paris in 1687. This work of reconciliation and synthesis was justified in these terms:

> Pourquoi ne pourrions-nous pas rapporter leurs témoignages, bien qu'en autres passages ils se contredisent et y mêlent leurs opinions? Ne voyons-nous pas l'Apôtre des gentils et les premiers Pères de L'église se servir des écrits et des témoignages des vains poètes, des sybilles et d'autres païens? C'est comme si, pour ainsi dire, ils recueillaient des perles dans la boue et les ordures, ou bien ils discernaient dans les ténèbres certaines places lumineuses ou des étincelles brillantes qui auraient été insérées par l'auteur de la nature dans les esprits des hommes pour amener les peuples à la première connaissance de la lumière éternelle.[10]

Ten years later Father Bouvet, in his effort to demonstrate that the *I-ching* was as philosophically sound as Plato and Aristotle, stated the case as clearly as anyone:

> I do not believe that there is anything in the world more proper to dispose the spirit and the heart of the Chinese to embrace our holy religion than to make them see how it is in conformity with the principles of their ancient and legitimate philosophy.[11]

This effort at "translating" closely resembles the work of the early Buddhists in China. One might suggest that there is a parallel between the stage of presentation of foreign ideas represented by the *Li-huo Lun* and by Ricci's *T'ien-chu Shih-i;* research might well show further parallels in the later phases of the domestication of the two systems. The reactions against this type of "translation" which seeks to capitalize on indigenous thought may also be seen as similar in type though different in expression. The Buddhists, without any centralized world church organization, became conscious of the defects and dangers of these early experiments and began slowly to work out a technical terminology and methods of explication which they hoped would guard Buddhist ideas against the danger of deformation through coalescence with their Chinese counterparts. The Jesuit missionaries were subject to the criticism of Rome, and the dangers in the early Jesuit use of Confucianism were recognized by the Propaganda and by rival orders. It was typical of the Catholic system that the Propaganda, responsive to Dominican arguments, decided that *T'ien* and *Shang-ti*—terms for a supreme deity in a millennial Chinese tradition—could not be used as equivalents for the Christian "God" and sent the DeTournon legation (in China, 1705–10) to interdict these terms and the related practices which the Jesuits had followed in spreading the faith. Thus, while the Buddhists in China modified their practices out of their own experience, the Jesuits were compelled to modify theirs by outside fiat.[12] It is significant that both groups, in subsequent stages of their missionary activity, resorted to neologisms —translations into Chinese characters used in a specified technical sense (e.g., *fa* for *dharma*) or new or rare combinations of characters (e.g., *T'ien-chu* for God).

The Protestants in the nineteenth century faced the same problems, tried many of the same solutions, but made little effort to capitalize on the experience of their predecessors. Protestant attitudes toward China differed sharply from those of the Buddhist and Catholic missionaries. Tolerance born of compassion generally characterized Buddhist devotees, both foreign and Chinese, while the Jesuit attitude was informed with Renaissance humanism and moderated by prevailing notions of "natural religion." The Protestants, on the other hand, saw themselves as representatives not only of the one true faith but of a progressive and triumphant civilization which was bound to prevail throughout the whole world, especially among such backward heathen as the Chinese.[13]

Many able and distinguished scholars labored long and patiently to render the Bible into acceptable Chinese. But they were subject to incessant carping criticism from those who chaffed at the barriers which "heathen" language and custom placed in the path of religion. One of these critics attacked concessions made to Chinese classical usage:

> What an unreasonable elevation of heathen writers have we here by Christian missionaries! What does the principle here laid down amount to but this:—"If the words used in the translation of the New Testament into a heathen language cannot be found used in the same sense in the writings of the heathen classical writers of said language, the whole work is unclassical and contemptible." When laying down this canon—"unclassical and contemptible," the writers, I am sure, could not have reflected upon the sentence they were passing upon our Greek Testament unless they design to claim more for the Chinese classical writers than for the Greek. There are many, many Greek words whose use in the New Testament does not correspond with that in the classical writers. This Dr. Medhurst and his friends would not deny, and yet, I am sure, here is a case in which they would not say "unclassical, ergo contemptible." Why then should the Chinese Classics be elevated into a Christian man's standard of what is contemptible or otherwise?[14]

More than half a century later there was still a strong note of both arrogance and despair in Protestant writing on the translation problem:

> Is there any convenient method of stating the doctrine of the Trinity which does not imply the grossest materialism? Who has been fortunate enough to discover a name for sin which does not dash us on the Scylla of civil crime or engulph [*sic*] us in the Charybdis of retribution for the faults of a former life? Use whatever language you please to express the resurrection, and the uninitiated will understand it to mean transmigration.[15]

Although there was considerable enlightened discussion in the course of the "term" controversies—essays, for example, which adduced parallels between the problems facing the Protestant translators in China and those which had faced the translators of the King James and the Revised English versions of the Bible—the extreme and naïve position taken by Mateer as late as 1908 would have amused a seventeenth-century Jesuit:

> Existing translations reveal a distinct disposition to adapt the Bible to the Chinese in the process of translating it. Things that are obscure are made plain by paraphrase or substitution. Things that might offend prejudice are modified. Metaphors and personifications not familiar to the Chinese are expanded into comparisons. Phrases and forms of speech growing out of the customs of Biblical times are turned about into what is supposed the Chinese would now say in like circumstance. . . . [This] is wrong in principle and should be entirely and conscientiously avoided.[16]

Obviously Mateer's injunction is impractical, since translation always involves compromise. Indeed, the Protestant choice of *shang-ti* for "God" was far more of a compromise with Chinese usage than the Catholic choice of the relatively unfamiliar term *t'ien-chu*. And, as the tormented missionary translators must have observed, it was the Sinicized term, the most "compromising" term, that had the strongest appeal. The T'ai P'ing rebels, in putting together their pseudo-Christian ideology, chose the word *shang-ti* for "God" and deliberately rejected both *t'ien-chu* and *yeh-ho-hua* (Jehovah) as foreignisms.[17]

Research would, I suspect, show that, with the decline of European self-confidence following the first World War, there was a steadily increasing disposition to admit or even encourage the Sinicization of Protestantism. For example, the cleric Frank Rawlinson, in a plea for what he terms "Christo-centric broadmindedness" wrote in 1927:

> There is need that those who go to work among people of another civilization than their own keep in mind the *inferiorities* of their own civilization. . . . There are also common world problems which must be kept in mind if Western Christians would avoid the charge of self-righteousness. The "Christian" West has no solutions to offer to China as to the social snarls of race prejudice, war, narcotic addiction, industrial discontent, or the stabilization of family life.[18]

More recently a missionary has argued that the Christian failure to recognize the value and truth of Confucian teachings and the missionary effort to undermine the values of Chinese society prepared the way for communism. In attempting to explain the Christian failure in China, he emphasizes Christianity's unacknowledged debt to Chinese thinkers:

> It is a sorry commentary on Christianity that although it produced scholars who translated the Bible faithfully by adapting the idea of "Shang Ti" from Confucius and the idea of "Tao" from Lao Tzu, yet the use of these terms by the Church has not been accompanied by the same degree of appreciation that the translators had for the teachings

of the great sages who first conceived them. . . . The terms used for God in the Chinese version of the Bible are not the terms used by Abraham, Moses, Isaiah, Jeremiah, Micah, or Jesus. They are the thoughts of Confucius and Lao Tzu woven into the Chinese Bible to give meaning to God and Jesus. . . . Unless the Christian humbly and loyally acknowledges its debt to China's sages for the terms used for God and the Son Incarnate, found in the Chinese translation of the Bible, it is guilty of theft of the noblest ideas of Lao Tzu and Confucius while attempting to supplant them in their own land.[19]

It is not clear how repeated acknowledgments of conceptual indebtedness would have had any effect save to force the terms adopted by the Protestants back into their Chinese literary contexts and thus strip them of the new meanings which Christianity sought to give them. The Protestant experience seems to have produced no new solutions to the vexing problems of translation. The dilemma stated earlier remained, and the Protestants who made their translations conform to Chinese usage and adopt established Chinese terms saw their sacred writings distorted by and absorbed into the stream of Chinese literature; those who used neologisms and technical terms saw educated Chinese reject their translations as barbarous.

By the middle of the nineteenth century, Chinese leaders themselves were beginning to feel that—for the preservation of their country—they *must* take over and apply certain Western ideas and techniques; there was no comparable pressure in earlier times to adopt alien religious ideas. The language reform movement, starting from Lu Kan-chang (1854–1928) and gradually attracting the attention of the upper class, was a reflection of this sense of urgency, of an impatience with the traditional written language and doubts about its capacity to become the medium of communication for a literate nation or a medium for modern scientific studies.[20]

Meanwhile, however, Western secular works were being translated and distributed, first by missionaries and later by Chinese official and private agencies. Neologisms were coined at a fantastic rate, different translators coining or borrowing from Japanese different compounds as equivalents for the same Western terms. This chaotic stage is reminiscent of the early decades of Buddhist translating activities: translators with different backgrounds chose different Chinese equivalents for foreign terms; translators had different degrees of knowledge of the language from which they were translating; communication among translators was infrequent; different versions or editions of foreign works were used by different translators; different stylistic preferences produced different versions of the same work.

The technical problems in translating Western scientific statements were somewhat less acute than those involved in translating literary and philosophical works. As Mr. Richards points out elsewhere in this volume, a scientific utterance has a limited number of functions. It does not "value"; it does not "influence"; etc. Nevertheless, serious difficulties remained. The English Preface to a translation of a Western anatomy of 1851, *Ch'uan-t'i Hsin-lun*, remarked: "There has been much difficulty experienced in fixing upon new terms, and finding suitable words for unnamed or improperly described parts of the human body."[21] Nevertheless, "equivalents" were found and proliferated to produce immeasurable confusion. Standardization of equivalents has been and still is being attempted by governments and by professional groups. The question, then, is: Even when standardized, how efficient are these symbols in communicating Western scientific ideas with a minimum of distortion? This is a much disputed subject. Forrest argues that the revival of little-used characters and the composition of new characters for scientific names—e.g., 鋃 for lanthanum, 鈀 for palladium, and 氬 for the gas argon are efficient and expansible means of accurate symbol creation. He further maintains that *li-hsüeh* 力學 is a perfectly accurate rendering of "dynamics" and is unlikely to be deformed in the mind of an educated reader by the earlier meanings and associations of the word *li*.[22]

Purcell takes a negative position which leads him to urge the adoption of a Western language as a medium for Western ideas, particularly scientific ideas. He comes to this conclusion through a dual etymological analysis: first of the original term and second of its Chinese translation. And his conclusion would seem to be that, whereas Western abstract and scientific terms do not tend, in the minds of Western readers, to preserve earlier meanings of their components—thus distorting the sense—the Chinese terms do have this tendency. In the case of such a neologism as *she-hui chu-i*, "socialism," Purcell seems to me to overestimate the influence of the galaxies of meanings of the component characters on the compound term. As we have mentioned in connection with Buddhist and Christian translations, the neologism, by its very strangeness, is a signal to the reader that it has a special meaning. However, when he discusses the ambiguities of *ch'üan*, used by Sun Yat-sen for both "powers" and "rights" in the modern political senses, he does demonstrate a very real weakness in the Chinese language as a medium for expressing Western ideas, namely, the variety of alternate meanings of a character.

The problem of widely varying meanings of a single character and the effect of this on translation can be illustrated by a consideration of one of the key statements of Western philosophy, *Cogito, ergo sum*. Purcell analyzes a Chinese translation of this, but some of his argument loses force because he selected a rather inferior vernacular version.[23] But even a comparatively good translation such as in Fan Ping-ching's *Dictionary of Philosophy* shows some of the difficulties involved.[24] He renders the statement: *Wo ssu, ku wo tsai*. This would appear to be "literal" and to parallel precisely an English translation of the phrase. With the pronoun there seems to be no ambiguity; *ku*, "therefore," "it follows that," has had such meanings in similar contexts since the philosopher Mo Tzŭ (*ca.* 479–381 B.C.). *Tsai* retains overtones of "to be in or at a place" but is commonly used in approximately the sense intended here. But *ssu*, "think," has a galaxy of meanings, many of them involving emotions. Waley, who has analyzed this term as it occurs in the *Analects* of Confucius, concludes:

> Never is there any suggestion of a long interior process of cogitation or ratiocination, in which a whole series of thoughts are evolved one out of the other, producing on the physical plane a headache and on the intellectual an abstract theory. We must think of *ssu* rather as a fixing of the attention (located in the middle of the belly) on an impression recently imbibed from without and destined to be immediately re-exteriorized in action.[25]

I do not wish to imply that *ssu*, as used in the *Analects*, was used in precisely this sense throughout Chinese history. Chu Hsi (d. A.D. 1200), for example, paraphrased *ssu* as "seeking within the heart."[26] And one finds in any good Chinese dictionary a whole further series of meanings. What should be emphasized is that no one of these varied meanings is equivalent to Descartes's *cogito*, and such of them as remain in the mind of a Chinese reader would tend to suggest quite a different range of meanings than that intended by the translator.

To use a character of multiple meanings to translate a new Western concept is hazardous. A further defect of the neologistic translation appears at the level of mass communication. When the foreign term is translated, as often happens, by a compound of many characters, the Chinese, in the interests of conciseness, abbreviate, using only a few of the characters to suggest the whole term. Such abbreviations can produce confusion in the minds of the semieducated. Derk Bodde recounts a conversation with an unsophisticated Chinese lady in 1949 who startled him by stating that the United States was ruled by an emperor. She had been led to this conclusion, first, by the Chinese translation of "White House," which is literally "White Palace," and, second, by one of the most common abbreviations. "American imperialism" is translated by the clumsy term *Mei-kuo ti-kuo chu-i*, literally "American country emperor-country-ism." The newspapers commonly abbreviate this to *Mei-ti*, literally "American emperor." Hence the confusion.[27] The proliferation of this type of abbreviation in recent years must have produced innumerable similar cases of defective communication.

The preceding discussion, together with the evidence which will be given in the discussion of transliteration below, seems to support the contention that Chinese characters are more apt to distort foreign ideas than are the syllables of one Western language used to translate another. This, as has often been noted, is a product of the unchanging composition of the individual character and its tendency to suggest a wide range of meanings accumulated through the centuries, connotations derived from certain well-known contexts in which it has frequently been used. In closing this discussion of translation, it might be observed that, with the inevitable decline of classical learning in China and with—as seems likely—the development of a literate but classically uneducated public, many foreign terms will cease to be subject to distortion by prior meanings of the Chinese characters used to express them, simply because the readers will be generally unaware of those meanings. Such a development would mean that *she-hui chu-i* would cease to suggest—if it still does—anything but "socialism" as expounded in current speech and writing, just as "socialism" has, with us, long ceased to suggest the Latin *socius*, "companion."[28] The pattern would follow that of the history of foreign loan-words which have long become part of the Chinese language and whose origins are known only to philologists (e.g., *yen-chih* for "rouge"). This would perhaps solve some of the problems of terminology; it would leave other problems of translation unsolved; for example, multiple meanings of single characters, poverty of terms of relationship (cause, etc.), ambiguities arising from unexpressed subjects, etc.

2. *Transliteration*

Transliteration, which has been used extensively since the early days of Buddhism, avoids some of the problems of translation but brings peculiar problems of its own. Since the foreign words so rendered are usually polysyllabic, transliteration creates units of vocabulary which are awkward and attenuated. In the classical style they destroy the compactness and balance of a sentence; in a vernacular style they are destructive of rhythm. It is difficult if not impossible to write a pleasing sentence in any Chinese style when one of the words is, for example, *ya-po-la-han* (Abraham) or *Ma-ho-p'o-lo-nei-han* (*Maha parinirvana*). One of the disadvantages of transliteration, then, is uncouthness. The following comment refers both to neologistic translation and to transliteration, but it is particularly applicable to the latter:

> Finally, there are things in the sacred Scriptures to express which no established terms are found in some heathen languages. When these occur, they must either be left untranslated, and the bare sounds given, or a new mode of expression employed, both of which are uncouth; and when a disaffected Christian or heathen happens to meet with them, it is ten to one if he does not condemn the whole book.[29]

Such condemnations were commonly made of foreign works, and it was the strings of sound syllables that always struck the Chinese as barbaric and silly.

I have already suggested one advantage which both the neologism and the transliterated term have over the established terms: this is that they "flag down" the reader, send him to a dictionary or glossary or commentary, and thus prompt him to master for himself the technical meaning of the term. It might be added, however, that such a process in its turn leads to many of the difficulties and distortions resulting from translation into accepted Chinese terms. The Buddhist dictionaries, for example, often give abbreviated translations of a transliterated term, using only a character or two, so that the user can easily be misled by taking the characters of the dictionary translation in another sense than that which was intended. Thus one might say that the advantage of the transliterated term is often vitiated by the means through which its meaning is explained.

A further and more serious disadvantage is the tendency for sound-syllables to retain their meaning. It is obviously a psychological wrench for a Chinese reader to stop and tell himself that characters, which he is accustomed to take as individually meaningful, are simply there to render the sounds of a foreign word especially since, until very recently, characters used thus were not graphically differentiated from characters used for meaning. In the case of Buddhism the tendency for sound characters to reassert their meaning content was strengthened by the fact that the Chinese Buddhists did not preserve an Indian language as a church language; Chinese was the language of the sacred writings, and very few Buddhist scholars throughout the centuries had studied an Indian language; they were thus unprepared to read back through the transliteration to the Indian word or to comprehend the meaning of the original term in its own context.[30]

There are numerous examples in Chinese Buddhist literature of the recrudescence of the meanings of characters used to transliterate syllables. For example, the great Buddhist cleric Chi-tsang (549–623) was asked, "What is the meaning of the character *shih* in Chiu-mo-lo-shih?" Instead of answering that it is meaningless, merely a transliterated syllable in the name of the foreign monk Kumārajīva, he replied that the character had the meaning of *fu-shih*, "honorableness" (?).[31]

A friend of mine recalled from his boyhood a precisely parallel case from Christianity. The foreign preacher was away for a Sunday, and the Chinese pastor took the service. He chose as the text for his sermon "Adam" (transliterated *ya-tan*) and, with a prodigious display of learning, traced the *meanings* of the characters *ya* and *tan* from the earliest dictionaries down through later literature. Sifting and selecting from among the many possible meanings of these two characters, he built up a remarkable and ingenious discourse.[32]

A slightly different example of the same phenomenon was described to me by a missionary long resident in China. A Chinese pastor was anxious to show conclusively that Jesus Christ was the son of God. He first pointed out that Jehovah was rendered into Chinese as Yeh-ho-hua and Jesus as Yeh-su. Then, treating the syllables not as mere transliterations but as parts of Chinese style names, he said that both bore the surname of the Yeh family, that Jehovah's personal name was Ho-hua and Jesus' was Su.[33] This example demonstrates the power of one of the cultural constants, here the ideas and terminology of Chinese kinship. It is as difficult for Chinese to think of the names of people apart from the kinship relations which govern Chinese personal nomenclature as it is for us to comprehend the nomenclature of a society which does not use inherited surnames (e.g., Burma).

In one of his stories Lu Hsün satirizes the vain and silly intellectual of the 1920's caught in the same web of transliteration. The object of his barbs is a certain Mr. Kao who affected Western manners and claimed wide acquaintance with the "new literature." Mr. Kao appears one day with a new visiting card on which he has had printed a new personal name, Kao Erh-ch'u. A friend, surprised, asks the reason for the change. Mr. Kao condescendingly points out that there is a great Russian writer called Kao-erh-chi (transliteration of Gorki).[34] He has tried with his new name to suggest a relationship to a great writer with whom he fancies he shares the surname Kao. And, in choosing a new personal name, he has taken the middle syllable of the transliteration of "Gorki" and added a second character whose *meaning* is the same as that of the last syllable.

A final example shows this phenomenon in a secular political expression of recent date. Chiang Kai-shek is lecturing to the Officers Training Corps at Kuling in July, 1934:

> The Japanese call China "Chihna." What is the Japanese meaning of Chihna? It means "half dead man." In their sight there is no China. . . . What do they call Russia? They call it "Lusiya." Lu means dew. What is the significance of "Lu"? It means that the Japanese compare Japan to the sun and Russia to dew. Once the sun shines, the dew

dries instantly. From this it is obvious that long ago Japan had decided upon her national policy. She is determined to destroy Russia. What do the Japanese call the United States of America? We Chinese call her "Meilichien" or "Beauty Sharp Strong." But the Japanese call her "Milichi" or "Mikuo." The word "Mi" means rice. In using this word as the name for America the Japanese reveal that they have long intended to eat her up. From this we can understand how painstaking the enemy has been making preparations to acquire supremacy.[35]

It does not matter whether Chiang believed in the logic of his argument; what matters is that he seemed to think that it would have enough effect on his audience to make it worth saying; more surprisingly his information service thought it worth translating and distributing in English. This statement reveals, as do the similar examples given above, the persistence of a rather primitive attitude toward written symbols: that they are endowed with some efficacy that makes them more than mere notations and gives them a semimagical control over the phenomena symbolized.

Thus in the long period covered by these examples, transliteration has proved an extraordinarily treacherous medium for rendering alien terminology. It would appear that, as long as the characters exist, their emblematic force will, to some degree, tend to distort the terminology expressed through the characters used as syllables.

3. Cultural Factors: Some Questions

Elements of Chinese culture inevitably have their place in any estimate of the effectiveness of the language for expressing foreign ideas. Here I shall discuss some of these elements and their effects on this type of communication. What follows is of course not intended as an inventory of all such elements; it is meant rather to raise certain types of questions which merit further investigation.

The Chinese family system had an enormous influence on the reception of foreign ideas. The effort to justify Buddhist celibacy, for example, as a "higher form" of filial piety undoubtedly tended to distort the original Indian concept.[36] A reflective missionary has pointed out that, although *t'ien-fu* is, on the surface, an adequate and "literal" translation of the Christian "Heavenly Father," "the concept 'father' however, is not the one best adapted for use in China to suggest the character of the Supreme Father, as the father, together with the teacher and emperor, was expected to hold himself aloof and be reticent. It does not, therefore, easily suggest the idea of intimate relationship with the Supreme Father so prominent in Jesus' thought."[37] Nakamura has remarked on the Chinese Buddhist emphasis on the genealogy, the line of descent of successive teachers of a set of doctrines, and he feels that this emphasis—qualitatively different from that of Indian Buddhism—is the result of Chinese esteem for genealogies, family pedigrees, and the like.[38] The Chinese pastor's attempt to prove the "true" kinship between Jehovah and Jesus is another example of the influence of familistic patterns of thinking.

The Chinese emphasis on the self-cultivation of the individual might be expected to have its effects on foreign ideas. I suspect that Father Vagnoni's Chinese essay catering to this interest, "Doctrines de l'occident pour se gouverner soi-même, sa famille et l'état," would provide examples of the changes in the meanings of a good many Western ideas when they are adapted to this purpose.[39] Certainly Chinese Communist leadership has been greatly concerned to transmute Communist doctrine into guiding principles of self-cultivation—an emphasis that did not characterize Communist ideological writings elsewhere. It is interesting that Liu Shao-ch'i, in his authoritative work *Lun Kung-ch'an Tang-yüan Ti Hsiu-yang* ("The Training of a Communist Party Member"), should quote extensively from the Chinese Classics on the meaning and purpose of self-cultivation, using such tags as "Everybody can be a Yao or a Shun" ("adapted" from *Mencius*, IV, Part 2, chap. 32) to urge a type of self-cultivation for which the Marxist scriptures provide no authority. Chinese-Communist writers take the Marxist-Leninist concept of struggle (Chinese *tou-cheng*) and extend it to become a principle of inner cultivation, a psychological state which is to be nurtured in the interests of personality development. This extension—together with other efforts to transcendentalize the concept—have given an entirely different complex of meanings to the term than it has in other Communist literature.[40]

In the highly ritualized social life of traditional China, such distinctions as that between right and left have accumulated a vast number of symbolic associations. The left is east, *yang* (the male force), the rising sun, spring, etc. It is the place of honor, the location of the residence of the crown prince in relation to the ruler, etc.[41] What then happened—under the influence of this group of symbols—to the meaning of the statement in the New Testament that Jesus is seated on the right hand of God? (Col. 3:1.) The translators were obviously facing a difficult dilemma: they could translate the passage literally (as they did), do no violence to holy writ, but create the impression that someone other than Jesus occupied the place of honor on the left; or they could have translated so as to give Jesus the place of honor—on the left—and have been laid open to the charge of tampering with God's word. And what was a Chinese to make of the passages in chapter 25 of Matthew where the left is specified as the place of dishonor, whose occupants were to depart "into the eternal fire which God prepared for the devil and his angels"?

The basic pattern of life—in China, farming—has a profound and pervasive influence on metaphor. In communicating foreign ideas born of a different environment and hence expressed in a different metaphor, a degree of distortion is inevitable. Thus the metaphors of pastoral life which pervade the Old Testament make that work seem very strange, often incomprehensible, even to modern Western readers.[42] For a Chinese, accustomed to regard herding as an inferior way of life of frontier barbarians, and herdsmen as the natural enemies of Chinese farmers, the metaphor of the Old Testament plus the prophets' expressed disdain for agriculturalists must have set up serious resistances. Soothill describes a Chinese pastor at Ningpo dealing with some of these resistances in a sermon on the parable of the lost sheep. By an ingenious excursion into etymology he showed that many key words in Chinese contained the graphic element "sheep"; such are the characters *i*, "righteousness," *keng*, "ancestral sacrifice," etc. He drew from this the conclusion that the ancestors of all Chinese had been herdsmen.[43] Thus, he implied, his audience should respond more sympathetically to biblical teachings cast in pastoral metaphor.

Research might reveal certain parallels in the history of Marxist ideas whose terminology and metaphor were developed in an urban and industrialized Europe and had, in China, to be communicated to a predominantly agricultural people. It need hardly be added, however, that, to the degree that urban and industrial life continues to develop in China, such disparities will gradually disappear.

It is interesting to speculate on the process of the total transformation of culture and life now being attempted by the Chinese Communists and its significance for the types of problems we have been discussing. It would appear that, in the case of earlier bodies of alien thought, the continuing vitality of indigenous thought and literature acted to distort alien ideas in China. Cultural factors such as the sample mentioned before had—in the manner suggested—a further deforming effect. Now, if we assume that the Communists gain a measure of success, both the influence of the old literature and the force of the traditional cultural factors will be reduced or nullified. How far all this may go is a much argued question. It is one of the most important questions of our day.

NOTES

1. Some reference is made to these variables in the Wright-Wilhelm-Schwartz symposium, "Chinese Reactions to Imported Ideas," *Journal of the History of Ideas*, XII (January, 1951), 31–72.

2. Marcel Granet, *La Pensée chinoise* (Paris, 1934), p. 51.

3. *Kao-seng Chuan* ("Lives of Eminent Monks"), chap. 2, *Taisho* ed., L, 332*b*–*c*. Cf. also J. Nobel, "Kumārajīva," *Sitzungsberichte der Preussischen Akademie der Wissenschaften*, XX (1927), 225.

4. "In What Form Shall We Give the Bible, etc.," *Chinese Recorder*, 1890, p. 454. S. Wells Williams took much the same view: "The language itself, as we have had opportunity to observe, is an unwieldy vehicle for imparting new truths" (*The Middle Kingdom* [New York, 1888], II, 370).

5. Victor Purcell, *Problems of Chinese Education* (London, 1936), p. 16.

6. Cf. John De Francis, *Nationalism and Language Reform in China* (Princeton, 1950), p. 46.

7. Cf. T'ang Yung-t'ung, "On Ko-yi," in *Radhakrishnan: Comparative Studies in Philosophy* (New York, 1950), pp. 276–86.

8. Though the Protestants later standardized *tao* as the translation of *Logos*, few seemed to be aware of the dangers inherent in such an equivalence. Mr. Levenson has called my attention to the fact that the Jews at Kaifeng early chose *tao* for the Hebrew "God." In so doing, they passed on to later members of their community a term which, with its strong flavor of immanence, radically changed the character of their transcendental God.

9. Cf. Henri Bernard-Maitre, *Sagesse chinoise et philosophie Chrétienne* (Sien-sien, 1935), pp. 92–100. His material on the language controversy is largely drawn from Schurhammer, *Das Kirchliche Sprachproblem in der Japanischen Jesuiten-mission des 16 und 17 Jahrhunderts* (Tokyo, 1928).

10. Quoted in Bernard-Maitre, *op. cit.*, pp. 133–34.

11. Translated from a letter of August 30, 1697, quoted *ibid.*, p. 145.

12. Cf. A. H. Rowbotham, *Missionary and Mandarin* (Berkeley, 1942), pp. 128–29, 149.

13. A rather extreme expression of this attitude is that of S. Wells Williams: "The universal practice of lying and dishonest dealings; the unblushing lewdness of old and young; harsh cruelty towards prisoners by officers, and tyranny over slaves by masters—all form a full unchecked torrent of human depravity, and prove the existence of a kind and degree of moral degradation of which an excessive statement can scarcely be made, or an adequate conception hardly be formed" (*op. cit.*, I, 836). I recall that the great Robert Morrison is somewhere reported as describing the Chinese as "ignorant, deluded, guilty men."

14. "Testimony to the Truth of Christianity . . . ," *Chinese Repository*, XX (1851), 46.

15. "In What Form Shall We Give the Bible, etc.," *op. cit.*, p. 454.

16. C. W. Mateer, "Lessons Learned in Translating the Bible into Mandarin," *Chinese Recorder*, November, 1908, p. 608.

17. Eugene P. Boardman, *Christian Influence upon the Ideology of the Taiping Rebellion, 1851–1864* (Madison, 1952), pp. 59–60.

18. *The Naturalization of Christianity in China* (Shanghai, 1927), pp. 4–6.

19. Leonard M. Outerbridge, *The Lost Churches of China* (Philadelphia, 1952), p. 27.
20. Cf. De Francis, *op. cit.*, pp. 31–54.
21. *Chinese Repository*, XX (August, 1851), 538–39.
22. R. A. D. Forrest, *The Chinese Language* (London, 1950), pp. 240–41.
23. Purcell, *op. cit.*, pp. 101–2.
24. *Che-hsueh Tz'u-tien* ("Dictionary of Philosophy") (Shanghai, 1926), p. 253.
25. Arthur Waley, *The Analects of Confucius* (London, 1938), p. 45.
26. *Ibid.*, p. 46.
27. *Peking Diary* (New York, 1950), pp. 190–91.
28. Fu Ssu-nien, writing in *Hsin Ch'ao*, Vol. I, No. 3 (1919), suggested that the development of a Chinese phonetic writing would hasten this process. When a friend challenged him, saying that the terms (*ming-tz'u*) of scholarship would lose their meaning, he replied, "This is not so. Meaning whose expression must rely on the shape of the characters and cannot rely on the language is not worth much. . . . As to the word philology, Westerners do not mistake it to mean love of learning. Hence one can see that the patent origin of a word is not important" (p. 408). For foreign words he proposes that, except in unusually difficult cases, they be translated into Chinese and then written in phonetic symbols on the pattern of Biologie-Lebenskunde.
29. E. C. Bridgman, "The Bible: Its Adaptation to the Moral Condition of Man," *Chinese Repository*, IV (November, 1835), 305.
30. It would be interesting to know how far and in what ways the use of Latin by the Chinese Catholic church preserved Catholic doctrine from this type of distortion.
31. Quoted in Nakamura, *Tōyōjin Shii Hōō*, II, 354. Cf. *Taisho*, XLII, 235*c*.
32. Recounted to the author by Charles J. Stanley.
33. Related to the author by Dr. Lucius C. Porter, July 24, 1952.
34. Lu Hsün, "Kao Lao-fu-tzŭ" in *Huang-fang* (written 1925) (Shanghai ed. of 1944), p. 79.
35. *Resisting External Aggression and Regenerating the Chinese Nation* (Hankow: China Information Committee, 1938), p. 15. Much the same attitude was displayed by various pro-Japanese propagandists during the war in China. To denigrate the allied powers, it was thought effective to add the degrading "dog" element to the characters usually employed to signify England, America, etc.
36. Cf. the argumentation in my translation of the biography of the nun An-ling-shou, *Harvard Journal of Asiatic Studies*, XV (1952), 193–96.
37. Rawlinson, *op. cit.*, p. 128.
38. Cf. Nakamura, *op. cit.*, I, 428–33.
39. Cf. Bernard-Maitre, *op. cit.*, p. 123.
40. Cf. my paper, "Struggle versus Harmony: Symbols of Competing Values in Modern China," to appear in the forthcoming report of the Thirteenth Annual Conference on Science, Philosophy and Religion.
41. Cf. Granet, *op. cit.*, pp. 367–68, and *passim*.
42. Logan Pearsall-Smith in *All Trivia* (New York, 1934) has an amusing account of the effects of certain Old Testament rewards of virtue when they descended on the occupant of a London flat. The multiplication of he-goats and she-goats proved as embarrassing as having the head continuously anointed with oil.
43. W. E. Soothill, *A Mission in China* (London, 1907), p. 133.

INDEX[1]

1. Prepared by Shen-yu Dai.